THE FUTURE OF
SCHOOL INTEGRATION

THE FUTURE OF SCHOOL INTEGRATION

Socioeconomic Diversity as an Education Reform Strategy

Richard D. Kahlenberg, *editor*

A CENTURY FOUNDATION BOOK

The Century Foundation Press • New York

LIBRARY OF CONGRESS CATALOGING-IN-PUBLICATION DATA

The future of school integration : socioeconomic diversity as an education reform strategy / edited by Richard D. Kahlenberg.
    p.   cm.
"A Century Foundation Book."
Includes bibliographical references and index.
ISBN 978-0-87078-522-1 (alk. paper)
    1. School integration—United States. 2. Educational sociology—United States.
3. Discrimination in education—United States. 4. Educational equalization—
United States. 5. Educational change—United States. I. Kahlenberg, Richard D.

LC214.2.F88 2012
379.2'63—dc23

2011046595

Manufactured in the United States of America

Cover design by Lili Schwartz.
Text design by Cynthia Stock.

Foreword

Much has been made of growing economic inequality in this country. America's once-thriving middle class has been disappearing for decades, as the nation has split into two groups: a prosperous upper class that has seen their share of the nation's wealth and income increase in ever-greater amounts, and the rest, who struggle to see any improvement whatsoever in their economic prospects.

One troubling aspect of this cleaving of American society that has received scant attention is the rising economic segregation of Americans by neighborhood. New research shows that, as the middle class has shrunk, the rich and poor in this country increasingly live in separate areas, as mixed-income neighborhoods become a thing of the past. This residential segregation by income in turn has led to the increasing economic segregation of schools—and this is a very worrying trend for the future of public education. Economic segregation undercuts public education's goals of providing academic opportunity and promoting social mobility, because schools that serve mostly children from poor families rarely are as good as those that serve mostly the more affluent.

Furthermore, growing economic segregation undermines the important role that American public education has in forging social cohesion and national unity among diverse populations.

The good news is that an increasing number of school districts recognize the importance of socioeconomic school integration and are taking active steps to promote it. In 2001—the year that The Century Foundation published Richard D. Kahlenberg's book *All Together Now: Creating Middle-Class Schools through Public School Choice*—only a handful of districts were pursuing conscious policies to bring children of different economic backgrounds together under one roof. Today, more than eighty districts, educating some 4 million students, are pursuing such strategies. In the volume before you now, *The Future of School Integration,* a new, younger generation of researchers has taken on the challenge of studying the important effects of socioeconomic integration policies at the Pre-K, elementary, and secondary levels.

The publication of this research is well timed, not only because increasing residential sorting makes economic integration policies more urgent, but also because today's very tough budgetary circumstances make policies that produce greater educational bang for the buck in high demand. As research in this book suggests, economic school integration can be one of the most cost-effective means for producing what the nation desperately needs: more highly skilled graduates.

The Future of School Integration is part of The Century Foundation's long-running commitment to studying the effects of economic school segregation and policies to counteract it. Our publication of *All Together Now* in 2001 was followed the next year by *Divided We Fail: Coming Together through Public School Choice,* the Report of The Century Foundation Task Force on the Common School, chaired by former Connecticut Governor Lowell P. Weicker, Jr. Later on, we published two reports by Kahlenberg—*Rescuing Brown v. Board of Education: Profiles of Twelve School Districts Pursuing Socioeconomic School Integration* in 2007, and in 2009, as the Obama administration put a new focus on improving the nation's worst performing schools, we published *Turnaround Schools that Work: Moving Beyond Separate But Equal.*

Our interest in public education extends beyond socioeconomic integration to include many aspects of preserving and promoting the mission of public education as a whole. Our books in that vein include Kahlenberg's *A Notion at Risk: Preserving Public Education as an Engine for Social Mobility,* as well as a collection of essays he edited, *Public School*

Choice vs. Private School Vouchers. In addition, we have published works on improving student performance, including Richard Rothstein's *The Way We Were? The Myths and Realities of America's Student Achievement;* Joan Lombardi's *Time to Care: Redesigning Child Care to Promote Education, Support Families, and Build Communities;* Gordon MacInnes's *In Plain Sight: Simple, Difficult Lessons from New Jersey's Expensive Effort to Close the Achievement Gap,* and *Improving On No Child Left Behind: Getting Education Reform Back on Track,* another volume edited by Kahlenberg.

The need to ensure that a good education remains accessible for students across the income spectrum does not end with high school, and so The Century Foundation has also published three volumes edited by Kahlenberg that look at how to increase the prospects for low-income students in college: *America's Untapped Resources: Low-Income Students in Higher Education* (2004), *Rewarding Strivers: Helping Low-Income Students Succeed in College* (2010), and *Affirmative Action for the Rich: Legacy Preferences in College Admissions.* In addition, The Century Foundation also has just established its Task Force on Preventing Community Colleges from Becoming Separate and Unequal, which will begin its work this year. More can be found about the work of the task force, as well as our other ongoing efforts in the area of education, on our website, www.tcf.org.

The need to preserve public education as an engine of social mobility is vital. Socioeconomic school integration, where it has been put into place, has shown very promising results and should be the next frontier for increasing the return from our public schools. On behalf of the Trustees of The Century Foundation, I thank Richard Kahlenberg for assembling another pathbreaking body of research, and his colleagues for their work on this important topic.

Janice Nittoli, *President*
The Century Foundation
January 2012

Contents

1

Introduction:

Socioeconomic School Integration

RICHARD D. KAHLENBERG

Almost fifty years ago, the federally authorized Coleman Report—which is "widely regarded as the most important educational study of the twentieth century"[1]—found that the most powerful predictor of academic achievement is the socioeconomic status of a child's family, and the second most important predictor is the socioeconomic status of the classmates in her school. In other words, being born poor imposes a disadvantage; but attending a school with large numbers of low-income classmates presents a second, independent, challenge.

Until very recently, the second finding, about the importance of reducing concentrations of school poverty, has been consciously ignored by policymakers, despite publication of study after study that confirmed Coleman's findings.[2] And in Washington, D.C., to this day, the education debate has centered on trying to "fix" high-poverty schools by investing greater resources into them, paying educators more to teach in them, or turning them into charter schools.

But in recent years, across the country, a number of local school districts have quietly begun pursuing a promising strategy to reduce the proportion of high-poverty schools altogether by integrating students from rich and poor families. These efforts at socioeconomic school integration seek to avoid the problems associated with compulsory busing from the 1970s by relying primarily on voluntary choice, using integration incentives such as magnet schools. The number of such districts employing socioeconomic integration has risen from just a few a decade ago to more than eighty today, educating some four million students. The districts are large (Chicago, Illinois) and small (Burlington, Vermont); northeastern (Amherst, Massachusetts), southern (Jefferson County, Kentucky), western (San Diego, California), and midwestern (Omaha, Nebraska). (See the Appendix for a full list.) Districts measure socioeconomic status by looking at a student's eligibility for free or reduced-price lunch, or by examining census data, including such factors as parental education, single-parent household status, and median income.

Four forces appear to be driving the socioeconomic integration movement. First, as a matter of law, integrating by socioeconomic status offers substantial advantages over integrating by race. In 2007, the U.S. Supreme Court restricted the ability of school districts to use race as a factor in student assignment in the cases of *Parents Involved in Community Schools v. Seattle School District No. 1* and *Meredith v. Jefferson County Board of Education.*[3] When the Supreme Court struck down racial integration plans in Seattle and Louisville, many districts seeking to preserve racial diversity turned to socioeconomic plans as a legally bulletproof way of achieving diversity without using race per se. In 2008, the *New York Times Magazine* called socioeconomic plans "The Next Kind of Integration."[4]

Second, districts, under increasing pressure to raise the achievement of low-income and minority students, are beginning to heed the evidence suggesting that one of the most effective ways to do so is to give low-income and working-class students a chance to attend predominantly middle-class schools. Although the media shower tremendous attention on high-poverty public schools or charter schools that have positive results (such as KIPP), the fact remains that it is extremely difficult to make high-poverty schools work on a system-wide basis. According to research by the University of Wisconsin's Douglas Harris, middle-class schools are twenty-two times as likely to be high performing as high-poverty schools.[5] Likewise, on the National Assessment of Educational Progress, low-income fourth grade students given the chance to attend more-affluent schools in math are two years ahead of low-income students stuck in high-poverty schools.[6]

The reasons for better performance are straightforward. Low-income students in middle-class schools are, on average, surrounded by peers who are more academically engaged and less likely to act out than those in high-poverty schools; a community of parents who are able to be more actively involved in school affairs and know how to hold school officials accountable; and stronger teachers who have high expectations for students.[7]

Third, in an era of tight budgets, some school districts appear to be attracted to socioeconomic integration as a more cost-effective means of raising student achievement than pouring additional dollars into high-poverty schools. As is outlined below in further detail, socioeconomic integration is highly cost-effective.[8] In North Carolina, for example, Charlotte-Mecklenburg has sought to raise achievement through an innovative Pre-K program and extra expenditures in high-poverty schools; by contrast, Wake County, North Carolina, has sought to raise achievement through socioeconomic integration. Both had measures of success, but according to a study by the Center for American Progress, Wake County's integration approach was more cost effective.[9]

Fourth, the problem of poverty concentrations is growing, and the type of district grappling with the issue is no longer confined to those in urban areas. According to the U.S. Department of Education's *Condition of Education,* 47 percent of elementary school students now attend majority low-income schools, and the proportion of high-poverty schools has grown from 34 percent in 1999 to 47 percent in 2008.[10] A 2010 Brookings Institution report, "The Suburbanization of Poverty," found that in the nation's largest metropolitan areas, more poor people live in large suburbs than in their primary cities.[11]

With the number of school districts integrating by socioeconomic status growing, The Century Foundation thought it would be appropriate to assemble leading scholars to analyze in further detail this new approach to narrowing the achievement gap.[12] In particular, this volume seeks to analyze the benefits, costs, logistics, and politics of socioeconomic school integration, as well as its relevance to ongoing policy debates about turnaround schools and charters.

Part I of this volume asks: Do students learn more in socioeconomically integrated schools—and Pre-K programs—than in high-poverty institutions? What are the financial costs of integration programs, and do the benefits outweigh the expense? If so, by how much?

In Part II, we ask: Is socioeconomic integration logistically and politically feasible? What proportion of high-poverty schools (those with more than 50 percent of students receiving subsidized lunch) could be reduced through intradistrict integration? What proportion through interdistrict integration? Are there more affluent, higher-performing public schools within reasonable driving distance that have space to accept low-income transfer students? If logistically feasible, is socioeconomic integration politically viable? Do some approaches make integration more politically palatable than others?

Finally, in Part III, we examine the relevance of socioeconomic integration strategies being pursued by states and localities to ongoing policy debates in Washington, D.C., where the issue of integration remains largely off the table. Should the effort to turn around the nation's lowest-performing schools incorporate the lessons of socioeconomic integration programs? Would the burgeoning charter school movement benefit from taking affirmative steps to promote economic diversity?

Part I: The Benefits and Costs of Socioeconomic Integration

The volume begins with a chapter by Heather Schwartz of the RAND Corporation, which analyzes the educational outcomes of low-income elementary school students who had access to a wide variety of neighborhoods and schools in Montgomery County, Maryland, a diverse and high-achieving district outside of Washington, D.C. The study, when first released in October 2010, was featured on the front page of the *Washington Post,* and later in a column in the *New York Times.*[13]

Schwartz's research takes advantage of a rare opportunity to compare two education approaches.[14] On the one hand, the Montgomery County school district has invested substantial extra resources in its lowest-income schools to employ a number of innovative educational approaches. On the other hand, the county also has a longstanding inclusionary housing policy that allows low-income students to live in middle- and upper-middle-class communities and attend fairly affluent schools.

Thus, Montgomery County offers an interesting experiment: Do low-income students perform better in higher-poverty schools that receive greater resources, or in more-affluent schools with fewer resources? Which matters more for low-income students: extended learning time, lower class size, and intensive teacher development programs—all made available in Montgomery County's higher-poverty schools—or the types of advantages usually associated with wealthier schools, such as positive peer role models, active parental communities, and strong teachers?

Schwartz's results are unmistakable: low-income students attending lower-poverty elementary schools (and living in lower-poverty neighborhoods) significantly outperformed low-income elementary students who attend higher-poverty schools with state of the art educational interventions. By the end of elementary school, Schwartz finds, students living in public housing who attended the lower-poverty schools cut their initial, sizable math achievement gap with non-poor students in the district by half. For reading, it was cut by one-third. In math, students in public housing achieved at 0.4 of a standard deviation higher in more affluent schools than less-affluent ones, which is substantially larger than the 0.1 effects size often found for educational interventions. The study did not specifically measure the effect of the inclusionary housing program on the achievement of middle-class students, but Montgomery County's non-poor students are among the highest-achieving in the state and the nation.

What is particularly remarkable about the comparative success of students in public housing attending Montgomery County's more-affluent schools is they were not besting students stuck in lousy schools but rather students in schools that saw improvement. Indeed, the school system's interventions in its less-affluent schools, have been generally effective, and widely lauded. Under the leadership of then-Superintendent Jerry Weast, school officials divided county schools in two roughly equal groups—more-affluent "green zone" elementary schools and less-affluent "red zone schools"—and then poured an extra $2,000 per student into red zone schools, much to the chagrin of many wealthy parents. As Stacey Childress, Denis Doyle, and David Thomas write in their 2009 book, *Leading for Equity,* Weast's strategies helped decrease the achievement gap with whites in third grade reading from 35 percentage points in 2003 to 19 points in 2008 for African Americans, and from 43 points to 17 points for Hispanics. "Improvements of this magnitude in a district of this size in so little time are rare in public education," they wrote.[15] Schwartz's research confirms that students in Montgomery County's red zone schools had higher performance on state tests than students in demographically similar schools statewide.

The success of this red zone/green zone intervention deserves acclaim. But it was Montgomery County's "inclusionary zoning" policy, long advocated by researchers such as David Rusk, that had a far more pronounced positive educational effect. Under a policy adopted in the early 1970s, developers of large subdivisions are required to set aside between 12 percent and 15 percent of units for low-income and working-class families. The housing authority purchases up to one-third of the inclu-sionary zoning homes to operate as public housing apartments that are scattered throughout the county. Families eligible for public housing enter a lottery and are randomly assigned to public housing apartments.

Schwartz's study traces the academic progress of 850 students in pub-lic housing in red zone and green zone elementary schools between 2001 and 2007. The average family income of these students was $21,047, and 87 percent were from female-headed households. By race, the stu-dent population was 72 percent African American, 16 percent Hispanic, 6 percent Asian, and 6 percent white.

The study has national significance not only because it found a very large longitudinal effect from economic integration, but also because it helps answer a question about whether the superior performance of low-income students in more-affluent schools nationwide is simply an artifact of self-selection. We know that low-income students in more-affluent schools routinely outperform low-income students in high-pov-erty schools, but researchers wondered: Might the result reflect the high level of motivation among families who scrape to get their children into good schools? Schwartz's study controls for that factor by comparing students whose families were assigned by lottery into red zone and green zone schools. (And, unlike research based on charter school lotteries, the attrition rate in Montgomery County public housing is extremely low.) Professors Jeffrey Henig and Henry Levin, who advised Schwartz in her research as part of a dissertation at Columbia University, applaud her "rigorous" analysis of "a unique and original data set."[16]

On the surface, Schwartz's study would seem to contradict results from a federal housing income integration program known as Moving to Opportunity (MTO), which saw few academic gains for children. But MTO involved students who moved to schools that were mostly still high poverty, with an average free and reduced-price lunch population of 67.5 percent (compared to a control group attending schools with 73.9 percent of students receiving subsidized lunches). The Montgomery County experiment allowed low-income students to attend some very-low-poverty schools, similar to the wildly successful Gautreaux program in Chicago.[17] Schwartz found the achievement benefits extended to stu-dents in public housing attending schools with up to 30 percent low-income student populations.

Does this research suggest that 30 percent is a "tipping point," after which low-income students generally will cease to benefit from economically integrated schooling? Schwartz concludes that it does not. The vast majority of the schools in Schwartz's sample had low-income populations of between 0 percent and 60 percent. Because other research has found that the negative effects of concentrated poverty are compounded in very-high-poverty schools, it may well be that low-income students in, say, 30 percent to 50 percent low-income schools perform better than students in 60 percent to 100 percent low-income schools, but Montgomery County does not have enough truly high-poverty schools to test the hypothesis.[18]

One interesting question raised by the study is to what extent students benefited from living in more-advantaged neighborhoods, compared with attending more-advantaged schools. Schwartz finds that roughly two-thirds of the benefit comes from the school, and one-third from the neighborhood.[19] This suggests there may considerable value in programs that integrate at the school level alone, though greater benefits clearly accrue from integration at both the neighborhood and school levels.

If socioeconomic integration shows such promise at the elementary school level, would students in Pre-K programs also benefit from socioeconomic integration? Very little research has been conducted to date on the issue, but in chapter 3, Jeanne Reid outlines the findings of her important new study, which draws on her dissertation at Teachers College, Columbia University. She concludes that socioeconomic integration can improve learning for students in early childhood educational settings, a finding that should make policymakers rethink the way we currently educate many students.

Socioeconomic integration in preschool is not a new concept. Edward Zigler, one of the founding fathers of the federal Head Start program, originally hoped it would be socioeconomically integrated, but his view did not prevail.[20] Unfortunately, today many public Pre-K models, including the federal Head Start program, employ explicit means testing that effectively promotes concentrations of poverty, which actually may limit the effectiveness of these interventions.

As Reid notes, however, today's push for universal Pre-K programs provides a fresh opportunity to try a new socioeconomically integrated model. For example, one study of 169 state-sponsored Pre-K classrooms found that half had 38 percent or fewer students from households at or below 150 percent of the poverty line.[21]

In her study, Reid examines the performance of 2,966 four-year-old students in 704 Pre-K classrooms located in eleven states. After carefully controlling for a number of factors, including the individual socioeconomic status of student families, and the racial composition of the classroom, Reid finds that being in a classroom with an above-average socioeconomic composition had a positive impact on achievement in three areas: receptive language, expressive language, and math learning. (In a fourth area, social skills learning, socioeconomic composition did not have an impact, perhaps because of the subjective nature of the evaluation.)

The positive impact of being in a socioeconomically integrated preschool on growth in receptive language, expressive language, and math learning was telling, Reid says, especially because children in her study spent relatively little time in the preschool classroom itself. The average time between the fall and spring assessments, she notes, was five months, and more than half of the children attended half-day programs. These part-time students spent an average of just 2.7 hours per day in preschool, of which only 32 minutes were spent on language and literacy, and just 10 minutes on math.[22]

"Despite this limited exposure," Reid finds, socioeconomic classroom composition had an effect on receptive language, expressive language, and math learning "comparable in size to two other aspects of children's learning that we know from other research are very important: children's own SES [socioeconomic status] and instructional quality."[23] The socioeconomic composition of a preschool classroom, she concludes "was a significant and positive predictor" of learning.[24] This was true even though low-SES classrooms were twice as likely to offer meals, 1.4 times more likely to offer family services, and 1.9 times more likely to offer health services than high SES classrooms.[25]

Why did schoolchildren tend to make larger gains in more-affluent preschool classrooms? Reid finds that higher instructional quality in higher SES classrooms cannot fully explain the gains, and concludes that the impact of peers is likely to be important.

Reid finds that children benefit from moving from a below-average SES classroom to an above-average SES classroom, but what happens to the students in the more-affluent classrooms? Up to a point, the increasing presence of low-SES students actually increases receptive language learning in Pre-K classrooms, she finds. However, the benefits of socioeconomic integration dissipate as the SES for the classroom approaches the mean SES for all classrooms, so as a policy matter, "middle- and high-SES children should represent a majority of the children in the classroom."[26] (In Reid's study, "middle-SES children" come from families with a mean income of $27,868 and mothers with a mean of 12.6 years of education.)

Overall, Reid's research on socioeconomic integration of Pre-K programs shows strikingly similar results to those found at the K–12 level. Controlling for individual family socioeconomic status, children's learning is greater in more-affluent Pre-K programs, even though special support services may be less prevalent. Increased teacher quality cannot fully explain the gains; peer effects seem to be significant. And the optimal mix is one that involves a majority of students who are middle- and high-SES.

Chapter 4 takes up the important issue—particularly in times of tight budgets—of whether socioeconomic school integration provides substantial "bang for the buck." Opponents of integration have long claimed that money used to transport children to integrated schools should instead be devoted to classroom education. It is a nice political slogan, but as the Schwartz chapter demonstrates, integration can produce far better achievement gains than pouring extra funds into high-poverty schools. And, according to a new paper by Marco Basile, a former Century Foundation employee now pursuing a law degree and Ph.D. in history at Harvard University, the total public and private return on investment in socioeconomic integration appears to greatly exceed the costs.[27]

The McKinsey and Company consulting firm, as Basile notes, has found that "school spending in the United States is amongst the least cost-effective in the world,"[28] yet little attention has been paid to the question of whether our relatively high rates of economic school segregation play a role in this problem. Early in the tenure of the Obama administration, I met with a high-ranking education department official (who himself had worked at McKinsey), and he asked me whether anyone had performed a cost-benefit analysis on socioeconomic school integration. When I mentioned this question to some friends in the civil rights movement, they balked, suggesting that integration is a moral imperative that should not be subject to such analysis. But socioeconomic school integration is also an education reform strategy, which means its effectiveness needs to be gauged, and so Basile undertook what appears to be the first attempt nationally to quantify the costs and benefits of socioeconomic integration.

Given research findings that indicate most economic segregation occurs between districts rather than within them, Basile estimates the costs and benefits of a model in which two-way public school choice interdistrict programs are enacted. Recognizing the political obstacles of integration under old-style compulsory busing plans, he examines the costs of programs that create incentives for middle-class families to participate voluntarily in integration: the creation of magnet schools in disadvantaged areas (which adopt special themes or pedagogical approaches) to attract middle-class students by choice; and a design for financial incentives to entice more-affluent schools to accept low-income transfer students voluntarily.

Rather than examining the effects of complete socioeconomic integration (which is probably unachievable), Basile's model looks at the effect of reducing socioeconomic segregation by one-half nationally—a level of integration enjoyed in many individual communities already.[29] He estimates that in order to cut economic segregation in half, one-fourth of low-income students would need to transfer to more affluent schools while one-fourth of more-affluent students would need to transfer to newly created magnet schools located in more-disadvantaged neighborhoods.[30]

Drawing upon a wide body of research, Basile estimates the costs of creating magnet programs with special themes and pedagogical approaches (transportation costs, special teacher training, and additional equipment) at roughly 10 percent greater than the costs of regular public school education.[31] Likewise, he estimates the cost of creating financial incentives to "magnetize" low-income students in order to make transfers attractive to middle-class schools at a 10 percent premium overall. (Because only one-fourth of low-income students would move to middle-class schools under the model, the effective funding bonus per low-income student is 40 percent, to be shared with all students in the receiving school.) This funding premium is far more generous than several existing metropolitan interdistrict integration programs in places such as Boston and Hartford.[32] Averaged out over all pupils, Basile estimates the per pupil net present value of total costs over seven years of integrated schooling at $6,340.[33]

In measuring the benefits, Basile points to a comprehensive study of segregation and high school graduation rates, which suggests that decreasing socioeconomic segregation to one-half the national average is associated with a ten-percentage-point increase in high school graduation.[34] Basile examines the effects on increased high school graduation rates (as opposed, say, to increased academic achievement) because there is a much broader consensus among researchers about the economic benefits.[35] The net lifetime public benefits of having a student graduate high school are estimated at $209,200 in constant 2004 dollars, coming in the form of increased tax revenue due to greater earnings; decreased health care spending, decreased criminal justice system costs, and decreased spending on welfare.[36]

Averaged out over all students, the public benefit per student is over $20,000, and the combined public and private benefits amount to about $33,000 per student, far exceeding the cost of $6,340 per student. Put differently, Basile estimates that the public return on investment in socioeconomic integration exceeds costs by a factor of 3.3 and the total return (public and private) exceeds costs by a factor of 5.2.[37] This type of return exceeds almost all other investments in education (private school vouchers, reduced class size, and improvements in teacher quality) with the exception of investments in very high quality early childhood education.[38]

Basile suggests his estimate probably undervalues the full benefits of socioeconomic integration, for a number of reasons. He uses a conservative estimate of the impact of socioeconomic integration on high school graduate rates; individual districts such as St. Louis and Hartford have seen larger rises in graduation than the ten-percentage-point increase Basile relies upon.[39] He employs conservative estimates of the economic benefits of high school graduation. He estimates only the benefits that magnet schools bring because of socioeconomic integration, excluding potential ancillary benefits from providing a closer fit between student interests and curriculum.[40] He does not count the civic benefits to our democracy of having more highly educated citizens; nor the benefits to the children of high school graduates in the form of improved life chances. And he does not count the benefits to the workplace of having employees who know how to get along with workers of different socioeconomic and racial backgrounds.[41]

In sum, rather than representing a diversion of funds to "busing" or transportation, spending that reduces socioeconomic school segregation, Basile concludes, is among the wisest possible investments in all of education.

Part II: The Logistics and Politics of Socioeconomic Integration

While socioeconomic integration is a good investment, is it logistically feasible, given the distances between rich and poor neighborhoods in America? And can socioeconomic integration be made politically palatable to middle-class Americans?

In chapter 5, educators Ann Mantil, Anne G. Perkins, and Stephanie Aberger address whether public policy can do much to reduce socioeconomic segregation, asking the key logistical question: Is class segregation "an ugly but immutable reality," as some suggest?[42] They conclude it is not, though they acknowledge that the challenges are certainly significant. Today, Mantil, Perkins, and Aberger find, nearly 15 million American public elementary school students attend "high-poverty" schools, which they define as those in which a majority of students are eligible for free or reduced-price lunch.[43] They point out that the percentage of high-poverty elementary schools has increased significantly, from 34 percent in 1999 to 47 percent in 2008. But in what appears to be the first national estimate of the viability of socioeconomic school integration, the authors conclude that "dramatic reductions in the number of high-poverty schools across the United States are within reach."[44]

The authors' study draws upon the National Center for Education Statistics' Common Core of Data from 2007–08 in forty-six states for which data are available. Their study focuses on students in public elementary schools, because subsidized lunch eligibility at that level is thought to be a more reliable indicator of true socioeconomic status than in middle and high schools, where students may avoid the program because they feel stigmatized when receiving free or reduced-price meals.[45] Mantil, Perkins, and Aberger draw several important conclusions.

First, they find there is "dramatic variation" in the presence of high-poverty schools by state, from just 4 percent of elementary schools in New Hampshire to 85 percent in Mississippi.[46] Significantly, the authors find a strong correlation between socioeconomic school segregation in a state and the size of the achievement gap between low-income and higher-income students. Examining achievement gaps on the National Assessment of Educational Progress (NAEP) for math and reading in 2007 and 2009, the authors found "a strong positive relationship between the SES achievement gap and the degree of socioeconomic school segregation," ranging from a correlation of 0.64 to 0.74.[47]

Second, the authors find a strong relationship between race or ethnicity and attendance of high-poverty schools. Blacks and Latinos are twice as likely to attend high-poverty elementary schools as non-Hispanic whites. "While it is increasingly difficult in the United States to predict a family's income based on their race, more often than not one *can* predict whether a child attends a high-poverty school simply by knowing whether she is black, Latino, Asian, Native American, or white."[48]

Importantly, the authors found variation by state in the degree to which minority students were likely to attend high-poverty schools, and black and Latino students had smaller gaps with whites when they were less likely to be stuck in high-poverty school environments. Examining NAEP data, Mantil, Perkins, and Aberger find that "states with larger black-white and Latino-white gaps in high-poverty school enrollment tend to have larger achievement gaps," with "moderate to large correlations," ranging from 0.56 to 0.75.[49] While policymakers and analysts often point to different levels of performance of minority students in different states—and suggest that teacher practices and school leadership may be possible explanations[50]—variations in socioeconomic isolation, a factor not often mentioned, may play a significant role.

Third, the authors conclude that the potential for reducing the number of majority low-income schools through intradistrict solutions is relatively modest in most states. Overall, states could reduce the number of high-poverty schools by 5 percent with intradistrict strategies, benefitting 0.5 million students. Intradistrict efforts would have modest effects, the authors find, because most high-poverty schools are located in high-poverty districts. But in seven states—New Hampshire, Wyoming, Maryland, Utah, Nevada, North Dakota, and Virginia—intradistrict integration could reduce the number of high-poverty schools by more than 20 percent.[51]

Finally, the authors conclude that while intradistrict integration plans usually would have a modest effect, interdistrict integration efforts could have a very substantial impact in reducing the proportion of high-poverty schools in the United States. Inter-district racial or socioeconomic integration programs already exist in numerous jurisdictions, including Minneapolis, Omaha, Boston, Rochester, St. Louis, Hartford, Milwaukee, San Diego, and Bergen County, New Jersey, the authors note.[52]

To examine the potential impact of interdistrict integration plans, the authors examine six sample states—Massachusetts, Virginia, Colorado, Nebraska, Missouri, and Florida—that "represent a diverse cross-section in terms of enrollment, district size, population density, and student demographics."[53] In modeling the effects, they assume, rather conservatively, that transfers would be made only to contiguous school districts.[54] (In fact, many existing interdistrict integration plans, such as the Boston METCO program, involve students traveling farther distances to noncontiguous suburban districts.)

The authors conclude that the benefits of interdistrict programs range widely, from reducing the number of high-poverty schools by 7 percent in Florida to 52 percent in Nebraska. Virginia could see a 36 percent reduction, Colorado and Massachusetts a 34 percent reduction each, and Missouri a 17 percent reduction.[55] Taking intra- and interdistrict strategies together in these six states could result in substantial reductions of high-poverty schools in five of those states. While Florida could see a relatively modest 13 percent reduction, two states could see a reduction of more than one-third (37 percent each in Missouri and Massachusetts), and three states could see a reduction of more than one-half (52 percent in Colorado, 58 percent in Nebraska, and 60 percent in Virginia).[56]

In sum, the authors conclude, a great deal could be done to reduce the proportion of high-poverty public elementary schools in the United States. Socioeconomic integration strategies, particularly those that aim to reduce interdistrict segregation, could "dramatically reduce the national number of high-poverty schools."[57]

Chapter 6, written by Meredith P. Richards, Kori Stroub, and Jennifer Jellison Holme, all of the University of Texas at Austin, takes a look at the logistics of interdistrict choice through a related lens: the feasibility of interdistrict transfers out of failing high-poverty schools under the No Child Left Behind Act (NCLB).[58] In important ways, the work by Richards, Stroub, and Holme complements the analysis of the Mantil, Perkins, and Aberger study by examining key additional issues, such as whether there is space at transfer schools within a reasonable driving distance.

The right of students to transfer from "failing" Title I schools to attend a better-performing public school within their district was originally one of the most talked about provisions of NCLB. Many conservatives supported the provision as a way of promoting competition among schools. Meanwhile, some liberals supported the idea as a way of liberating low-income students from segregated high-poverty schools.

Today, the existing public school choice provision is widely seen as an example of one of the ways in which NCLB is "broken." Very few eligible students—fewer than 2 percent—take advantage of public school choice under NCLB, and the rates are lower among black and Hispanic students than white students.[59] Some believe that low transfer rates suggest that parents want neighborhood schools, even if those schools are weak. Education Secretary Arne Duncan has criticized "federally dictated . . .

school-transfer options" as doing little good.[60] But research by Richards, Stroub, and Holme suggests that low-income parents may fail to utilize transfer rights not because they are necessarily satisfied with their local school but because other schools within the district are not much better.

Using comprehensive data from the 2004–05 school year (the most recent year available), the authors examined 61,000 schools in forty-five states, educating 65 percent of the nation's students. They find that under current intradistrict choice policies, students in 94.5 percent of failing schools have "no meaningful access to higher-performing schools," because other schools in the district either do not perform better, or have no capacity for transfers.

One obvious solution—to allow students to cross school district lines to attend better-performing public schools—raises an empirical question: Is there space in suburban schools within a reasonable driving distance? A 2008 study published by Education Sector, a think tank that advocates charter schools and online learning, suggested that interdistrict choice would not help many students because of space and distance constraints.[61] But Richards, Stroub, and Holme point out that the study was deeply flawed by arbitrarily assuming that receiving schools could expand student populations by no more than 10 percent and that driving distances could not exceed twenty minutes. The latter assumption was undermined by evidence from existing programs in Boston, Hartford, and elsewhere that suggest that students are willing to travel substantially farther if what is at the end of the bus ride is sufficiently attractive. The 10 percent capacity assumption, Richards, Stroub, and Holme note, had no empirical basis whatsoever.

Richards and colleagues have produced a far more sophisticated analysis, drawing upon a "gravity model" used to predict traveling behavior and to model accessibility to such resources as grocery stores, bus stops, and health clinics. The gravity model considers both distance and the attractiveness of the destination. In the case of schools, the model suggests that families will be willing to travel farther for very high performing schools than those that are only marginally better than a sending school. In contrast to the earlier Education Sector study, Richards, Stroub, and Holme calculate school capacity not by assuming an arbitrary amount of space but by examining the actual student-teacher ratio in schools and considering a facility full when it reaches the seventy-fifth percentile student-teacher ratios for the state.[62]

Using this more sophisticated model, they find that interdistrict choice would vastly expand options for students in failing schools. Richards, Stroub, and Holme conclude: "Contrary to the findings of previous research, the current study finds than an NCLB interdistrict choice policy, if implemented nationally, has the potential to meaningfully expand access to higher-performing schools for students in over 80 percent of eligible sending schools."[63] The average number of slots available to students in struggling schools would increase by 128 percent. Most importantly, the average sending school's "accessibility value," a measure that incorporates both increased access to receiving schools and the comparative quality of those schools, would increase five-fold.[64]

Moreover, interdistrict choice would disproportionately benefit students in schools with high proportions of low-income and minority students, their research finds. For example, a school with a low-income population of 95 percent would see gain in access under interdistrict choice "more than twice as large" as a school in which 45 percent of students were low-income.[65] This finding obviously has important implications for socioeconomic school integration.

Of course, just because interdistrict choice is logistically feasible and educationally sound does not make it politically palatable. Upper-middle-class families, who have considerable political power, often purchase homes in a certain neighborhood with the idea of having their children attend the neighborhood school. Can integration be made politically palatable? What sort of incentives can be offered to encourage all families to see socioeconomic integration as beneficial?

Politics is the subject of chapter 7, written by Sheneka Williams of the University of Georgia. Williams conducted in-depth interviews in three communities that have pursued socioeconomic integration plans: Wake County (Raleigh), North Carolina; Jefferson County (Louisville), Kentucky; and Champaign, Illinois. While acknowledging the tough political challenges associated with integration policies, she draws important lessons about how the particular mechanics of integration plans can significantly enhance the political attractiveness of socioeconomic diversity policies.

The Wake County School District, which encompasses the city of Raleigh and the surrounding suburban areas, has received a great deal of media attention in recent years for the political controversy surrounding its socioeconomic integration plan. The eighteenth-largest school district nationally, Wake is the largest district in North Carolina, with more than 140,000 students. The 800-square-mile district was created in 1976 by the merger of the Raleigh and suburban Wake school districts.[66] The district's student population is 50 percent white, 25 percent African American, 15 percent Latino, and 6 percent Asian, with 32 percent of students eligible for free or reduced-price lunch.[67]

In the early 1980s, Wake County adopted a voluntary racial integration plan with the goal that all schools should be between 15 percent and 45 percent black. In order to achieve integration largely through choice, almost all of the Raleigh schools were turned into magnets. In 2000, given legal concerns about the use of race, and a sense among school researchers that poverty concentrations were of great educational concern, Wake County shifted to a socioeconomic diversity plan, with a goal that all schools should not exceed student populations that were more than 40 percent low income.[68]

For many years, academic achievement rose, the program drew wide support, and pro-integration candidates continued to be elected to the school board.[69] But over time, Wake County became, in a sense, the victim of its own success. In part because the schools were highly regarded, Wake County's business climate thrived, new families moved to the area, and large numbers of students were added each year. In order to accommodate skyrocketing growth, increasing numbers of students were reassigned to fill new schools, generating anger among parents. Moreover, increasing numbers of families relocated from other areas of the country, and the newcomers did not fully understand the county's history of integration and its importance as an educational strategy. District officials, Williams notes, were "playing to a parade, and not a crowd."[70]

At the same time, the booming economy attracted a large influx of Latino students, many of them low-income. A relatively small presence in 2000, Latinos made up 15 percent of the student population by 2010, creating new challenges to maintaining the 40 percent low-income student cap in any given school.[71] Parental anger at the school district peaked when exploding growth led some families to have their children mandatorily assigned to schools with a staggered year-round calendar (rather than a traditional schedule with summers off) in order to make better use of building capacity.

In October 2009, with an influx of funding from the Koch brothers and other conservative interests, including the Tea Party, opponents of the socioeconomic integration plan gained a 5–4 majority on the school board and vowed to establish a system of neighborhood schools.[72] The majority did succeed in officially eliminating the 40 percent low-income cap for schools, but it ran into major community resistance in efforts to establish a system of de facto segregated neighborhood schools.

Resistance to re-segregation, Williams notes, came from an interesting coalition of civil rights groups and teachers on the one hand, and white magnet school parents and business leaders on the other. Furthermore, critical centrist voters became disillusioned with the conservative school board majority following a series of events.

First was the resignation of superintendent Del Burns, who said that he could not, in good conscience, play a part in re-segregating Wake County schools. Then, when the school board moved to immediately reassign a small number of low-income and minority students, the NAACP filed a complaint with the U.S. Department of Education's Office for Civil Rights. An accreditation agency also began reviewing Wake County's status.

Civil rights groups organized protests at board meetings, which drew national attention, including a front page *Washington Post* story highlighting the turmoil. As Williams notes, television comedian Stephen Colbert ridiculed Wake County's board, suggesting, "What's the use of living in a gated community if my kids go to school and get poor all over them?" By 2011, a survey of local residents found that 51 percent of local residents viewed the school board unfavorably, compared with just 29 percent who viewed it favorably.[73]

The Chamber of Commerce, which supported integration as a way of strengthening schools and preparing employees to work with a diverse set of colleagues, commissioned a plan, released in February 2011, to use public school choice to accommodate growth and also produce diversity. The plan tweaked the earlier socioeconomic goal to employ, instead, diversity measured by academic achievement, a very close cousin of socioeconomic status. It was clear that business leaders did not appreciate national publicity suggesting that a world-class community was planning to consciously re-segregate its schools.

In the fall 2011 school board elections, Democrats swept into office, ousting the Republican school board chair who had led the effort for neighborhood schools. As of this writing, the Wake County situation is still in flux, but it appears that the school district is likely to embrace a third way. Eschewing both a continuation of integration by mandatory assignment and proposals to re-segregate through neighborhood schools, policymakers appear ready to pursue a hybrid: integration by achievement levels through school choice.[74]

In contrast to Wake County, Williams writes, in Jefferson County (Louisville), Kentucky, a coalition of civil rights groups, teachers, and the business community organized early to support integration and thus avoid a conservative school board takeover.

Like Wake County schools, the Jefferson County schools, which educate 96,000 students, were created by a merger of city and suburban schools in the mid-1970s. After a period of court-ordered mandatory busing for racial desegregation, Jefferson County schools adopted a plan, in the mid-1990s, using magnet schools to create racial integration, with the goal that all schools should be between 15 percent and 50 percent black. In 2002, Williams notes, white parents sued, charging that the use of race in student assignment violated the Fourteenth Amendment's Equal Protection Clause; in 2007, the U.S. Supreme Court agreed.[75]

Jefferson County leaders did not give up on integration, however, and in 2008, the county adopted a new plan that emphasizes socioeconomic status, along with race, in student assignment. Instead of looking at the individual race or socioeconomic status of students, the county's plan looks at the geographic areas in which students live and labels them as either Area A (having a below-average income and education level, and above-average minority population) or Area B (the converse). In the plan, students choose the schools they want to attend, and county officials honor choices with an eye to having Area A students constitute between 15 percent and 50 percent of the student body.

In the 2010 school board elections, supporters of diversity feared they might face the same upheaval that Wake felt in its 2009 elections, but in fact a pro-integration school board majority remained in power. How was Jefferson County able to avoid most of the political turmoil associated with the Wake County plan? Williams suggests that teachers and the business community, cognizant of what had happened in Wake County, aggressively supported pro-diversity candidates with strong financial contributions. By emphasizing the choice mechanism, Jefferson County also avoided large-scale redistricting that so angered many Wake County parents. According to Williams, 80 percent of parents in Jefferson County favor retaining a diversity component in the student assignment plan.[76]

The third district studied by Williams—Champaign Unit 4 Schools in central Illinois—has seen the least amount of political resistance of all. Located in a college community that is sharply divided between blacks in the north end and whites in the south end, Champaign educates 10,000 students. District-wide, 42 percent of students are eligible for free or reduced-price lunch.[77]

The district originally adopted a "controlled choice" plan for race, in which parents ranked their preferences among a variety of magnet schools and were assigned in compliance with fairness guidelines to ensure racial integration. In 2009, after a consent decree for racial integration was lifted, district officials shifted to a program of controlled choice based on socioeconomic status. Parents are now asked about such factors as family income, parental education, number of parents in the household, and number of children in the household. The goal is for schools to be within fifteen percentage points of the district-wide average for low-income students.[78] Significantly, Williams notes, "Champaign faced fewer political tensions than did Wake County or Jefferson County."[79] The use of choice, combined with magnet programs that give middle-class families an incentive to integrate, may have been particularly critical.

Looking broadly at the experience in Wake County, Jefferson County, and Champaign, Williams draws four lessons about how to make socioeconomic integration politically sustainable. First, public school choice is a far more popular way to promote integration than compulsory assignment. Choice gives parents a feeling of "ownership," and magnet school offerings provide students with special themes or pedagogical approaches to match their particular interests. As illustrated in Wake County, choice can also provide a much better way to accommodate rapid growth in student populations because schools can be filled through election rather than reassignment.

Choice and incentives can also make interdistrict integration more politically palatable. Strong financial incentives could encourage middle-class students to accept more low-income transfers. Just as the right kind of magnet themes or pedagogical approaches have successfully drawn affluent students into schools in tougher neighborhoods, programs that "magnetize" low-income students can overcome opposition to interdistrict choice. In the St. Louis area, for example, Republican suburban state legislators were among those who backed an interdistrict choice program that allowed substantial numbers of African-American students to attend suburban schools—bringing school funds with them in the bargain.[80]

Second, Williams suggests that constant communication on the part of school officials regarding the rationale for integration policies is critical, particularly in communities such as Wake County, which have seen large increases in new families. Third, to be effective, civil rights groups should build strong alliances with other groups that support integration, including the business community, teachers, and magnet school parents. Finally, national leadership matters. Support from U.S. secretary of education Arne Duncan, and even the comedian Stephen Colbert, may have helped make a difference in turning the Wake County public against a school board seeking to re-segregate the public schools.

Part III: Socioeconomic Integration and the Washington, D.C., Policy Debate over Turnarounds and Charters

Finally, chapter 8 takes up the issue of how socioeconomic integration strategies might be used to address two current policy debates in Washington, D.C.: how to turnaround persistently failing schools, and how to increase the performance of charter schools.

Early in the Obama administration, Education Secretary Arne Duncan courageously took on the most important—and most difficult—problem in American education: turning around America's lowest-performing schools.[81] Duncan noted that for years districts allowed failing schools to slide, and he has called, instead, for "far-reaching reforms" that fundamentally change the culture in the country's worst five thousand schools.[82] Ironically, Duncan's approach, which focused almost entirely on changing the faculty and school governance, was itself too timid.

Duncan wrote in an *Education Week* piece, that in Chicago, "we moved the adults out of the building, kept the children there, and brought in new adults."[83] But the exclusive focus on changing the principal and teachers misses two-thirds of the larger school community—which also includes students and parents. This partial turnaround approach in Chicago was met with "mixed" results, education consultant Bryan Hassel told the *New York Times*.[84] The Civic Committee of the Commercial Club of Chicago noted in a 2009 report that "most students in Chicago Public Schools continue to fail."[85]

Changing the principal and teachers in a school is not enough, in part because it ignores the effects of socioeconomic segregation. As chapter 8 details, in high-poverty schools, a child is surrounded by classmates who are less likely to have big dreams, and, accordingly, are less academically engaged and more likely to act out and cut class. Classmates in high-poverty schools are more likely to move during the school year, creating disruption in the classroom; and less likely to have large vocabularies, which in turn limits the ability of peers on the playground and in the classroom to learn new words.

As chapter 8 outlines, parents are also an important part of a school community. Students benefit when parents regularly volunteer in the classroom and know how to hold school officials accountable when things go wrong. Low-income parents, who may be working several jobs, may not own a car, and may have had a bad experience themselves as students, are four times less likely to be members of a PTA, and are only half as likely to volunteer.

The student and parent makeup of a school, in turn, profoundly affects the type of teachers who can be recruited. Polls consistently find that teachers care more about "work environment" than they do about salary. They care about school safety, whether they will have to spend large portions of their time on classroom management, and whether parents will make sure kids do their homework. That is why it is so difficult to attract and keep great teachers in high-poverty schools, even when bonuses are offered.

Chapter 8 outlines evidence that the most promising "turnaround" model is one that recognizes these realities and seeks to turn high-poverty schools into magnet schools that change not only the faculty but also the student and parent mix in the school. Failing schools can be shuttered and reopened with new themes and pedagogical approaches that attract new teachers and a mix of middle-class and low-income students. Meanwhile, some low-income students from the old school will be given the opportunity to fill the spots vacated by middle-income children who had been attending more-affluent schools.

A leading example comes, as noted earlier, from Wake County, North Carolina. As Gerald Grant notes in his important book, *Hope and Despair in the American City: Why There Are No Bad Schools in Raleigh,* Wake County provided virtually every Raleigh school with a special theme such as science and technology, arts and theater, and International Baccalaureate. Raleigh's inner-city schools, which had been marked by white flight, were soon filled with economically and racially diverse student bodies. Many of the schools had waiting lists.[86] To prevent the creation of enclaves of privilege, the Raleigh magnets are nonselective. The results have been very promising. Wake County, writes Grant, "reduced the gap between rich and poor, black and white, more than any other large urban educational system in America."[87]

Of course, there are plenty of examples of places where magnet schools have failed to attract middle-class families. The most famous is probably the Kansas City high school that featured a $5 million swimming pool, an indoor track, and a model United Nations wired for language translation, yet failed to draw white middle-class students. But well-designed plans poll parents ahead of time and find out what sort of programs would be attractive to them. For example, in Cambridge, Massachusetts, which has a system of universal choice and seeks an economic balance among schools, officials turned the struggling, predominantly low-income Tobin school, located near a large low-income housing complex, into a Montessori school, which emphasizes student-directed learning in mixed-age classrooms. In the 2006–07 school year, Tobin had attracted only twelve first-choice applicants to fill sixty Pre-K and kindergarten seats. The next year, when it reopened as a Montessori, Tobin attracted 145 applicants, with twice as many middle-class as low-income students applying, says Michael Alves, who administers the student lottery.[88]

These types of successful magnet school turnaround efforts appear, finally, to have caught the attention of Washington policymakers. In October 2011, a major proposal in the U.S. Senate would include magnet schools as a turnaround school option.[89]

Using magnet themes to turn around failing high-poverty schools will not work everywhere. Some schools located in extremely dangerous neighborhoods may be unable to attract middle-class children. In those cases, efforts should be made to improve high-poverty schools. But the socioeconomic integration option can be pursued far more often than it currently is, and simply accepting segregation should be a last resort, not the first.

Likewise, the data on the damaging effects of socioeconomic segregation have direct relevance to the future of charter schools. While many educators stand in awe of the impressive efforts of a few efforts—like the Knowledge Is Power Program (KIPP)—to make high-poverty schools work, the fact is that the vast majority of high-poverty charters fail. While in theory charter schools, as schools of choice, could be more socioeconomically integrated than traditional public schools, in fact, they are more segregated. In the 2007–08 school year, 54 percent of charter school students were in high-poverty schools, compared with 39 percent of public school students. Meanwhile, 28 percent of charter school students were in extremely high-poverty schools (more than 75 percent low income) compared with 16 percent of regular public school students.[90] High concentrations of poverty may help explain why the most comprehensive study of charter schools, by the Stanford Center for Research on

Education Outcomes, found that only 17 percent of charter schools out-performed comparable traditional public schools in math, while 46 percent performed the same, and 37 percent performed worse.[91]

Even KIPP schools have succeeded only with self-selected groups of students who apply to, and persist in, a rigorous program. (In San Francisco-area KIPP schools, 60 percent dropped out.) The one time KIPP tried to educate every student in a public school catchment area—in Denver, Colorado—it failed, and got out of the business.[92]

Fundamentally, we need to rethink the basic theory of both charter schools and turnaround schools. The unspoken assumption of current approaches is that teachers in high-poverty schools (and their union protectors) are to blame for academic failure, and that if we could fire those teachers and bring in union-free charter schools, we can fix the problem. Mountains of research, however, suggest that the reason high-poverty schools fail so often is that economic segregation drives failure: it congregates the kids with the smallest dreams, the parents who are most pressed, and burnt out teachers who often cannot get hired elsewhere. How have we come to the point where creating high-quality integrated schools is hardly even part of the charter and turnaround discussions?

Conclusion

Fifty years of research suggests that high-poverty public schools—like high-poverty housing projects—more often than not create negative environments for children. There is ample evidence to suggest that poor kids—given the right environment and the right supports—can achieve at high levels, but an increasing number are stuck in high-poverty schools.

Most public policies today are willfully ignorant of these findings, which are a matter of consensus among social scientists. Our public education system is supposed to provide genuine equal opportunity to students of all walks of life. It is supposed to be the American answer to the European social welfare state. As the evidence in this volume amply demonstrates, socioeconomic integration has substantial benefits that far outweigh the costs; is logistically and politically feasible, if done right; and is directly relevant to some of the key policy debates in Washington. For how long will we continue to ignore the evidence and provide good educations to one set of children while subjecting another set to separate schools of concentrated poverty that simply compound the disadvantages of poverty itself?

The Benefits and Costs of Socioeconomic Integration

2

Housing Policy Is School Policy:

Economically Integrative Housing Promotes Academic Success in Montgomery County, Maryland

HEATHER SCHWARTZ

"School enrollment patterns are closely tied to residential patterns. *In short, housing policy is school policy.*"

—DAVID RUSK[1]

Introduction: Montgomery County as an Exemplary Case of Economic Integration

Montgomery County, Maryland, operates one of the most acclaimed large public school systems in the United States. Although an increasing share of the population of this suburban school district just outside Washington, D.C., is low income, and the majority of its students belong to racial minority groups, the county graduates nine in ten of its students. Two-thirds of its high school students take at least one Advanced Placement course, and the average SAT score in the district greatly exceeds the national average. A recent book has lauded its educational reforms intended to close racial and economic achievement gaps.[2] A large education publisher, Pearson, has acquired rights to sell the district's elementary school curriculum.[3]

Montgomery County also ranks among the top twenty wealthiest counties in the nation, and has done so since its inception in the 1950s. Less than 5 percent of its residents live in poverty, compared to a national rate of 15 percent. Despite the increasing share of low-income students within its school system, a little less than one-third of its approximately 142,000 students qualified for free and reduced-price meals (FARM) in 2010—a ratio that is somewhat lower than the national average (42.9 percent) and far lower than that in most of the largest urban districts such as Los Angeles, Chicago, and New York City, where about three out of every four students qualify.[4]

Montgomery County's reputation as both an affluent area with good schools and a district that serves low-income students relatively well is firmly established. Much less known is the fact that it operates the nation's oldest and by far the largest inclusionary zoning program—a policy that requires real estate developers to set aside a portion of the homes they build to be rented or sold at below-market prices. The zoning stipulation has caused the production of more than 12,000 moderately priced homes in the county since 1976. Similar inclusionary zoning policies have since spread to over one hundred high-cost housing markets in California; Massachusetts; New Jersey; New York City; Santa Fe, New Mexico; Denver and Boulder, Colorado; the greater Washington, D.C., metro area; and Burlington, Vermont, among other places.[5]

A singular feature of Montgomery County's zoning policy is that it allows the public housing authority, the Housing Opportunities Commission, to purchase one-third of the inclusionary zoning homes within each subdivision to operate as federally subsidized public housing, thereby allowing households that typically earn incomes below the poverty line to live in affluent neighborhoods and send their children to schools where the vast majority of students come from families that do not live in poverty. To date, the housing authority has purchased about 700 apartments that are located in market-rate apartment complexes that it operates as public housing. All told, it operates 992 public housing family apartments (some clustered in small public housing developments) that are located in hundreds of neighborhoods throughout the county and are zoned into almost every one of the school district's 131 elementary schools. Families that occupy the public housing apartments in Montgomery County have an average income of $22,460 as of 2007, making them among the poorest households in the county. The apartments are leased at a fraction of the normal market rates: whereas the average monthly rent for a two-bedroom apartment in Montgomery County in 2006 was $1,267, public housing tenants' average rent contribution was $371 (equal to one-third of their income, per federal regulation) in the same year.

The Housing Opportunities Commission randomly assigns applicants to the public housing apartments. Since almost all of the county's elementary schools have neighborhood-based attendance zones, children in public housing thus are assigned randomly to their elementary schools via the public housing placement process. This feature prevents families' self-selection into neighborhoods and elementary schools of their choice, which in turn allows for a fair comparison of children in public housing in low-poverty settings to other children in public housing in higher-poverty settings within the county.

Building on the strength of the random assignment of children to schools, I examine the longitudinal school performance from 2001 to 2007 of approximately 850 students in public housing who attended elementary schools and lived in neighborhoods that fell along a spectrum of very-low-poverty to moderate-poverty rates. In brief, I find that over a period of five to seven years, children in public housing who attended the school district's most-advantaged schools (as measured by either subsidized lunch status or the district's own criteria) far outperformed in math and reading those children in public housing who attended the district's least-advantaged elementary schools.

In this report, I describe the study, the findings, and their ramifications. First, I review why economic integration in neighborhoods and schools might matter in the first place. Then I provide greater context about the Montgomery County school district and the housing policies in question, and briefly describe the methods by which I compare the schooling outcomes of children in public housing. Following that, I set out the results of the study by describing the influence of school poverty (as measured by two different metrics) and neighborhood poverty on children's math and reading outcomes. Then I clarify what can and cannot be learned from this study. Finally, after reviewing my findings, I consider how Montgomery County's experience might pertain to that of similar suburbs, as well as to the challenges facing policymakers concerned with the issues of affordable housing and education.

To anticipate the lengthier discussion below, the following list sets out the main educational and housing-related effects of Montgomery County's economically integrative housing policies.

School-related Findings

- *School-based economic integration effects accrued over time.* After five to seven years, students in public housing who were randomly assigned to low-poverty elementary schools significantly outperformed their peers in public housing who attended moderate-poverty schools in both math and reading. Further, by the end of elementary school, the initial, large achievement gap between children in public housing who attended the district's most advantaged schools and their non-poor students in the district was cut by half for math and one-third for reading.

- *The academic returns from economic integration diminished as school poverty levels rose.* Children who lived in public housing and attended schools where no more than 20 percent of students qualified for a free or reduced-price meal did best, whereas those children in public housing who attended schools where as many as 35 percent of students qualified for a free or reduced-price meal performed no better academically over time than public housing children who attended schools where 35 to 85 percent of students qualified for a free or reduced-price meal. (Note that fewer than 5 percent of schools had more than 60 percent of students from low-income families, and none had more than 85 percent in any year, making it impossible to compare the effects of low-poverty schools with truly high-poverty schools, where 75 percent to 100 percent of the families are low-income.)

- *Using subsidized meals as the metric for measuring school need might be insufficient.* The two different measures of school disadvantage used in this study—subsidized school meal status and Montgomery County's own criteria—each indicate that children from very poor families benefited over the course of five to seven years from attending low-poverty schools. A comparison of the district's own measure of school disadvantage to the most commonly employed measure (subsidized meals) yielded differently sized estimates of the benefits to low-income elementary school children of attending advantaged schools. The differences suggest the shortcoming of the free and reduced-price meal metric as a single indicator of school need.

Housing-related Findings

- *In Montgomery County, inclusionary zoning integrated children from highly disadvantaged families into low-poverty neighborhoods and low-poverty schools over the long term.* The county's inclusionary zoning program generally, and its scattered site public housing program in particular, have been a highly successful means of exposing low-income persons to low-poverty settings. As of the years in which this study took place, families with school-age children living in public housing had stayed in place for an average of eight years, which resulted in long-term exposure of their children to low-poverty settings.
- *Residential stability improved students' academic outcomes.* Even though the families living in public housing in Montgomery County earned very low incomes, they stayed in place for longer periods of time than is typical of public housing families nationally with similar incomes. Their residential stability was a crucial aspect that allowed their children to reap the long-run benefits of attending low-poverty schools.
- *Children in public housing benefited academically from living in low-poverty neighborhoods, but less from attending low-poverty schools.* There is suggestive evidence that, above and beyond which schools they attended, low-income children who lived in very-low-poverty neighborhoods (where 0 percent to 5 percent of families live in poverty) experienced modest academic benefits as compared to those children in public housing who lived in low-poverty neighborhoods (where 5 percent to 10 percent live in poverty). School-based economic integration had about twice as large an effect as neighborhood-based economic integration on low-income children's academic performance. However, the prevailing low poverty rates within Montgomery County allowed for only a limited test of neighborhood poverty effects.

How Economic Integration Matters to Children

With few exceptions, schools in the United States with high concentrations of students from low-income families perform less well than schools with low concentrations of poverty. In 2009, more than one-half of fourth and eighth graders who attended high-poverty schools failed the national reading test, compared to fewer than one in five students from the same grade levels who attended low-poverty schools.[6] The average achievement gap between high- and low-poverty schools has remained virtually unchanged over the past ten years, and slightly exceeds the black-white student achievement gap.[7]

Given the large, persistent academic achievement gap between low- and high-poverty schools, many social scientists and policymakers engaged in housing and education argue that children in low-income households derive substantial benefits from living and attending schools in economically integrated neighborhoods. The concept first gained credibility with the extremely positive results stemming from the 1976 Supreme Court case *Hills* v. *Gautreaux,* which caused the relocation of some Chicago public housing families to affluent suburban settings.[8] Research on those families that moved to suburbs because of *Gautreaux* suggested that poor children typically required a period of one to six years in which to make academic gains, but that after seven years, there were substantial, positive effects on the children's school outcomes. However, the Moving to Opportunity experiment, a subsequent and more exacting test of integrating poor families into non-poor neighborhoods that was conducted in several cities across the country, failed to obtain the same positive educational results for low-income children, in part perhaps because students saw only minor changes in school poverty levels. Students in the treatment group attended schools with a mean subsidized lunch population of 67.5 percent, compared to 73.9 percent for the control group.[9]

The most common hypotheses about the positive impacts that low-poverty neighborhoods have on children include *decreasing stress levels* through less exposure to crime, gang activity, housing mobility, unemployment, weakened family structure, and through better access to services and resources such as libraries and health clinics; *increasing academic expectations and performance* through increased access to positive role models and high-performing peers, skilled employment opportunities close to home for their parents, quality day care and out-of-school resources, and prevailing norms of attending and staying in school; and *promoting the adoption of pro-social attitudes and behaviors,* with less exposure to peers and adults engaged in violent behavior, drug use, or other antisocial activities.[10]

Prevailing theories about the advantages of low-poverty schools are that they not only benefit from having more material resources, but also reap the stability-conferring benefits from having greater parental stewardship as well as attracting and retaining a better-prepared corps of teachers, administrators, and students. Put another way, changing the poverty level among the student body could affect school practice through five primary mechanisms: *teacher quality,* since teachers are sensitive to the student composition of the school and are more likely to transfer or exit when placed in poor schools; *school environment,* because high-poverty schools experience greater churn in staffing and students as well as higher levels of confrontation; increased *parent involvement,* where middle-class parents tend to establish a norm of parental oversight by customizing their children's school experiences; *teacher-student interactions,* since teachers calibrate their pedagogical practice to the perceived levels of student skills and preparedness; and *peer interactions,* since peers form the reference group against which children compare themselves, and by which they model behavior and norms.[11] By contrast, high-poverty schools and neighborhoods may receive bursts of investment— for example, a stellar school principal, an infrastructure project, a new curricular mandate—but the investments typically form a succession of short-term reforms and churning leadership that fails to achieve sustained improvements.[12] While these inequities do not determine a school's academic performance, they do influence them.

Considering the disparities between low- and high-poverty schools and neighborhoods, it might seem obvious that any child would benefit from living in a low-poverty neighborhood and attending a low-poverty school. Yet, it has proved quite difficult to quantify the degree to which economic integration benefits children.[13] Further, it is quite possible that economic integration of children from low-income families could isolate or otherwise alienate children, detracting from their performance. Policy-induced economic integration in schools is a small but growing intervention,[14] while residential sorting along economic and racial lines is quite common, yielding a relatively small proportion of poor children who live in low-poverty settings and attend low-poverty schools. However, it is difficult to generalize from the experiences of these children, since their families may particularly value—and thus be more likely to benefit from—access to low-poverty places.[15]

In view of this research challenge, Montgomery County's unusual and successful economically integrative housing program offers a rare look into a subject that has been hard to research well: how poor children fare in affluent settings.

Setting and Methods of the Study

Montgomery County is a large, affluent suburb of Washington, D.C., that is home to almost one million people. The median household income in 2008 was $93,895, which is 80 percent higher than the national figure. While aggregate statistics establish the area's affluence and privilege, they gloss over its substantial heterogeneity. Although the county is primarily suburban, it is best understood as a large region (almost five hundred square miles) that contains urban, suburban, and rural communities. Approximately two-thirds of its residents are white, with the rest comprised of equal shares of African Americans, Hispanics, and Asians. Almost one-third of its residents are foreign-born, which is more than double the national rate. Montgomery County was one of the first suburbs nationally to host more jobs than residences; as early as 1970, a majority of its residents both lived and worked there.[16] There are roughly 550 neighborhoods,[17] and, in the vast majority of them, less than 10 percent of residents live in poverty.

Portrait of the School District

The rate of poverty in Montgomery County schools is higher and more varied than that of its neighborhoods. Of the school district's 114 elementary schools that students in public housing attended during the study period of 2001–07, the percentage of students who qualified for FARM ranged from as low as 1 percent of the student body to as high as 72 percent in 2006.[18] Figure 2.1 reveals that, in this study, about one-half of the elementary schools that children in public housing attended had less than 20 percent poverty, as measured by the percentage of students who were eligible for a subsidized meal.

Subsidized meal status is the first measure of school need considered in this study. The second is the district's own metric for schools that it considered most "impacted"—presumably by poverty. This designation arose out of the district's decision to invest more heavily in its most disadvantaged elementary schools after a county commission in the late 1990s found that students' demographic characteristics and academic performance in third grade could perfectly predict their subsequent level of participation in Advanced Placement and honors courses in high school.[19] In response, the school district created in 2000 its own measure of school disadvantage for the purposes of directing additional investments to its neediest schools. The neediest half of the elementary schools

FIGURE 2.1. Distribution of Poverty among the Elementary Schools Attended by Students in Public Housing (2006)

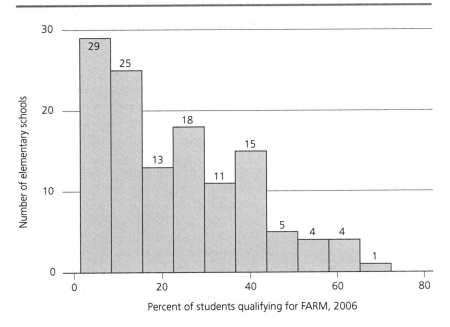

Percent of students qualifying for FARM, 2006

in the system—sixty schools—were designated as "red zone" schools, while the balance were designated as "green zone" schools. Red zone schools typically had the largest number of students living in poverty, and the schools clustered along a main north-south interstate bisecting the county. By 2006, though, there was no single criterion that cleanly delineated green zone schools from red zone schools; for example, the red zone schools had subsidized meal rates ranging from 17 percent to 72 percent, while white and African-American students accounted for 0 percent to 50 percent and 10 percent to 74 percent, respectively, of any given red zone school's population.

After designating the least-advantaged half of its schools as belonging to a red zone, the district proceeded to make a series of extra investments in them. Red zone schools were the first in the district to phase in full-day kindergarten, they reduced class sizes in kindergarten through third grade, invested in more than one hundred hours of professional development for teachers, and adopted specialized instruction for high-needs students, including ninety-minute blocks for a balanced literacy curriculum and sixty-minute blocks for mathematics in first and second grade.[20] Reflecting these investments, the average class size as of 2006 was 19 in red zone schools, compared to 23 in green zone schools.

Portrait of Public Housing in Montgomery County

Compared to other housing authorities nationally, Montgomery County's Housing Opportunities Commission has placed an unusual focus on deconcentrating poverty over the past thirty years by eschewing large-scale public housing projects in favor of placing scattered-site public housing units and two- or three-story family developments throughout the county's many neighborhoods. The housing authority's success in so doing is largely attributable to Montgomery County's adoption in the early 1970s of a mechanism known as inclusionary zoning.[21] As stated previously, this zoning policy mandates that real estate developers of all housing subdivisions with thirty-five or more homes set aside between 12 percent and 15 percent of the homes to be sold or rented at below-market prices. The housing authority has the right to purchase up to one-third of inclusionary zoning homes in any given subdivision. To date, the housing authority has acquired about seven hundred scattered-site public housing homes.

To qualify for public housing during the years examined in this study, a household first had to sign up on a waiting list and, if selected, pass a criminal background check and provide proof of income eligibility. Income-eligible households could get onto the waiting list only by submitting an application to the housing authority during a fourteen-day window that occurred every other year. Several thousand households did so each time (applicants must resubmit each time the waiting list is reopened), so any given applicant had approximately a 2 percent chance of being selected via rolling computerized lotteries. The lottery selection of applicants is without respect to seniority. As public housing apartments became available, the housing authority offered to each randomly selected household up to two size-appropriate public housing apartments of the housing authority's own choosing. Approximately 93 percent of public housing households selected the first offer, and they typically did not know the location of the second unit at the time the first offer was made.[22] Households that rejected both offers were removed from the waiting list. The initial random assignment of families to apartments persisted, due to tight restrictions by the housing authority on internal transfers and to low turnover among public housing families with children;

FIGURE 2.2. Public Housing in Montgomery County

Pictured above are three of the five public housing family developments in Montgomery County. The developments each range from fifty to seventy-five public housing units.

Examples of market-rate developments where 12 percent to 15 percent of the homes are set aside as inclusionary zoning units to be sold or rented at below-market rates. The housing authority has the option to purchase up to 40 percent of the inclusionary zoning units in any given subdivision and operate them as scattered-site public housing units for families. To date, there are about seven hundred such scattered-site public housing units in the county.

Sources: Housing Opportunities Commission and Montgomery County Department of Housing and Community Affairs.

96 percent of children in public housing remained enrolled in Montgomery County public schools during the study period, and 90 percent of the children in public housing in the sample remained in the original elementary school to which they were assigned. (See Appendix 2.1 and Appendix 2.2 for more details about attrition from the sample and for descriptive characteristics of students enrolled in the lowest-, medium-, and highest-poverty elementary schools in the district.)

The large discrepancy between prevailing rent levels and the amount of rent that public housing families paid (the average market rate rent for a two-bedroom apartment in 2006 was $1,267, whereas public housing tenants' average rent contribution in the same year was $371) created a large incentive for poor families to apply to enter and, if selected from the waiting list, remain in the subsidized housing. Once admitted to public housing, tenants had to pay rent to the housing authority that was equal to one-third of their adjusted gross monthly income.

Children in the Study

To test whether affluent schools or neighborhoods improve low-income students' academic achievement, this study examined all elementary-age children of families who lived in public housing during 2001–07 in Montgomery County.[23] Approximately 850 children in public housing attended district elementary schools for at least two years during this period of time. These families comprised some of the very poorest households living in the county; their average income was $21,000, 72 percent were African American, and 87 percent of these families were headed by females. (See Table 2.1.)

TABLE 2.1. Characteristics of Children and Families in the Study

Criteria for selection	Children living in public housing enrolled in elementary grades K–6 for at least two consecutive years within the 2001–07 school-year period who (a) have at least one test score, and (b) do not qualify for special education services of more than fourteen hours per week.[a]
Number	858 students, with 2,226 reading scores and 2,302 math scores
Race	
African American	72 percent
Hispanic	16 percent
White	6 percent
Asian	6 percent
Average family income[b]	$21,047
Average family assets[b]	$775
Female-headed household	87 percent
Average length of tenancy	8.4 years

Sources: Housing Opportunity Commission and Montgomery County Public Schools.

[a]Children receiving more than fourteen hours of services per week are frequently enrolled in Learning and Academic Disabilities classrooms that are often smaller in size and are designed to provide more intensive services to children that are deemed to have a disability that "significantly impacts" academic achievement. Children receiving more than thirty hours per week of special education services generally are removed from their home school and enrolled in one of the district's special education schools. These special education schools are excluded from this analysis. Those students receiving one to fourteen hours of special education services were retained in the sample. Over half of public housing students receiving such services are classified with a speech or language disability.

[b]Since the housing authority collects annual recertification data for every household, income and assets figures were first converted into 2006 real dollars, then averaged within each household across up to seven years of data (2001–07), and then that figure was averaged across the sample.

School Economic Integration Effects

Figure 2.3 graphically depicts the average math performance of children in public housing who respectively attended Montgomery County's lowest-poverty and moderate-poverty schools over the period of 2001 to 2007. The technical appendix (see page 61) describes how these estimates were derived; it also describes the Maryland standardized tests and the test score scales.

As Figure 2.3 demonstrates, after two years in the district, children in public housing performed equally on standardized math tests regardless of the poverty level of the school they attended.[24] This helps to confirm the random assignment of children in public housing to schools, establishing the comparability of the two groups of students. By the fifth year in the district, statistically significant differences ($p < 0.05$) emerged between the average performance of children in public housing in low-poverty schools compared to those in moderate-poverty schools. By the

FIGURE 2.3. Effect of Low-poverty Schools on the Math Scores of Children in Public Housing

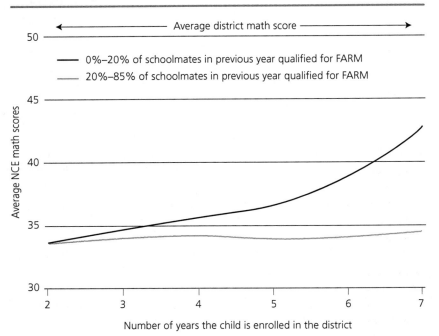

seventh year in the district, children in public housing in low-poverty schools performed an average of eight normal curve equivalent (NCE) points higher than children in public housing in higher-poverty schools. This difference is equal to 0.4 of a standard deviation in math scores— a large effect size in education research, where a typical effect size is one-tenth of a standard deviation for educational investments such as increased years of teacher experience or increased teacher cognitive ability as measured on state teacher tests.[25]

The positive slope for the average math performance of children in public housing in low-poverty schools indicates that public housing students in the least-poor schools were catching up to their average non-poor district-mates over the course of elementary school. (Note that the test score scale is constructed such that 50 was the average math score in Montgomery County, regardless of elementary grade level or year.) This means that the average child in public housing started out performing about 17 points (NCE score of 33) below the typical Montgomery County student (NCE score of 50) in math—0.8 of a standard deviation, which comports with the national income achievement gap. Over time, however, children in public housing in the district's low-poverty schools began to catch up to their non-poor district-mates in math; by the end of elementary school, the math achievement gap halved from an initial disparity of 17 points to 8 points. In contrast, the achievement gap between the children's average (non-poor) district-mate and the average child in public housing in the district's poorest elementary schools held constant.

Notably, the children in public housing benefited from attending the lowest-poverty schools even though they were more likely to cluster within non-accelerated math courses in their given schools, where greater proportions of their classmates were poor, nonwhite, and did not qualify as academically gifted or talented. This grouping occurred because each elementary school in the district provided differentiated math offerings starting in the second grade, by which point a student could have tested into either accelerated or standard math. By third grade, a child could place into one of three levels of math, and by sixth grade the offerings split into a total of four levels. Since the children living in public housing typically performed substantially lower than other children in the district, it is not surprising that they often placed into the non-accelerated math courses. Consequently, within low-poverty schools, the math classmates of children in public housing scored an average of nine points lower than their grademates as a whole. Likewise, the proportion of their

FIGURE 2.4. Effect of Low-poverty Schools on the Reading Scores of Children in Public Housing

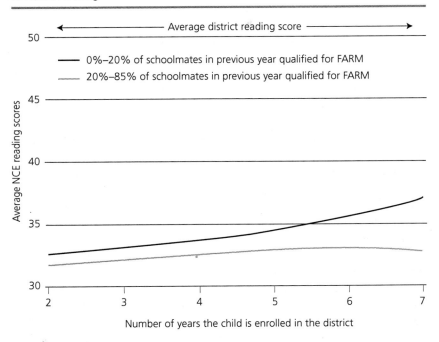

math classmates who were gifted and talented was fourteen percentage points lower than the rate among their grademates. By contrast, the math classmates of children in public housing who attended moderate-poverty schools were more similar to that of their grademates and schoolmates as a whole.

Unlike the differentiation in math, the district offered only one reading course per grade. The heterogeneous grouping of students for literacy instruction did not, however, yield larger reading than math effects for the children in public housing attending low-poverty schools. As shown in Figure 2.4, a more modest but similar improvement trend held for reading as for math. Unlike in math, however, the difference between reading scores for children in public housing across low- and moderate-poverty schools was never statistically significant at high levels of certainty; by the end of elementary school, the children in public housing in the lowest-poverty elementary schools performed an average of five points higher in reading (0.2 of a standard deviation, p < 0.20) than children in public housing attending moderate-poverty schools. As in math, they started out far behind their district-mates in their reading achievement. Those enrolled in low-poverty schools made modest gains relative to their district-mates, such that the achievement gap narrowed from 17 to 13 normal curve equivalent points (from 50 to 37). Also as in math, however, children in public housing attending moderate-poverty schools never caught up to their district-mates over the course of elementary school.

To determine whether there were diminishing academic returns to low-income students as school poverty levels rose, the graphs in Appendix 3 show the same analyses as above, but with successively higher school poverty cutoff rates. As expected, the positive effect on the math scores of students in public housing dissipated as school poverty rates rose: the average student in public housing in a school with a poverty rate as high as 35 percent performed no better in math than the typical student in public housing in an elementary school with 35 percent to 85 percent poverty. Note here that the comparison largely excludes high-poverty schools—less than 5 percent of schools in the district had poverty rates in excess of 60 percent, and only one school had a poverty rate in excess of 80 percent in any single year. The *effective* comparison, then, is between children in public housing in schools where 0 percent to 35 percent of schoolmates qualified for subsidized meals, who performed no better than children in public housing in schools with 35 percent to 60 percent subsidized-meal students. Given the lack of truly high-poverty schools in this sample, this study does not suggest that 35 percent school poverty is a tipping point, after which low-income students no longer benefit from socioeconomic integration. We cannot know from this study, for example, how students in 35 percent to 60 percent low- income schools perform compared with students in 60 percent to 100 percent low-income schools.

Regarding reading scores, by contrast, it was only at the low poverty rate of 20 percent or less that children in public housing outperformed their peers in public housing attending higher-poverty schools. Note again that the comparison here primarily was between children living in public housing who attended schools with 0 percent to 20 percent subsidized meal students, to peers in public housing who attended schools with 20 percent to 60 percent subsidized meal students. Absent higher levels of school poverty in Montgomery County, it is impossible to contrast reading results for students in public housing who attended

FIGURE 2.5. Characteristics of Low- and Moderate-poverty Schools

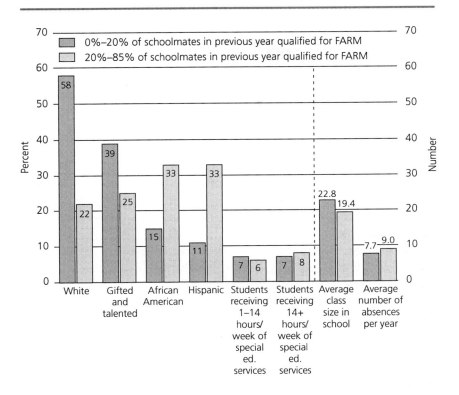

high-poverty schools, although national trends suggest that it is in high-poverty schools that students perform least well.[26]

The lowest-poverty elementary schools in the county had characteristics correlated with better student performance. Figure 2.5 shows the demographics of Montgomery County's low- and moderate-poverty elementary schools. For example, a majority of students were white, a demographic characteristic that is positively associated with teacher quality, since the lowest rates of teacher mobility typically occur in such schools.[27] (Note that teacher and administrator characteristics, an important potential source of advantage, were not available for this study.) More than one-third of students qualified as gifted and talented.[28] Based on statistical tests, no single characteristic shown in Figure 2.5 fully accounted for the low-poverty school effect, suggesting that the benefit of low-poverty schools derived from multiple sources (or possibly from an aspect of school that is not measured here).

Measuring School Disadvantage a Different Way

As described above, beginning in 2000, the Montgomery County school district created its own measure of school need, designating 60 of 131 elementary schools as being in a "red zone." Today, about one-half of the district's elementary age students attend red zone schools, while the other half attend "green zone" schools. During the years examined in this study (2001 to 2007) the district directed substantial resources to red zone schools so that they could extend kindergarten from half- to full-day, reduce class sizes from 25 to 17 in kindergarten and first grade, provide one hundred hours of additional professional development to red zone teachers, and introduce a literacy curriculum intended to bring disadvantaged students up to level by third grade.

The red/green zone designation provides an alternate way to categorize negatively impacted schools, against which to compare the commonly used but limited metric of subsidized meal status. Red- and green-zone comparisons reveal similar but even more marked impacts of school advantage on the performance of children in public housing over time. Figures 2.6 and 2.7 depict the average performance of students in public housing in both math and reading in the county's green zone and red zone schools. After seven years, children who lived in public housing and attended green zone schools performed about nine points higher in math and eight points higher in reading (0.4 of a standard deviation, respectively, significant at the $p < 0.12$ level) than their peers in red zone schools, despite having started out with statistically similar achievement levels.[29]

In math, the cumulative positive effect of attending a green zone school by the end of elementary school (nine points, $p < 0.12$) was about the same as that of attending the lowest-poverty elementary schools (eight points, $p < 0.05$). However, in reading, the cumulative effect of attending a green zone school (eight points, $p < 0.12$ level) was larger than attending the lowest-poverty schools (five points, $p < 0.20$ level). In the case of the green and red zone reading comparison, the larger effect was attributable to the erosion in average reading test scores toward the end of elementary school among children in public housing who attended red zone schools. One possible explanation for the negative turn was that the fourth and fifth grades did not receive the same level of intensive investments within

FIGURE 2.6. Effect of Red Zone/Green Zone Designation on the Math Performance of Children in Public Housing

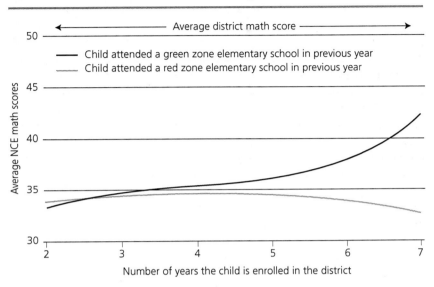

FIGURE 2.7. Effect of Red Zone/Green Zone Designation on the Reading Performance of Children in Public Housing

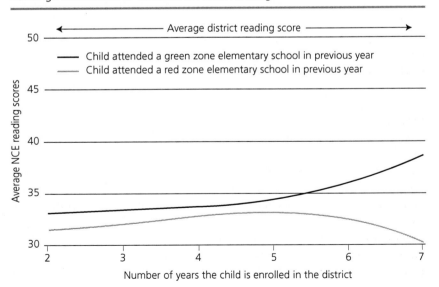

red zone schools, which focus resources on getting children on level by grade three. In other words, the extra attention paid to grades K–3 could have caused the scores of children in public housing attending red zone schools to improve, as shown in years two through five in Figures 2.6 and 2.7. But the positive effect faded and even reversed after the extra investments stopped, as shown in the scores of children in public housing from fifth and sixth grade (that is, years six and seven in Figures 2.6 and 2.7).[30] If true, this trend would not necessarily have emerged in the comparison of school poverty levels shown in Figures 2.3 and 2.4, since both green and red zone schools comprised the set of schools with 20 percent to 85 percent of schoolchildren qualifying for a free or reduced-price meal. Disturbingly, children in public housing enrolled in red zone schools not only did not keep pace with their green zone peers in public housing, but also by the end of elementary school they fell even further behind their average district-mate (who earned a score of 50 in any given year) than when they first enrolled in the district.

This loss of ground is especially striking when one considers the positive impact the school district's red zone investments had on students' campus-wide performance. To test whether red zone investments improved students' performance relative to the absence of those investments, I conducted an analysis comparing school-wide achievement on Maryland state tests in the red zone schools to school-wide achievement in other demographically similar elementary schools throughout the state (see Figure 2.8). (Note that this analysis considers the aggregate achievement of all fifth grade students in each school, not just that of fifth graders who lived in public housing.) Each dot on the graph represents the percentage of students in a given elementary school that scored "advanced" on the Maryland reading assessment in fifth grade. Black dots and the black line show the trend for the red zone schools, and gray dots and the gray line show the trend for demographically similar elementary schools throughout Maryland. In 2003, the state migrated from the Maryland School Performance Assessment Program (MSPAP) to the Maryland State Assessment (MSA), which had the effect of increasing the percentage of students scoring "advanced" within almost all schools. In 2001, the red zone elementary schools first received investments (as described above).

The school district's investments in the red zone schools was associated with a statistically significant 4.9 point increase and a 3.3 point increase in the percentage of fifth grade students in the school who scored

FIGURE 2.8. Red Zone Investments Associated with Increased Percentage
of Students Who Scored "Advanced" on Reading

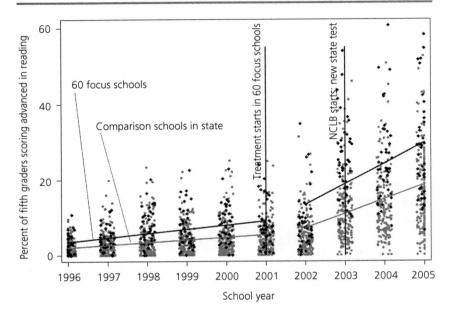

"advanced" on the MSA in reading and math, respectively. The red zone
investments were *not* associated with gains in the percentage of students
scoring "proficient" relative to demographically similar elementary
schools in Maryland. This may be because red zone schools were more
likely than their demographically similar school counterparts to raise
student performance from the "proficient" to the "advanced" level on
the state standardized test. If so, the pattern would be consistent with the
school district's explicit goal that students achieve at the advanced level
on the state standardized reading test by grade three, one of the district's
often cited "seven keys to college readiness."[31]

To reconcile the seemingly contradictory results shown in Figures 2.6
and 2.7 with those shown in Figure 2.8, recall that public housing students were a small proportion of the total student body in any given
school. It is possible, then, that there were distributional effects of red
zone investments *within* red zone schools, such that students not in public housing benefited from investments in ways that the students who
lived in public housing did not. Absent detailed data about students who

did not live in public housing but attended red zone schools, it is difficult to identify the sources of within-school differences. An insufficient number of students in public housing, for example, attended any single red zone school to conduct subgroup analyses.

Given the boost to scores shown in Figure 2.8, it is possible that, in the absence of the district's red zone intervention, the achievement gaps between red zone public housing students and their green zone public housing peers as well as their district-mates would have been even larger. The persistence of the gap in achievement between students in public housing in green and their peers in red zone schools points to the formidable challenge of raising student achievement in disadvantaged schools. It also implies that economic integration could be a more effective tool to improve the achievement of low-income students over the long run than even well-designed and sustained interventions (such as the red zone policy) in needy schools.

Effects of Very-low- to Low-poverty Neighborhoods on Academic Performance

Given the random assignment of families entering public housing to neighborhoods throughout Montgomery County, data from this study also provide information about the effects of poverty in neighborhoods— over and above the effects of schools—on low-income children's academic achievement. However, the more restricted variation in neighborhood poverty in Montgomery County, as compared to school poverty, narrows the window for the detection of possible neighborhood effects. In a county with approximately 550 neighborhoods (defined here as census block groups), only ten had poverty rates in excess of 20 percent. The prevalence of household poverty in any given neighborhood ranged from 0 percent to 32 percent, but 90 percent of neighborhoods possessed less than 10 percent of households in poverty. Not surprisingly, public housing was overrepresented in the higher-poverty neighborhoods, but only to a limited degree; 20 percent of the 854 children in public housing examined in this study lived in a neighborhood with a poverty rate higher than 10 percent.

Despite limited variability in poverty, living in a neighborhood with 0 percent to 5 percent poverty was suggestive of a modest increase (approximately four points) in math scores for children in public housing and a small (two point) increase in reading scores for children in public

FIGURE 2.9. Effect of Living in a Very-low-poverty Neighborhood on Math Performance of Children in Public Housing (above and below 5 percent poverty rate)

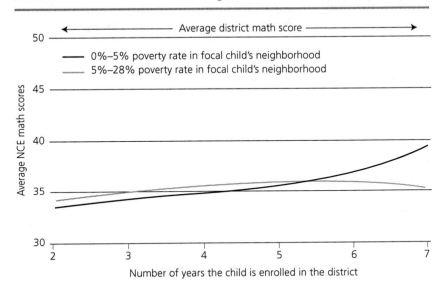

FIGURE 2.10. Effect of Living in a Very-low-poverty Neighborhood on Math Performance of Children in Public Housing (above and below 10 percent poverty rate)

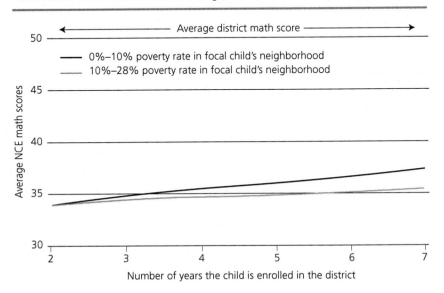

housing, relative to children in public housing living in neighborhoods with 5 percent to 28 percent poverty (and after controlling for school poverty levels). These differences in average math scores were statistically significant only at low statistical significance rates of 80 percent or less. It is possible that larger and presumably largely negative neighborhood effects accrue at higher rates of poverty than it is possible to study in Montgomery County.

Put side by side, the effect size of living in a very-low-poverty versus a low-poverty neighborhood (over and above school poverty rates) is half that of the school poverty effect. This finding is consistent with that of other studies, which have also found smaller neighborhood effects than school effects on students' achievement.[32] Although the comparison to other studies is limited, because most other neighborhood effects studies typically examine higher poverty rates among neighborhoods than it is possible to do here, this study nevertheless adds to a growing literature that can help policymakers weigh the relative benefits of neighborhood- and school-based interventions on student academic outcomes.

Limitations of the Study

Montgomery County's random assignment of families to public housing apartments helps to answer with some certainty that, for children in public housing, attending low-poverty schools improved reading and math performance on standardized tests relative to attending moderate-poverty schools. The effect of economic integration in schools on children's academic achievement also was larger than that of neighborhood economic integration alone. These results suggest that children from highly disadvantaged circumstances benefit from long-term exposure to advantaged school settings. The integrative housing policy was the means by which children living in public housing gained access to advantaged school settings.

Although households living in Montgomery County's public housing are quite disadvantaged, there is some indication that they are more advantaged than their counterparts in public housing nationwide. As of 2008, Montgomery County public housing households earned less than one-third of the national average household income, and the vast majority earned incomes that fell below the poverty line. Yet, they earned almost 25 percent more per household member than public housing households nationally (although less than public housing households in the neighboring suburban, but less-advantaged, Prince Georges County). Put another way, families living in Montgomery County public housing are among the more advantaged of an *extremely* disadvantaged public housing population nationally.

Although it is not possible in this study to identify the degree to which public housing families chose Montgomery County based on schooling preferences,[33] it is quite likely that the county's economically integrative housing program promoted academic success for the kind of families in public housing that choose such a setting in the first place. In other words, the results from this study might generalize to other low-income families with a tolerance or a preference for living in suburban, low-poverty locations. In this sense, the most directly correlative populations might be low-income families who have opted into low-poverty places through private, unsubsidized choices; through federally subsidized housing vouchers or other affordable housing vehicles, such as low-income housing tax credit projects; or through the more than one hundred other inclusionary zoning programs that operate in the United States.[34]

It also is worth noting that this study tracked the performance of students in public housing up through sixth grade. The study did not follow children through middle or high school, where there conceivably might be different effects from economic integration in neighborhoods or schools. On the one hand, elementary school might be a time when the effects of socioeconomic integration on low-income children are greater, since elementary schools are less likely to sort students internally into academically tracked classes than middle or high schools, where course differentiation is greater, and where exposure to advantaged peers and teachers is potentially more limited. Alternately, if low-income students benefit most from positive peer models in economically integrated schools, research indicates that those effects might be greater at secondary rather than at primary grade levels.[35]

Review of Findings

Children in public housing who initially were academic equals but attended either a low- or moderate-poverty school were set on two different academic trajectories over the course of elementary school. Comporting with previous studies, I find that length of exposure was the crucial factor mediating the effects of economic integration on children's performance. After seven years (the end of elementary school), children in public housing in Montgomery County's most affluent half of elementary schools performed eight points higher in math (0.4 of a standard deviation, p <0.05) and five points higher in reading (0.2 of a standard deviation, p <0.20) than otherwise similar children in public housing who attended schools with greater than 20 percent poverty. Within education research, these are large effects since relatively few educational reforms demonstrate positive effects of this magnitude.

Perhaps most important, the children in public housing who attended low-poverty schools began to catch up to their non-poor district-mates over the course of elementary school; by the end, they had cut their initial achievement gap in half. The benefit of attending low-poverty schools held, even though the students in public housing attended math classes and, to a lesser degree, reading classes in which other disadvantaged students within their given school were clustered.

As expected, the academic returns from economic integration diminished as school poverty levels rose. For the low-income children examined in this study, the benefits from economic integration were greatest when they attended schools where less than 20 percent of the students qualified for a free or reduced-price meal. Students also benefited (though to a lesser extent) from attending schools with less than 30 percent of students eligible for subsidized lunch. Students in public housing in schools where 0 percent to 35 percent of students qualified for subsidized meals performed no better over time than those in schools where 35 percent to 85 percent of students qualified for subsidized meals. Without the presence of schools with poverty in excess of 85 percent in any year, it is difficult to identify whether public housing students in the schools with poverty as high as 35 percent would have performed better than students in schools with 85 percent to 100 percent low-income students. Further, since 90 percent of elementary schools in any given year served student populations where less than 60 percent of students qualified for a free or reduced-price meal, the effective comparison described above is between the performance of public housing students in schools where 0 percent to 35 percent of students qualified for subsidized meals to public housing students in schools where 35 percent to 60 percent of students qualified for subsidized meals.

As measured by the district's own indicator of school need, an indicator that is more nuanced than subsidized meal status, the benefits to students in public housing from attending a low-need school were even greater. After seven years, students in public housing who attended green zone schools, the more-advantaged half of the district's elementary schools, performed about nine points better in math and eight points better in reading (0.4 of a standard deviation, respectively) than students in public housing who attended red zone schools, the less-advantaged half of the district's elementary schools. This academic benefit held, even though the school district made large investments in red zone schools, such as extending kindergarten from half-day to full-day, and reducing class sizes, which improved campus test scores relative to other demographically similar elementary schools throughout Maryland during this period of time. This implies that economic integration could be a more effective tool to improve the achievement of low-income students over the long run than even well-designed and sustained interventions such as the one Montgomery County has made in its most impacted schools.

Regardless of the measure of school disadvantage used, this study provides a lower-limit estimate of the effects of economic integration, since there were very few highly disadvantaged schools in Montgomery County against which to compare the low-poverty/low-need schools. For example, less than 1 percent of elementary schools in the district classified as high-poverty, compared to 40 percent of urban elementary schools nationally.[36] Since student achievement typically is depressed in high-poverty schools, the gaps between the academic performance of children in public housing in low-poverty schools versus those in high-poverty schools might well be larger than the gaps reported here.

In another sense, however, the results of this study provide an upper-limit estimate of the effect of economic integration in neighborhoods and schools on disadvantaged children. The housing-based approach that Montgomery County adopted offered low-income families up to three benefits that each could have contributed to their children's improved school performance: a supply of affordable housing, which could promote stability; residence in a low-poverty neighborhood; and enrollment of their children in a low-poverty school. The remarkable residential stability of families living in the county's public housing supplied their children with a strong dose of economic integration in the form of extended exposure to low and moderate poverty levels in their neighborhoods and schools.

Relevance to Other Settings

In many ways, the environment examined here represents a best-case scenario for housing-based economic integration. A group of very-low-income students lived in federally subsidized housing that was not only affordable (promoting residential stability), but also was unusually well-dispersed into hundreds of neighborhoods within an especially affluent county. Montgomery County is exceptional in a number of respects, but its circumstances and policy choices forty years ago forecast the current direction of national affordable housing policy and the economic conditions a growing proportion of high-cost, high-tech suburbs have come to experience. To that end, the county's experience and the results obtained in this study speak to the concerns of at least four audiences: high-cost suburbs that need to attract lower-income workers into their jurisdiction, localities with low but increasing rates of poverty, housing mobility counselors for tenant-based assistance programs, and school districts seeking to mitigate school segregation.

The integration of public housing into non-poor neighborhoods benefited not only the children who lived in public housing over the long run, but also served several of Montgomery County's own ends. A review of the politics surrounding the county's voluntary adoption in the 1970s of integrative housing policies suggests that a combination of altruistic and self-interested motives were at work. As the county's population rapidly grew in the 1960s and 1970s, a growth in the highly paid, highly skilled workforce spilled over to an attendant demand for lower-skill and lower-wage workers who were steadily priced out of the jurisdiction. Thus, the economically integrative housing policy provided a supply of workers for the county's lower-wage jobs, an approach to stem the concentration of poverty in any one area of the county, and a solution to public outcry over a heated housing market that was pricing out moderate-income residents. Indeed, the particular mechanism that the county adopted, inclusionary zoning, has become an increasingly popular tool that has spread to high-cost housing markets in other parts of the Washington, D.C., metro area, as well as in California, Massachusetts, New Jersey, New York City, Santa Fe, and Colorado, among other places.[37]

Over the same period that suburban economies have grown and diversified, the federal government's affordable housing policies steadily have shifted in emphasis from building and maintaining a supply of low-cost housing via programs such as public housing (supply-side) to subsidizing housing mobility (demand-side). The federal housing voucher program, which provides low-income households with a voucher that they can utilize in the private market anywhere within the United States, began in 1974 and has since grown to become the U.S. Department of

Housing and Urban Development's largest rental assistance program. Today, the housing voucher program serves about 1.5 million households, whereas only 1.2 million households live in public housing. As the housing voucher program has matured, housing authorities increasingly have appreciated the need for housing mobility counseling that goes beyond statutory requirements (which overlooks the role schools play in voucher families' selection of neighborhoods) to educate voucher recipients more meaningfully about their mobility options. Better information about how low-income children have fared in suburban districts and in schools of varying poverty levels could provide useful guidance for low-income households as they weigh their residential options.

Housing and education have traditionally been considered the primary instruments of social mobility in the United States.[38] Since education is an investment with both individual and societal benefits, improving low-income students' school achievement via integrative housing is a tool that can not only reduce the income achievement gap but also help stem future poverty. Furthermore, the experience of Montgomery County shows that it can be in the self-interest of both localities and low-income families to create economically integrated neighborhoods and schools.

Although most education research attempts to quantify the effects of various promising school-based reforms for low-income children, many of which Montgomery County has embraced—for example, full-day kindergarten, smaller class sizes in early grades, a balanced literacy curriculum, increased professional development—the results from this study suggest that the efforts to enroll low-income children in low-poverty schools has proven even more powerful. Although the county's inclusionary zoning policy occurs outside the school walls, it has had a powerful educational impact, even as measured by the most demanding but perhaps most meaningful test. Namely that, over the course of elementary school, highly disadvantaged children with access to the district's lowest-poverty neighborhoods and schools began to catch up to their non-poor, high-performing peers, while similar disadvantaged children without such access did not.

Appendix 2.1
Analysis of Attrition from the Public Housing Student Sample

A total of 1,198 children lived in public housing and enrolled in any one grade in K–6 in Montgomery County Public Schools during 2001–07. As described below, only the 877 out of 1,198 children living in public housing that had at least two years of test scores and received less than fourteen hours per week of special education services were considered in the analysis. But of the entire population of 1,198 children in public housing who were enrolled in the district at some point during 2001–07, 4 percent exited the district during 2001–07 before reaching seventh grade. (When children rise into seventh grade, they drop from the sample.) There is no evidence that the 48 exiting children (4 percent of 1,198) were different in aggregate from their remaining peers in public housing in terms of family income, initial test scores, or initial school poverty levels. Of the 48 children who exited the sample for nonstructural reasons, the first school in which they enrolled had an average of 26 percent of schoolmates qualified for free and reduced price meals (FARM), versus an average of 29 percent of schoolmates qualified for FARM in the first year of school for the balance of the public housing students. Of the 48 exiting students, 21 were enrolled in at least one grade level that was tested, and the remaining 27 were not. (Recall the district tested second through sixth graders for at least some of the years between 2001 and 2007.) For those with at least one test score, exiting children's first math and first reading scores were not statistically different from the first scores of their peers in public housing.

Putting this in a regression framework, students whose first test score was above the average of their peers in public housing and whose first school had moderately high poverty (that is, more than 20 percent of students qualified for FARM) were no more likely to exit the sample than their peers in public housing who also first scored above average but were enrolled in the district's lowest-poverty schools (where less than 20 percent of students qualified for FARM).

A total of 877 out of 1,019 children living in public housing met the three sample restrictions—(a) enrolled in elementary grades K–6 for at least two consecutive years within the 2001–07 school-year period, (b) have at least one test score and (c) do not qualify for special education services of more than fourteen hours per week. Of these 877 children, a total of 2 percent of the sample (19 children) exited, leaving a total of

858 children for the analysis. The 19 children that met the sample criteria and that exited the district were not systematically higher (or lower) performing than their peers, nor did they first attend public schools that were poorer or wealthier on the whole than their peers.

Looking at attrition from a different angle, approximately one hundred public housing family apartments become available to new admittees in any given year in the county. Most of the turnover occurred in public housing situated in the poorer neighborhoods within the county. This means that a disproportionate share of the newest families in the public housing system lived in the highest-poverty areas where public housing is located. However, families *without* elementary-age children drove the turnover. In other words, families in public housing whose children originally were assigned to the highest-poverty schools (that is, more than 40 percent of schoolmates qualify for FARM) were no more likely to switch schools or to leave the district during the 2001–07 window of this study than families with children originally assigned to low-poverty elementary schools (that is, where less than 20 percent of schoolmates qualify for FARM).

Appendix 2.2
Randomization of Children across School Poverty Levels

	Low-poverty Schools (0–20% of first grademates qualify for FARM*)	Moderate-poverty Schools (20–40% of first grademates qualify for FARM*)	Moderately-high-poverty Schools (40–85% of first grademates qualify for FARM*)
Characteristics of students in public housing in the first year of school within the district			
African American	73%	69%	71%
Asian American	4%	7%	7%
Hispanic	16%	15%	17%
White	5%	7%	5%
Female	48%	52%	55%
Earliest grade level in district	1.85	2.07	1.80
English as a second language	9%**	13%	16%**
Receives 1–14 hours a week of special education services	9%	12%	8%
Average math score (percentile rank)	39	36	37
Average reading score (percentile rank)	42	37	42
Characteristics of families in public housing in child's first year of school within the district			
Average household income	$21,147	$20,253	$20,571
Average household assets	$448	$986	$743
Average number of children age 0–18 in family	3.26	3.26	3.31
Household headed by a female	88%	86%	85%
Age of head of household (years)	40.19**	39.97	38.66**
Wages is a primary source of income	69%	76%	71%
Head of household is disabled	8%	7%	7%

Note: The results include 958 children in public housing, 345 of whom attended low-poverty, 353 moderate-poverty, and 260 moderately-high-poverty schools in their first year. Only 235 of 958 children were in grade levels such that they had test scores in their first year within the district. The 958 children are distributed across 114 of the elementary schools in the district. Note that, for completeness, the sample includes all forms of special education students, which exceeds the number of students included in the regression analyses.

*FARM stands for free and reduced-price meals, which is the only income measure public schools collect.

**Within the same row, the t-statistic indicates that there is less than a 5 percent likelihood that the difference in the distribution of that row's characteristic is solely due to chance.

Appendix 2.3
Effects of Four Levels of School Poverty

FIGURE A1. Comparing Math Scores of Children in Public Housing Who Attended Schools with 0–20 Percent versus 20–85 Percent Poverty

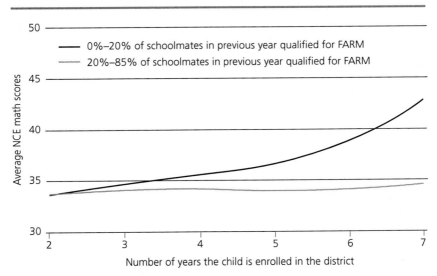

FIGURE A2. Comparing Math Scores of Children in Public Housing Who Attended Schools with 0–25 Percent versus 25–85 Percent Poverty

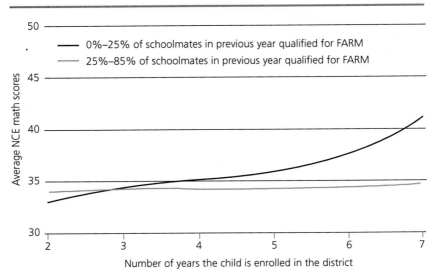

FIGURE A3. Comparing Math Scores of Children in Public Housing Who Attended Schools with 0–30 Percent versus 30–85 Percent Poverty

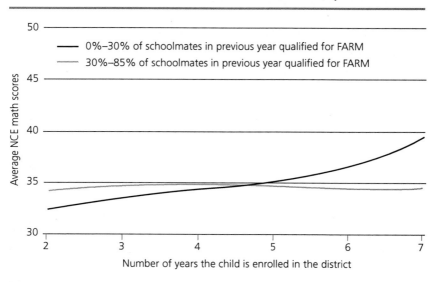

FIGURE A4. Comparing Math Scores of Children in Public Housing Who Attended Schools with 0–35 Percent versus 35–85 Percent Poverty

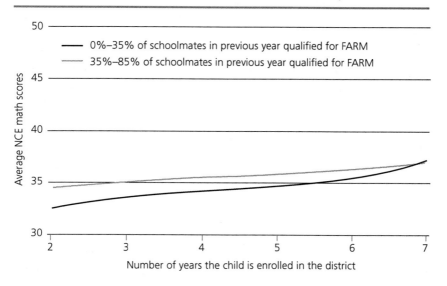

Appendix 2.4
Technical Appendix

Test Scores

To maximize the number of students, grades, and years analyzed, the results of analyses shown in Figures 3, 4, and 6–10 draw on individual students' norm-referenced test scores from the CTBS TerraNova, CTBS TerraNova2, and Stanford 9 (which were part of the Maryland State Assessment) tests administered to second, fourth, and sixth grades in 2001 and 2002, and second through sixth grades in 2003 through 2007. The national percentile rank norm-referenced scores of students in public housing were available for each test type. In each case, individual students' national percentile rank scores first were converted using a published conversion equation to normal curve equivalent (NCE) scores using grade- and year-specific Montgomery County district data. This conversion from percentile rank scores to normal curve equivalent (NCE) scores was necessary to place the individual students' test scores on an equal interval scale.

An NCE score measures where a student falls on the normal curve of test scores for that grade and year within the school district. NCE scores range from 1 to 99, and have a mean score of 50 and a standard deviation of 21.06. Put another way, the average NCE math score in the school district for any grade level in any year is 50, and two-thirds of students in the district in any given grade level scored between 28.94 and 71.06 (50 ± 21.06).

To check whether the results shown in the figures were biased due to the use of public housing students' test scores from two test types (Stanford 9 on the Maryland State Assessment and CTBS), I performed separate sensitivity analyses using scores from only one of the tests (the Maryland State Assessment), first with students' norm-referenced scores and then with their criterion-referenced scale scores. (Note that students obtained both a norm-referenced score and a criterion-referenced score from the MSA derived from subsets of the MSA test questions. The criterion-referenced scores on the MSA were used for accountability purposes to determine whether schools passed or failed Adequate Yearly Progress. The norm-referenced scores, which are the ones used in the primary analysis and in figures throughout the report, had no accountability stakes attached to them.) The MSA was administered to third and fifth graders in 2003 and to third through sixth graders in 2004–2007. Analyzing only the scores from the MSA and not the CTBS TerraNova reduced the number of scores included in the regression analysis from 2,034 math NCE scores and 2,001 reading NCE scores to 1,344 math and 1,249 reading scale scores from the Maryland State Assessment. Nevertheless, the trend lines and effect sizes from the MSA scale score-only analyses are largely the same as those for the NCE scores shown in the narrative that combines scores from both the MSA and the TerraNova. The differences between the scores of children in public housing in the lowest-poverty versus moderate-poverty schools using the MSA-only tests are also statistically significant at the 10 percent level in year five to year seven.

Empirical Analysis

Since children in public housing across the county are assigned randomly to neighborhoods and schools, the concept behind estimating the effect of school and neighborhood poverty levels is relatively simple: compare the average performance of children in public housing according to the poverty levels of their schools and neighborhoods. Call Y the outcome measure (that is, reading or math score) in year t for student i. The estimated effect for children in public housing of moving from moderately-high-poverty to the lowest-poverty schools equals:

Equation 1
$$\delta = E[Y_{it} \mid Lowpov.school_{i(t-1)} = 1] - E[Y_{it} \mid Modpov.school_{i(t-1)} = 1]$$

where *Lowpov.school* is a dichotomous variable that either equals 1 if less than 20 percent of the student's schoolmates in the previous year $(t-1)$ qualified for FARM or equals 0 if not. Likewise, *modpov.school* is a binary variable that equals 1 if more than 20 percent of the student's grademates in the previous year $(t-1)$ qualified for FARM. Schoolmates from the year prior to the test score are chosen since the outcome measure (Y) is a test administered before the end of the school year. The estimated effect of neighborhood poverty rates is identical, with the substitution of indicators for *lowpov.neighborhood* and *modpov.neighborhood*, respectively.

In Equation 1, δ represents the average effect of shifting from a moderate-poverty to a low-poverty school for all the children in public housing in the sample, regardless of how many years those children have been enrolled in the district during 2001–07. It is important to recall that the population parameter δ applies to children of families who signed up for and then won admission to public housing in an affluent suburb. Strictly speaking, this means the impacts are generalizable to this kind of student.

However, the structure of the longitudinal data is such that typically there are multiple test scores per child, multiple children in public housing per school, and multiple children in public housing per neighborhood.[39] To take advantage of the multiple years of information about children, the unit of analysis in the study is not the student but rather a test score Y obtained by student i in year t. However, test scores corresponding to single students should be highly correlated with one another. To a lesser degree, test scores corresponding to students who live in the same neighborhood or attend the same school should also be correlated. To account for the dependencies among the test scores, I fit a multilevel regression model where test scores (level 1) are nested within students (level 2A) who are, in turn, nested within schools (level 3) and separately nested within neighborhoods (level 2B). Since neighborhoods as defined in this study (that is, census block groups) are unaligned with school boundaries,[40] the fitted model has both a nested and non-nested structure.

Equation 2:
Three-level model to estimate impact of school (neighborhood)
poverty level on the test scores of children in public housing

Level 1: test score-level equation

$$Y_{it} = \alpha_i + \alpha_{j[it]} + \beta 1 \; low.povschool_{it-1} + \beta 2 \; mod.povschool_{it-1} + X_i\beta + \varepsilon_{it}$$

where:
Y = standardized math or reading score
i = student
t = time t = school year 2001 . . . 2007
j = neighborhood where student i lived at time t
X = vector of five predictors to control for random differences in student characteristics across the three treatment groups and for time trends—i.e., student ESL status and school year dummies

$$\varepsilon_{it} \sim N(0, \sigma_\varepsilon^2)$$

Here, each test score Y for student i at time t is modeled as a linear function of: a mean for the student i who produced the score; the contribution of school s in which student i was enrolled at time t; the contribution of neighborhood j in which student i lived at time t; the poverty level of the school student i attended in the year $t - 1$; and student i's ESL status at time t and year fixed effects (contained in X). The residual term ε_{it} represents the unexplained difference between the student i's test score at time t and the sum of the fitted model predictors. It is assumed that ε_{it} is normally distributed and has a mean of zero and a standard deviation of σ_{it}.

Level 2A: student-level regression

$$\alpha_i = \alpha_{s[it]} + \varepsilon_i$$

where $i = 1, \ldots$ students and $s = 1, \ldots n$ schools, and $\varepsilon_i \sim N(0, \sigma_\varepsilon^2)$

The level 2A equation models the child-level variation within each school, where $\alpha_{s[it]}$ is the average standardized test score of children in public housing who attended the school s that student i attended at time t. ε_i is normally distributed, with a mean of zero and a standard deviation of $\sigma_{\alpha[i]}$. The error term, ε_i, represents the variation among students that is not explained by the data-level predictors (level 1) and the school-level predictor.

Level 3: school-level regression

$$\alpha_{s[it]} = \mu_{\alpha[s]} + \varepsilon_{s[it]}$$

where $s = 1, \ldots n$ schools, and $\varepsilon_s \sim N(0, \sigma_\varepsilon^2)$

The level 3 equation models the school-level variation between the elementary schools that children in public housing attended. The index term s refers to the school student i attended at time t. The error term, ε_s, is normally distributed with a mean value of zero and a standard deviation of $\sigma_{\alpha[s]}$.

Level 2B: neighborhood-level regression

$$\alpha_{j[it]} = \mu_{\alpha[j]} + \varepsilon_{j[it]}$$

where $j = 1, \ldots n$ neighborhoods, and $\varepsilon_j \sim N(0, \sigma_\varepsilon^2)$

The level 2B regression models the neighborhood-level variation between the neighborhoods where children in public housing lived. The error term, ε_j, is normally distributed with a mean value of zero and a standard deviation of $\sigma_{\alpha[j]}$.[41]

The slopes $\beta1$ and $\beta2$ from level 1 of the model—which are fixed in the sense that the two coefficients do not vary over the observations whereas the two random effect intercepts do—indicate the average effect of the two respective poverty levels (low and moderate) among schools in the year prior to a student's test score in the following year. For example, taking the difference between fitted coefficients for $\beta1$ and $\beta2$ provides the estimated average effect of moving from a low-poverty school to a moderate-poverty school in the prior year on a public housing student's subsequent-year test score. The standard deviation of the respective coefficients for α_s, α_j, and α_{i-s} indicate what proportion schools, neighborhoods, and students respectively comprised of the variability in public housing students' test scores.

For the purposes of this study, taking the difference between the estimated coefficients $\beta1$ and $\beta2$ answers the primary question: Do poor students benefit academically from exposure to low-poverty schools? But they do not address the more policy-rich questions of when effects occur. To test when effects occur, I expand the baseline model (equation 2) by introducing nine additional predictors: the interactions of three time-related predictors—time (in days) elapsed since student i first entered the school district and time t of the test score, time elapsed squared, and time elapsed cubed—with each of the two poverty-related predictors ($\beta1$ and $\beta2$). The interaction terms are included to see if the effects of poverty differ according to the number of years the child has been enrolled in the district.

3

Socioeconomic Diversity and Early Learning:

The Missing Link in Policy for High-Quality Preschools

JEANNE L. REID

Introduction

"We know that each child brings different strengths, styles, and experiences into the mix, and that sparks cognitive growth. The diversity in experience and knowledge among the children naturally creates a larger scaffolding for learning, expanding a child's base of knowledge and problem-solving skills," says Steffani Allen, director of early childhood education in Norman,

The chapter is adapted from material that originally appeared in the author's dissertation, completed at Teacher's College at Columbia University, May 2011. The Multi-State Study of Pre-Kindergarten and SWEEP data used in the study described in this chapter were collected by the National Center for Early Development and Learning (NCEDL), using funds from the U.S. Department of Education, National Institute for Early Education Research (NIEER), Pew Charitable Trusts, and Foundation for Child Development. The contents of this chapter do not necessarily represent the positions or policies of NCEDL or the funding agencies, and endorsement by these agencies should not be assumed.

a suburb of Oklahoma City. "That's why so many of us believed so strongly in the concept of universal preschool, instead of just targeting kids based on need. We recognized that if you put peers together in a classroom—all at-risk or all wealthy, all black or all white—you would automatically limit their experience and their learning."[1]

What the preschool director quoted above knows about the value of socioeconomic composition in her classroom is often missing from policy and research discussions regarding early education. Amidst concerted efforts to identify the components of preschool quality and searching debates regarding the quality of Head Start, policymakers rarely consider the potential benefits of fostering socioeconomic diversity in preschool classrooms. Moreover, despite growing support for universal access to public preschool programs, the press to increase preschool quality generally sustains a "separate but equal" model, in which policymakers strive to improve high-poverty programs, rather than offer low-income children access to higher-income settings.[2]

The current policy context of early education, however, presents a historic opportunity to consider how socioeconomic diversity in preschool classrooms may promote children's learning relative to high-poverty settings, and thereby support policy efforts to expand access to high-quality preschool programs. While research on socioeconomic composition and children's learning in K–12 classrooms is plentiful, it is sparse in preschool settings. This study helps to fill that gap by exploring how the socioeconomic composition of classrooms may affect children's preschool learning.

In this chapter, I present my study that empirically tests the hypothesis that the socioeconomic composition of preschool classrooms is associated with children's learning. Using empirical data from eleven state Pre-K programs for four-year-olds, I examine whether children learn more in classrooms with a high average socioeconomic status (SES) relative to classrooms with a low average SES, and whether this is true for all children, regardless of their own SES and the racial/ethnic composition of their class. I also explore the mechanisms for this relationship, such as whether any association between average SES and children's learning is due to the presence of better teachers in high-SES Pre-K classrooms. Finally, I ask whether the relationship between average SES and children's learning is stronger in certain classrooms, such as when instructional quality is high or the classroom is relatively diverse in terms of children's family income. The results of the analysis, in brief, indicate:

- A positive association between the average SES of the children in a preschool classroom and their receptive language, expressive language, and math learning, regardless of their own SES and the racial/ethnic composition of the class. As the average SES of the class increased, children learned more during the Pre-K year, and this relationship did not depend on whether children in the classroom were from high-, middle-, or low-SES backgrounds.
- The association between average SES and children's learning was comparable in size to the relationship between children's own socioeconomic background and their learning during the Pre-K year. This suggests that policy measures to alter the SES composition of children's classrooms could prevent the gap in skills and knowledge between high- and low-SES children from widening during the Pre-K year.
- No association between social skills learning and socioeconomic composition after controlling for children's own SES and the racial/ethnic composition of their classrooms.
- The socioeconomic compositional effect appears to operate through direct peer interactions, not instructional quality or other aspects of quality in preschool classrooms.
- At the same time, the presence of high instructional quality and income diversity in the classroom interacts with average SES to further promote children's learning in high-SES classrooms.

The Policy Context

Three recent policy and research developments have created a fertile landscape for considering how the socioeconomic composition of preschool classrooms may relate to young children's learning. Together, these developments create an extraordinarily dynamic context to consider how policies that promote socioeconomic diversity in preschool classrooms may support the goal of expanding access to high-quality early education programs.

Pressure to Close Gaps in Readiness for Kindergarten

First, the pressure exerted by the No Child Left Behind (NCLB) law to close achievement gaps between children of different racial, ethnic, and socioeconomic backgrounds has aggravated concerns regarding the wide disparities in skills and knowledge among children entering kindergarten.[3]

With little explicit reference to early childhood, NCLB has raised expectations that preschool educators close these "readiness" gaps by assuring that all children, regardless of their race, ethnicity, or SES, are prepared for the academic demands of kindergarten.

This political pressure poses a formidable policy challenge. At a remarkably early age, children demonstrate substantial differences in their skills and knowledge that are primarily related to their social class.[4] The influential study by David T. Burkam and Valerie E. Lee, *Inequality at the Starting Gate,* found that, on average, children in the lowest SES quintile scored a full standard deviation below children in the highest SES quintile on both math and reading assessments, and that SES accounts for more of this variation than any other factor.[5] States have responded with a concerted push to give more parents access to preschool options that meet state standards of quality and improve children's outcomes.

While devoting substantial resources to close both readiness and achievement gaps, policymakers have found that making significant learning gains in high-poverty settings is extremely difficult. In early childhood education, the experience of Head Start demonstrates the challenge of fostering high-quality educational programs that serve only children living in poverty. As the federal government's largest effort to eradicate inequities in preschool enrollment, Head Start has successfully engaged thousands of parents in their children's development, and in the aggregate, the program produces modest, but significant improvements in children's learning. A randomized evaluation found that Head Start improved children's language, cognitive skills, and school-related behavior by 0.10 to 0.24 standard deviations, relative to a control group of children who may have attended other types of preschool.[6] These results place Head Start on par with good child care programs, and often it is the best option for many low-income parents who enjoy few affordable choices.

The uneven quality and modest results of many Head Start programs remain a concern, however.[7] A 2007 study found that 96 percent of Head Start classrooms scored in the low range on a measure of instructional quality; the average score for Head Start was 1.9 on a 7-point scale.[8] Moreover, its programs do not compare well, at least in the short run, with universal Pre-K programs.[9] One study compared children in Head Start with children who were eligible for Head Start but who attended Georgia's Pre-K program.[10] Although the two groups were statistically similar at the beginning of preschool, by the beginning of kindergarten, children in Georgia's Pre-K demonstrated better outcomes on five of six cognitive and language assessments and fourteen of seventeen teacher assessments of children's academic and social skills, health, communication, and "general readiness."

This research has raised difficult questions for supporters of Head Start, who have responded with efforts to boost the quality of its programs. The 2007 Head Start reauthorization required that half of its teachers nationally have at least a bachelor's degree in early childhood education or a related degree with preschool teaching experience by 2013.[11] In addition, federal regulators are proposing to force lower quality programs to "re-compete" for their funding, an attempt to hold them accountable for meeting quality expectations.[12] But at least part of the problem may be related to the composition of the Head Start classroom. Even within state Pre-K programs, the quality of classrooms is lower when more than 60 percent of children come from poor families.[13]

Nevertheless, the practice of serving poor children separately from higher-income children is an enduring tradition in early childhood education, and Head Start enjoys a large contingency of supporters, many of them parents, who actively advocate for the program. From the earliest days of the republic to the advent of Head Start, early childhood policy has usually addressed the care and education of young children in low-income families separately from their higher-income peers.[14] Reimagining our approach to early education in ways that do not divide children by family income would be a momentous departure from this obdurate past.

New Research on Socioeconomic Composition of Classrooms in Early Childhood Education

Second, in the wake of legal decisions that have discouraged policies to pursue racial integration in K–12 settings, more school districts are considering the feasibility of integration by income for children from high-poverty schools.[15] As these policy efforts have grown, research on the benefits of socioeconomic diversity has also surged.[16]

Although early childhood researchers have only just begun to explore how socioeconomic composition of classrooms affects early learning, their focus has been mostly on kindergarten and elementary school data. One national study examined children's reading trajectories from kindergarten through third grade and found that, while family background made the largest contribution to initial reading disparities, school composition (such as poverty concentration) and neighborhood conditions were more important in predicting SES differences in learning rates.[17] The authors concluded that student socioeconomic composition was "a critical component" of school context, more important than "teacher experience, preparation, and classroom literacy instruction."[18] Although other studies have found similar results among children, almost no attention has focused on preschool settings.[19] One small-sample study looked at preschool classrooms in Connecticut and found that, by the spring of preschool, low-income children who attended economically diverse programs learned more than children in high-poverty programs.[20] For children who spoke English at home, the gains were so substantial in the diverse programs that their spring scores did not differ significantly from those of their more affluent peers.

Each of these studies, of course, is subject to concerns regarding selection bias; that is, parents who enroll their children in more diverse schools may nurture their children's learning in ways that have nothing to do with the composition of their schools. Answering this critique, Heather Schwartz's longitudinal study, which forms the basis of chapter 2 in this volume, used a dataset of 850 low-income children who had been randomly assigned to housing and elementary schools in Montgomery County, Maryland, and found that from 2001 to 2007, children who attended the district's most-advantaged schools (measured by either subsidized lunch status or the district's own criteria) far outperformed in math and reading those children who attended the district's least-advantaged elementary schools.

This small but growing body of research indicates that the relationship between socioeconomic composition and children's learning extends down to kindergarten, and perhaps to preschool as well. Yet few early childhood researchers and policymakers, who together conduct the critical discussion about what constitutes high-quality preschool, explicitly consider the role of socioeconomic composition in early childhood learning. While the question of whether socioeconomic diversity in preschool classrooms promotes children's learning has not been fully explored, early results suggest it is fertile ground for nurturing children's growth and achievement.

The Expansion of State Pre-K

The third and perhaps most significant development in early education, and the one that makes this policy question so urgent, is the recent dramatic increase in state Pre-K programs. As neuroscience and developmental research has highlighted the remarkable growth in children's development during the early years of life, the effectiveness of model preschool programs in promoting children's learning and long-term success in school and life has fostered broad support for publicly funded preschool.[21] In 2010, forty states enrolled 1.3 million children in Pre-K programs at a cost of $5.4 billion, representing one out of every four (26.7 percent) four-year-olds in the country.[22] Despite state budget woes caused by the dreary economic climate, total enrollment increased in 2010, and two states added Pre-K programs—a reflection of not only the enduring bipartisan support for such efforts but also the historic chance to promote effective learning opportunities for young children.

Although efforts to integrate high-poverty K–12 schools or to move their students into more diverse settings face an uphill political battle, early education is not bound by the same constraints. Unlike the K–12 system, parents of preschool-age children choose whether and where to enroll their children within the realm of affordable programs. Low-income parents usually have fewer high-quality options, however, than do high-income parents.[23] To expand access to quality programs, most states target their Pre-K programs so that they enroll only children from poor families, though many aspire to a universal framework that would serve low- and middle-income families who cannot afford private programs but do not qualify for public options.[24] In effect, states (and some urban areas, such as Washington, D.C., and Chicago) that are moving toward universality are inviting middle-income families to participate in public programs that previously had focused only on low-income children, a contrast to the K–12 experience of trying to integrate solidly middle-income K–12 schools in the 1970s by bringing in low-income children.

To expand Pre-K enrollment, states have generally taken one of two approaches, or a combination of the two. Some states offer enrollment in state-funded Pre-K programs (a supply-side approach); others offer vouchers or subsidies to low-income families for use in any state-approved Pre-K program (a demand-side approach).[25] In 2009, one-third of state-funded Pre-K children attended preschool in programs that also received private funding.[26] As long as the supply-side approach attracts middle-income families, both supply- and demand-side strategies create the possibility of socioeconomically diverse preschool classrooms.

Indeed, these policy strategies already are creating unprecedented diversity in Pre-K classroom. An analysis of 169 Pre-K classrooms found that, in half of the classrooms, 38 percent or fewer of the children were poor (that is, had a family income up to 150 percent of the poverty line).[27] This suggests that state Pre-K programs have begun to alter the historical separation of preschool children in poor families from those in higher-income families. Whether policymakers should design their programs in ways that further encourage this diversity depends on the benefits they offer to children.

How Socioeconomic Composition May Affect Children's Preschool Learning

Early education research is playing an important role in this dynamic policy environment by delineating the components of preschool quality that are associated with children's learning.[28] Rarely are compositional aspects of preschool classrooms the focus of these efforts, however. For many policymakers, the model programs, such as the High Scope/Perry Preschool program, remain the gold standard of quality, and much of the preschool research considers quality in the context of such programs that serve mostly or entirely low-income children.[29] This perspective represents a narrow lens on the dimensions of quality. Reconsidering how socioeconomically diverse classrooms may contribute to children's learning requires a conceptual shift that creates new possibilities for how to support broad access to high-quality preschool.

The formation of effective policy requires an understanding of whether and how class composition may affect children's early learning. It is possible, for example, that any benefits associated with preschool classroom composition could be addressed through policies that do not require socioeconomic integration, such as the recruitment of good teachers to low-SES programs who might otherwise gravitate to higher-SES settings. Yet other benefits associated with high-SES classrooms, such as direct peer effects, might be inextricably linked with the assets of diverse middle- or high-SES classrooms, and therefore call for policies that promote diversity by social class in order to capture the benefits associated with such diversity.

To explore how the socioeconomic composition of preschools may affect children's learning, I look first to the literature from K–12 schools and then suggest how its findings might relate to preschool settings, given the lack of such research in early childhood. In general, K–12 research has focused on two theories for the underlying mechanisms that explain the relationship between class composition and learning: one suggests that socioeconomically diverse schools promote children's learning through superior resources, such as better teachers, demanding curricula, and engaged parents; the other suggests that school composition influences how much children learn through direct peer effects that operate in the classroom. There are reasons to believe that both of these mechanisms operate in preschool settings as well.

Teaching and Curriculum

High-poverty K–12 schools are less likely to have qualified teachers than mostly middle-class schools, as defined by their educational degrees, experience, and credentials.[30] Schools with mostly low-performing students, often in high-poverty neighborhoods, have difficulty retaining their best teachers, and school composition appears to be more important than compensation in teachers' decisions to leave.[31] This suggests that, even when high-poverty and middle-class schools have equal financial resources, high-poverty schools are less able to keep the best teachers. Other studies also have found that low-SES schools tend to have less advanced coursework, less curricular emphasis on reasoning in addition to basic skills, less homework, lower teacher expectations, fewer teachers with experience relevant to their subject area, and less positive disciplinary climates than middle-SES schools.[32]

Some evidence suggests that disparities in teacher quality and curriculum exist in Pre-K classrooms as well. Pre-K programs that serve mostly low-SES children attract teachers with fewer qualifications and tend to offer lower quality instruction than Pre-K programs with higher-SES children.[33] In some high-poverty preschool classrooms, moreover, teachers favor didactic instruction of basic or nominal skills over more child-directed learning of analytic and problem-solving skills.[34] Critics view this detour into direct instruction, described as "drill and kill instruction," as deeply troubling.[35] Though direct instruction may improve the scores of children in the short-run, their academic success may wane when the curriculum requires more analytic and problem-solving skills.[36] Direct instruction has also been associated with lower levels of motivation and self-perceptions of competence.[37]

If higher-SES preschools attract better teachers who use a more demanding curriculum than do high-poverty settings, then socioeconomic composition could be an important factor, albeit indirectly, in promoting children's learning. While the K–12 literature indicates that the most qualified teachers often prefer not to teach in high-poverty settings, it

is unclear whether recent efforts to increase teacher education requirements and compensation in Pre-K and Head Start programs may alter
this inequity.[38] But if Pre-K programs follow the pattern found in K–12
schools, higher-SES settings are more likely to offer low-SES children
the quality of teaching that is most predictive of abundant learning by
children. Alternatively, policy that expands access for low-SES children
to high-poverty settings with poorer quality teaching could aggravate,
rather than alleviate, the disadvantages that these children experience.[39]

The Power of Parents

Another important school resource is parents who actively promote their
children's academic success. On average, low-SES schools are more likely
to have parents with lower levels of education, higher rates of mental
health issues, and highly stressful lives that may hinder participation in
their children's education at home and school.[40] One study found that low-
SES parents are more likely to delegate the job of educating children to the
schools, while middle- and high-SES parents are more likely to communicate high academic expectations to their children and actively demand
that schools help children fulfill such aspirations.[41] Higher-SES parents
may also be able to garner larger and more stable financing for their public
schools.[42] Together, these resource disparities among parents pose a formidable advantage for middle- and high-SES schools over their high-poverty
counterparts, and it is plausible that the same advantages would accrue in
a universal preschool system that engages middle- and high-SES parents.

Peer Effects for Lower-Skilled Children

The theory of "peer effects" in K–12 schools is that lower-skilled children who interact with higher-skilled peers learn more than they would
in classrooms with only lower-skilled peers. Direct contact with higher-
skilled peers may stimulate the learning of language, communication,
social, and problem-solving skills among lower-skilled children. In addition, higher-skilled peers may nurture higher expectations among teachers, encourage a faster instructional pace, provide academic role models,
and foster a positive disciplinary environment, all of which may enhance
the learning of lower-skilled students.[43] While SES is by no means a proxy
for ability, as measured by assessment scores, the two are strongly correlated due to the disadvantages of living in poverty. The result is that
socioeconomically diverse classrooms are often higher in average skill
level than are high-poverty classrooms.

Preschool scholars have only begun to explore the influence of peers on children's preschool learning, but their work suggests a positive association between the average ability of peers and how much children learn. One multi-state study found that the expressive language ability of children's Pre-K classroom peers, as measured by an assessment in the fall, was positively related to children's learning of expressive and receptive language skills during the Pre-K year.[44] The analysis controlled for children's race, ethnicity, and mother's education, and program variables such as class size, teacher-child ratio, and the quality of teacher-child interactions. Another study, using data on children who attended Pre-K in Georgia, similarly found that higher peer abilities were positively related to children's growth in receptive vocabulary, familiarity with print materials, and oral comprehension skills, regardless of children's own socioeconomic background and program variables such as class size, teacher experience and qualifications, and observed classroom quality.[45] A third study, using different data, found positive peer effects for low-skilled children with higher-skilled peers, while high-skilled children were largely unaffected by peer skills.[46]

Peers could influence children's preschool learning in myriad ways. Higher-SES children who have been socialized to engage assertively and verbally in learning activities could engage and stimulate their lower-SES peers who may not have been similarly socialized.[47] They may also encourage teachers to increase the pace of instruction and the level of content, which could foster greater learning among all children. In either case, the influence of peer effects may be particularly important in preschool due to the uniquely social aspect of early learning.[48] Most preschool classrooms are designed to exploit this fact by emphasizing child-to-child interactions more than the teacher-directed lessons commonly found in K–12 settings. While ability grouping is frequent in kindergarten, collaborative and play-based interactions predominate in preschool classrooms.[49]

Perhaps most prominently, the critical developmental task of acquiring language is inherently a social process. Higher-skilled children may serve as models of language use and vocabulary knowledge to their lower-skilled peers. One longitudinal study of children found that language-rich preschool settings promoted children's receptive language skills, particularly when they came from home environments with lower levels of language stimulation.[50] This finding is consistent with evidence that dramatic differences in children's early vocabulary growth seem to be explained, at least in part, by the amount and type of speech to which children are exposed, such as the use of open-ended questions, expansions, and recasts.[51] Some scholars have suggested that peer interactions are especially beneficial to children who are learning English as a second language because they provide opportunities to hear and test communication skills, to expand their understanding of the sociolinguistic rules of a particular culture, to form cross-cultural friendships, and to take on positions of authority in the context of play.[52]

The mechanisms for peer effects on children's math skills have been less studied. While language skills permeate multiple activities in the classroom, math skills may be less salient and explicit. Nevertheless, children who possess stronger math skills might stimulate their less-skilled peers with their use of math and verbalization of math concepts in everyday interactions. Their presence in the classroom may also encourage teachers to increase the content and pace of math instruction.

While we do not know the exact mechanisms for peer effects in preschool settings, we do know that the social context for early learning is highly influential. This suggests that the socioeconomically diverse classroom is likely to be a fertile ground for the eager minds of young children.

Peer Effects for All Children

Peer diversity may evoke social and cognitive benefits that are not exclusive to lower-skilled children. Children from a variety of social class backgrounds may benefit from interactions and friendships with children who are different from them, and the effects may be enduring and profound. In K–12 settings, research on racial and ethnic diversity suggests that heterogeneous schools can reduce the prejudices and social isolation of children by race and class, and promote cross-cultural relationships that have long-term benefits such as greater social capital, employment opportunities, and comfort in multi-racial settings.[53] Supporters of diversity in higher education settings argue that racially and socioeconomically diverse peer interactions also create a rich forum for cognition that pushes students to consider new ways of understanding the world.[54]

In early childhood, research in this area is relatively sparse. By kindergarten, children have formed beliefs regarding racial, ethnic, and socioeconomic identities, and they are likely to have developed awareness of social status and skills of social comparison.[55] Exposure to peers from a variety of racial, ethnic, and socioeconomic backgrounds may inform these categorizations and destabilize emergent prejudices. One study found that in racially diverse kindergartens, children's acceptance of peers and friendships transcends racial and ethnic identities.[56] Although this research does not focus on social class identities, it is plausible that friendships in socioeconomically diverse classrooms could diminish the social isolation that characterizes children in socioeconomically homogenous neighborhoods—whether they are high-, middle-, or low-SES.

In addition, it is plausible that diverse classrooms stimulate young children cognitively with the different perspectives of peers, pushing children to engage in active learning. This hypothesis is not unlike Piaget's theory of early cognitive development in which young children learn when their knowledge constructs and understandings (called "schema") are pushed into disequilibrium by new experience and, through assimilation and accommodation, new constructs and understandings take hold.[57] A preschool setting in which children come from diverse socioeconomic backgrounds could thus stimulate cognitive and social growth for all children through daily interactions, collaborative learning activities, and simply by playing together.

The Importance of Good Teaching in Socioeconomically Diverse Pre-K Programs

The possibility that all children benefit from socioeconomically diverse classrooms does not mean that they benefit equally, or that teaching in those classrooms is an easy task. Indeed, it is important to recognize that socioeconomically diverse classrooms may pose challenges as well as learning opportunities for children. Assuring that all children benefit may require teachers to adapt their pedagogy and raise the quality of their teaching.

It is unclear whether low- or high-SES children benefit the most from having high-ability peers. One study found that, on average, lower-skilled children benefited the most from sharing a preschool classroom with higher-skilled peers.[58] Yet another study found that, while the expressive language skills of peers positively affected children's language learning, the effect was larger for children who began preschool with more language skills.[59] One concern is that lower-skilled children may be less likely to engage in active conversation with their peers because they lack the vocabulary, grammar, and narrative discourse skills to participate fully with higher-skilled peers. They may also be valued less as play partners by their peers if they are perceived as lacking in the communication skills that facilitate collaborative play. If this is the case, teacher intervention may be crucial to capture the full benefits of a diverse classroom.

Indeed, to assure that all children benefit in socioeconomically diverse classrooms, teachers likely will need to address several pedagogical obstacles. Wide skill disparities among children may pose instructional challenges that require the stimulation of high- and low-skilled children simultaneously. This does not mean, however, that teachers must juggle multiple curricula. Early education research has identified the use of a comprehensive curriculum as an important organizing tool in preschool programs (that is, a curriculum that addresses the multiple developmental domains of early learning).[60] Within this curricular framework, teachers may need to offer individualized approaches to instruction that stimulate children with multiple skill levels.[61] Importantly, research in K–12 classrooms indicates that, when all children receive the same curriculum, high-scoring students appear unlikely to be "hurt" by the presence of lower-scoring students, as long as high-scoring students remain the majority.[62]

Children in socioeconomically diverse classrooms also are likely to vary in their cultural backgrounds and perhaps their home language. Such cultural and linguistic differences necessarily influence pedagogy in complex ways. For example, while research has found that "sensitive and stimulating teaching" predicts children's learning regardless of their socioeconomic background, the practices that constitute this measure may look quite different in programs that vary by class composition.[63] One study examined a sample of preschool programs that predominantly served African-American children and found that their version of "developmentally appropriate practice," a standard of practice in many early education programs, was infused with "African American cultural traditions, such as religiosity and community mothering."[64]

Teachers in culturally diverse classrooms likely will need to accommodate a variety of cultural expectations and reference points in their pedagogy:

- Effective classroom management may vary across cultures, with Latino, African-American, and poor families more likely to emphasize unquestioning obedience than white and non-poor families.[65]
- Fulfilling the goal of "parent engagement" could look different among different families. European-American parents may be more likely to volunteer in school, for example, while Chinese-American parents may be more likely to engage in systematic home schooling.[66]
- Teachers may need to reconsider their perceptions of "normal" behavior among their students. Whether and how children

demonstrate assertiveness, cooperation, independence, and internalizing or externalizing of social-emotional problems may vary widely across cultural identities.[67]

- If a teacher's expectations of children differ by their socioeconomic backgrounds, the result may be differential treatment that hinders low-SES children with low expectations.[68]
- In classrooms with children who are emergent bilinguals, pedagogy that is culturally *and* linguistically relevant can be even more challenging for teachers.

Cultural and linguistic differences between teachers and children thus require that teachers adapt their practice to the families they serve. While these differences do not reliably fall along social class lines, culturally competent teaching would likely be particularly important in socioeconomically diverse classrooms, where cultural gaps may open between teachers and children and between children themselves. In addition to adjusting their own pedagogy, teachers play an important role in nurturing the social-emotional skills and peer exchanges that support children's learning in the social setting of preschool. Their ability to foster positive peer interactions could be highly influential in diverse classrooms when children need a teacher to facilitate such interactions.[69]

Together, these multiple research findings suggest that, while the possibilities for learning may be greater in diverse classrooms, and not only for low-SES children, the demands of good teaching may also be higher. The K–12 desegregation experience showed how schools and teachers who serve racially and socioeconomically diverse students need an "educational logic" for how to meet the disparate needs of incoming students.[70] This challenge may loom large in diverse preschool settings as well. To capture the full benefits of socioeconomic diversity classrooms, teachers should be ready to bridge cultural and linguistic gaps between themselves and their children, attend to skill disparities that require individualized instruction, and nurture the peer interactions that may be highly influential in the social context of preschool learning.

Methods and Data

The study presented in this chapter empirically tests the hypothesis that the socioeconomic composition of preschool classrooms is associated with children's learning. After accounting for how children's own SES might affect their learning, I explore the extent to which the socioeconomic composition of preschool classrooms affects learning outcomes, how it may do so, and whether the relationship between classroom composition and children's learning varies in different classroom contexts. Finally, I discuss the policy and research implications of the findings and suggest how policymakers could try to capture any apparent benefits of socioeconomic diversity in the context of parental choice regarding preschool education.

First, it is worth defining some terms. *Early childhood* refers to the years from birth to age eight. Learning before kindergarten takes place in a variety of settings—at home with family, in home- or center-based care, Head Start programs, private preschools, state Pre-K programs, and public or private elementary schools. In this study, a *preschool* experience refers to center-based care, Head Start programs, state Pre-K programs, and private preschools. This study focuses on a sub-set of preschools: *Pre-K* programs, whose provision is mostly funded by the states. Furthermore, the analysis considers four-year-olds, who have been the priority of state Pre-K efforts to date. *High-quality* programs connote programs that effectively nurture children's learning.

Consistent with other research in the social sciences, I consider children's family income and their mothers' level of education as measures of SES, or *social class*.[71] For the purposes of this study, I weight these two measures equally to create an SES measure. Children whose families are described as *poor* in this study have incomes below 150 percent of the poverty line, or about $22,000 for a family of three when the data were collected.[72] Finally, the focus of this study is *classroom* composition. Some of the relevant K–12 research looks at *school* composition, which can be an unreliable proxy for classroom composition.

Analytic Approach

An important contribution of the study is the use of multi-level modeling to explore the relationship between classroom composition and children's preschool learning. The dataset contains information on children and their preschool classrooms, a nested data structure that allows for a multi-level approach in which hierarchical linear modeling (HLM) partitions the variance in the dependent variable (the outcome) into two parts, the portion that lies between children within preschools and the portion that lies between preschools.[73] Children's learning is modeled simultaneously as a function of their own characteristics (*child-level* variables), as well as characteristics of the preschool classrooms they attended (*class-level* variables). Multi-level modeling represents a significant improvement in the precision of analytic methods over single-level, ordinary least squares (OLS) regression, which has been employed in much of the research on school effects, including the Coleman Report.[74]

Using an eleven-state database of 2,966 children who attended 704 Pre-K classrooms, I employed multi-level modeling to assess the gains in receptive language, expressive language, math, and social skills, measured on fall and spring assessments, among children in classrooms with different socioeconomic compositions. Using spring assessment scores as an outcome and fall assessment scores as a covariate (an ANCOVA approach), I was able to interpret the parameter estimates as to how much the children learned between the two assessments. I had three research questions:

- RQ1: To what extent is the socioeconomic composition of preschool classrooms related to children's language, math, and social skills learning, above and beyond the association between their own SES and learning?
- RQ2: To what extent do aspects of preschool classrooms, such as instructional quality, explain the relationship between socioeconomic composition and children's preschool learning?
- RQ3: Is this relationship more important in certain classroom contexts, such as when income diversity or instructional quality is high?

I built a succession of models to address these three questions. First, I established whether socioeconomic composition is positively related to children's learning on each of the four outcomes, after accounting for their own SES and other background characteristics (such as race/ethnicity, single-parent status, and primary home language), and the racial/ethnic composition of the classroom. Then, because socioeconomic composition may act as a proxy for other aspects of classroom quality, I added class-level measures of quality to the model (such as instructional quality, teacher education level, and class size) to explore how such measures may explain this relationship. Finally, I considered interactions between class-level measures of quality and SES composition to see if SES composition is particularly important in certain contexts.

To measure the socioeconomic composition of classrooms, I combined the average family income and average level of mothers' education in the class to get a single measure of average class SES. I also used a measure of the standard deviation of family incomes within classrooms to assess the extent to which the diversity of income within classrooms relates to children's learning.

The Data: Children in Pre-K Classrooms

For the analysis, I used data from two studies conducted by the National Center for Early Development and Learning (NCEDL): the Multi-State Study of Pre-Kindergarten, sponsored by the U.S. Department of Education's Office of Educational Research and Improvement, and the State-Wide Early Education Program Study (SWEEP), sponsored by the National Institute for Early Education Research, Pew Charitable Trusts, and Foundation for Child Development. Collecting data from eleven state Pre-K programs (California, Illinois, Georgia, Kentucky, New York, Ohio, Massachusetts, New Jersey, Texas, Washington, and Wisconsin), the two studies had the same research team and measures, similar sampling designs, and the common goal of understanding the relationship between features of Pre-K programs and child outcomes.[75] Both studies included extensive classroom observations and child assessments in the fall and spring of a Pre-K year. Though the eleven states represented 80 percent of the national Pre-K population at the time the studies were conducted, the sample was not meant to be nationally representative.

Within each state, NCEDL chose a stratified random sample of centers/schools to maximize variation in teacher credentials, program setting, and intensity. Within each center/school, NCEDL then chose one classroom, collected demographic data on families of children in the classroom, and randomly selected four children for assessment in the fall and spring of preschool. Children were eligible for assessment if they (1) would be old enough for kindergarten in the following year, (2) did *not* have an individualized education plan (IEP) in the fall, and (3) could follow simple instructions in English or Spanish. Because the average class size was eighteen, the children assessed represent about 22 percent of all children who were enrolled in the class.

Class-Level Variables

My primary variable of interest at the class level is the combined measure of class mean family income and class mean level of mothers' education, which represents the average SES in the class. Another variable of interest is a measure of the standard deviation of mean family income *within* classrooms, an indicator of the diversity of incomes in classrooms. While high-poverty classrooms by definition have a narrow distribution of family income, as class mean income rises, so does the potential for income diversity. Indeed, class mean income and the standard deviation of incomes within classrooms are strongly correlated ($r = 0.597$; $p < .01$). However, some high-SES classrooms may have little diversity at all. By using both class mean SES and the standard deviation of income, I am able to consider what portion of a compositional effect might relate to having high-SES children in the classroom, and what portion might relate to having a wide distribution of income within the classroom.

The data offer additional measures of classroom composition that I consider as covariates: the percentage of children in the classroom who are white or racial/ethnic minorities; whether 15 percent or more of the children in a classroom are English language learners (ELLs), and whether 15 percent or more of the children have IEPs or referrals for IEPs, by the spring of the preschool year. Most children (at least 70 percent) attended classrooms that had fewer than 15 percent ELLs or fewer than 15 percent children with IEPs or IEP referrals.

To account for other aspects of classroom quality that may relate to a compositional effect, I included a measure of teacher quality, which has two dimensions: (1) instructional interactions and (2) social/emotional interactions. I also included a global quality measure of the classroom (the ECERS). Details regarding these measures appear in Appendix 3.1 (see page 123). I also considered variables that represent particular aspects of structural quality, such as the child-teacher ratio; class size; whether the program was full-day; whether the class was part of a Head Start program; whether it was located in a public school; whether the program offered meals, family services, and/or health services, as well as measures of teacher education; whether the teacher had been certified for less than four years; whether the teacher spoke Spanish; and whether the teacher used a comprehensive curriculum, such as High/Scope or the Creative Curriculum. In the final models, I included only those variables that were statistically significant for at least one of the four outcomes.

Child-Level Variables

In the fall and spring of the pre-K year, four children in each classroom participated in direct assessments of their receptive language, expressive language, and math skills. (Children demonstrate receptive language skills when they show their understanding of language implicitly, as when they follow a directive such as "Put the book on the shelf." Expressive language skills are demonstrated explicitly, such as when children answer a question in a way that indicates comprehension.) In addition, in the fall and spring, teachers completed a behavioral rating scale to assess children's social competence. Details regarding these assessments appear in Appendix 3.2 (see page 124).

To account for the associations between children's own background characteristics and their learning during the preschool year, I included child-level covariates such as age, gender, race/ethnicity, single-parent status, ELL status, IEP status in the spring, and days absent from preschool. To represent children's own SES, I combined their family income and mother's education level to make a single measure of SES. This allowed me to compare the relative importance in children's learning of their own SES and the average SES in their classrooms.

Portrait of the Children and Their Pre-K Classrooms

I began with a descriptive analysis of children in the sample and how they were distributed among classrooms, and then examined how their classrooms differed in terms of various aspects of quality. The results of these analyses suggest that, while the data represent unusual levels of socioeconomic diversity within public preschool programs, the pattern of concentrating low-SES children in lower-quality classrooms persists.

The Children

A threshold requirement for a study of socioeconomic diversity in preschool classrooms is the presence in the dataset of children with a range of socioeconomic backgrounds, some of whom share the same classrooms. The data in Figure 3.1 indicate that roughly half (49.2 percent) of the children in the combined dataset were from families with incomes of $25,000 or below, which was just above 150 percent of the poverty line for a family of three at the time the data were collected.[76] A quarter (25.4 percent) of the children came from families whose incomes were from $25,001 to $45,000. Another quarter (25.4 percent) came from families whose incomes exceed $45,000, which was above the median family income ($43,000) at the time the data were collected.[77] Though the dataset contains a disproportionate number of children from low-income families, they reflect a mix of children that is unusual among public preschool datasets.

The results of the analysis also indicate that many children attended classrooms that were reasonably diverse in terms of family income. As

FIGURE 3.1. Children's Family Income

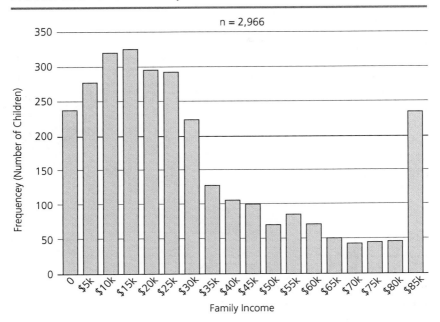

shown in Figure 3.2, about half of the children (51.3 percent) attended classrooms that could be considered high-poverty (more than two-thirds of the children were poor). But a quarter of the children (25.2 percent) attended classrooms that were more mixed (one-third to two-thirds of children were poor), and another quarter of the children (23.5 percent) were in classrooms that could be considered low-poverty (less than one-third of children were poor). While about half of the children attended high-poverty classrooms, the results suggest that a significant number attended classrooms that were more diverse.

Another way to examine the diversity of classrooms is to look at how widely family income varied within classrooms. The analysis indicates that half of the children attended classrooms in which the standard deviation of family incomes was more than $15,927. This finding suggests that, in those classrooms, roughly one-third of the children were more than $31,854 apart in family income. Together, these results suggest that, while many children attended high-poverty classrooms, as might be expected in publicly funded preschools, a substantial number attended

FIGURE 3.2. Percent of Children in Low-, Medium-, and High-Poverty State Pre-K Classrooms

classrooms in which there was a wide mix of family incomes, reflecting states' efforts to reach beyond the poorest families as they have expanded their Pre-K programs and to give low-SES children access to programs that may serve higher SES families.

While other early childhood databases reflect a socioeconomically diverse mix of children in public and private settings, only the Multi-State and SWEEP data, to my knowledge, provide a large-scale, nested data structure regarding children from a wide spectrum of socioeconomic backgrounds in publicly funded preschool classrooms. This creates a unique opportunity to explore the extent to which socioeconomically diverse preschool classrooms promote children's learning.

To assess further how children in the dataset differ among classrooms, I compared those in low-, middle-, and high-SES classrooms. As shown in Figure 3.3, the class mean income in low-SES classrooms was $17,300, slightly more than half of the mean family income in middle-SES classrooms, which was $30,366 (p < .001). Children in high-SES classrooms had a mean family income of $58,711 (p < .001), nearly twice the average of children in middle-SES classrooms and more than three times the average in low-SES classrooms.

Mothers of children in the three types of classrooms differed significantly by the average number of years of education they had attained. On average, the mothers of children in low-SES classrooms lacked a high

FIGURE 3.3. Mean Income in Low-, Middle-, and High-SES Classrooms

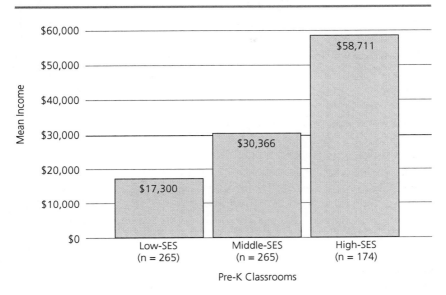

school diploma (11.7 years of education; p < .001), while mothers of children in middle-SES classrooms had eight months of education beyond high school (12.7 years). Mothers of children in high-SES classrooms had the highest levels of education with an average 2.6 years of postsecondary education (14.6 years; p < .001).

Stratification by other socio-demographic characteristics was also evident. Children were disproportionately distributed among classrooms by race/ethnicity (p < .001). Black and Latino children were much more likely to attend low-SES classrooms. Together, they comprised 63.9 percent of children in low-SES classrooms (compared to 45.1 percent of the sample), while white children comprised 69.8 percent of children in high-SES classrooms (compared to 41.2 percent of the sample). Middle-SES classrooms had roughly equal portions of white children (39.7 percent) and black or Latino children (45.8 percent).

The results suggest a strong relationship between whether children had single parents and their likelihood of attending a low-SES classroom (p < .001). Children in low-SES classrooms (50.0 percent) were more than twice as likely to have single parents as those in high-SES classrooms (20.5 percent). The analysis also indicates a strong association between ELL status and the average social class of children in preschool classrooms (p < .001). Children in low-SES classrooms (32.7 percent) were three times more likely to be learning English as a second language than children in high-SES classrooms (10.1 percent). Children in low-SES classrooms also missed more days of preschool than their peers in middle-SES classrooms (p < .001), while children in high-SES classrooms missed even fewer than those in middle-SES classrooms (p < .001). Children in low-, middle-, and high-SES classrooms did not differ significantly in age, gender, and whether they had an IEP or IEP referral by the spring of their preschool year.

The differences among children in low-, middle-, and high-SES classrooms are most striking in terms of the skills they possessed at preschool entry. Children in low-SES classrooms began preschool with receptive language skills that were one-third of a standard deviation below those of children in middle-SES classrooms (p < .001), while children in high-SES classrooms began preschool with receptive language skills that were two-thirds of a standard deviation above those of children in middle-SES classrooms (p < .001). This suggests that children in low- and high-SES classrooms were, on average, a full standard deviation apart in receptive language development when they began Pre-K.

The disparities in expressive language and math skills followed the same pattern, though with somewhat smaller disparities. Children in low- and high-SES classrooms were, on average, more than three-quarters of a standard deviation apart on both expressive language skills and math skills when they began Pre-K. The gap in social skills, however, was statistically significant only when comparing children in high-SES classrooms with those in middle-SES classrooms. Children in high-SES classrooms demonstrated social skills that were more than one-quarter of a standard deviation higher than those of children in middle-SES classrooms (p < .001).

Overall, even while a substantial number of classrooms were characterized by socioeconomic diversity, the predominant pattern is the clustering of advantaged children in high-SES classrooms and disadvantaged children in low-SES classrooms, measured by family income, mother's education, single-parent status, race/ethnicity, ELL status, days absent, and children's skills at the beginning of the Pre-K year.

The Classrooms

The descriptive analysis of class-level measures reveals some of the same patterns of concentrated disadvantage that were evident in the child-level

FIGURE 3.4. The Range of Incomes in Low-, Middle-, and High-SES Classrooms

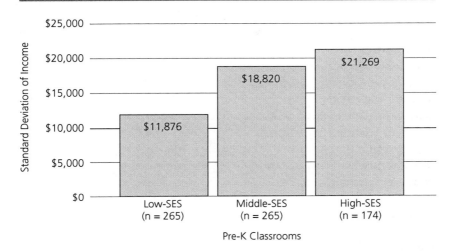

data. For example, the results indicate the unequal distribution of poor children among classrooms. Children living in poverty comprised 85.2 percent of children in low-SES classrooms (p < .001) and only 17.5 percent of those in high-SES classrooms (p < .001). Even so, it is striking that one in six children in high-SES classrooms was poor. Indeed, the presence of low-income children in higher-SES classrooms indicates that some state Pre-K programs have achieved a remarkable degree of classroom diversity, which makes this study possible.

Importantly, the class-level results reveal a significant relationship between the diversity of income within classrooms and the average SES in those classrooms.[78] As shown in Figure 3.4, the average standard deviation of family incomes in low-SES classrooms, $11,876, was about two-thirds of the average standard deviation of income in middle-SES classrooms, $18,820 (p < .001). The average standard deviation of family income in high-SES classrooms, $21,269, was higher still (p < .001), and almost twice as high as that of low-SES classrooms. In other words, as average classroom SES increased, so did the diversity of family income. Low-SES classrooms were likely to represent a concentration of children whose families were poor or near poor, while middle- and high-SES classrooms were likely to offer more economic diversity.

The descriptive results also indicate that classrooms of varying socioeconomic composition differed significantly in terms of quality, affirming concerns that despite concerted policy efforts to standardize levels of quality across publicly funded classrooms, more work remains to be done. As measured by the ECERS, the average quality level in high-SES classrooms was almost one-third of a standard deviation higher than the average quality level in middle-SES classrooms (p < .01), and a half a standard deviation higher than the average quality level in low-SES classrooms (p < .001). Low-SES classrooms were most likely to have teachers who lacked a BA (p < .01) and least likely to have teachers who have earned more than a BA (p < .01). However, low-SES classrooms appeared most likely to have teachers with a Child Development Associate certificate (CDA) (p < .01), and to have teachers who spoke Spanish (p < .001), which corresponds with the higher number of ELL students in those classrooms.

Some aspects of structural quality did not differ across classrooms. Variations among the classrooms in size, the child/teacher ratio, whether they were full-day, and whether they were located in a public school were not statistically significant. Yet children in low-SES classrooms attended Pre-K for fewer hours per week than did children in high-SES classrooms (p < .05). Combined with higher rates of absenteeism in low-SES classrooms (found in the child-level analysis), this is cause for concern.[79] As might be expected, low-SES classrooms were twice as likely to offer meals (p < .001), 1.4 times more likely to offer family services (p < .001), and 1.9 times more likely to offer health services (p < .001) than high-SES classrooms.

Aspects of process quality were significantly related to the SES level of classrooms, mostly suggesting lower quality in low-SES classrooms. The quality of emotional support offered by teachers in the course of the preschool day was much higher in high-SES classrooms than in either middle- or low-SES classrooms (p < .001). The average level of emotional support in high-SES classrooms was almost one-half standard deviation higher than the average level of emotional support in middle-SES classrooms (p < .001), and two-thirds a standard deviation higher than the average level in low-SES classrooms (p < .001). Differences in the quality of instructional support in high-, middle-, and low-SES classrooms followed the same pattern, but were not large enough to be statistically significant. Surprisingly, the use of a comprehensive curriculum was 1.7 times more common in low-SES classrooms than in high-SES classrooms (p < .001), where some teachers may have followed a flexible curricular path to meet the needs of more-advantaged students.

Overall, the class-level findings reveal some important differences between low-, middle-, and high-SES classrooms in terms of their composition and quality, with lower-SES classrooms more likely to have had higher numbers of disadvantaged children and more teachers who possessed lower levels of education and who offered less emotional support to their children. Differences in instructional quality among the three types of classrooms, however, were not large enough to be considered statistically significant. Despite the wide gaps in initial skills among low- and high-SES children, children in low-SES classrooms spent fewer hours there than did children in high-SES classrooms.

The Findings

In the multivariate analysis, I explored the relationship between socio-economic composition and children's learning during the preschool year. I began with a simple child-level model for each of the four outcomes to establish the relationship between children's characteristics and their preschool learning, without adjusting for any variables at the class level. Then I built a series of models to answer the three research questions.

The unadjusted child-level model establishes a baseline of how much children learned during the preschool year. Across each of the four outcomes, the findings indicate a moderately strong and highly significant relationship between children's SES and their preschool learning, controlling for other aspects of their background such as their race/ethnicity, whether English was their second language, and whether they had an IEP. This means that the skills gap between lower- and higher-SES children widened during the Pre-K year. For each standard-deviation increase in their SES, children's receptive language learning improved by 0.077 standard deviations ($p < .001$) and their expressive language learning improved by 0.078 standard deviations ($p < .001$). The relationship between children's SES and their learning was even stronger for math skills (Effect Size [ES] = 0.122; $p < .001$) and somewhat weaker for social skills (ES = 0.057; $p < .001$).

The skills gap between white and minority children also grew on most outcomes during the preschool year. Regardless of SES and other aspects of children's background, black children learned fewer receptive language (ES = -0.293; $p < .001$), expressive language (ES = -0.142; $p < .001$), math (ES = -0.224; $p < .001$), and social skills (ES = -0.077; $p < .10$) than white children. Latino children similarly learned fewer receptive language skills than white children (ES = –0.313; p < .001), and fewer expressive language skills (ES = –0.182; p < .001). Asian children also learned fewer expressive language skills than white children (ES = –0.241; p < .01).

The finding that low-SES and minority children in Pre-K learned less, on average, than high-SES and white children is an urgent policy concern, given the near-universal goal of using Pre-K to help close the wide readiness gaps among these children that are apparent in kindergarten. A common explanation for this troubling finding is that low-SES and minority children are likely to attend lower-quality programs, an argument that finds some support in the descriptive findings here.[80] The obstacle remains, then, to identify the components of quality that allow low-SES and minority children to learn as much as, or more than high-SES and white children. This study explores the extent to which socioeconomic composition may help to address this challenge.

RQ1: Socioeconomic Composition and Children's Learning

The first research question asks: To what extent is the socioeconomic composition of children's preschool classrooms associated with their learning of language, math, and social skills, above and beyond the association between their own SES and preschool learning? To answer this question, I built five models. The first model simply asked whether class mean income was related to children's learning, controlling for children's SES, race/ethnicity, single-parent status, ELL status, IEP status, gender, and age. In Model 2, I added the standard deviation of income within classrooms to assess the extent to which the class mean-income coefficient reflects the diversity of income in classrooms, rather than the presence of high-income children. In Model 3, I added the average level of mothers' education, and in Model 4, I use only the average SES level to estimate the relationship between the socioeconomic composition of the class and children's learning. Finally, in Model 5, I added a measure of the racial/ethnic composition of the class (the percentage of children who are white) to assure that the estimate of socioeconomic composition is not attributable to racial/ethnic composition.

RQ1: Receptive Language Learning.
The results from Model 1 indicate that class mean income was significantly associated with children's receptive language learning, beyond their own SES and other background characteristics (ES = 0.036; p < .10). In Model 2, the standard deviation of family income within classrooms was not statistically significant, but

was strong enough to render class mean-income non-significant. This suggests that, by itself, income diversity was not a significant predictor of children's learning, but it was an important aspect of the relationship between high-SES classrooms and learning. In Model 3, I added the mean level of mothers' education and found that it was a stronger predictor of children's receptive language learning than was class mean income. For each one standard-deviation rise in the average level of mothers' education in the classroom, children's learning rose by 0.057 standard deviations (p < .05), compared to 0.036 standard deviations for a comparable rise in class mean income (p < .10).

The single measure of socioeconomic composition, used in Model 4, suggests a significant relationship between socioeconomic composition and children's learning of receptive language skills (ES = 0.055; p < .05). The addition of the percentage of white children in the classroom in Model 5 attenuated the effect of socioeconomic composition, though it remained significant (ES = 0.042; p < .10). It is noteworthy that the effect of socioeconomic composition was comparable to the coefficient for children's own SES (ES = 0.051; p < .05).

RQ1: Expressive Language Learning. The results from Models 1 and 2 indicate that neither class mean income nor income diversity was significantly related to children's learning of expressive language skills, adjusting for their background characteristics. However, in Model 3, the mean level of mothers' education in classrooms was significantly related to children's expressive language development, controlling for children's own SES and other background characteristics (ES = 0.066; p < .001).

When class mean income and mean mothers' education were combined in Model 4, the results indicate a significant relationship between the socioeconomic composition of preschool classrooms and children's expressive language learning, regardless of their own SES and other background characteristics (ES = 0.061; p < .05). This association persisted in Model 5, which included racial/ethnic composition (ES = 0.052; p < .05). Once again, the estimate for the relationship between socioeconomic composition and children's learning was comparable in size to the coefficient for children's own socioeconomic background (ES = 0.047; p < .05).

Interestingly, the main effect for the percentage of white children in the classroom was positive (ES = 0.133; p < .10), but the so-called quadratic term was negative (ES = −0.108; p < .10). This means that, on average, attending a classroom that was high-minority/low-white (that is, two standard deviations below the mean) was associated with a 0.697 standard-deviation decline in how much children learned relative to children at the mean. As the percentage of white children increased, children's learning improved; a classroom with a percentage of white children that was one standard deviation above the mean was associated with a 0.026 standard-deviation rise in children's expressive language development. Yet above that level, the advantage of having white children in the classroom dissipated; classrooms that were two standard deviations above the mean were associated with a 0.165 standard-deviation decline in learning relative to children at the mean. This nonlinear relationship implies that racial/ethnic diversity improves children's expressive language learning when neither whites nor minorities are in the overwhelming majority, once we control for classroom SES.

RQ1: Math Learning. The results from Model 1 indicate that class mean income was significantly related to children's math learning, after adjusting for their own SES and background characteristics (ES = 0.065; p < .01). The quadratic term for class mean income was also significant and positive (ES = 0.032; p < .10), which suggests that the beneficial effect of higher class mean-income grew stronger as the mean income increased. Again, the measure of income diversity was not significant in Model 2. In Model 3, the classroom average of mother's education was significantly associated with children's math learning (ES = 0.053; p < .05).

When mean class income and mothers' education were combined in Model 4, the results indicate a significant relationship between socioeconomic composition and children's math learning, controlling for their SES and other background characteristics (ES = 0.061; p < .01). The coefficient decreased slightly in Model 5 with the addition of racial/ethnic composition (which was not statistically significant), but the effect of socioeconomic composition remained significant and positive (ES = 0.058; p < .05). It is again striking that the socioeconomic composition coefficient was comparable to that associated with children's own SES (ES = 0.092; p < .001).

RQ1: Social Skills Learning. In contrast to the other three outcomes, the relationship between class mean income and children's social skills learning was significant but negative (ES = -0.060; p < .01). This result suggests that for each standard deviation increase in the socioeconomic level of the classroom, children's social-skills learning was 0.06 standard deviations *less* than in classrooms where the SES level was average. In Models 2 and 3, neither the measure of income diversity within classrooms, nor the measure of mothers' education was significant.

Combining class mean income and mother's education, the results in Model 4 indicate a significant and negative relationship between socioeconomic composition and children's social skills learning, adjusting for children's SES and background characteristics (ES = –0.044; p < .10). However, this estimate was no longer significant when the percentage of white children was incorporated into Model 5 (ES = –0.045; p < .10).

Of the four outcomes, the social skills measure is the only one that relied on teacher evaluations and the sole outcome for which socioeconomic composition was not significant when I included the racial/ethnic composition of the classrooms in the model. In my analysis, I explored the implications of this finding and will discuss the results below.

RQ2: Socioeconomic Composition, Classroom Quality, and Children's Learning

The second research question asks: To what extent do aspects of preschool quality, such as instructional quality, explain the relationship between the socioeconomic composition of preschool classrooms and children's learning? To answer this question, I added measures of classroom quality to the last model in RQ1 (Model 5) to create a new model (Model 6). These variables included measures of instructional quality and emotional support, teacher education, class size, whether the program consumed a full day, whether the classroom was a Head Start program, and whether the teacher used a comprehensive curriculum. If a covariate was significant for any one of the four outcomes, I included it in the models for all four outcomes to make them comparable. In the final version of the models, six class-level covariates were significant for at least one outcome, and hence included in the models for all four outcomes.

To the extent that the coefficient for socioeconomic composition decreases upon the inclusion of these covariates, the compositional effect can be interpreted to be spurious. For example, if the inclusion of instructional quality diminishes the coefficient for socioeconomic composition, we could infer that the compositional effect was related to the fact that higher-SES classrooms are likely to attract higher-quality teachers. But if the inclusion of instructional quality, or other measures of classroom quality, does not diminish the compositional coefficient, then we would need to consider alternative explanations for how socioeconomic composition relates to children's learning.

RQ2: Receptive Language Learning. Only one of the six covariates was significantly related to children's receptive language learning: instructional quality (ES = 0.034; p < .10). When this measure and the other five class-level covariates were incorporated into the model, the coefficient for socioeconomic composition remained constant (ES = 0.046; p < .10). Because the class-level covariates did not reduce the estimate for socioeconomic composition, they do not explain its relationship to children's receptive language learning.

RQ2: Expressive Language Learning. Again, among the six covariates, only one, instructional quality, was significantly related to children's expressive language learning (ES = 0.057; p < .001). With the inclusion of the class-level covariates, the estimate for socioeconomic composition remained constant (ES = 0.064; p < .05). Because none of them reduced the coefficient for socioeconomic composition, the covariates do not explain its relationship to expressive language learning. Their inclusion in the model, however, rendered the measure of racial-ethnic composition non-significant. This finding suggests that the association between the percentage of white children and expressive language learning is explained, at least in part, by the preponderance of higher-quality instruction in classrooms with more white children.

RQ2: Math Learning. Two of the classroom covariates were significantly associated with children's math learning: instructional quality (ES = 0.034; p < .05) and a small class (ES = –0.056; p < .10). Somewhat surprisingly, the coefficient for class size was negative, suggesting that children in smaller classes learned fewer math skills than children in larger classes. In the presence of these and the other classroom covariates, the socioeconomic compositional estimate remained constant (ES = 0.061; p < .05), indicating once again that the covariates do not explain the relationship between socioeconomic composition and children's math learning.

RQ2: Social Skills Learning. Several of the classroom quality measures were significantly related to social skills learning. After adjusting for their SES and other background characteristics, children in classrooms with higher levels of instructional quality developed more social skills (ES = 0.041;

$p < .05$), as well as children whose teachers had a BA (ES = 0.092; $p < .10$) or more than a BA (ES = 0.153; $p < .01$), when compared to those whose teachers lacked a BA. Children in Head Start classrooms learned more social skills than children in non-Head Start classrooms (ES = 0.104; $p < .10$), but children in full-day programs acquired fewer social skills than those in half-day programs (ES = –0.078; $p < .10$).

Despite the significance of these covariates, the association between socioeconomic composition and social skills development remained non-significant. The results of the social skills analyses represent the only findings, thus far, when socioeconomic composition was not significantly related to children's learning. For the other three outcomes, it has remained a durable predictor of learning, even in the presence of classroom covariates that are commonly thought to be important aspects of high-quality preschool classrooms.

RQ3: Socioeconomic Composition, Classroom Contexts, and Children's Learning

The third research question asks: Is the relationship between socioeconomic composition and children's learning stronger in certain classroom contexts, such as when income diversity or instructional quality is high? To answer this question, I began by creating interaction terms between each class-level covariate and two measures: (1) classroom SES and (2) the standard deviation of family income within classrooms. I then added the interaction terms to Model 6 to create a new Model 7. If an interaction term was not significant, I excluded it from the model. Though the measure of income diversity within classrooms was not significant by itself in Model 2, I included it here to test whether it was a significant predictor of children's learning when combined with aspects of classroom quality. For each of the four outcomes, only one interaction term was significant. Yet the findings have important research and policy implications.

RQ3: Receptive Language Learning. The results indicate that socioeconomic composition and income diversity interacted to promote receptive language learning (ES = 0.046; $p < .01$). When socioeconomic composition and income diversity were both one standard deviation above the mean, children's learning improved by 0.103 standard deviations, compared to classrooms where both measures were only average. Conversely, when socioeconomic composition and income diversity were both one standard deviation below the mean, children's receptive language learning declined by 0.103 standard deviations relative to children's learning in classrooms that were average on both measures.

This result indicates that classrooms in which both the SES level and income diversity were high enjoyed an advantage beyond the sum of the two coefficients by themselves. On the other end of the spectrum, high-poverty classrooms in which there was little variation in family income suffered a double disadvantage that substantially suppressed children's receptive language development. The finding that above-average SES and above-average income diversity combine to promote learning also implies that there is a "tipping point" above which high SES and high diversity promote learning, and below which income diversity pulls down the SES average so much that it no longer confers a learning advantage. (I discuss the issue of tipping points further below.)

RQ3: Expressive Language Learning. The results indicate that socioeconomic composition and instructional quality interacted to promote children's expressive language learning (ES = 0.032; p < .05). When socioeconomic composition and instructional quality were both one standard deviation above the mean, children's expressive language learning improved by 0.147 standard deviations, compared to children's learning in classrooms where both measures were only average. Conversely, when socioeconomic composition and instructional quality were both one standard deviation below the mean, children's expressive language learning declined by 0.147 standard deviations relative to children's learning in classrooms that were average on both measures.

This finding indicates that classrooms in which both the SES level and instructional quality were high enjoyed a big advantage that promoted children's expressive language development. At the same time, high-poverty classrooms in which instructional quality was low endured a big disadvantage that significantly suppressed how much children learned.

RQ3: Math Learning. The results indicate that the diversity of income within classrooms interacted positively with teachers who had more than a BA to promote children's math learning (ES = 0.089; p < .05). When income diversity was one standard deviation above the mean and the teacher had more than a BA, children's math learning improved 0.089 standard deviations relative to children's learning in classrooms where income diversity was average. When the teacher had only a BA or less and income diversity was a standard deviation below the mean, children's acquisition of math

TABLE 3.1. The Combined Effects of Socioeconomic Composition, Instructional Quality, Income Diversity, and Teacher Education (n = 2,966)

	Receptive Language	Expressive Language	Math Skills
Child-level SES[a]	0.049*[b]	0.048*	0.093***
Class-level effects:			
SES composition[c]	0.057*	0.054*	0.059~
Instructional quality	0.031~	0.061***	0.033~
SES composition + income diversity	0.046**		
SES composition + instructional quality		0.032*	
Income diversity + teacher has > BA[d]			0.089*
Total of class-level effects[e]	0.134	0.147	0.181

~ p < .10 *p < .05 **p < .01 ***p < .001 [a]All measures are z-scored; socioeconomic status is the average of two z-scored variables: child's family income and mother's education. [b]Coefficients are empirical Bayes estimates adjusted for child-level characteristics, such as race/ethnicity, IEP status, and fall assessment score, and class-level characteristics, such as teacher education, class size, use of a comprehensive curriculum, and whether the site is a Head Start program. [c]Socioeconomic composition is the average of two z-scored variables: class mean income and class mean mothers' education. [d]Comparison group is "no BA." [e]The totals do not include the discrete coefficients for income diversity and teachers with more than a BA because, by themselves, they were close to zero and not statistically significant.

skills declined by 0.089 standard deviations relative to children's learning in classrooms with only an average level of income diversity.

This finding suggests that classrooms in which income diversity was above average and teachers had more than a BA, children's math learning improved. At the same time, when income diversity was low and teachers had only a BA or less, children suffered a double disadvantage that suppressed their math development.

RQ3: The Combined Effects of High Classroom SES, Instructional Quality, Income Diversity, and Teacher Education. The results of the analysis indicate that classrooms that offer above-average SES, instructional quality, income diversity, and teacher education levels may substantially benefit children, regardless of their own SES. Table 3.1 summarizes the combined effects of these variables in classrooms, including the value of their interactive effects. For receptive language learning, the combined effect of above-average classroom SES, instructional quality, and income diversity is 0.134 standard deviations. For expressive language learning, the combined effect of above-average classroom SES and instructional quality is 0.147 standard deviations. For math learning, the combined effect of above-average classroom SES, instructional quality, and teacher education levels is 0.181 standard deviations. In each case, these combined effects are roughly twice the size of the coefficient for children's own SES.

Because these aspects of the classroom interact to promote children's learning, combining them creates additional benefits for children, beyond the sum of their discrete coefficients. Policy that tries to capture these interactive effects by supporting diverse preschool classrooms with high-quality, highly qualified teachers could thus offer substantial advantages to children.

RQ3: Social Skills Learning. For social skills learning, the coefficient for socioeconomic composition continued to be non-significant, but the interaction term for socioeconomic composition and instructional quality was significant and negative (ES = –0.033; p < .10). This means that when both the SES level and instructional quality were one standard deviation above the mean, children's social skills learning improved by a negligible 0.008 standard deviations, compared to a more substantial improvement of 0.041 standard deviations associated with instructional quality when the SES level was average. Moreover, in the presence of these covariates, the measure of racial/ethnic composition (the percentage of white children) remained significant and negative (ES = –0.073; p < .01).

These findings are somewhat puzzling. Throughout the social skills analysis, the fact that the coefficients for socio-composition (though non-significant) and racial/ethnic composition were negative calls for explanation. The interaction findings add to this puzzle by suggesting that a high SES-level virtually eliminated the benefits associated with instructional quality. Together, do these findings imply that high-poverty, high-minority classrooms promoted children's social skills learning?

A plausible explanation for this negative coefficient is that it reflects a ceiling effect on the social skills measure (that is, high-SES children began Pre-K with higher skills and thus had less room to improve on the social skills assessment), which made it appear that children in high-SES classrooms were not learning as many social skills as children in low-SES classrooms. Yet, the negative correlation between initial skills and gains, which indicates a ceiling effect, was not stronger on this outcome than on the other three, and this was the only outcome for which the coefficient was negative. It is also possible that teachers in mostly white classrooms had higher expectations for their children's social development and were less generous with their evaluations of them, which would produce "less" social skills learning in those classrooms.

Another explanation, however, is that high-poverty, high-minority classrooms somehow supported children's social skills development in ways that high-SES, predominantly white classrooms did not. Other research has found that common disciplinary practices among low-SES, minority parents may differ from those of high-SES, white parents.[81] Perhaps teachers in high-poverty, high-minority classrooms can take advantage of this common approach to create consistent social expectations for children that, in turn, foster their social development.

To explore this possibility, I tested a model in which I used the percentage of children in poverty and the percentage of children who are minorities for my class-level compositional variables. I also included an interaction term for the two measures to explore if they interacted to promote children's social development.

The results suggest that classrooms that were both high-poverty and high-minority conferred a *disadvantage* in terms of children's social skills learning. The relationship between the percentage of minority children in the classroom and children's social skills learning was positive (ES = 0.121; $p < .01$), and the relationship between the percentage of children in poverty and their social development was also positive, though non-significant. But their interaction term was negative and significant (ES = −0.138; $p < .05$). When both compositional measures were one standard deviation above average, which means the classroom was both high-poverty and high-minority, children's social skills learning was 0.017 standard deviations less than when both measures were average. Conversely, in low-poverty and low-minority classrooms (that is, both one standard deviation below the mean), children's social development improved by 0.017 standard deviations relative to when both measures were average.

These findings indicate that the negative coefficients for the socioeconomic and racial/ethnic compositional measures do not imply that high-poverty, high-minority classrooms somehow promote children's social development. In the absence of an alternative explanation, this result provides support for the hypothesis that the negative coefficient for racial/ethnic composition may reflect higher teacher expectations in predominantly white classrooms, which would produce the appearance of less learning on the social skills assessments. At the same time, teachers in mostly minority classrooms may have had relatively low expectations for their children's social skills, and subsequently rated them higher in terms of their progress over the preschool year. Because only the estimate for racial/ethnic composition was statistically significant, these expectations would appear to relate more to the racial/ethnic composition of the classroom than to its socioeconomic composition.

Again, it is noteworthy that with the exception of the social skills analysis, socioeconomic composition remained a reliable predictor of children's learning, even with the inclusion in the final model of numerous classroom measures and interaction terms that prior research had found to be associated with children's learning. Only one other aspect of the classroom, instructional quality, was an equally reliable predictor.

Limitations of the Study

The nature of the dataset introduces three limitations to the study related to (1) the narrow scope of the outcomes, (2) the possibility of selection bias, and (3) the inability to determine whether certain groups (such as low-SES students) are more or less influenced by the socioeconomic composition of their classroom than other groups (such as high-SES students).

Choosing the Right Outcomes

Though the Multi-State/SWEEP data are remarkably rich in aspects of children's learning and classroom quality, the short time-span between assessments precludes the analysis of longer-term outcomes that may be relevant to an analysis of socioeconomic composition and children's learning. While short-term pre-academic outcomes predict later achievement, they represent necessary, but not sufficient measures of how young children may benefit from attending high-quality preschools.[82] Economist James Heckman, for example, has posited that the most enduring benefit of high-quality preschool is the nurturance of motivation, perseverance, and self-esteem.[83]

Short-term pre-academic outcomes are also likely to neglect the particular benefits of early education in diverse classrooms that may extend to all children in the class. In fact, learning in such classrooms may create a durable imprint on all children's minds that affects how they perceive the meaning of social class and the strengths and challenges of living in a diverse community. Children from any socioeconomic background may learn how to befriend and work with a variety of children with ease and confidence, a skill that would serve them well in the labor force and their

social and civic lives. Diverse classrooms may also nurture parental interactions across social classes, easing the social isolation that segregated
communities create and the structural inequalities that result.

Is it realistic to think that socioeconomically diverse preschool classrooms would contribute to such profound social and economic outcomes?
We know that children in early childhood absorb stereotypes about particular groups that affect their cross-cultural beliefs and relationships,
and that as children grow into middle childhood, racial and cultural perceptions solidify and in-group biases that favor sameness often develop.
During this time of foundational development, which Piaget called "the
construction of reality in the child," the experience of a diverse preschool
classroom is likely to provide rich learning opportunities that foster long-
term cross-cultural skills and friendships, and perhaps an appreciation of
the strengths of diverse communities.[84]

Selection Bias

The problem of selection bias deserves careful consideration when interpreting the findings of this and any quasi-experimental study. Separat-
ing the effect of treatment from the effect of selection has long been a
critical challenge to the researcher.[85] One could argue that parents who
seek out socioeconomically diverse preschool programs are different in
ways that positively affect a child's learning, and thus inflate the apparent effect of socioeconomic composition. It is also possible that the effect
of socioeconomic composition is, at least in part, reflecting the effect of
a child's neighborhood. At the same time, it may be that parents whose
special-needs children are having trouble in their local preschools seek
out higher-quality programs, which could suppress the apparent effect
of socioeconomic composition if those children land in diverse programs
but tend to learn less. Moreover, though the Multi-State/SWEEP data
collectors randomly chose children for assessment, they could choose
only children whose parents had allowed them to participate. How these
varieties of selection may have affected the results is hard to discern precisely and demands caution when interpreting these results.[86]

To address this concern, the models tested here control for an unusually wide variety of children's background characteristics, including
maternal education, which has been found to account for a large portion
of the relationship between child care quality and children's learning.[87]
Such characteristics can be expected to account for many if not most
aspects of the home environment that affect children's learning while

they attend preschool. Though not perfect, the ANCOVA approach also helps to address non-equivalency between families in low- and high-SES preschools by comparing the treatment effect on different groups as if they had started with the same pretest scores.[88]

Moreover, other research has suggested that distortions due to selection bias in early education research may be less substantial than previously thought. In an attempt to address such bias, one study employed propensity score matching and found a significant relationship between high-quality child care and children's academic achievement.[89] Another study analyzed data on low-income elementary school children who were randomly assigned to high- or low-poverty elementary schools, which should eliminate selection bias, and found significant learning benefits for children in low-poverty schools.[90]

Differential Sensitivity

Some researchers (including James Coleman) found different levels of sensitivity among groups of students to classroom socioeconomic composition. In particular, Coleman found that low-income and black students were more influenced by school environment, including school SES, than wealthier and white students. The sample used in this study, which included only four assessed children per classroom, did not allow me to determine whether some groups of children benefit more from SES composition than others.

The Policy and Research Implications

The findings indicate that the socioeconomic composition of preschool classrooms was a significant and positive predictor of children's receptive language, expressive language, and math learning during the preschool year, regardless of children's own SES, other background factors, and the racial/ethnic composition of the class. Socioeconomic composition was not significantly related to children's social skills development after controlling for children's SES, other background factors, and the racial/ethnic composition of the class.

The relationship between socioeconomic composition and children's language and math learning was not explained by an association with structural or instructional aspects of preschool quality that other research has found to be related to children's learning. Children who benefited from attending higher-SES classrooms were not learning more purely because they enjoyed higher levels of instructional quality or smaller classes, for example. Socioeconomic composition promoted children's learning through some other pathway, which, I argue, is likely to be direct peer effects.

The strength of the relationships between socioeconomic composition and children's language and math learning depended on whether other aspects of preschool quality were present in the classroom. For receptive language skills, socioeconomic composition and income diversity interacted to increase children's learning beyond the sum of the two coefficients. For expressive language skills, instructional quality and socioeconomic composition combined to promote more learning, and for math skills, income diversity and teachers' education levels combined to increase how much children learn. These results underline the value of income diversity and the importance of highly competent teaching, or the education that may support it, to capture the full benefits of diverse classrooms.

The results have multiple and important ramifications for the current policy dialogue regarding the expansion of access to quality preschool programs, as well as ongoing research to help inform this debate. In the following sections, I discuss these ramifications, as well as the overarching implications for policy and research on how to pursue high-quality preschool programs. Finally, I address whether policies to promote socioeconomically diverse preschool classrooms are feasible and the implications for Head Start.

The Substantive Significance of Socioeconomic Composition

The results from the analysis indicate that across three of the four outcomes, socioeconomic composition, as measured by the average SES in the classroom, was significantly related to children's preschool learning, regardless of their own SES and other background characteristics, the racial/ethnic composition of preschool classrooms, and other aspects of classroom quality. The relationship between socioeconomic composition and children's receptive, expressive, and math development was statistically significant, but modest, which raises the question of whether it is substantively significant.

I would not expect the association between socioeconomic composition and the growth in children's language and math skills to be large, given how little time the children in the dataset spent in preschool. The average time between the fall and spring assessments was five months (157.1 days), and more than half (54.1 percent) of the children attended half-day programs. For them, the average number of hours per week spent in preschool was only 13.3, a mere 2.7 hours per day. Such limited exposure to diversity in the classroom is unlikely to produce large effects on children's learning. Moreover, on average, in the Multi-State/SWEEP data, children spent only 20 percent of their day on literacy and language activities and 6 percent of their day on math activities.[91] For children in half-day programs, this amounts to an average 32 minutes on language and literacy and only 10 minutes on math.

More troubling, the descriptive analyses indicate that low-SES children were more likely than their higher-SES peers to be absent from Pre-K and, when they did attend, to be there for fewer hours per week. Other research has found that low-SES children in kindergarten also were more likely to have teachers who spent fewer hours per week on instructional activities, even while time on instruction was associated with their learning.[92] These findings suggest that low-SES children are receiving an even smaller "dose" of preschool than their higher-SES peers, further constraining the effects that we would expect to find.

Despite this limited exposure, the findings also indicate that the coefficient for socioeconomic composition on the three outcomes is comparable in size to two other aspects of children's learning that we know from other research are very important: children's own SES and instructional quality.[93] The equally modest coefficients for the relationships between these aspects of children's lives and their learning suggest that the short time between assessments is indeed a cause of their small size in this study, and that the socioeconomic composition of children's preschool classrooms belongs on the list of important components of children's early learning.

To explore further the substantive significance of the findings here, I looked at other research for context and comparability. To do so, I used two approaches: (1) comparing the results to policy-relevant gaps, and (2) comparing the results to those from relevant studies.[94]

Policy-Relevant Gaps. The first approach examines the effects found here in the context of the skills gaps between low-, middle-, and high-SES children. The descriptive analyses indicate that children in low- and high-SES classrooms were, on average, a full standard deviation apart in receptive language skills when they began Pre-K, and that children in low- and high-SES preschool classrooms were, on average, more than three-quarters of a standard deviation apart on expressive language and math skills. (The gaps in achievement between low-, middle-, and high-SES children are similar to those between low-, middle-, and high-SES classrooms.) The findings suggest that, on average, if more low-income children could attend higher-SES classrooms, their learning would improve by 0.06 standard deviations in receptive language skills, 0.05 standard deviations in expressive language skills, and 0.06 standard deviations in math skills for each standard deviation increase in the average SES-level of the classroom (Table 1). In the context of such wide gaps in skills, an improvement of 0.05 to 0.06 standard deviations looks like small progress.

However, a more reasonable goal might be to try to move more low-income children into middle-SES classrooms. The descriptive analyses indicate that the skill disparities between children in low- and middle-SES classrooms were one-third of a standard deviation (0.322) in receptive language, one-fifth a standard deviation (0.208) in expressive language, and one-quarter a standard deviation (0.249) in math when they began Pre-K. In this context, a coefficient of 0.05 to 0.06 looks more substantial. In expressive language and math, the gains in learning represent a quarter of the initial gap between low- and middle-SES students.

Moreover, if the classrooms offer above-average SES levels, income diversity, instructional quality, and teacher education levels, then we could capture the interactive effects among these aspects of the classroom, and the gains would be even greater: 0.134 standard deviations in receptive language skills; 0.147 standard deviations in expressive language skills; 0.181 standard deviations in math learning. If such increases were cumulative over several years in higher-SES classrooms, they would represent very important improvements in low-SES children's learning.[95]

Even in a single year of preschool, the results suggest that moving a child who attends a very low-SES classroom (that is, two standard deviations below the mean) to a classroom that is in the middle (that is, the mean for all classrooms) would boost their language and math skills substantially and would prevent the skills gap from widening. First, an increase in classroom SES of two standard deviations could boost children's receptive language learning by about 0.12 standard deviations (0.06 × 2). By comparison, the Head Start Impact Study found that children's receptive language skills improved by 0.12 standard deviations during one year in Head Start.[96] This means that moving Head Start children from a very-low-SES classroom to one where the average SES-level is the average for all Pre-K classrooms could substantially improve how much they learn. In math, moving from a very-low-SES school to a more affluent classroom that is three standard deviations higher in SES could result in a substantial gain of 0.18 standard deviations (0.06 × 3).

Second, this and other studies have found that the skills gap between children from low- and high-SES families may widen during the preschool year, a serious policy concern given the devotion of substantial resources to close these gaps. The findings here indicate the potential for creating access to higher-SES, higher-quality settings for low-SES children. For example, for each standard-deviation increase in children's SES, the receptive language skills they learn between the two assessments increases by 0.049 standard deviations (see table 3.1). The findings here suggest, however, that for both the receptive and expressive language outcomes, this disadvantage for low-SES children would be erased by moving them into higher SES classrooms because the coefficient for socioeconomic composition is comparable in size to the coefficient for children's SES. Similarly, for math learning, the socioeconomic composition coefficient is nearly as large as the estimate for children's SES. Moving children out of high-poverty classrooms could thus largely prevent the widening of socioeconomic learning gaps during a year in preschool.

From a policy perspective, even small effects may be worth pursuing if their benefit-to-cost ratio is better than alternative policy measures. This type of calculation requires careful consideration of the full benefits of a policy measure, as well as the related costs, which are beyond the scope of my study. But it is worth remembering as researchers explore the benefits of diverse preschool classrooms.

Comparisons with Relevant Studies. The second method for evaluating the substantive significance of the findings compares their magnitude with the results from other studies that have addressed similar questions and populations. Two lines of research are useful for comparison with the current findings: those that have looked at the relative contribution of socioeconomic composition to children's learning, and those that have assessed the magnitude of preschool peer effects.

The results appear to contradict a key finding of the Coleman Report, which stated that children's own family background was by far the most important predictor of their achievement in high school, with school composition a distant second.[97] In contrast, the findings here indicate an association between classroom socioeconomic composition and language and math learning that is comparable in size to the association between children's SES and their language and math development. However, these findings are consistent with recent research that has exploited the strengths of multi-level modeling and reanalyzed Coleman's ninth-grade data, finding that socioeconomic composition had an equal or even larger effect on children's learning than their own social class.[98] The implication is not that we have overestimated the importance of children's social class in the long-term trajectory of children's achievement, but rather that we have underestimated the potential of classroom composition to narrow learning gaps between low- and high-SES children.[99]

Although no similarly large-scale, multivariate, multi-level analyses have assessed the extent to which socioeconomic composition promotes children's preschool learning, studies on preschool peer effects, measured by peer assessment scores, offer relevant findings for comparison, given the high correlation between children's SES and assessment results. Compared to my findings, a study of data from Georgia's Pre-K programs found larger coefficients for the relationship between peer abilities and receptive language learning (ES = 0.28; p < .05) and math learning (ES = 0.36; p < .05), and a smaller coefficient for the relationship between peer abilities and expressive language learning (ES = 0.02; p < .10).[100] The authors noted that their findings were larger than those from most peer effects studies in K–12 settings, but suggested that peers may be more important in early childhood due to the emphasis on direct peer interactions in preschool.

In sum, the estimates for socioeconomic composition look slight at first. Yet, upon further consideration in the context of policy-relevant benchmarks and related research, socioeconomic composition appears to be an important aspect of preschool quality that deserves policy and research attention

The Salience of Mothers' Education

The analysis indicates that for both receptive and expressive language, the average level of maternal education in preschool classrooms is more strongly related to children's learning than average family income. For math skills, the coefficient for family income is slightly higher than the coefficient for maternal education, but both are significant and positive. These results are consistent with a substantial body of research that has indicated the salient contribution that mothers' education makes to their children's early learning and development.[101] This contribution appears to operate independently from family income and to be mediated by children's home experience. Such findings have inspired early childhood interventions that seek to foster children's learning at home by directly nurturing parenting skills in low-SES families.[102]

My findings add to this body of work by providing evidence that the development of mothers' own children is associated not only with maternal education, but also with the learning of their peers in preschool classrooms. This "spillover effect" for maternal education could enhance the returns attributed to policy interventions that seek to promote educational attainment among mothers. It also serves as a cautionary example to researchers who use family income as a lone proxy for classroom composition; they may miss an important aspect of classroom learning.

Socioeconomic and Racial/Ethnic Composition

For receptive language skills, the findings indicate that both socioeconomic composition and racial/ethnic composition are significant and positive aspects of classroom quality. For expressive language and math learning, only socioeconomic composition was a significant predictor of children's learning.

These results suggest that, although socioeconomic composition is a more reliable, positive predictor of children's learning, racial/ethnic composition is also an important aspect of classroom quality, at least in terms of receptive language learning. Clearly, one is not an adequate proxy for the other in either research or policy discussions. These findings are consistent with research in K–12 settings, which suggests that the socioeconomic composition and racial/ethnic composition of classrooms are independently associated with educational outcomes.[103] The results here may be especially important for children who are both low-SES and minority, because they often enter kindergarten with substantially lower skill levels than peers who are either minority or low-SES.[104] The findings indicate that attending preschool classrooms that are diverse both by SES and race/ethnicity may help address this double disadvantage.

Classroom Composition and Social Skills Learning

Despite the consistently positive and significant estimates for socioeconomic composition on the language and math outcomes, the coefficient for socioeconomic composition and children's social skills learning was negative, and when racial/ethnic composition was incorporated in the model, non-significant. I have suggested that this finding is the result of higher teacher expectations in classes that are predominantly white. While I cannot say so definitively, the explanation for this finding may

JEANNE L. REID | **113**

relate to the fact that the social skills assessment was the only instrument of the four that relied on teacher ratings of children's progress. To clarify the nature of the association between social skills development and compositional aspects of classrooms, future research could explore this relationship with alternative instruments that rely on independent observations, rather than teacher assessments.

Capturing Peer Effects

The apparent role of peer interactions as the mechanism for the compositional effect suggests that efforts to improve the quality of high-poverty programs, such as Head Start, are limited in their effectiveness. To capture the effects found here, policymakers may need to expand access for low-SES children to higher-SES preschools

Can we assume that the durable significance of socioeconomic composition, even in the presence of multiple measures of classroom quality, indicates that it operates through direct peer effects? Other research suggests that we can. One study of Pre-K classrooms, which found a compositional effect and tested its durability by including numerous class-level covariates, similarly concluded that peer effects were likely to be the mechanism for the persistent compositional effect.[105] Using an even more abundant array of covariates, I similarly find that a significant compositional effect remains after their inclusion. If peer effects do not explain this relationship between SES composition and children's learning, what would?

One possible answer is the influence of a child's neighborhood, a context that is probably shared by many children in the preschool classroom. However, I would argue that in this dataset, neighborhood measures are an unlikely explanation for a compositional effect, given that in socioeconomically diverse classrooms, children are less likely to share the same neighborhood than in classrooms that are low-SES and homogenous. Another possible answer is that, despite the inclusion of a wide variety of covariates, the analysis fails to control for teacher expectations and efficacy, which may be higher in diverse classrooms than in high-poverty classrooms, and consequently promote children's learning. However, the study of children in Georgia's Pre-K programs included these two measures and found no change in their compositional estimates.[106]

I suggest, therefore, that direct peer effects are likely to be the mechanism for the relationship between socioeconomic composition and children's language and math learning. If so, the policy strategy of promoting

children's learning by trying to improve the quality of high-poverty programs will not capture this important aspect of classroom learning.

High SES, Income Diversity, and the Tipping Point

The findings do not suggest that income diversity within classrooms, as
measured by the standard deviation of income, is *by itself* related to children's learning. But importantly, such diversity appeared to work in con-
cert with higher-SES levels to promote children's learning.

For receptive language learning, the estimate for high-income classrooms fell into non-significance when the measure of diversity was incorporated into the model as a separate variable, rather than one embedded
in the variable of socioeconomic composition. In other words, both high-
income levels and income diversity were important parts of the learning
equation. Moreover, the combination of above-average SES and income
diversity in classrooms promoted children's receptive language learning
more than when the two measures were only average for all classrooms.
This further suggests that, in terms of receptive language, the combination
of higher-SES and economically diverse classrooms offers a powerful and
positive context for children's learning. (It is worth noting that the nonlinear relationship between the racial/ethnic composition of classrooms
and children's expressive language learning implies that racial/ethnic
diversity also promotes children's expressive language learning, regardless of the average SES in the classroom.)

To capture the benefits of classrooms that are both high-SES and
relatively diverse by income requires a balance, of course. Introducing
lower-SES children to high-SES classrooms will necessarily bring down
the SES average. Hence, if you have a homogenous, high-SES classroom,
you would increase learning in the classroom if you make the class more
diverse in terms of income. But if you add so many lower-SES children to
the classroom that the class falls to the mean SES for all classrooms, then
you lose the benefit of high-SES classrooms *and* the additional benefit of
combining high SES with high diversity.

This tipping point has important policy implications. First, it suggests that encouraging the creation of more mixed-SES classrooms will
promote children's learning relative to high-poverty settings, but that
middle- and high-SES children should represent a majority of children in
the classroom. This, in turn, suggests that policymakers need to attract
more middle- and high-SES families to public Pre-K programs, given
the current predominance of low-income families, or create access for

low-SES children to higher-SES settings. Indeed, the results indicate that policymakers cannot escape the disadvantages associated with high-poverty classrooms by attracting a few higher-SES children to such programs. To capture the apparent benefits of more diverse classrooms, early education policy should support as many middle- and high-SES preschool classrooms as possible and open them to low-SES children. I discuss below how to pursue this outcome through either supply-side or demand-side strategies.

The Combined Power of Socioeconomic Composition and High-Quality Teaching

On the expressive language outcome, socioeconomic composition interacts positively with instructional quality to improve children's learning; on the math outcome, income diversity and teachers who have more than a BA interact positively as well. While other research has not found teacher education to be a reliable predictor of children's learning, it appears that in economically diverse classrooms, teachers with postgraduate degrees may be better able to promote the math development of their children. Why would the quality of instruction, or the teacher education that may support it, be so important in high-SES and diverse classrooms?

High-SES classrooms are more likely to be socioeconomically diverse classrooms, and this diversity may pose both opportunities and challenges to teachers. In such classrooms, children may come to preschool with different behavioral norms, cultural reference points, and communication styles. They may demonstrate skill levels that are relatively high on average, but also widely divergent. Together, these characteristics create possibilities for learning as well as obstacles to curricular and social cohesion in the classroom. The teachers in these classrooms may need to be especially skilled at creating individualized instructional support and facilitating peer interactions, such as exploring books, solving math puzzles, and engaging in dramatic play together.

Does this mean that policy should encourage postgraduate education for preschool teachers? Not likely, given the inconsistent relationship between even secondary education for teachers and children's learning.[107] Instead, many scholars have argued that preparing preschool teachers demands sustained and cohesive professional development.[108] This type of teacher training could nurture teacher skills and strategies to manage the disparate skill levels and cultural norms in socioeconomically diverse classrooms, while exploiting the rich learning opportunities they offer. These challenges also deserve research attention as an important component of effective pedagogy in socioeconomically diverse preschool classrooms.

Socioeconomic Composition and the Policy Dialogue about Quality

The findings indicate that the current policy debate about preschool quality is critically inadequate. Although early childhood researchers and policymakers are engaged in a constructive conversation about how to nurture high-quality preschool programs, rarely mentioned in this dialogue is the potential of classroom composition, and socioeconomic composition in particular, to bolster quality. When the relationship between socioeconomic composition and children's learning is mentioned, it often comes with an implicit acknowledgment of the need for more empirical evidence to support the idea.[109] The results of this study help to address the urgent need for empirical evidence and represent an important step toward changing the conversation regarding preschool quality to include a fundamental piece of the policy equation: the children with whom a child learns in a preschool classroom.

The historic omission of classroom composition from preschool policy and research has had two important consequences. First, any study on preschool quality that has not included classroom composition may suffer from omitted variable bias that may have produced inaccurate results.[110] Researchers should routinely include measures of classroom composition in models of preschool quality.

Moreover, lack of attention to the potential of socioeconomic diversity in preschool classrooms may lead policymakers to miss an important opportunity to cultivate both excellence and equity in the nation's emerging preschool landscape. While the argument for diversifying K–12 classrooms has often been made in terms of social justice, the empirical evidence here indicates that allowing children from different social classes to attend the same classrooms is a component of preschool quality. Without this recognition, concerted efforts to design policies that expand access to high-quality preschool are neglecting an important piece of the puzzle.

Is Socioeconomic Diversity Feasible?

Even if policymakers decide that reducing the number of high-poverty preschool classrooms would offer worthwhile benefits to children's learning, the policy challenge remains of how to expand access to higher-SES classrooms. Across the country, a premise of early education policy is that parents should be allowed to choose whether and where to send their children to preschool, which demands a voluntary approach to any attempt to encourage socioeconomic diversity. In this context, parents are the ultimate arbiters of quality within the constraints of supply and will be the determinants of whether socioeconomic diversity is possible.

Accordingly, I argue that a voluntary framework that could foster socioeconomically diverse settings requires three policy steps: (1) giving parents high-quality choices beyond their neighborhoods, (2) making these choices practically feasible with support services and adequate funding, and (3) re-imagining the role of Head Start.

Giving Parents Choices

Much of current state and federal preschool policy already is focused on expanding the menu of high-quality choices when parents consider preschool for their children. As noted earlier, these options can be fostered with a supply-side approach, in which the government funds or subsidizes programs, such as Head Start, public school, and nonprofit or for-profit Pre-K providers. They also may proliferate with a demand-side approach, in which the government lets parents choose among preschool programs that meet state requirements and pays public money to the program to serve the family. Either approach, or a combination of the two, has the potential to foster socioeconomic diversity, if certain policy choices are made.

One threshold requirement for fostering diversity is avoiding the neighborhood assignment that is common in K–12 school districts. If policymakers rely on neighborhood assignment for Pre-K programs, they are likely to replicate the residential segregation by race, ethnicity, and income that characterizes many communities across the country. Expanding choices beyond neighborhood boundaries creates possibilities for socioeconomic diversity that otherwise would be unlikely. With a geographically expanded menu of choices, for example, parents may decide that preschools close to their place of employment are more desirable than a neighborhood preschool, creating opportunities for diversity that would otherwise not occur.

When taking a supply-side approach to pursue universal access, state policymakers who want to encourage socioeconomic diversity could do so by making careful choices regarding location. Rather than fund new programs in the heart of high-poverty neighborhoods, they could seek locations on the borders of urban or suburban neighborhoods that might attract families from nearby low-income and higher-income communities. In more rural areas, choosing locations that are reasonably convenient for all residents makes it more likely that residents of all incomes may choose to attend the same preschool when few alternatives exist. Funding or subsidizing preschool centers that are located within employment settings, such as hospitals, may also attract a broad spectrum of income levels that represents the parents who work for the organization.[111]

The demand-side approach introduces low-SES children to programs that are privately funded and possibly serving higher-SES children as a result. This funding strategy offers a practical advantage over supply-side approaches in that it does not depend on the large-scale recruitment of middle-income families into entirely state-funded programs to expand access to higher-SES classrooms. The existence of socioeconomically diverse classrooms in the Multi-State/SWEEP data is suggestive evidence that such policies are already allowing children from different social classes to mix in preschool classrooms, despite the residential segregation that persists. In this context, the question is not whether socioeconomic diversity is feasible, but how to encourage it.

Making Choices Feasible for Parents

If state Pre-K policies avoid neighborhood assignment and allow parents to choose from a range of providers, will socioeconomically diverse programs naturally emerge? Without empirical evidence, we do not know when parents, given high-quality options both within and beyond their neighborhood, might choose preschools that offer such diversity. However, existing research on preschool and K–12 choices offers some ideas on what key components will make their choices informed and practically feasible.

- The provision or subsidizing of transportation is perhaps an obvious necessity for policy that strives to allow low-SES parents to travel outside their neighborhood to a preschool.[112] In families with multiple children attending different child-care, preschool, and K–12 locations, transportation would be particularly important.
- Parent-friendly information about preschool choices likely would be necessary to help parents learn about programs both within and outside their neighborhoods. State QRIS initiatives, for example,

may enable parents to make informed choices about preschools and consider aspects of quality beyond proximity.[113] Culturally sensitive outreach, which attends to the values and cultural expectations that shape preschool choices, may help to engage parents who might otherwise disregard publicly funded, center-based options.[114]

- Structural components of preschool quality, such as the provision of full-day preschool, also could be important to foster parent participation across different social classes. Low-SES parents who often are subject to welfare-to-work program requirements, and middle-SES parents who may also be working long hours, might consider only full-day programs.[115]

- Adequate financing is critical as well so that voucher or subsidy levels are sufficient to fund capacity for both low-SES and higher-SES children in quality programs. A sliding scale of Pre-K subsidies, which vary by a family's income, can assure that no one is excluded on the basis of cost.[116]

In short, the mere presence of high-quality choices likely will not be enough to foster broad participation in socioeconomically diverse programs. Each of these factors—transportation, accessible and culturally sensitive information about the choices and their relative quality, full-day programs, and adequate funding—may be essential components of policy to support parents' preschool decisions that, in turn, foster the socioeconomic diversity that my findings suggest will enhance children's learning.

The Future of Head Start

Despite Head Start's challenges, the success of the model programs indicates that high-poverty programs can indeed be effective. At the same time, how to "bring to scale" what appears to work in model programs at considerable cost is an obstinate challenge, and rising child poverty rates and income inequality only add to the urgency of such an endeavor.[117] The policy moment created by the state Pre-K expansion offers an opportunity to consider the strengths and weaknesses of Head Start, and the possibility that expanding the number of quality slots for children might better be achieved in more diverse settings.

The role of Head Start—a program that, by design, clusters poor children in the classroom—is uncertain in the evolving terrain of preschool choices. As support for universal programs has grown, Head Start programs have found themselves under fire for practicing "reverse discrimination," "deliberately segregating" poor children, and failing to provide many of them with the high-quality preschool settings they deserve.[118] There is some poignancy to this critique because Head Start began with the hope of providing preschool services primarily to low-income children and families to compensate for the extreme disadvantages they experienced. Head Start's founders also presciently envisioned a program that could be socioeconomically diverse by trying to reserve up to 10 percent of its slots for children whose family incomes were above the poverty line, a vision that never came to be. Today, some of Head Start's strongest supporters argue that the program's enactment as a preschool solely for poor children is untenable.

In this heated context, the accusation that the quality of Head Start is inadequate has been growing in the face of disappointing results.[119] The consensus response, if one exists, is to apply a rigorous standard of "what works," based on empirical evidence, to improve Head Start: a laser focus on teaching and learning, higher-quality instruction, better-educated and trained teachers, and the de-funding of consistently low-quality programs. The findings from my study, however, suggest that this approach neglects an important element of what works in promoting children's language and math learning: diverse classrooms that do not segregate poor children.

The accumulation of empirical evidence that children often learn less in high-poverty classrooms calls for a fundamental re-imagining of Head Start's purpose and structure. Certainly, it would be irresponsible to abandon a program that thousands of families rely upon when policymakers are struggling to create sufficient capacity for families who need and desire full-day preschool services. And it is worth noting that being a Head Start classroom was a positive predictor of social skills learning in this study. While helping to fill gaps in capacity, Head Start represents a valuable nationwide repository of expertise on how to serve culturally diverse families who face the harsh realities of poverty. Yet it is time to re-imagine Head Start's place in a preschool policy environment that is increasingly informed by empirical evidence and broadening its reach to serve middle- and high-SES families.

Looking forward, one option is that Head Start could open its doors to families from all socioeconomic backgrounds. As state Pre-K programs expand and middle-income families increasingly enroll, new families could be invited to attend Head Start and non-Head Start programs alike. While it is hard to imagine that Head Start centers located in high-poverty neighborhoods would attract significant numbers of higher-SES families, Head Start locations that are closer to middle-income neighbor-hoods could appeal to a broader array of families, particularly if they offer needed services such as full-day coverage for working parents. In the short run, this approach seems sensible. But in the long run, as state Pre-K programs approach universality, it might make more sense to reorient Head Start, particularly where its programs are lower or incon-sistent in quality, as a complement to universal state Pre-K programs that focus on providing high-quality preschool education to children from all socioeconomic backgrounds.

What would this complementary role be? Sally Styfco of the Yale Cen-ter on Child Development and Social Policy has posed three possibili-ties for Head Start's reformation, which are not mutually exclusive: (1) Head Start would no longer provide preschool for four-year-olds and instead focus its efforts on families with children from birth to age three, as it already does with Early Head Start. (2) Head Start would become a general family support program for families with children from birth to age eight. Its mission would be to provide comprehensive services, such as social, physical, and mental health services, crisis intervention, housing assistance, and adult education—all of which are highly needed and yet beyond the scope of state Pre-K programs. These services could be focused on families in poverty, but not limited to them as resources allow. (3) Head Start could offer a therapeutic preschool setting for chil-dren with disabilities and/or mental health needs when Pre-K programs do not have the capacity to do so.[120] Unlike state Pre-K programs, Head Start has long been required to serve children with disabilities and har-bors valuable expertise as a result.

Each of the three options would build on Head Start's considerable experience addressing the multiple strengths and challenges of families who are living in poverty, and which lie beyond the resources of Pre-K programs. None of these options requires that Head Start abandon its goal of nurturing young children's school readiness. On the contrary, Head Start as "a multi-faceted program designed to promote whole child and family development" could very significantly promote children's readiness for academic success and life's challenges.[121] This role would be quite important and pressing. Even as universal Pre-K programs expand, the substantial needs of families in poverty continue to be demanding and complex. Head Start is perfectly positioned to address them and thus could honor its past by serving and empowering families who face urgent challenges, but leaving the core mission of preschool education to universal Pre-K programs, which offer the possibility of socioeconomically diverse classrooms.

Rethinking Preschool Quality

With a wealth of research pointing to the benefits of intensive preschool programs that foster learning opportunities through high-quality teaching and play, many policymakers are admirably committed to funding quality programs in a time of severe fiscal austerity. In this context, it is critical to identify the necessary components of programs that produce positive outcomes. The results from this study suggest that socioeconomic composition is a significant aspect of quality that is frequently missing from this dialogue.

Policymakers are imagining an early childhood system that allows all children to learn, develop, and thrive in high-quality preschools. In a challenging political context, adding socioeconomic diversity to this ambitious goal may seem unrealistic. The findings here suggest that it is not. The presence of children in socioeconomically diverse classrooms in the Multi-State/SWEEP data indicates that, whether by design or accident, some state Pre-K systems are already fostering such diversity, and the findings indicate they are getting a reward for doing so in terms of children's learning.

Socioeconomically diverse preschool classrooms are by no means a panacea, and they may pose pedagogical challenges. But the evidence suggests that providing universal Pre-K with the possibility of socioeconomically diverse classrooms should be our goal as we design policy that systematically supports preschools of the highest quality. Putting together the quality equation accurately and reliably is more than an academic exercise. At stake is the effective use of billions of taxpayer dollars and, most important, the learning opportunities offered to millions of young children.

Appendix 3.1
Classroom Quality Measures

Classroom Assessment Scoring System

The Classroom Assessment Scoring System (CLASS) is an instrument that measures several dimensions of teacher-child interactions in classrooms.[122] Based on the theory that interactions between teacher and children are the primary mechanism through which children learn, the CLASS observes two main types of these interactions: social/emotional and instructional. Social/emotional features of the CLASS include the extent to which teachers are sensitive and responsive to children's needs and cues. Instructional features of the CLASS include the extent to which teacher behaviors promote children's concept development, and provide quality feedback and language modeling. Each feature is rated on a scale of 1 to 7 (1 or 2 = *low quality;* 3, 4, or 5 = *mid-quality;* and 6 or 7 = *high quality*).

Early Childhood Environment Rating Scale

The Early Childhood Environment Rating Scale (ECERS) is a global measure of classroom quality.[123] The instrument includes thirty-six items that try to capture several dimensions of classroom quality: space and furnishings, routines, language reasoning, activities, interactions, and program structure. The average of the thirty-six items provides a single overall measure; scores range from 1 to 7 (1 = *inadequate quality;* 3 = *minimal quality;* 5 = *good quality;* and 7 = *excellent quality*).

Appendix 3.2
Child Outcome Measures

Peabody Picture Vocabulary Test

The Peabody Picture Vocabulary Test (PPVT) is a norm-referenced instrument for measuring the receptive (listening) vocabulary of children.[124] For each item on the assessment, the examiner shows the child four pictures and says a word; the child responds by selecting a picture that best illustrates the word's meaning. Raw scores are converted to standard scores (m = 100; SD = 15), which reflect the child's performance relative to children in the population of the same age.

Oral and Written Language Scales

The Oral Expression Scale from the Oral and Written Language Scales (OWLS; Carrow-Woolfolk, 1995) is an instrument to assess children's comprehension and use of spoken language. For each item on the assessment, the examiner shows the child a picture and offers a verbal stimulus; the child responds by completing a sentence, answering a question, or making new sentences. Raw scores are converted to standard scores (m = 100; SD = 15), which reflect the child's performance relative to children in the population of the same age.

Woodcock-Johnson-III Test, Applied Problems

The Woodcock-Johnson-III Applied Problems Subtest seeks to measure children's basic math skills, such as counting, numeracy, comparisons, and word problems.[125] Items on the assessment include questions of addition, subtraction, how to read a thermometer, and how to tell time. Raw scores are converted to standard scores (m = 100; SD = 15), which reflect the child's performance relative to children in the population of the same age.

Teacher-Child Rating Scale

In the fall and spring, children's preschool teachers completed the Teacher-Child Rating Scale (TCRS), a behavioral rating scale that seeks to measure social and emotional skills.[126] Following directions from the scale authors, NCEDL researchers created a social competence scale for the Multi-State and SWEEP studies with four sub-scales: assertiveness, peer social skills, task orientation, and frustration tolerance. Items include "participates in class discussions" on the sub-scale for assertiveness, "well-liked by classmates" on the sub-scale for peer social skills, "completes work" on the sub-scale for task orientation, and "copes well with failure" on the sub-scale for frustration tolerance (NCEDL, 2005). Teachers use a five-point scale (1 = *not all;* 2 = *a little;* 3 = *moderately well;* 4 = *well;* and 5 = *very well*) to indicate how well the statements describe the child. I use a mean of the four sub-scales as a measure of social competence.

4

The Cost-Effectiveness of Socioeconomic School Integration

MARCO BASILE

Introduction

The benefits that primary and secondary education convey to students and to society as a whole can never be exactly quantified. But this inability to put a firm price tag on the benefits of education does not diminish the usefulness for education policymakers of assessing the extent of a proposed education reform's economic impact relative to its costs.[1] Such an approach is more valuable than ever given that, according to a recent major study by the consulting firm McKinsey and Company, "school spending in the United States is amongst the least cost-effective in the world."[2] Determining the cost-effectiveness of a given education reform can

The author would like to thank Duncan Chaplin, Jeff Guo, Jennifer Jellison Holme, Richard Kahlenberg, and Bernard Wasow for their invaluable reviews of previous drafts of this chapter as well as Christopher Swanson for graciously sharing his data on the relationship between graduation and segregation.

provide vital insights into maximizing the economic return from each taxpayer dollar spent on education.

Indeed, a careful review of the costs and benefits of breaking up concentrations of school poverty through socioeconomic integration suggests that this particular education reform intervention might be highly cost-effective. Previous research suggests that schools with socioeconomic segregation that is half the national average level experience high school graduation rates that are ten percentage points higher.[3] Other research indicates that higher graduation rates deliver economic gains to the new graduates and their communities.[4] Combining these two research topics together in the present study allows us to explore the benefits of improving socioeconomic balance in schools and the costs of such an intervention.

In this chapter, I estimate the cost-effectiveness of socioeconomic school integration based on research regarding segregation's effect on graduation rates, the economic payoff of increased graduation, and the costs of programs that encourage families to choose to cross neighborhood borders for their children's schooling. On the benefits side, I trace how reducing socioeconomic segregation by half would increase the graduation rate by ten percentage points and result in a public gain—that is, the gain from increased tax revenues plus the savings from reduced spending associated with health care, crime, and welfare—of over $20,000 per student. The total gain—which includes both the public gain as well as increased private earning—is estimated at around $33,000 per student. On the cost side, I draw on studies suggesting that mechanisms to achieve voluntary integration would raise total public school expenditure about ten percent and estimate the cost of an intervention that halved socioeconomic segregation at just under $6,500 per student. Accordingly, the expected public return of socioeconomically integrating a particular set of schools is estimated at more than three times the cost, and the total return on this investment is estimated to exceed the costs by a factor of greater than five. These estimates exclude less tangible benefits to our democracy from gains in educational attainment generally and from socioeconomic integration specifically, such as increased civic participation.

The potential for such results lies in the fact that the critical factors for successful education and increased graduation are more likely to be found in socioeconomically mixed schools than in high-poverty schools. Consider the three key groups of actors in education: teachers, parents, and students. At a school that is significantly middle-class, one can expect to find stronger teachers with higher standards of and expectations for their students. Schools that are predominantly middle-class also are more likely than high-poverty schools to have an active parent population, which holds the school more accountable for its results, as well as a more stable student culture focused on finishing school and getting into college.[5] In contrast, high-poverty schools suffer from higher teacher attrition and a higher proportion of teachers instructing classes outside their respective fields;[6] less parent participation in PTA, school committees, and as volunteers in the classroom;[7] and a student body that is more mobile and disruptive while holding lower aspirations for college.[8] As a result, high-poverty schools have trailed significantly behind middle-class schools in terms of performance: it has been found that middle-class schools are twenty-two times more likely to be consistently high performing than high-poverty schools.[9]

Striving for socioeconomic integration is not a novel concept. More than seventy-five school districts, educating over four million students, already take socioeconomic status into account when considering student transfers, in drawing school boundaries, and/or in their assignment of students to schools of choice such as magnet schools.[10] The first districts to do so were La Crosse, Wisconsin, in the 1970s and Wake County, North Carolina, at the turn of the century.

Recent U.S. Supreme Court decisions, most notably *Parents Involved in Community Schools v. Seattle School District No. 1,* have been unreceptive to the use of race in the assignment of students to schools.[11] This has resulted in an increased interest in the use of socioeconomic status in student assignment, a legally promising strategy that has demonstrated greater success in improving education outcomes than integration by race alone has.[12] Many large, prominent school districts have adopted successful socioeconomic integration plans, including Cambridge, Massachusetts; Omaha, Nebraska; and St. Louis, Missouri,[13] and, most recently, at the end of 2009, the school district of Chicago, Illinois.[14]

Unfortunately, from a cost-effectiveness perspective, school districts that have implemented this intervention have not collected and amalgamated the necessary longitudinal cost and benefit data before and after actual implementation of this intervention—perhaps because of a lack of sufficient resources. In the absence of these data, cost-effectiveness can be measured by drawing upon various studies that inform both the expected costs and benefits of socioeconomic integration and applying these results to a hypothetical scenario of the intervention.

In this chapter, I construct such an estimate of the costs and benefits of socioeconomic school integration by modeling a hypothetical interdistrict transfer plan in which:

- Schools in poorer areas are magnetized to attract students from more affluent school districts;
- And these more affluent districts are encouraged through incentive payments to receive low-income transfer students.

I envision the plan's execution through a system of "controlled choice," in which parental choice of schools is honored with an eye to maximizing socioeconomic integration.[15] In our country's many metropolitan areas, this scenario might play out by urban students commuting to middle-class schools in the suburbs and by magnetizing urban schools to attract suburban students. I often will refer to this particular example for explanatory reasons; however, I recognize that the suburbanization of poverty makes this dichotomy less clear than it once was.[16] In the 2008 election cycle, one major presidential candidate proposed a plan along these lines that would provide $100 million to suburban districts accepting low-income transfer students and granting an additional $100 million in federal funding for urban magnet schools to attract suburban students.[17]

My scenario's interdistrict approach might overestimate the costs of socioeconomic integration in many cases, particularly in the South, where urban and suburban communities often fall into a single jurisdiction, in which case costs such as incentive payments to suburban schools outside the urban district would be unnecessary. But I base my model on an interdistrict approach because research finds that there is more socioeconomic segregation between districts than within them.[18] Further, my estimate of the intervention's benefits might be biased downward because, firstly, I use moderate to conservative estimates of the economic consequences of high school graduation and, secondly, I look only at the benefits that the creation of magnet schools delivers via socioeconomic integration. It may well be that magnet schools confer other benefits associated with the close fit between student interests and the school curriculum and/or with the feeling of ownership engendered by school choice.[19] However, because of this chapter's focus on measuring the cost-effectiveness of socioeconomic integration alone, I do not attempt to estimate the additional benefits of magnet schools.

In order to assess the costs and benefits of my scenario, certain assumptions must be made about the scenario's parameters. First, complete integration is probably unachievable. Therefore, I model the economic consequences of reducing socioeconomic segregation by half of its national level, or from a high school socioeconomic segregation index level of about 0.47, to approximately 0.24.[20] These index numbers, which refer to intradistrict segregation rather than interdistrict segregation, are provided by an Editorial Projects in Education research effort led by Christopher Swanson that analyzed the effect of segregation on high school graduation across the country. The segregation index, also known as an isolation index or a P* index, is a form of an exposure metric that measures the extent to which students eligible for free or reduced-price lunches (FRL), a proxy for low socioeconomic status, are isolated from non-FRL students within the district. The index represents how likely an FRL student will interact with another FRL student in school relative to how likely that student will interact with a non-FRL student. In a school district in which all of the FRL students are concentrated in one school that is fully FRL, the segregation index is 1.0; in other words, each FRL student is 100 percent more likely to interact with another FRL student than with a non-FRL student. The lower the index level, the more likely the FRL student is to interact with non-FRL peers. The segregation index is commonly found in the social science literature.[21]

A similar but not directly related metric known as a dissimilarity index, commonly used since the 1950s, measures the fraction of students within a given geographic unit who would need to move in order to reach complete integration.[22] According to Duncan Chaplin, the national dissimilarity index level for primary schools based on socioeconomic status is 0.5. If segregation were reduced by half, the new dissimilarity index level would be 0.25, indicating that one-fourth of the student population would have had to move in order to decrease segregation by half. (This presupposes, under a system of controlled choice, that middle-class students would not move from an urban district to the suburbs and that low-income students from the suburbs would not move to magnet schools in an urban district, given that such moves would exacerbate socioeconomic segregation.)[23] Within this framework, I develop my second assumption. I assume that one-quarter of the students in the interdistrict network would travel for their schooling: one-eighth would choose to commute full-time from more affluent areas to magnet schools in less-affluent areas, and one-eighth would choose to commute full-time from poorer areas to middle-class schools in more-affluent areas (see Figure 4.1). This post-intervention treatment condition can be contrasted with

FIGURE 4.1. Interdistrict Distribution of Students, Before and After Intervention

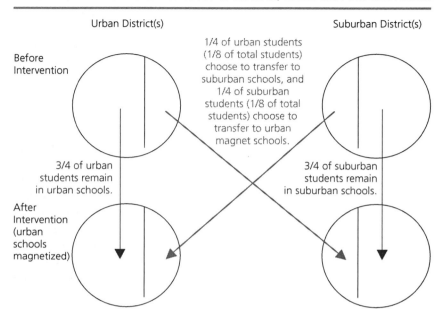

a pre-intervention comparison condition in which these students would attend their neighborhood schools full-time.

It is important to keep in mind that my scenario is built around districts with average—not complete—levels of segregation. Thus, the voluntary movement of students across district lines is intended to augment existing levels of socioeconomic diversity, rather than to constitute the entirety of integration. In other words, the movement across district boundaries of one-quarter of more-affluent suburban students (that is, one-eighth of total students) to magnet schools will not, on its own, lead to middle-class schools in the urban areas. But these students will be joining a student population that already has some level of socioeconomic diversity (recall that the national average segregation index level is 0.47), and the expectation is that these new students will raise previous levels of diversity dramatically—especially in any subset of magnet schools to which they are targeted.[24]

Third, I assume that graduating students within the scenario have attended socioeconomically integrated schools for half of their K–12 tenures, or seven years. (I round up to the nearest full year from six and a half years in order to facilitate annual compounding for net present value cost estimates.[25]) In the studies cited below on the benefits of attending integrated schools, there is no indication about the duration of integrated schooling, so I assume a midpoint estimate. (I also estimate the cost of the intervention over other durations, such as four years for high school and thirteen years for an entire K–12 tenure.)

Costs

The expected costs of an interdistrict desegregation plan are principally driven by two factors. One, the additional expense of implementing and operating magnet schools in order to attract middle-class suburban students to urban schools. And two, the cost of instituting mechanisms by which to bring urban students to the suburbs for their education—mainly, an incentive payment to non-magnet schools that receive transfer students in order to reduce the very real possibility of political opposition from suburban residents resisting an influx of low-income students. The extra cost of transporting students across district boundaries comprises a key component of both of these factors.

Urban Magnet School Costs

Magnet schools develop particular strengths around given curricular themes or pedagogical approaches and market themselves accordingly. For example, a magnet school might be especially strong in math and science or in the performing arts, or it might use a Montessori teaching approach. Because of these unique themes, magnet schools often require additional equipment, singular facilities, and/or specially trained teachers, which lead to costs that traditional schools normally might not incur. Transportation costs are also greater than for neighborhood schools. However, as the studies mentioned below indicate, the extent of these costs is muted considerably by two factors. Magnet schools tend to spend less on fringe benefits for their personnel, given that magnet school teachers are generally higher-salaried, and their improved retention rates reduce the financial obligations of unemployment compensation.[26] Second, magnet schools are more likely to use their facilities cost-effectively because they often maximize student enrollment and retention from a pool of applicants eager to attend the themed school.[27]

The most systematic studies of the additional expense of magnet schools were conducted in the 1980s, when magnet schools were first created. Although these studies are not new, the core factors that contribute to higher magnet school costs have not changed: staff development, personnel costs, materials/equipment, facilities, publicity, and transportation. These studies reveal that, as a general rule, the marginal increase in the cost of a magnet school, including transportation, is about 10 percent, +/– 2 percent in the school's initial start-up years—and even lower as the school becomes operational. The landmark study on magnet schools, including their costs, was conducted in 1983 by Rolf Blank and colleagues, with researchers at Abt Associates and Lowry and Associates, by looking at data from fifteen urban school districts that represented a range of student populations and geographic locations across the country. The school districts were selected randomly from among all urban districts in the country—stratified by size, region, and other characteristics—that applied for federal funding for magnet schools and that had the requisite number of magnet schools, whether with a merit admissions process or, as in my scenario, the more common lottery admissions process.

Blank and his colleagues found that the cost difference between magnet schools and traditional schools is about 8 percent, the largest factor of which is transportation (about one-fourth of the additional expense), and "narrows over time" as initial sunk costs are spread out over successive school years.[28] In his separate analysis of the Blank study's data, Kent John Chabotar, who was one of the original study's authors, stresses not only this point about the change from start-up costs to operational costs, but also the effects on start-up costs of increased enrollment: "Magnet schools in general cost more than non-magnets; however, most of these extra costs tended to be fixed. As magnet school enrollments increased, their per pupil costs decreased to a point near and often below per pupil costs at non-magnets."[29] Studies on the eve of the 1990s reiterated the Blank study's findings. After studying "nine urban high schools that prepare students for specific occupational fields as well as for college entrance," Vernay Mitchell and colleagues found that "differentials in operating or recurring costs appear to be relatively small when the exemplary schools are compared to other schools."[30] Lorraine McDonnell cites William Snider's 1987 conclusion that "magnets are from 10 percent to 12 percent more expensive to run than traditional schools" and includes the caveat that "a system of public school choice may impose start-up costs, but its operational costs should be no more than the current system's."[31] Finally, a 2008 report that "analyzes a recent survey of several hundred teachers and administrators affiliated with magnet schools across the country" confirms the consensus amongst these earlier studies that the additional cost of magnet schools is about 10 percent of non-magnet school expenditure.[32] In this chapter's scenario, I assume that some students will cross district lines to attend magnet schools, which may involve higher transportation costs than intradistrict magnet schools; but given the long-run reductions in operating costs, the 10 percent premium seems reasonable to apply. Because only half of the schools in the hypothetical integration scenario are magnet schools (that is, every urban school), total additional expenditure due to magnet school expenses (including transportation) would be half of the 10 percent premium, or about 5 percent system-wide.

Suburban Transfer Costs

The scope and structure of state financing for transferring students to suburban schools have varied widely in states that have implemented school choice programs, whether voluntarily or by court order. Along with transportation costs, some states provide additional funding to the receiving suburban districts. Such supplementary payments serve as incentives to encourage suburban districts to admit urban transfer students.

The size of these incentive payments varies among states. In their review of the incentive payments made by states in eight school choice integration programs across the United States, Jennifer Jellison Holme and Amy Stuart Wells found that incentive payment designs range from arrangements in which the state pays the receiving district a fixed fee to ones in which the state pays the average per-pupil expenditure of the receiving district, the home district, or the state.[33] (These expenditure numbers vary because districts generate different amounts of funding from three main sources: federal, state, and local governments.) For example, in the interdistrict transfer programs in Milwaukee and Indianapolis, the state's incentive payment to the receiving suburban district is equal to the suburban district's per-pupil expenditure. This means that, for each transfer student, the receiving district collects funding from the state equal to what the local government spends on each of its home students in addition to the usual federal and state funds.[34] In the Rochester and East Palo Alto programs, the incentive payment is equal or nearly equal to the home urban district per-pupil expenditure. In other words, receiving districts receive all or most of the federal, state, and local funds that would have been allotted for the transfer student in the student's home district. In general, the former funding scheme (Milwaukee and Indianapolis) generates larger incentive payments than the latter scheme (Rochester and East Palo Alto) because suburbs generally, but not always, spend more than urban areas on education. As alternatives to both of these funding schemes, the state might allocate only the state's average per-pupil funds for the receiving district, such as in the case of Minneapolis's program, or the state might pay an incentive payment to the receiving district and a "shadow payment" to the home district, such as in the case of Little Rock's Majority-to-Minority program in Arkansas.[35]

Further insight into the structure and costs of incentive payments is provided by the experience of St. Louis's interdistrict racial desegregation program, which was established in 1983 and, as one of the country's largest school choice programs, has incorporated different incentive payment schemes over the years. For each transfer student, Missouri formerly allocated federal and state funds to receiving suburban districts equal to the district's total per-pupil expenditure. But the state recently switched to providing only the state's average per-pupil expenditure after suburban districts opted to continue voluntarily in the program despite the expiration of a court-supervised desegregation order. In its incipient stages, the program's financial arrangement was "the key" to its success, according to William Freivogel. Under the original plan, for each transfer student, the state paid the receiving school district the amount that the district spent educating each of its students. This fee would range from as little as $3,000 to as much as $10,000.[36] In theory, a suburban district does not gain financially from such an arrangement because the state covers only the district's cost of educating a new student; but, in practice, suburban districts would find this financial arrangement advantageous because, due to economies of scale, the marginal cost of educating each additional (transfer) student is below the per-pupil cost of educating the district's original core cohort of students.[37] Under the original plan, the state would, in addition, also pay the transfer student's home district (that is, St. Louis) half of the state's average per-pupil expenditure with the presumed intention that this money would be used to improve the quality of education in urban schools and would prevent urban districts from discouraging its students from transferring. In 2008 the payment to the receiving district was fixed at $8,000, roughly the state's average per-pupil allotment of funds (that is, it does not include local funds) and the "shadow payments" to home districts were discontinued.[38] The St. Louis experience with incentive payments offers a gloss on how these payments function—in two different forms, one above average state per-pupil expenditure and one equivalent to it.

Historically, incentive payments have not been included in all inter-district transfer programs. Some suburban districts determine that their schools benefit from the diversity fostered by transfer programs and will-ingly absorb a financial hit under the program's arrangement. State fund-ing for these particular receiving suburban districts is below the state's average per-pupil expenditure. Under the interdistrict school choice designs of Boston's Metropolitan Council for Educational Opportunity (METCO) program and Hartford's Project Choice program, state fund-ing per student was as low as $3,700 and $2,500 respectively in 2008. Rather than an incentive payment to the receiving district, this funding constituted a below-cost per-pupil tuition payment.[39]

Whether or not deemed politically necessary, financial incentives have a historical track record of encouraging voluntary desegregation success-fully. Most school districts in the South hesitated on integration for more than a decade after *Brown v. Board of Education* (1954). In 1965 Con-gress passed legislation to provide federal Title I grants under the Elemen-tary and Secondary Education Act and made the aid contingent on efforts to desegregate. Research finds that federal aid significantly affected the behavior of local officials in the South in the 1960s by encouraging them to desegregate their schools voluntarily. As a result, the incentives reduced "the burden that desegregation had long placed on the courts."[40]

As Holme and Wells's review of eight interdistrict transfer programs reveals, incentive payment designs vary widely—to the point where, in the case of Boston and Hartford, receiving districts effectively lose rather than gain funding by accepting urban transfer students. Because of both variance in current state funding schemes and uncertainty as to whether incentive payments are necessary, I model an amount of funding that has often proven effective in attracting students across school district lines: the 10 percent premium for additional magnet school costs (which cov-ers both transportation and other special costs). A 10 percent premium for suburban districts receiving transfer students would cover transpor-tation costs and would acknowledge the possibility of some political opposition to such transfer programs (even though some progressive communities might not need a financial carrot to encourage their adop-tion of a program whose potential benefits for suburban and urban stu-dents alike they recognize). Because only half of schools would receive this funding under my scenario, incentive payments would constitute an increase in total expenditures of 5 percent (that is, half of 10 percent). The "shadow payments" to urban districts, used in places such as St. Louis under its original transfer plan, would be unnecessary because urban districts would be receiving an additional flow of students and resources into their magnet schools, which would offset the loss of students and resources to the suburbs.

The 5 percent increase in total spending given to receiving districts would cover the additional cost of transferring more students to the suburbs, which is important because providing transportation free of charge to transfer students is essential to guaranteeing access to this opportunity to transfer to suburban schools, especially for low-income students.[41] Based on the studies of magnet school costs, the 5 percent increase in total expenditure seems to far exceed transportation costs for moving the same sized cohort of students across neighborhood school boundaries. Blank and colleagues found that about one-fourth of this additional expenditure covers transportation costs.[42] Assuming that the transportation mechanics for magnet students and transfer students to the suburbs would be roughly equivalent (in both cases, students would be transported from a selected group of pick-up points in one neighborhood to schools in another), the proportion of magnet school costs spent on transportation should serve as a rough guide for the proportion of the incentive payment that suburbs would need to spend on transportation.[43]

Indeed, for suburban transfer students, interdistrict transportation costs would likely constitute a quarter of the incentive payment. Given variance in the distances these students would travel, it is reasonable to assume that the average inter-district transportation cost per transfer student in the scenario would fall somewhere between the national average transportation expenditure per student transported, about $750 in 2005–06, and the high-end transportation costs of inter-district programs with ambitious transportation schemes. These latter high-end costs can reach, according to Holme and Wells, $2,000 per year, and perhaps more.[44] Accordingly, I estimate the transportation cost per non-magnet transfer student at the rough midpoint of this range, or $1,375. Under the scenario's assumptions, only one-eighth of the total students transfer from cities to suburbs, and, given that just over half of the country's students already use transportation, it can be further assumed that only about one-sixteenth of the total students would incur new non-magnet transfer student transportation costs of $1,375 each.[45] The other half of non-magnet transfer students (one-sixteenth of total students) would incur only the additional transportation cost between $1,375 and the current national average expenditure, resulting in a new cost of $625 per student. When the new costs incurred by all of the non-magnet transfer students are spread out across all students within the inter-district network, the cost amounts to $125 per student, or roughly 1.3 percent of total per-pupil public expenditure nationally in 2005–06.[46] Thus, these calculations indicate that one-fourth of the receiving district's incentive payment would cover new transportation costs and the balance would constitute a true incentive.[47]

When the additional costs incurred by the development and operation of magnet schools (5 percent) and incentive payments (5 percent) are considered, the total increase in public expenditure of inter-district socio-economic integration is estimated to be 10 percent.[48] Using the 2004–05 school year as a base year, the net present value of the investment in socioeconomic integration over half of a student's K–12 tenure (seven years), rounded to the nearest ten, is estimated at $6,340. This cost calculation is outlined in the formula below, where t equals the years since the present (understood as the 2004–05 school year) and c equals the national average per-pupil expenditure for each year.[49]

Per-pupil NPV of total cost over seven years, with 2004–05 as $t = 0$
$$= \sum_{t=-6}^{0} \frac{c}{10} (1.035)^{-t} = \$6,340$$

Benefits

The link between increased and improved education on one hand and increased employment, earnings, and productivity on the other is well-established.[50] This premise is at the heart of the desire to better quantify the economic payoff that students receive as the result of a given education intervention, namely its net impact on lifetime earnings. The benefit of integrated schools can be approximated by looking at the effect on high school graduation rates, and through this lens, on lifetime earnings. The economic gain of an intervention goes beyond simply the private gain as expressed by the high school graduate's higher earnings; it also includes public gain, such as all the benefits that are experienced by people other than the person who received the extra education. It includes increased tax revenues, as well as savings from reduced spending associated with health care, crime, and welfare. Inevitably, estimates for both private and public gain will fail to capture other less tangible benefits to society, some of which I detail below.

An intervention's impact on high school graduation rates is particularly revealing for a cost-effectiveness study given that high school graduation is a significant indicator of an individual's economic prospects, especially because of the strong correlation between high school graduation and college matriculation.[51] Claude Fischer and colleagues write that "social scientists have long established that people's educational attainments are the strongest immediate determinants of their economic fortunes."[52] Indeed, this fact is a large part of the reason that there has been a recent upswing of interest in graduation rates, especially since the enactment of the No Child Left Behind Act in 2002.[53] As President Barack Obama insisted in his first address to the U.S. Congress, "Dropping out of high school is no longer an option. It's not just quitting on yourself, it's quitting on your country."[54] The particular failure of schools to graduate underprivileged students makes this measurement especially critical for assessing how well an economic intervention addresses the needs of the huge proportion of students in "dropout factories."[55] Moreover, relative to other modes of educational assessment, such as test scores, the long-run consequences of high school graduation rates have been better established, and their economic impact has proven more conducive to economic analysis.[56] In his endorsement of the use of graduation rates in cost-effectiveness studies, Clive Belfield concludes: "Given the empirically identified economic benefits to the state of high school graduation (higher tax payments, lower expenditures on criminal justice, health, and welfare), a large fraction of investments that are effective in this domain should be cost-effective."[57]

High school graduation does not capture all the benefits of socioeconomic integration, such as higher academic performance or better preparation for laboring in a global and diverse workforce. But it does arrive at a central consequence with quantifiable results, and it avoids double counting benefits through overlapping measures of success.[58] At a minimum, the benefits of a socioeconomic integration program can be approximated through its effects on graduation rates; these provide a low bound on the full social benefits. Nevertheless, it is worth considering additional benefits, at least qualitatively. Among these benefits, for example, is the fact that a more highly educated population will be more civically and politically engaged. Although more than half of high school graduates tend to vote in major elections, just over one-third of

Americans without a high school degree voted in the 2000 and 2004 elections.[59] Other social benefits from increased education include an echo effect leading to more highly educated subsequent generations, healthier families, more efficient consumer choices (constituting an effect similar to that of increased earnings), and reduced teenage pregnancy.[60] Further, students who attend integrated schools are better prepared to participate in a global and diverse workforce. Employers believe that employees are more productive if they know how to work and get along with colleagues of various backgrounds. The 553 social scientists who authored an *amici curiae* brief for *Parents Involved v. Seattle School District* in support of the Seattle School District's integration program presented research results before the U.S. Supreme Court that support this link between past experience in an integrated environment and future productivity. Tellingly, the social scientists stressed that "the U.S. military has found that policies that encourage the participation and leadership of African Americans are essential for the effective functioning of the military in a multiracial society."[61]

Another benefit of socioeconomic integration that I do not include in the quantitative estimates—outside of their correlation with increased attainment—are gains of increased academic achievement, especially increased test scores and the deeper knowledge and understanding that these might imply.[62] Again, research suggests that economic and racial desegregation improve test scores.[63] Increased test scores are tied to increased earnings, although the size of the effect is disputed. In his review of the relevant literature, Belfield highlights three studies. In one, Eric Hanushek writes that a one standard deviation increase in test scores raises annual earnings by as much as 12 percent.[64] However, in the second study, James Heckman and Edward Vytlacil's study found a much weaker association.[65] Finally, Heather Rose found mixed results based on gender.[66] As Belfield writes, although it is clear that higher educational achievement leads to higher earnings, "the magnitude of the gain from higher achievement is open to debate."[67]

Socioeconomic Integration and Graduation Rates

A link between socioeconomic school integration and increased high school graduation is suggested by Christopher Swanson's recent study on graduation rates across the country and the factors influencing these rates. His study marks "the most extensive set of systematic empirical findings on public school graduation rates in the United States available to date."[68]

FIGURE 4.2. Estimated Graduation Rates, by SES Segregation Index Level

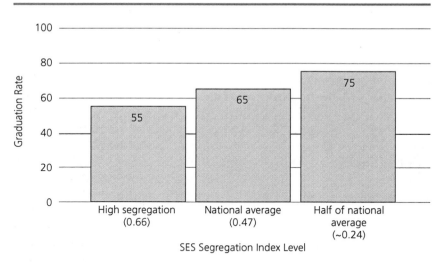

After controlling for other pertinent district characteristics, Swanson found a modestly strong negative correlation (r = –0.45) between graduation rates and socioeconomic segregation within districts.[69] In fact, there is a "more dramatic pattern" between socioeconomic segregation and graduation rates than between racial segregation and graduation rates.[70] Swanson's analysis of the differences in graduation rates in a cohort of sixteen southern states plus the District of Columbia suggests a difference in graduation rates of roughly ten percentage points between school districts whose high schools are at the national average socioeconomic segregation index level of 0.47 (approximately 65 percent graduation rate) and school districts whose high schools experience half that level of segregation (approximately 75 percent) (see Figure 4.2).[71] Other research suggests that the changes in graduation rates connected to integration do not constitute a zero-sum phenomenon: when low-income students do better, middle-class students are not hurt.[72] Ten percentage points is also the difference that Swanson found between the graduation rate of highly socioeconomically segregated schools with a segregation index level of 0.66 (55 percent) and the graduation rate of schools with an average segregation index level of 0.47 (65 percent).[73]

One promising area for future study is measuring the impact on graduation rates of the implementation of a socioeconomic integration plan by comparing graduation rates in the two different contexts—before and after integration—as it would help us understand the relationship between socioeconomic integration and high school graduation. A longitudinal study that examined the relationship would offer more confident conclusions about integration than those provided by my use of Swanson's data, which compare graduation rates between segregated and integrated schools rather than documenting an actual switch in segregation context. However, given the current paucity of research on this topic, the ten percentage point graduation rate difference between economically segregated and integrated schools suggested by Swanson's data is the most reliable estimate available and is consistent with the findings of research studying the effect of actual implementations to decrease racial segregation.[74]

Moreover, the ten percentage point graduation rate differential is supported indirectly by a recent longitudinal study of Charlotte-Mecklenburg's school choice program in which ninth-grade students from low-quality neighborhood schools could enter a lottery to attend schools outside their neighborhoods. The study found that the program increased the high school graduation rate of lottery winners by about nine percentage points. Although the study did not specifically measure the amount of socioeconomic integration engendered by Charlotte-Mecklenburg's school choice program, the program prioritized FRL-families' preferences to attend FRL-minority schools and was thus oriented toward significant socioeconomic integration.[75]

Thus, despite the limitations of the current research literature, the experiences of urban-suburban school choice programs in Charlotte-Mecklenburg and elsewhere help corroborate that such an increase in graduation rates due to socioeconomic integration—and, in the case of St. Louis's school choice program, racial integration as well—is realistic. In St. Louis, the graduation rates in 1993 for black students who were freshmen in 1989 and either attended an urban magnet school or transferred to a suburban school were around thirty percentage points higher than they were for black students who were enrolled neither in the magnet schools nor in the suburban schools.[76] The St. Louis example suggests that integration might raise graduation rates even more than ten percentage points, especially given the additional positive effect of improved educational quality at the magnet schools.

As in St. Louis, integration is associated with high graduation rates in Cambridge, Massachusetts and Hartford, Connecticut. Since the early 1980s, Cambridge has integrated its schools by race and, more recently, by socioeconomic status. Cambridge's 2009 graduation rates for black (79.8 percent), Hispanic (90.6 percent), low-income (85.3 percent), and limited English proficiency (79.1 percent) subgroups exceeded—in each case—the state graduation rates by roughly ten to over thirty percentage points. Cambridge's graduation rate for low-income students (85.3 percent) far exceeded Boston's (60.4 percent) and the commonwealth's (66.9 percent).[77]

A study from the 1960s through the 1990s followed the progress of 700 urban students in Hartford, nearly all black, who participated in the city's urban-suburban transfer program known as Project Concern. Along with keeping track of the graduation rates of a cohort of urban students, virtually all of whom were randomly selected to transfer to the suburbs, the study also followed a control group of students who remained in urban schools. Whereas 36 percent of the control group dropped out of high school, all of the transfer students graduated.[78]

The possibility of such a striking relationship between integration and increased graduation is plausible for several reasons. As was mentioned at the beginning of this chapter, the factors that educators consistently cite as essential to successful education—better teachers with higher standards, more active parents, and a student culture conducive to graduating from high school and matriculating at college—are more likely to be found at middle-class schools than at high-poverty schools. The influence of a student's peer environment is particularly critical for improving the chances of the student's graduation. A student is likely to perform better in a school where the student's peers study, do their homework, expect to graduate, and plan on going to college. Research indicates that poor children are particularly sensitive to their school environment. In the absence of strong family backgrounds—which are more prevalent amongst middle-class students—the aspirations of students from low-income families are more heavily influenced by the peers they meet at school.[79]

The Economic Benefits of Graduation

Although uncertainty exists regarding the magnitude of the economic gain of increased achievement, as measured by test scores, there is a growing consensus on the economic magnitude of increased attainment, as measured by high school graduation rates. This development is due to the recent work of several researchers from Columbia, Princeton, Harvard, Tel Aviv University, City University of New York, and the University of California-Berkeley on the economic consequences of high school graduation. Their findings were brought together and published by Clive Belfield and Henry Levin in *The Price We Pay: Economic and Social Consequences of Inadequate Education.*

In exploring what it costs taxpayers not to make an investment regarding a given intervention that increases high school graduation rates, the group of researchers led by Belfield and Levin found that the net lifetime public cost-savings per additional high school graduate is, on average, $209,200 in constant 2004 dollars. Given the difference between a dollar spent today and one received in the future, Belfield and Levin discount future gains at a rate of 3.5 percent per year (the same rate I applied in my cost calculations) and present all of their estimates at present value for a cohort of individuals who were twenty years old in 2005. Their estimate of the net lifetime public cost-savings per additional high school graduate accounts for public savings from four factors: increased tax revenue due to increased earnings ($139,100), decreased health care spending ($40,500), decreased costs associated with the criminal justice system ($26,600), and decreased welfare spending ($3,000). Potential savings from graduating more black males—the demographic whose graduation rates are most likely to be improved by inter-district socioeconomic integration—are even higher. Belfield and Levin calculate that the public savings for each additional graduate who is a black male is as high as $268,500.[80] Indeed, a study by Mark Cohen and Alex Piquero concludes that the public gain of graduating a high-risk youth can range into the millions of dollars.[81]

A 2009 study by Northeastern University's Center for Labor Market Studies confirms the findings of Belfield and Levin's group in calculating that "the average high school dropout will cost taxpayers over $292,000 [2007 dollars] in lower tax revenues, higher cash and in-kind transfer costs, and imposed incarceration costs relative to an average high school graduate."[82] In constant 2004 dollars, the study's estimate of the cost of a high school dropout is roughly $266,030, or about Belfield and Levin's estimate for the cost of a black male high school dropout.[83]

Further, in addition to these public economic gains are private gains for high school graduates resulting from increased earnings due to higher wages and increased working hours and weeks per year. Indeed, it is precisely these increased earnings that are fueling the increased tax revenue attained by the public at large. Nobel laureate James Heckman and Pedro Carneiro summarize the research consensus that the rate of private return to an additional year of schooling "exceeds 10 percent and may

TABLE 4.1. Cost Savings per Additional High School Graduate

Study	Public, Private, or Total	Savings per Average Youth ($)	Savings per Higher-risk Demographic ($)		Discount Rate (%)
Belfield and Levin	Public	209,200	Black male	268,500	3.5
(with Rouse)	Private	260,000		—	3.5
	Total	330,100[a]		370,900[b]	3.5
Center for Labor Market Studies	Public	266,030	—	—	Not reported

Note: All dollar figures are constant 2004 dollars.

[a]$139,100 is subtracted from the summation of public and private gains in order to avoid double counting this tax revenue (income, property, and sales).

[b]Rouse's study does not report a separate private earnings estimate for a black male high school graduate, so the total estimated savings for a black male is a summation of the public savings estimate for a black male and the private earnings estimate for an average youth, minus $157,600, the estimated additional tax revenue—income, property, and sales—for a black male graduate (in order to avoid double counting this tax revenue).

be as high as 17 to 20 percent."[84] According to a recent study by Cecilia Elena Rouse, also included in Belfield and Levin's volume, that assumes an annual discount rate of 3.5 percent and annual income growth of 1.5 percent, the lifetime difference in earnings between a high school graduate and a dropout is $260,000.[85] This research suggests that an individual's completion of high school results in lifetime private gains that exceed even the substantial lifetime public gains.[86]

The Economic Benefits of Socioeconomic Integration

The association between integration and graduation rates highlighted by Swanson's study—which, despite its limitations, is the most promising empirical analysis of the relationship between integration and graduation currently available—suggests that an intervention that reduces current segregation from the national average to half of that average could raise overall graduation rates by ten percentage points and lead to each new graduate saving the public approximately $209,200 over the student's lifetime—and perhaps even more, to the extent that socioeconomic integration will raise the graduation rates of black males in particular, saving the public $268,500 for each male who completes high school.

Using student population data from 2005–06, during which 3.84 million students began ninth grade nationwide, increasing this cohort's graduation rate by ten percentage points would mean 384,000 more graduates would each save the public $209,200 for a total present value of more than $80 billion in constant 2004 dollars over the students' lives. To put that savings into perspective, averaged out over the cohort of 3.84 million students, the gain would be $20,920 public dollars per student.[87]

When the public and private gains are amalgamated using the more conservative estimate of the link between graduation rates and earnings suggested by Rouse's more recent study, the total gain from the investment in integration would be $33,010 per student in constant 2004 dollars.[88] Put differently, increasing the graduation rate of the nation's 3.84 million freshmen by ten percentage points through socioeconomic integration would result in a gain of nearly $127 billion, on the order of 1 percent of GDP.

As mentioned, it is possible that in some cases the economic benefit of socioeconomic integration would be dramatically higher than the estimates presented above suggest. For example, consider the well-documented case of Hartford's Project Choice program. The graduation rate of the mostly randomly selected urban students who transferred to the suburbs was thirty-six percentage points higher than that of a randomly selected control group of urban students who did not transfer (yet, unlike in my proposed scenario, did not receive the advantage of integrating with incoming suburban students transferring to magnet schools). Further, most of the beneficiaries of increasing graduation rates through integration would be black males, each of whom is projected to save the public $268,500 by graduating from high school. (This figure is similar to the one the Northeastern University study suggested as the average public benefit of each additional high school graduate, regardless of the student's race or gender.) Using this public benefit estimate and Hartford's level of increased graduation, the public benefit of socioeconomic integration would average out across all students to $96,660 per student. The total benefit, public and private, would be $133,520 per student.[89] These figures suggest an enormous yet latent economic potential might exist in heavily segregated districts with low-socioeconomic-status schools.

Returning to the more conservative estimate of benefits, how do these benefit projections compare to the intervention's cost projections? Recall that the model's assumption that seven years of integration—a midpoint estimate of a K–12 tenure—costs a total present value of $6,340 per pupil. The public benefit of a ten percentage point increase in the

TABLE 4.2. Benefit-cost Ratios of Socioeconomic School Integration

Graduation Rate Increase (percentage points)	Public or Total Benefits	Lifetime Benefit per High School Graduate, Using Belfield and Levin Estimates ($)	Total Benefit for National Cohort ($)	Benefit-Cost Ratio		
				Four Years of Expenditure (High School Tenure) or $3,690	Seven Years of Expenditure (Half of K–12 Tenure) or $6,340	Thirteen Years of Expenditure (K–12 Tenure) or $11,400
10	Public	20,920	80 billion	5.7	3.3	1.8
10	Total	33,010	127 billion	8.9	5.2	2.9
36	Public	96,660	a	b	b	8.5
36	Total	133,520	a	b	b	11.7

Note: All dollar figures are constant 2004 dollars.

[a]Total benefit not calculated because a thirty-six percentage point increase in the national graduation rate would exceed 100 percent. The thirty-six percentage point graduation rate increase is offered as a possible high-bound estimate for integration's effects in heavily segregated districts with low socioeconomic status schools and not as a national estimate.

[b]The thirty-six percentage point graduation rate increase is drawn from the Hartford Project Choice experience, in which students participated for thirteen years.

graduation rate is estimated at $20,920 per student. Accordingly, such an intervention would exceed its costs by a factor of 3.3. The total benefits—public and private ($33,010 per pupil)—are estimated to exceed the intervention's costs by a factor of 5.2. Past experiences such as that of Hartford's inter-district program, however, suggest that the public benefits and total benefits might exceed costs by a factor ranging as high as 8.5 and 11.7, respectively.[90]

My assumption that the ten percentage point graduation increase reflects seven years of the intervention's implementation was generated out of uncertainty regarding the duration of integration in studies documenting the relationship between integration and graduation. Notably, Swanson's study looks at a snapshot of graduation rates and segregation levels in high school. The graduation rates he reports might reflect differences in integration for just the four years of high school. Alternatively, his findings might reflect longer exposure to integration, perhaps over students' entire K–12 tenures. Adjusting cost estimates accordingly, in the former case the public benefit-cost ratio of integration is estimated at 5.7, and the total benefit-cost ratio is estimated at 8.9. In the latter case, these ratios would be 1.8 and 2.9, respectively.

Conclusion

Cost-effectiveness studies of long-term education interventions necessarily require a chain of mutually dependent assumptions. In establishing my assumptions, I have tried to be consistently moderate to conservative in their impact on the net cost-effectiveness of the education reform. Thus the results—although gesturing toward a possible range of estimations—tend to constitute low- to medium-bound estimates of benefits and medium- to high-bound estimates of costs. Nevertheless, my analysis—which applies results of current research on the relationship between integration, graduation, and economic payoff—suggests that the benefits of a program to achieve voluntary socioeconomic integration through support of magnet schools and financial incentives constitute improvements in lifetime outcomes that exceed costs. Of course, the absence of direct evidence from longitudinal studies of those districts that have implemented programs of socioeconomic integration requires us to look at a hypothetical program. But, at the very least, I conclude with reasonable confidence that socioeconomic integration raises high school graduation rates and that greater graduation generates higher individual earnings and public savings to the point of exceeding integration's costs. As a useful benchmark, I have drawn on research suggesting that reducing socioeconomic segregation to half of its current level would raise graduation rates by about ten percentage points. Accordingly, I have estimated the cost-effectiveness ratio of socioeconomic school integration to be 3.3 for public benefits and 5.2 for total—that is, public and private—benefits.

This suggests that socioeconomically integrated schools might be more cost-effective than private school voucher programs, an intervention that has demonstrated only modest gains that do not offset the large adjustment costs of such programs.[91] My estimates also suggest that socioeconomic integration might be more cost-effective than the reduction of class size, which studies have indicated yields a public benefit-cost ratio of 1.46, as well as more effective than the improvement of teacher quality through increasing teacher salaries by 10 percent, which research has suggested yields a public benefit-cost ratio of 2.55. One intervention that some studies indicate is more cost-effective than my estimates of socioeconomic integration's cost-effectiveness is the implementation of specialized, publicly funded preschool programs such as the Chicago Parent-Child Center and the Tennessee First-Things-First programs.[92] Yet these programs have not proven themselves scalable. Head Start, the most ambitious attempt at scaling such preschool programs, has demonstrated much more limited results.[93] Moreover, the results of these specialized preschool programs might conflate the effects related to their particular intervention and the effects of their early timing. In other words, any intervention—including socioeconomic integration—may well have more impact the earlier it is administered. Indeed, studies have documented that socioeconomic integration at the pre-kindergarten level has had substantial effects.[94]

The research reviewed and amalgamated in this paper weighs strongly that segregated environments thwart students' achievement of their full potential. Focusing on one key variable, high school graduation rates, this study has sought to estimate the prospective gains of school integration as it affects lifetime earnings, tax payment, and demand on public services. Even though the study was moderately cautious, the existing evidence is promising for socioeconomic diversification strategies. It suggests that every one dollar spent today to promote socioeconomic integration might be expected to yield, through public saving and private earnings, more than five dollars in the future at present value. Such promise warrants further and more rigorous research of this education intervention.

Appendix 4.1
National Average Per-Pupil Expenditures
for Years Used in Cost Calculations

Number of School Years Included in Cost Calculation	t =	School Year	Average Per-Pupil Expenditure ($)
1	0	2004–05	9,316
2	−1	2003–04	8,900
3	−2	2002–03	8,610
4	−3	2001–02	8,259
5	−4	2000–01	7,904
6	−5	1999–2000	7,394
7	−6	1998–99	7,013
8	−7	1997–98	6,676
9	−8	1996–97	6,393
10	−9	1995–96	6,147
11	−10	1994–95	5,989
12	−11	1993–94	5,767
13	−12	1992–93	5,584

Source: "Table 181. Total and Current Expenditures per Pupil in Public Elementary and Secondary Schools: Selected Years, 1919–20 through 2005–06," Digest of Educational Statistics, IES National Center for Education Statistics, U.S. Department of Education.

The Logistics and Politics of Socioeconomic Integration

5

The Challenge of High-Poverty Schools:

How Feasible Is Socioeconomic School Integration?

ANN MANTIL, ANNE G. PERKINS, and STEPHANIE ABERGER

Introduction

More than forty years of research has consistently demonstrated a core reality of American education: students who attend high-poverty schools do worse academically than those who do not.[1] A school's socioeconomic makeup is in fact a stronger predictor of whether a child will succeed in school than any other factor, save the child's own family income.[2] Despite the high profile of the few high-poverty schools that do succeed with their students, these places remain the rare exceptions.

The authors would like to acknowledge Jal Mehta for his guidance throughout this project, Matt Klein for technical assistance with the maps, Erica Frankenberg for providing background on the exposure index, and Gary Orfield and The Civil Rights Project for comments on an early version of this draft. Any errors are attributable to the authors alone.

Such a consensus of the evidence is rare, yet the national debate on public education has largely ignored the growing number of high-poverty schools.[3] Instead, class segregation is accepted as an ugly but immutable reality, and efforts to improve student learning are limited to those that take as a given the current level of stratification in U.S. schools.

In contrast, this study finds that dramatic reductions in the number of high-poverty schools across the United States are within reach. Many such schools exist because of student assignment policies that can be changed if there is the political will to do so. Since most high-poverty schools are located in high-poverty districts, the change would largely involve strategies to promote integration across district boundaries.

The need for such reforms could not be more compelling. Today, nearly 15 million U.S. public elementary school children—47 percent of the total public elementary population—attend schools where the majority of students are low income.[4] Black and Latino children are concentrated disproportionately in these schools in virtually every state, as this study will show. Moreover, the number of high-poverty schools has grown significantly, from 34 percent in 1999 to 47 percent in 2008.[5] This increase outpaces both overall school growth and the growth in numbers of low-income students.[6]

This study provides the first national estimate of the viability of socioeconomic school integration. We develop quantitative measures, based on demographic data, of how many schools and districts could employ SES-based strategies to reduce or even eliminate high-poverty schools. The challenges to doing so are not insignificant. But no other strategy to close the achievement gap is as clearly linked to increased student achievement as the opportunity to attend a low-poverty school.

Given the tremendous educational costs of isolating low-income children in high-poverty schools, this study seeks to answer four questions:

1. What are the patterns and prevalence of U.S. high-poverty schools, and how do they vary by state?
2. To what extent is a child's likelihood of attending a high-poverty school impacted by his or her race or ethnicity?
3. What is the potential of intradistrict integration strategies to reduce the number of high-poverty schools?
4. What is the potential of interdistrict integration strategies?

The first research question focuses on the prevalence of high-poverty schools nationwide, and how states differ in their segregation of schools by income. We find that, while there is dramatic variation around the country, the socioeconomic segregation of American children frequently exceeds what would be necessitated by population demographics. In certain states, the percentage of students in high-poverty schools is far higher than what would be predicted by overall poverty rates. The gap appears to be greatest in states with dense populations and larger proportions of minority students.

We then look at the intersection between race and high-poverty school enrollment, and find that black and Latino children are twice as likely as white children to attend high-poverty schools. The degree of inequity varies markedly by state, with the gap between the percentages of white and minority students at high-poverty schools surpassing fifty points in the seven least-equitable states. By contrast, the gap between Asian and white high-poverty school enrollment is comparatively small.

Our exploration of the feasibility of socioeconomic school integration begins with intradistrict strategies, which are already in use in districts as diverse as Minneapolis, Louisville, Berkeley, Pittsburgh, and La Crosse, Wisconsin. Since most high-poverty schools are located in high-poverty districts, the potential for integration within individual districts is limited, with the exception of twelve states where such approaches would be effective.

Strategies involving more than one district, however, show considerable promise. Our analysis of regional demographics in six sample states found that in every state interdistrict partnerships or choice plans were more effective at reducing the number of high-poverty schools than single district approaches. States with urban patterns of poverty concentration and/or patchwork patterns of low- and higher-poverty districts are more amenable to interdistrict partnerships than the regionalized poverty found in areas like southern Missouri or the Appalachian region of Virginia. Such findings suggest the importance of recommitting to strategies that increase diversity in schools.

The political and policy challenges associated with brokering these kinds of arrangements are multifaceted and difficult, but should be placed in the context of the negative impacts associated with high-poverty schools and their failure to educate children. Efforts that focus on "turning around" these schools solely through more resources, better teachers, and new leadership discount considerable evidence of a persistent association between level of poverty in a school and low achievement. In many parts of the country, high-poverty schools are not a reality we must simply

FIGURE 5.1. 2009 NAEP, Fourth Grade Math

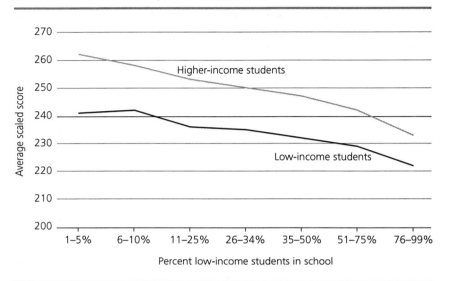

Source: U.S. Department of Education, Institute of Education Sciences, National Center for Education Statistics, National Assessment of Educational Progress (NAEP), Mathematics Assessment, 2009. Low-income students defined as those eligible for free and reduced-price lunch.

accept. If educational leaders brought a sense of urgency to tackling the prevalence of these schools, millions of children stand to benefit from the more equitable and successful learning environments that would result.

The Negative Impact of High-Poverty Schools

The negative impact of attending high-poverty schools affects every student in the school, regardless of their race or family income.[7] Figure 5.1 presents 2009 NAEP math results for both low-income and middle-class fourth graders by school socioeconomic status (SES). What becomes clear here is that even students from affluent backgrounds achieve at lower levels in high-poverty schools, which may be why families with other options choose to avoid them. In fact, the average middle-class student attending an extreme-high-poverty school (greater than 75 percent free or reduced-price lunch, or FRL) scores at or below the average among low-income students in affluent schools (10 percent or lower FRL).

A number of recent studies underscore the negative effects of high-poverty schools, first documented in the 1966 Coleman Report.[8] A review of fifty-nine articles on the relationship between school SES and mathematics outcomes concluded that "consistent and unambiguous evidence" supported the relationship between school poverty concentration and student learning, "irrespective of their age, race, or family's SES."[9] Similar results have been found for science achievement[10] and verbal achievement.[11] Most significant from a policy perspective, Heather Schwartz's research on Maryland's Montgomery County found that moving low-income students into more affluent school settings boosted academic achievement more than investing heavily in "turning around" high-poverty schools.[12]

The evidence also indicates that the negative effects of high-poverty schools accrue disproportionately to black and Latino children. Black students enrolled in high-poverty schools have significantly lower learning rates than white students, while in low-poverty schools the learning rates are equivalent.[13] For Latino students, a 2007 study found that a school's socioeconomic composition is an important predictor of test scores, while the school's racial composition is not: "Class integration matters more in raising academic achievement of Latinos than their racial integration. Further improvements of Latino educational status are impossible without addressing the question of poverty segregation."[14]

Why High-Poverty Schools Have Poor Outcomes. A body of research has tried to isolate *why* high-poverty schools are associated with low levels of student learning. James Coleman noted the importance of peer culture as early as 1966: "A child's learning is a function more of the characteristics of his classmates than those of the teacher."[15] Peer culture impacts the effectiveness of group learning, spreads or stifles motivation and career aspiration, and establishes the overall learning environment. Low-income students are likely to learn more in a middle-income school where many peers have large vocabularies, high levels of student engagement, and view education as part of a trajectory toward their greater goals.[16]

High-poverty schools also report less parental involvement than middle- and high-income schools.[17] Low-income parents volunteer and attend school events less often. Only 26 percent expect that their child will eventually earn a four-year college degree, compared to 43 percent of more-affluent parents.[18] Furthermore, higher-income parents often possess political clout and are more effective in insisting upon high academic standards, teacher quality, and financial resources.[19] Thus, schools serving the children of more affluent families are often held more accountable for their achievement outcomes.

Finally, other researchers have pointed to school-level factors such as curriculum, teacher quality, and student safety to explain the achievement differential for high-poverty schools. Students in such schools typically spend less time on homework and are less likely to take college prep courses or enroll in the academic track.[20] High-poverty schools not only report lower numbers of certified, experienced teachers but also suffer from higher teacher turnover.[21] These schools experience more violent crime, and their students' perceptions of feeling unsafe in school are correspondingly higher.[22] The cumulative effect of these negative school-level factors is detrimental to the achievement of students attending high-poverty schools.

Effects on Higher-Income Students. The possible impact of socioeconomic school integration on higher-income students is the subject of great concern in some communities. If such initiatives raised the achievement levels of low-income students while lowering those of higher income, their appeal could hardly be widespread. Although some work does raise the possibility of a tradeoff between equity and middle-class achievement,[23] a 2008 review of prior research concluded: "[W]ith desegregation, there is growing but still inconclusive evidence that the achievement losses among more advantaged groups are either small or nonexistent."[24] This finding is corroborated at the international level by the Organisation for Economic Co-operation and Development's 2006 Programme for International Student Assessment (PISA) tests, taken by fifteen-year-olds from fifty-seven countries, including the thirty OECD nations. These results showed that countries with more socioeconomically diverse schools produced a greater percentage of students who scored at the highest levels as compared with those whose schools were more segregated.[25]

However, if higher-income families fear negative repercussions for their children from school integration efforts, they could respond by sending their children to private school. This would effectively increase concentrations of poverty in neighborhood schools. One 2007 study of the twenty-one largest U.S. school districts found a twenty-six-percentage-point gap between the average neighborhood low-income percentage (34 percent), and that of the neighborhood's public school (60 percent): "Affluent students avoid neighborhood schools and this exposes poor and minority students to much greater rates of poverty in schools."[26] At the margin, this gap can be significant, the difference between the neighborhood public school being high-poverty or not. The implication for integration efforts is that the perception of these plans by middle-class families is critical; their concerns must be allayed to avoid flight from district schools as they become more socioeconomically balanced.

Socioeconomic Integration as a School Reform Strategy

The first and most noteworthy feature of SES-based integration strategies is their constitutionality. Although the U.S. Supreme Court ruled in the 2007 *Parents Involved in Community Schools v. Seattle School District No. 1*[27] decision that voluntary race-conscious choice plans violated the Fourteenth Amendment, scholars note that SES-based plans seem constitutionally uncontroversial: "The Supreme Court has many times held that a state may validly make legally binding distinctions based upon socioeconomic status in carrying out various public purposes, and that such choices need survive only a minimum level of federal judicial scrutiny."[28] A 2001 legal challenge to the Wake County School Board's use of SES in its assignment plan proved unsuccessful. Plans to achieve greater socioeconomic balance therefore appear to be on safe legal ground.

A broad range of SES-based strategies is currently being utilized to create more diverse school environments. There are two general ways to pursue this goal: *intradistrict* school assignment policies, which determine how students are assigned to schools within the district in which they reside; and *interdistrict* plans, in which two or more neighboring districts (usually an urban center and one or more of its surrounding suburbs) either consolidate or agree to allow students to enroll outside their home district. Most socioeconomic integration efforts to date have employed intradistrict plans, which are often more easily implemented because they involve only one jurisdiction.

The three districts of La Crosse, Wisconsin; Cambridge, Massachusetts; and Wake County, North Carolina[29] have the longest-running student assignment plans based on socioeconomic status. By 2009, however, at least forty districts were implementing or developing intradistrict SES-based plans,[30] including such large urban areas as Chicago and Pittsburgh;[31] some estimates of existing socioeconomic integration programs run as high as eighty districts.[32] The Omaha and Minneapolis metropolitan areas are currently implementing interdistrict student assignment plans based on SES. Housing policy has also been advocated as an approach to increasing socioeconomic diversity in schools.[33]

Besides academic outcomes, another key question concerning SES-based plans is their impact on existing levels of school segregation, both socioeconomic and racial. One study modeled the likely effect of socio-economic integration and concluded that reductions in racial segregation would probably result only in areas with already low levels of residential segregation by race. The study also found that the operational definition of SES was crucial; using a measure like parents' education or income would lead to a more positive impact on racial segregation than the more standard measure of FRL eligibility.[34]

While evidence based on actual SES-based plans remains quite limited, integration proponents point to broader research showing the positive link between diverse school settings and improved student achievement.[35] Integrated schools may also offer the potential for all students to acquire such twenty-first-century skills as collaborating with others, adaptability, and initiative.[36] A compelling research base exists on the benefits of racially integrated school settings, including their link with improved tolerance toward other groups, increased parent involvement, and better life opportunities for nonwhite students;[37] this work suggests important directions for future research on socioeconomic diversity, which may offer similar benefits.

Data and Methods

Data for this study was drawn from the National Center for Education Statistics Common Core of Data (CCD) for the 2007–08 school year. All tables, figures, and maps use CCD data unless otherwise noted. The forty-eight contiguous states[38] were initially considered for the prevalence and intradistrict analyses, and then states that were missing 10 percent or more of FRL data were excluded. Since North Carolina is missing 27 percent and Ohio is missing 100 percent of this data, the prevalence and intradistrict portions of the study include data from forty-six states. (See Map 5.1.) The more complex analyses required for the interdistrict section of the study limited that sample to six states, as explained in the section on policy implications (see page 207).

Since census poverty data is not collected annually or disaggregated at the school level, researchers and policymakers conventionally use participation in the FRL program as a proxy for poverty. FRL data is also used to determine low-income status for No Child Left Behind.[39] Students are eligible for free lunch if family income is up to 185 percent of the federal poverty level, which corresponds to an annual income of $40,793 for a family of four in the 2009–10 school year.[40]

MAP 5.1. United States, by Percentage of Students Receiving Free or Reduced Price Lunch

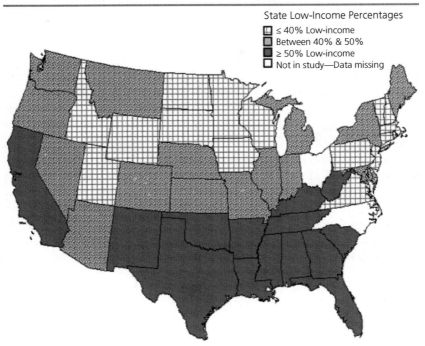

Source: Authors' compilations from National Center for Education Statistics Common Core of Data (CCD) for the 2007–08 school year.

However, FRL data is an imperfect measure of socioeconomic status. FRL eligibility is based on the federal poverty level and therefore does not account for cost of living differences between school districts across the country.[41] It also fails to express the range of poverty variations that exists in American families[42] since the measure is unable to distinguish, for example, between a family earning $50,000 and a family earning $150,000. Lastly, adolescents under-enroll in the program,[43] and as a result the FRL measure under-represents the number of low-income middle and high school students by as much as 20 percent.[44] Participation in the school lunch program occurs through completion of an application, and fear of stigma appears to reduce the number of older students who participate.

Despite the limitations of FRL as an indicator of poverty, it is the only socioeconomic measure consistently used in every school in the United States, and hence the measure used in this study. We did, however, restrict the sample to elementary schools[45] to maximize the accuracy of our findings. As a result, the district and statewide percentages of low-income students in this study are generally higher than those cited elsewhere, since they are calculated using only the more accurate elementary school numbers.

This study also focuses on district public schools, since these schools are the most eligible candidates for school integration strategies. Charter schools were therefore excluded, as were special education schools, due to the challenges associated with changing school assignments for this population. The study does not include data from schools serving only pre-kindergartners, given the wide variations in the percentage of this population enrolled from state to state, or schools with fewer than twenty-five total students. The charter school screen resulted in the removal of 2.4 percent of the K–12 population; the remaining screens excluded a total of 0.4 percent of the elementary school population.

Definitions

- *Low-income students* are defined as those eligible for free or reduced-price lunch.
- *FRL-eligible* and *FRL students* are used interchangeably with *low-income students*.
- *Higher-income students* are students who are not eligible for free or reduced-price lunch. For convenience, this population is referred to as *non-FRL* students in tables and charts.
- *High-poverty schools* are defined as those with 50 percent or more low-income students. While the U.S. Department of Education defines high-poverty schools as those with more than 75 percent low-income students, a cap that high was rejected for the purposes of this study because of the evidence of the negative impact of poverty concentrations less than 75 percent. A 40 percent low-income threshold, the level at which a school is eligible to run a school-wide Title I program, was judged too low to be a realistic goal, given that the FRL percentage in the majority of U.S. states exceeds 40 percent. A 50 percent FRL ceiling for individual schools thus seemed the best choice for a study focused on intra- and interdistrict socioeconomic integration strategies.

- *High-poverty states* are similarly defined as those with 50 percent or more low-income students.
- *Intradistrict integration strategies* to reduce high-poverty schools involve a wide range of approaches that can be undertaken by a single district. Examples include controlled choice, preferential magnet school enrollment policies, redrawing of attendance boundaries, and student transfers.
- *Interdistrict integration strategies* involve more than one district, thus enabling high-poverty districts to leverage the economic diversity in neighboring, lower-poverty school districts. Examples include cross-district school choice and magnet schools. District consolidation or regionalization can also increase SES diversity.

Prevalence and Patterns of High-Poverty Schools

Finding 1: High-poverty schools impact the education of nearly half of U.S. elementary school children. Their prevalence varies markedly by state, from a low of 4 percent in New Hampshire to a high of 85 percent in Mississippi.

Our study found that, of the elementary students in our sample, 10.3 million—48 percent of the total—attend high-poverty schools. Of the 47,099 elementary schools in our study, 22,487 were high-poverty, with the majority of students eligible for free or reduced price lunch. Table 5.1 shows the ten states with the highest percentages of students in high-poverty schools and the ten states with the lowest. In terms of sheer numbers, California ranks first, with 1.8 million students in high-poverty elementary schools. (See Appendix 5.1 for a listing of all states in this study.)

As one might expect, differences in high-poverty school enrollment rates are strongly linked to a state's overall percentage of low-income students: the poorer the state, the more likely its students are to attend high-poverty schools. (See Figure 5.2.) However, high-poverty school enrollment in states with similar low-income percentages can vary significantly. North Dakota and New Jersey, for example, have statewide low-income percentages of 35 percent and 32 percent respectively, yet New Jersey's high-poverty school enrollment rate is double that of North Dakota. Massachusetts' low-income percentage is two percentage points lower than Vermont's, yet its high-poverty school enrollment rate is nine points higher. Factors contributing to these disparities are explored in Finding 4 of this section.

TABLE 5.1. Prevalence of High-Poverty Elementary Schools

State	Low-Income Percentage	High-Poverty Elementary Schools		
		Number	Enrollment	As a % of Total
States with highest % of high-poverty schools				
Mississippi	72%	442	204,097	85%
Louisiana	69%	642	277,085	78%
New Mexico	69%	346	116,747	74%
Arkansas	61%	458	178,045	71%
Oklahoma	61%	761	240,667	69%
West Virginia	54%	309	86,982	63%
California	58%	3,289	1,779,914	62%
Kentucky	55%	510	210,361	62%
Tennessee	55%	673	294,667	61%
Alabama	56%	506	208,490	60%
States with lowest % of high-poverty schools				
New Hampshire	19%	15	3,992	4%
North Dakota	35%	49	7,128	15%
Vermont	33%	39	7,704	17%
Wyoming	36%	37	8,432	20%
Minnesota	34%	213	75,292	20%
South Dakota	35%	100	12,466	24%
Wisconsin	36%	279	95,664	24%
Iowa	37%	188	56,887	25%
Utah	37%	139	72,078	26%
Massachusetts	31%	303	117,881	26%

Source: Authors' compilations from National Center for Education Statistics Common Core of Data (CCD) for the 2007–08 school year.

Finding 2: The socioeconomic isolation of low-income students differs significantly between states, but is strongly related to overall state poverty levels.

Socioeconomic isolation is the degree to which children are segregated into schools with students of their same socioeconomic status. Our study used two measures to assess SES isolation:

- *Exposure index.* An exposure index measures the exposure of one category of students to another, and in this study is used to gauge

FIGURE 5.2. Correlation between High-Poverty School Enrollment and State Low-Income Percentage, r = 0.98

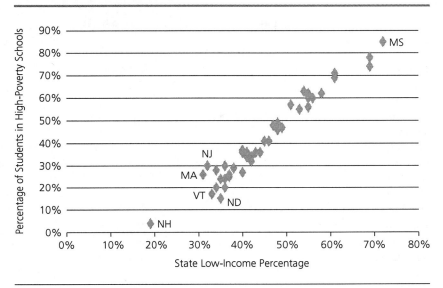

Source: Authors' calculations from National Center for Education Statistics Common Core of Data (CCD) for the 2007–08 school year.

the exposure of the average student to others in the same income group. For example, an exposure index of 70 for low-income students means that the average low-income student attends a school in which 70 percent of the students are also low-income. This measure is useful in providing a weighted average of segregation in a given state,[46] although the use of the exposure index alone can give an ambiguous picture in cases where the average masks the extremes.

- *Enrollment in hyper-segregated schools.* Like the exposure index, the percentage of students attending hyper-segregated schools is a variant of an approach typically used to measure racial segregation.[47] A hyper-segregated school is defined here as one in which enrollments of a given SES group exceed 90 percent. Atlanta's Grove Park Elementary School, where 95 percent of the students are low-income, is one example of a hyper-segregated school, as is Summit Hill Elementary, with 2 percent low-income students. Both schools are located in Georgia's Fulton County.

TABLE 5.2. Socioeconomic Isolation of Low-Income Elementary School Students

State	Low-Income Percentage	Hyper-Segregation: % of FRL Students at Schools with > 90% FRL	Exposure Index: FRL % of School Attended by the Average FRL Student
States with the most SES isolation			
New Mexico	69%	48%	79
Mississippi	72%	38%	78
Illinois	48%	38%	72
Connecticut	34%	35%	67
New York	49%	30%	72
Louisiana	69%	29%	76
Nevada	46%	27%	64
States with the least SES isolation			
Delaware	41%	0%	51
Idaho	40%	0%	47
New Hampshire	19%	0%	31
West Virginia	54%	1%	59
Maine	41%	1%	49
Wyoming	36%	2%	44
North Dakota	35%	2%	43

Source: Authors' compilations from National Center for Education Statistics Common Core of Data (CCD) for the 2007–08 school year.

Using these two measures, we find that in many states, low-income students experience extreme SES isolation. As shown by Table 5.2, the degree of isolation varies markedly between states.

In addition to the state-by-state comparison, Table 5.2 offers insights into the actual experiences of students in the states studied. We can tell, for example, that a low-income student in New Mexico, Mississippi, or Illinois has more than a one-in-three chance of being assigned to a hyper-segregated school, while in Delaware, Idaho, or New Hampshire, this likelihood drops to zero. Looking at the exposure index, we see that the average low-income student in Connecticut attends a school that is 67 percent low-income, while her counterpart in West Virginia attends a school that is 59 percent low-income. (SES isolation measures for all states are included in Appendix 5.2.)

Like the overall percentages of high-poverty schools, the SES isolation measures used here are heavily influenced by the state low-income percentage. In states with high FRL percentages, low-income students are more likely to attend school with one another and less likely to attend school with middle- and higher-income students. The correlation between state low-income percentage and the exposure index is an extremely strong 0.84, while that between state low-income percentage and hyper-segregated school enrollment is 0.54.

Finding 3: Higher-income students face similar degrees of socioeconomic isolation, which also vary significantly by state.

As would be expected, the socioeconomic isolation of low-income students goes hand in hand with that of higher-income students, depriving both groups of diverse learning environments. In Massachusetts, for example, low-income percentages in Boston, Chelsea, Holyoke, Lawrence, Lynn, and Springfield—where one-third of the state's elementary children attend school—exceed 75 percent, yet in half the state's school districts FRL percentages are below 10 percent. (See Table 5.3.) Looking nationally, the SES isolation of higher-income students varies markedly by state, and, as with low-income students, is strongly correlated with a state's overall low-income percentage. (SES isolation measures for all states are included in Appendix 5.3.)

Finding 4: In every state, SES school segregation exceeds the level predicted by statewide demographics. Controlling for state poverty, socioeconomic segregation tends to be higher in states with denser populations and more minority students.

While the exposure index and percent of students in hyper-segregated schools provide an important picture of the socioeconomic isolation of students, they are largely driven by the overall state poverty level. We therefore used a third measure to gauge the amount of SES segregation beyond the degree necessitated by each state's demographics. This is done by calculating a band of ±20 percentage points around the statewide low-income percentage, and then determining the percentage of schools that fall outside this band.[48] These schools are more segregated than statewide population demographics alone would dictate.

Table 5.4 shows the degree to which the enrollments at individual schools differ from the state's low-income average. In the states most segregated by SES, more than 55 percent of the schools fall outside the ±20 point state low-income percentage band, while in the least-segregated states this number drops below 35 percent. Future research might

TABLE 5.3. Socioeconomic Isolation of Higher-Income Elementary
School Students

State	% Low-Income	Hyper-Segregation: % of non-FRL Students at Schools with < 10% FRL	Exposure Index: non-FRL % of School Attended by the Avg. Non-FRL Student
States with the most SES isolation			
Connecticut	34%	55%	83
Massachusetts	31%	50%	82
New Jersey	32%	47%	81
New Hampshire	19%	40%	83
Illinois	48%	34%	74
Arizona	47%	33%	72
New York	49%	32%	73
States with the least SES isolation			
West Virginia	54%	0%	51
Mississippi	72%	1%	45
Arkansas	61%	1%	50
Louisiana	69%	2%	47
Oklahoma	61%	3%	53
Kentucky	55%	4%	54
Wyoming	36%	4%	69

Source: Authors' compilations from National Center for Education Statistics Common Core of Data (CCD) for the 2007–08 school year.

examine further the causes of the differences in SES segregation among states, although three observations are possible with the current data.

The first observation is a variation among the states by racial makeup. In the ten states most segregated by SES, the percentage of white students ranges from 27 percent to 70 percent; thus all but two states fall in the bottom two quartiles. In the ten states least segregated by SES, with the exception of Delaware, the percentage of white students ranges from 80 percent to 94 percent, the top quartile. The correlation between socioeconomic segregation and the statewide percentage of white students is −0.68, indicating a fairly strong relationship. Generally, states with higher proportions of black and Latino students also have high levels of socioeconomic school segregation. Delaware, where white students comprise 55 percent of public elementary schools, is unusual in that it is

TABLE 5.4. Factors in Socioeconomic Segregation of Schools

State	% Low-Income	Percent of Schools whose Low-Income % Varies from the State's by > 20 Points	Population Density Quartile [i]	% White Students Quartile
Most *segregated states*				
Arkansas	61%	80%	3	3
Connecticut	34%	68%	1	3
New York	49%	68%	1	4
Arizona	47%	65%	3	4
Illinois	48%	64%	1	4
New Jersey	32%	64%	1	3
Rhode Island	41%	63%	1	2
California	58%	63%	1	4
Massachusetts	31%	61%	1	2
Maryland	40%	57%	1	4
Least *segregated states*				
New Hampshire	19%	15%	2	1
Vermont	33%	20%	3	1
West Virginia	54%	20%	3	1
North Dakota	35%	21%	4	1
Wyoming	36%	25%	4	1
Idaho	40%	26%	4	1
Maine	41%	28%	3	1
Iowa	37%	28%	4	1
Delaware	41%	30%	1	3
Montana	42%	33%	4	1

Note: Population density quartiles ranked 1 to 4 from most to least dense, % white students ranked 1 to 4 from most to least white.

Sources: U.S. Census Bureau, Census 2000 Summary File 1, "GCT-PH1. Population, Housing Units, Area, and Density: 2000"; author's calculations from National Center for Education Statistics Common Core of Data (CCD) for the 2007–08 school year.

one of the nation's least-segregated states for black students. This comes as a result of a 1980 U.S. Supreme Court ruling that organized the state's school districts so as to prevent metropolitan segregation.[49]

A second difference between the most and least SES-segregated states is population density. The least segregated states include many—Montana, Wyoming, Iowa, North Dakota, West Virginia—in which the population is so dispersed that any sort of SES-based school segregation is unlikely. Many of the ten states most segregated by SES—Rhode Island, Massachusetts, Maryland, Connecticut, New York—are more densely populated, thus making it possible for districts to mirror existing neighborhood segregation by class. The correlation between socioeconomic segregation and population density is 0.47, indicating that states with higher densities are likely to also have high levels of segregation. While this correlation is not as strong as for race, Table 5.4 shows a clear relationship.

One final observation is that the differences among states shown in Table 5.4 appear largely unrelated to overall low-income percentage. The three states in which enrollments at individual schools vary most from the state's low-income average—Arkansas, Connecticut, and New York—have a wide range of poverty levels, with 61 percent, 34 percent, and 49 percent low-income enrollments, respectively. In fact, the correlation between a state's overall low-income percentage and socioeconomic segregation is 0.29, indicating a positive but relatively weak relationship.

Finding 5: States with greater degrees of SES school segregation also tend to have larger achievement gaps between low-income and higher-income students.

To explore how socioeconomic school segregation is related to student achievement, we used fourth grade national reading scores to calculate the achievement gap between low-income and higher-income students for every state in our sample. SES achievement gaps in the 2007 NAEP reading scores, for example, ranged from 16 scale score points in North Dakota to 38 points in Connecticut.

We found a strong positive relationship between the SES achievement gap and the degree of socioeconomic school segregation, as measured by the percentage of schools outside the ±20 point band around the state's low-income average. States where students were the most segregated by income generally had large achievement gaps between different income groups. Because of the sampling and measurement error associated with standardized test scores, we ran a series of correlations using NAEP achievement gaps from two different years (2007 and 2009) and two different subjects (reading and math). The correlations between each of these gaps and the degree of socioeconomic segregation ranged from 0.64 (2009 math and reading) to 0.74 (2007 reading). The strongest of the correlations is presented graphically in Figure 5.3.

FIGURE 5.3. Correlation between Socioeconomic Achievement Gap and Socioeconomic Segregation, r = 0.74

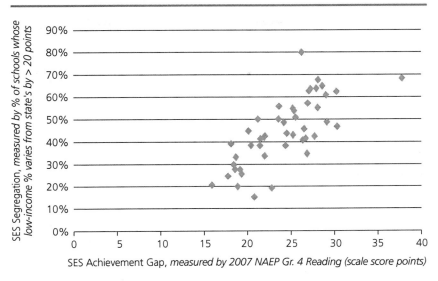

SES Segregation, measured by % of schools whose low-income % varies from state's by > 20 points

SES Achievement Gap, *measured by 2007 NAEP Gr. 4 Reading (scale score points)*

Sources: Authors' calculations from National Center for Education Statistics Common Core of Data (CCD) for the 2007–08 school year and National Assessment of Educational Progress (NAEP) 2007 Reading Assessment.

Table 5.5 presents data on the ten states with the largest SES gaps in high-poverty school enrollment. In all of these states, at least two-thirds of low-income students are attending high-poverty schools, while less than one-third of higher-income students do. The table shows that these ten states generally have quite large SES achievement gaps. Arkansas is the notable exception, ranking first on the degree of socioeconomic segregation, but only eighteenth on SES achievement gap. Overall, however, the evidence suggests that states with high degrees of socioeconomic segregation have high achievement gaps between low- and higher-income students as well.

Conclusion

More than 10 million elementary school students—48 percent—attend class each day in schools where the majority of students are low-income. The prevalence of high-poverty schools varies markedly between states, from a low of 4 percent in New Hampshire to a high of 85 percent in

TABLE 5.5. Socioeconomic Segregation and Achievement Gaps
(as measured by mean scale score in NAEP fourth grade reading)

National Rank, SES Segregation	State	% of Schools whose Low-Income % Varies from State's by > 20 Points	SES Achievement Gap	National Rank, SES Achievement Gap
1	Arkansas	80%	26	18
2	Connecticut	68%	38	1
3	New York	68%	28	7
4	Arizona	65%	29	6
5	Illinois	64%	28	9
6	New Jersey	64%	27	11
7	Rhode Island	63%	27	12
8	California	63%	30	3
9	Massachusetts	61%	29	5
10	Maryland	57%	27	13

Sources: Authors' compilations from National Center for Education Statistics Common Core of Data (CCD) for the 2007–08 school year and National Assessment of Educational Progress (NAEP) 2007 Reading Assessment.

Mississippi. The degree of socioeconomic segregation shows significant state-by-state differences as well, thus indicating the potential of state and local policy to reduce the number of high-poverty schools. Moreover, our data indicates that states with large degrees of segregation experience correspondingly high achievement gaps between low-income and higher-income students. The next section delves further into the disproportionate impact of high-poverty schools on black, Latino, Native American, and low-income students.

Race and High-Poverty Schools

Finding 1: Black and Latino students are more than twice as likely to attend high-poverty schools as white students.

The probability that a student will attend a high-poverty school is strongly related to race. Nationally, 29 percent of white elementary school students attend high-poverty schools, as compared with 75 percent of blacks and 72 percent of Latinos.[50] The white-Asian and white-Native American gaps are less pronounced, with 36 percent of Asian students and 67 percent of Native Americans attending high-poverty schools.

These findings come in the context of a moderate 0.55 correlation at the national level between race and poverty, a link that is significantly weaker than past correlations as high as 0.70.[51] While the association between race and poverty remains strong in areas with only two significant racial groups, the correlation weakens with the presence of multiple racial groups.[52] Thus, while it is increasingly difficult in the United States to predict a family's income based on their race, more often than not one can predict whether a child attends a high-poverty school simply by knowing whether she is black, Latino, Asian, Native American, or white.

Black Students and High-Poverty Schools. Of the 3.5 million black elementary school children in this study, 2.6 million—75 percent—attend high-poverty schools. The probability of a black student attending a high-poverty school varies significantly by state, and ranges from a high of 93 percent in Mississippi to a low of 12 percent in South Dakota. (See Appendix 5.4 for a list of all states and their high-poverty school enrollments by race.)

High-poverty school enrollment for black students is driven by two factors: a state's overall low-income percentage and its degree of inequity for blacks. The 63-point difference between black high-poverty school enrollment in Mississippi and South Dakota, for example, occurs in part because 72 percent of Mississippi's students are low-income, as compared with 35 percent in South Dakota. Black students in Mississippi are more likely to attend high-poverty schools than those in South Dakota because *all* students in Mississippi are more likely to attend high-poverty schools. Differing degrees of inequity, however, also explain the difference between the two states. In Mississippi, 93 percent of black students attend high-poverty schools as compared with 75 percent of whites—a gap of 18 percentage points. South Dakota, in contrast, has a black-white gap of −4 points, with black students being *less* likely to attend high-poverty schools than whites.

Nationally, the differences in black and white high-poverty school enrollment vary markedly by state. In the seven states with the greatest inequity for black students, the black-white gap exceeds 55 percentage points, while in the seven most equitable states this gap is less than 14 points. New York has the most inequitable conditions for black students, with 82 percent of black students attending high-poverty schools as compared with 17 percent of whites. Table 5.6 shows the ten states with the largest gaps between black and white high-poverty school enrollments.

TABLE 5.6. Black-White Gap: States with the Largest Gap between Black and White High-Poverty School Enrollment

	State	# Black Students	% Black Students	% of Blacks in High-Poverty Schools	% of Whites in High-Poverty Schools	Black-White Gap
1	New York	238,074	19%	82%	17%	65
2	Illinois	216,269	20%	83%	19%	64
3	Wisconsin	43,595	11%	75%	12%	63
4	Rhode Island	5,579	9%	78%	16%	62
5	Pennsylvania	122,074	16%	74%	15%	60
6	Massachusetts	32,882	7%	69%	12%	58
7	Michigan	128,297	18%	79%	23%	56
8	New Jersey	115,641	17%	63%	7%	55
9	Connecticut	39,465	14%	64%	9%	55
10	Indiana	58,542	12%	80%	25%	54

Source: Authors' compilations from National Center for Education Statistics Common Core of Data (CCD) for the 2007–08 school year.

Inequity for black students appears largely unrelated to the percentage of black students in a given state. As is shown by Figure 5.4, there is a weak correlation (0.2) between the overall percentage of black students and the size of the gap between white and black high-poverty school attendance.

Latino Students and High-Poverty Schools. Of the 5.2 million Latino elementary schoolchildren in this study, 3.7 million—72 percent—attend high-poverty schools. As with black students, the likelihood that a Latino student will attend a high-poverty school depends heavily on where she lives. In South Dakota, 18 percent of Latino students attend high-poverty schools, while Rhode Island, in stark contrast, educates 86 percent of its Latino children in high-poverty schools. The percentages in the remaining states fall between these two extremes, but in all but ten states the majority of Latino children attend high-poverty schools.

Latino students are highly concentrated in two states, California and Texas, which together educate more than half of all Latino children in the United States. As is shown by Table 5.7, however, conditions for Latino

FIGURE 5.4. Correlation between Statewide Percentage of Black Students and Black-White High-Poverty School Enrollment Gap, r = 0.20

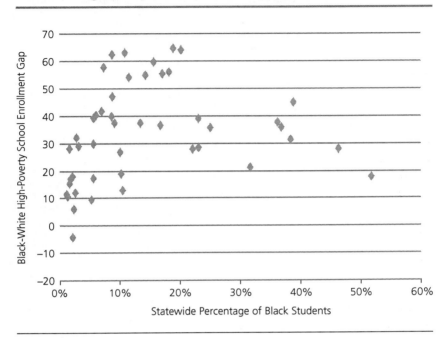

Source: Authors' calculations from National Center for Education Statistics Common Core of Data (CCD) for the 2007–08 school year.

children in Texas are better than for those in California. Texan Latino children have a 68 percent chance of attending a high-poverty school, whereas those in California have an 80 percent chance. While this difference reflects in part California's 62 percent low-income percentage—5 points higher than Texas—it also stems from greater Latino-white inequity. California's 49-point Latino-white gap is the ninth-largest in the nation, while this gap in Texas ranks twenty-fifth.

The gap between Latino and white high-poverty school enrollment appears nationally as well, and is similar in size and pattern to black-white gaps. In the seven states with the greatest inequity for Latino students, the Latino-white gap exceeds 50 percentage points, while in the seven most equitable states this gap falls below 12 points. Rhode Island has the most inequitable conditions for Latino students, with 86 percent

TABLE 5.7. Latino Elementary School Students—California-Texas Comparison

State	% Low-Income	# Latino Students	% Latino Students	% of Latinos in High-Poverty Schools	% of Whites in High-Poverty Schools	Latino-White Gap
California	62%	1,514,000	53%	80%	31%	49
Texas	57%	1,171,000	50%	68%	37%	31

Source: Authors' compilations from National Center for Education Statistics Common Core of Data (CCD) for the 2007–08 school year.

TABLE 5.8. Latino-White Gap: States with the Largest Gap between Latino and White High-Poverty School Enrollment

	State	# Latino Students	% Latino Students	% of Latinos in High-Poverty Schools	% of Whites in High-Poverty Schools	Latino-White Gap (percentage points)
1	Rhode Island	12,275	19%	86%	16%	71
2	Massachusetts	64,554	14%	73%	12%	61
3	New York	280,334	22%	78%	17%	61
4	New Jersey	148,231	22%	65%	7%	58
5	Connecticut	51,168	18%	67%	9%	57
6	Illinois	248,538	23%	75%	19%	56
7	Pennsylvania	63,152	8%	70%	15%	55
8	Nebraska	21,013	15%	71%	21%	49
9	California	1,514,358	53%	80%	31%	49
10	Colorado	115,897	31%	66%	18%	49

Note: States in italics are also among top ten most inequitable for black students.
Source: Authors' compilations from National Center for Education Statistics Common Core of Data (CCD) for the 2007–08 school year.

of Latino students attending high-poverty schools as compared with 16 percent of whites. Table 5.8 shows the ten states with the largest gaps between Latino and white high-poverty school enrollment.

Comparing Tables 5.6 and 5.8 makes clear that seven states—Connecticut, Illinois, Massachusetts, New Jersey, New York, Pennsylvania, and Rhode Island—are ranked among the top ten most inequitable for *both* black and Latino students. These states are highlighted on Table 5.8 above. Moreover, four of these states—Massachusetts, New York, Pennsylvania, and Rhode Island—rank among the ten most inequitable states for Asian students.

FIGURE 5.5. Correlation between Statewide Percentage of Latino Students and Latino-White High-Poverty School Enrollment Gap, r = 0.43

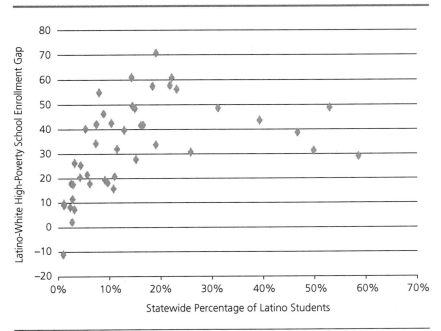

Source: Authors' calculations from National Center for Education Statistics Common Core of Data (CCD) for the 2007–08 school year.

Inequity for Latino students does grow somewhat as the percentage of Latino students in the state increases. As is shown by Figure 5.5, the data show a moderate 0.43 correlation between a state's percentage of Latino students and the size of its Latino-white gap in high-poverty school attendance. Eight of the ten states with the most equitable conditions for Latino students have Latino enrollments under 5 percent.

Asian Students and High-Poverty Schools. Of the 1 million Asian elementary schoolchildren in this study, 0.4 million—36 percent—attend high-poverty schools. Nationally, the percentage of Asian children attending high-poverty schools is seven percentage points higher than that of white children, and half that of blacks and Latinos. In only four states—Arkansas, Louisiana, Mississippi, and New York—do a majority of Asian students attend high-poverty schools.

TABLE 5.9. States with the Largest Numbers of Asian Students

State	% Low Income	# Asian Students	% Asian	% Asians in High-Poverty Schools	% Whites in High-Poverty Schools	Asian-White Gap
California	58%	338,474	12%	43%	31%	12
New York	49%	97,749	8%	62%	17%	44
Texas	51%	80,989	3%	31%	37%	−5
New Jersey	32%	57,799	9%	12%	7%	4

Source: Authors' compilations from National Center for Education Statistics Common Core of Data (CCD) for the 2007–08 school year.

The gaps between the percentages of Asian and white students who attend high-poverty schools are the smallest of any racial group. For two-thirds of U.S. states, the Asian-white gap is less than ten percentage points. In six states, the percentage of Asian students attending high-poverty schools is more than ten points lower than the corresponding percentage of white students.

As with Latino students, Asians are highly concentrated in a few states. California educates one-third of Asian students; the four states with the largest Asian enrollments—California, New Jersey, New York, and Texas—together educate more than half of all Asian children in the United States. Conditions for Asian students vary significantly in these four states, with the percentage of Asians attending high-poverty schools ranging from 12 percent in New Jersey to 62 percent in New York. Inequity in these four states differs as well, as shown by Table 5.9.

Given this context, the situation of Asian students in New York is particularly notable. New York educates nearly 100,000 Asian elementary school students, more than any other state except California. Yet the difference in high-poverty school enrollment for whites and Asians in New York is forty-four points, the highest in the nation. This gap is ten points higher than that of Rhode Island, the state with the next largest Asian-white gap.

Native American Students and High-Poverty Schools.

Of the 260,000 Native American elementary schoolchildren in this study, 173,000—67 percent—attend high-poverty schools. This number does not include schools located on reservations, which educate approximately 42,000 elementary and secondary Native American students.[53]

As with Asian students, Native Americans are highly concentrated in four states, which together educate more than half of the Native American students in the United States. In these four states—Arizona, California, New Mexico, and Oklahoma—the likelihood that a Native American child will attend a high-poverty school ranges from 64 percent to 89 percent, and the Native American–white gap ranges from 44 to 66 percentage points. Oklahoma has the highest percentage of Native Americans of any state in the study (20 percent), the largest percentage of the U.S. Native American school population (27 percent), and the highest Native American–white gap (66 points).

Finding 2: States with larger black-white and Latino-white gaps in high-poverty school enrollment tend to have larger achievement gaps.

Building on our exploration of achievement gaps in the previous section, we find that the segregation of minority students into high-poverty schools is strongly correlated with racial/ethnic achievement gaps. We used the fourth grade NAEP reading and math mean scale scores from 2007 and 2009 to calculate black-white and Latino-white achievement gaps. For example, black-white achievement gaps on the 2009 fourth grade math test ranged from 8 scale score points in West Virginia to 40 points in Wisconsin.[54]

These achievement gaps have moderate to large correlations with the black-white and Latino-white gaps in high-poverty school enrollment. In other words, when black and Latino students are disproportionately enrolled in high-poverty schools compared to their white peers, the corresponding gap in student achievement is likely to be large.

As with socioeconomic achievement gaps, we tested correlations using NAEP scores from two different years, 2007 and 2009, and two different subjects, fourth grade math and reading. For black students, the correlations between these achievement gaps and the black-white gap in high-poverty school enrollment ranged from 0.56 (2007 and 2009 math) to 0.67 (2007 reading). The Latino-white correlations were somewhat stronger and increased between 2007 and 2009. There were correlations of 0.58 and 0.59 between the high-poverty school enrollment gap and the 2007 reading and math achievement gaps, respectively. The corresponding correlations in 2009 were 0.66 and 0.75.

Figure 5.6 aids in visualizing this relationship for Latino and white students, using the 2009 math data:

FIGURE 5.6. Correlation between Latino-White Achievement Gap and Latino-White Gap in High-Poverty School Enrollment, r = 0.75

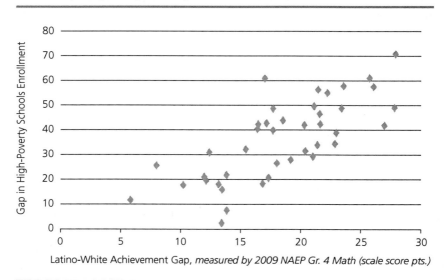

Sources: Authors' calculations from National Center for Education Statistics Common Core of Data (CCD) for the 2007–08 school year and National Assessment of Educational Progress (NAEP) 2009 Math Assessment.

This figure shows that states with high ranks on the Latino-white gap in high-poverty school enrollment also tend to have high ranks on the Latino-white achievement gap. As Table 5.10 demonstrates, there are exceptions to this overall pattern. New York has the third-largest gap between the percentages of Latinos versus whites in high-poverty schools, but ranks twenty-sixth on its Latino-white achievement gap in math based on 2009 NAEP scores. However, the overall relationship is quite pronounced and appears consistently across NAEP subjects and test administrations, as the above correlations make clear.

Conclusion

The likelihood that a child will attend a high-poverty school is strongly linked with race, with black and Latino students more than twice as likely as whites to attend high-poverty schools. We also find that the states with larger black-white and Latino-white gaps in high-poverty school enroll-ment also tend to have the largest achievement gaps. Large variations in

TABLE 5.10. Latino-White High Poverty School Enrollment Gaps and Achievement Gaps (as measured by mean scale score in 2009 NAEP fourth grade math)

National Rank, Latino-White High-Poverty School Enrollment Gap	State	Latino-White High-Poverty School Enrollment Gap (percentage points)	Latino-White Achievement Gap (scale score points)	National Rank, Latino-White Achievement Gap
1	Rhode Island	71	28	1
2	Massachusetts	61	26	5
3	New York	61	17	26
4	New Jersey	58	24	6
5	Connecticut	57	26	4
6	Illinois	56	21	13
7	Pennsylvania	55	22	10
8	Nebraska	49	21	15
9	California	49	28	2
10	Colorado	49	23	7

Sources: Authors' compilations from National Center for Education Statistics Common Core of Data (CCD) for the 2007–08 school year and National Assessment for Educational Progress (NAEP) 2009 Math Assessment.

black and Latino high-poverty school enrollment gaps, however, indicate the potential of state and local policy to reduce the inequitable treatment of minority children and reduce the overall numbers of high-poverty schools. The next two sections assess the viability of single and cross-district approaches to that end.

Viability of Intradistrict Strategies

Intradistrict strategies reduce the number of high-poverty schools through initiatives contained within a single district. Since such approaches are more common than those involving multiple districts, this study begins its viability assessment at the intradistrict level. This section explores the demographic viability of intradistrict strategies for each of the forty-six states in our study.

As of 2009, forty U.S. school districts were pursuing some form of SES-based school integration; more than 1.6 million children are enrolled in these districts, representing about 3.5 percent of total U.S. enrollment.[55]

Following recent work by Sean Reardon and Lori Rhodes, we identified five basic categories, listed here in order of the strength of the strategy.[56] The first category, parental choice, offers the greatest potential for reduction in the number of high-poverty schools; subsequent categories are weaker in terms of their potential impact.

- *Parental controlled choice.* A handful of districts give some or all parents the choice of a school outside their neighborhood assignment. Controlled choice expands upon traditional parental choice by including socioeconomic enrollment targets that try to ensure each school's percentage of low-income students falls within a certain range. For example, the district containing Louisville, Kentucky, utilizes controlled choice for all schools with a goal of keeping each school within a window of 15 to 50 percent of students from low-income neighborhoods.[57] Cambridge, Massachusetts, one of the longest running SES integration programs, uses a version of this model, as does the larger school system in San Francisco.[58]
- *Redrawing school attendance zones.* The original plan in La Crosse, Wisconsin, redrew attendance zones to ensure that each school's enrollment of low-income students approximated the district average,[59] and rezoning neighborhoods remains a common strategy for increasing socioeconomic diversity within a traditional school assignment system. Amherst, Massachusetts, instituted a flexible assignment plan in 2010 that closed one majority-low-income school and rezoned the affected students among three of the district's other schools.[60] Districts such as Burlington in Iowa, Manatee County in Florida, and McKinney in Texas have all redrawn attendance zones with increased SES diversity as one goal.
- *Student transfers.* Some districts have a policy in which the socioeconomic balance of their schools is considered when approving or denying student transfer requests. Seminole County, a district near Orlando, Florida, bases school attendance zones and student transfer decisions in part on its goal of achieving socioeconomic diversity across its schools.[61] Seminole is one of more than a dozen districts that consider SES as a factor in school assignment and/or transfer decisions.
- *Preferential admission to magnet schools.* Within-district magnet programs still educate more students in this country than do charter schools,[62] and approximately fifteen districts use preferential magnet school admissions policies to increase the SES diversity of their

schools. Chicago and Pittsburgh both weight socioeconomic status as one factor in magnet school lottery or admissions decisions.[63]

- *Hybrid approaches.* A number of districts employ some combination of the strategies listed above. For example, Wake County, North Carolina, currently uses a hybrid approach of magnet schools designed to attract more-affluent students to urban neighborhoods plus a flexible assignment policy that gives weight to socioeconomic diversity.[64] Troup County, Georgia, and Palm Beach County, Florida, both combine redrawn attendance zones and transfer priority based on socioeconomic status.[65]

For the purposes of our study, we assume that an individual district can reassign students to any school in the district. This assumption is most likely to be met under plans that include controlled choice, in which the concept of the neighborhood school is replaced by parental choice among all the schools in a district. Redrawing attendance zones is more limited in scope; each school's low-income percentage is still determined by the demographics within its zone, as opposed to those of the larger district. Plans that give SES preference for student transfers and magnet school admission are even narrower in terms of their potential impact, as the vast majority of students within a given district are unaffected by such policies.

Viability Measures

This study focuses on the extent to which districts around the nation could utilize one of the above approaches, most likely the strong strategy of parental controlled choice, to eliminate their high-poverty schools. We developed a viability measure for intradistrict integration based on the goal of bringing all schools in a given district below 50 percent low-income. Our examination of viability includes only demographic considerations; namely, whether the composition of a given district is such that a different student assignment plan could eliminate high-poverty schools. A state's intradistrict viability percentage, therefore, is defined as the percentage of the state's high-poverty schools that are located in districts that meet both the following criteria:

- *District size.* For intradistrict solutions to be feasible, a district must contain enough schools to enable the balancing of SES. Districts with fewer than three elementary schools were therefore deemed too small to be viable for intradistrict solutions.[66]

- *District low-income percentage.* Intradistrict strategies can be effective only in districts that have enough middle-income students to bring all district schools below the high-poverty level. For example, if a district's FRL average is 65 percent, it is mathematically impossible for all its individual schools to be below 50 percent regardless of how students are assigned. Districts with low-income percentages above 50 percent therefore cannot rely solely on intradistrict strategies if their goal is to eliminate all high-poverty schools.

However, even a district that is 50 percent low-income would find it challenging to redistribute students to achieve ideal levels of socioeconomic diversity. For example, a four-school district with a 50 percent low-income percentage would need every single school at exactly 50 percent to avoid having any high-poverty schools. This would be difficult to achieve in practice. Therefore, this study tested two different "district low-income cut-offs" for determining the viability of intra-district solutions: *districts at or below 50 percent low-income enrollment* and *districts at or below 40 percent.* The latter number may be more realistic from an implementation standpoint, since a district's individual schools could vary from the 40 percent district average by up to ten percentage points without exceeding the high-poverty threshold. To use another example, if a four-school district had a low-income percentage of 40 percent, it could include schools with low-income percentages of 31 percent, 38 percent, 42 percent, and 49 percent and still have no high-poverty schools. Given logistical and political constraints, a *district* SES ceiling of 40 percent low-income may be needed to ensure a *school* SES ceiling of 50 percent low-income for all schools in the district.

The above discussion and the following tables assume a goal of completely eliminating all high-poverty schools within a given district. This approach, however, is not meant to imply that other efforts to break up concentrations of poverty should not be considered. Integration strategies that can reduce a school's enrollment from 90 percent to 60 percent low-income, for example, could also prove effective, and might be possible in districts with low-income percentages deemed too high for the approach taken here.

Findings

Table 5.11 presents the percentage of high-poverty schools in each state that could be eliminated through intradistrict strategies. The table

TABLE 5.11. States Where Intradistrict Strategies Would Have the Most Impact: Using Two Different Viability Levels for District Low-Income Percentage

	State	% Reduction in High-Poverty Schools		Number of Students Affected	
		Using 50% cutoff	Using 40% cutoff	Using 50% cutoff	Using 40% cutoff
1	New Hampshire	80.0%	66.7%	3,891	3,254
2	Wyoming	70.3%	32.4%	6,123	2,881
3	Maryland	36.1%	32.4%	53,840	49,154
4	Utah	37.0%	28.0%	23,495	19,776
5	Nevada	97.2%	25.9%	83,718	14,295
6	North Dakota	30.6%	24.5%	3,044	2,696
7	Virginia	35.4%	23.5%	67,016	47,764
8	Colorado	23.9%	17.8%	35,796	26,925
9	Delaware	65.8%	15.8%	12,838	2,972
10	Idaho	44.9%	14.3%	16,836	4,952
11	Connecticut	21.8%	12.9%	14,353	7,585
12	Wisconsin	29.4%	12.2%	25,138	10,313
13	Minnesota	18.8%	8.9%	16,137	8,753
14	Arizona	15.7%	8.7%	42,799	25,000
15	Oregon	31.3%	8.3%	45,467	12,942
16	Washington	25.8%	8.1%	47,174	13,946
17	Kansas	11.7%	7.4%	10,495	7,940
18	Montana	20.2%	7.3%	7,802	2,741
19	South Dakota	12.0%	7.0%	1,906	1,673
20	Rhode Island	16.1%	6.5%	2,850	1,100
21	Iowa	17.0%	6.4%	8,545	2,832
22	Nebraska	26.3%	6.3%	13,085	2,626
23	Florida	27.5%	5.6%	171,185	37,397
	NATIONAL TOTAL	15.0%	5.0%	1,546,744	542,195

Source: Authors' compilations from National Center for Education Statistics Common Core of Data (CCD) for the 2007–08 school year.

includes the twenty-three states where intradistrict strategies could result in at least a 5 percent reduction in high-poverty schools, plus a total row that aggregates all forty-six states in our sample. In twelve of these states, the potential reduction in high-poverty schools exceeds 10 percent, and in seven states, it exceeds 20 percent.

Note the large differences in state-level viability, depending on whether the 40 percent or 50 percent low-income cutoff is used. Across the forty-six states, the percentage of high-poverty schools that could be remedied through intradistrict strategies falls from 15 percent to 5 percent if the 40 percent cutoff is employed. This difference varies markedly between states, with intradistrict viability dropping from 56 percent to 16 percent in Delaware, while in Maryland and Kansas the falloff is less than four percentage points.

This gap between the two viability measures reflects the percentage of high-poverty schools in each state that are located in districts with between 40 percent and 50 percent low-income enrollment. States with a large number of such districts, of course, have the most pronounced differences between the two measures.

Finding 1: Intradistrict strategies can reduce the numbers of high-poverty schools by 5 percent nationally.

Table 5.11 shows that the vast majority of high-poverty schools cannot be remedied through intradistrict integration policies. For a district to be able to eliminate its high-poverty schools solely by reassigning its own students, its overall low-income percentage must be below either 50 percent or 40 percent (depending on which cutoff is used). Not surprisingly, the percentage of high-poverty schools located in such districts was small, less than 6 percent in the majority of the forty-six states studied. Although there are school districts in virtually every state for which intradistrict socioeconomic integration carries tremendous potential, most districts with high-poverty schools have too many low-income students to eliminate high-poverty schools on their own.

While the overall percentage is low, it translates into a significant impact in terms of students. If intradistrict strategies were employed in every viable district, more than 500,000 elementary school students would no longer need to attend a high-poverty school.

Finding 2: In seven states, the potential effectiveness of intradistrict strategies is much higher than the national average.

New Hampshire, Wyoming, Maryland, Utah, Nevada, North Dakota, and Virginia all had intradistrict viability percentages larger than 20 percent, showing that more than one-fifth of high-poverty schools in these states could be eliminated through intradistrict approaches.

However, in examining the numbers in Table 5.11, one should keep in mind that they reflect none of the realities associated with the actual implementation of intradistrict integration strategies. Wyoming, for example, has large school districts with a widely dispersed population; for many if not most students there, the idea of attending a school other than the one geographically closest to their homes is not realistic. The viability levels in Table 5.11 should be viewed as the ceiling for what intradistrict integration strategies could possibly accomplish in each state, disregarding all other factors.

Finding 3: Intradistrict integration strategies are less viable in states with a larger share of poor students.

This study examined a range of factors that might be associated with higher and lower intradistrict viability percentages. The strongest correlation found was between a state's intradistrict viability and its low-income percentage, which was −0.56. This negative correlation indicates that more-affluent states have higher rates of intradistrict viability than do poorer states. This is logical, since more-affluent states have more low-poverty districts that meet the viability cutoff.

We had hypothesized that median district size would impact a state's ability to use intradistrict solutions, on the theory that a district with more students and more schools would have more flexibility in balancing SES across the district. However, the correlation between district size and viability was negligible. A wide range of other possible variables, including population density and student race,[67] were also tested, with none showing a strong relationship with intradistrict viability.

In conclusion, although there are school districts in virtually every state for which intradistrict socioeconomic integration carries tremendous potential, most high-poverty schools are located in high-poverty districts. Such districts cannot bring the low-income enrollment of all their individual schools below 50 percent by reassigning their students. The next section, therefore, focuses on a more promising alternative to intradistrict integration strategies: interdistrict plans that attempt to balance socioeconomic diversity across two or more districts or an entire metropolitan region.

Viability of Interdistrict Strategies

Our intradistrict analysis shows that most high-poverty schools are located in districts where the percentage of low-income students is too high for intradistrict integration efforts to be effective. However, initiatives that include more than one district offer an alternative approach to reduce the number of children attending high-poverty schools. This section addresses the viability of interdistrict strategies for increasing socioeconomic school diversity.

Although less common than integration initiatives within a single district, a number of interdistrict integration models currently exist. Four categories of interdistrict efforts show the multiple avenues that could be used to support greater socioeconomic diversity: SES-based models, race-based models, interdistrict choice, and district consolidation.

SES-based Models

While they are the only two such programs in existence, Omaha and Minneapolis offer working examples of comprehensive regional choice programs that increase socioeconomic diversity through partnerships between a metropolitan center and its surrounding suburban districts.

The Minneapolis program, The Choice Is Yours, began in 2001 as a result of a state court ruling, and enables low-income students from Minneapolis to transfer to a school in one of nine participating suburban districts. The program currently enrolls around 2,000 low-income students, or 9 percent of the total students receiving free and reduced lunch in Minneapolis. However, five times as many students apply to this program each year as are accepted due to seat constraints at the receiving schools.[68]

The Choice Is Yours provides academic and social support for transferring students and their families, as well as free transportation.[69] According to a study by Aspen Associates researchers, two-thirds of parents reported that they would make a different school choice for their child if this transportation provision were eliminated.[70] Participating suburban school districts receive per-pupil funding for every Minneapolis student they enroll, plus the compensatory funding that would have gone to the student's Minneapolis school.[71] Although there have been recent political challenges to the city's participation in interdistrict integration efforts, the Minneapolis School Board unanimously affirmed its commitment to existing programs through the 2010–11 school year.[72]

Omaha's interdistrict program began in 1999 as voluntary integration through school choice and magnet schools. In 2007, the state legislature supported a plan that called for all metropolitan Omaha schools to meet socioeconomic diversity targets through cross-district cooperation.[73] Beginning in the fall of 2010, student assignment in the newly merged Omaha "learning community" is based on open enrollment, with preference given based on SES. Free transportation is provided to students "who either qualify for free or reduced-price lunches or contribute to the school's socioeconomic diversity."[74] A 40 percent low-income target, reflective of the overall metropolitan average, has been established for each school in the learning community.

Race-based Models

Dating back to desegregation efforts in the 1960s, many school districts either sought or were compelled by court mandates to innovate in support of racial diversity. While not all programs remain intact following subsequent counter-lawsuits, notable current models include voluntary choice, magnet school, and dual programs that employ both of these methods. It is important to note that these plans are included in this section to highlight strategies that could be adapted by districts interested in pursuing socioeconomic integration, not to suggest that they might be replaced by SES-based plans.

Voluntary Interdistrict Desegregation Programs. Several long-standing programs create opportunities for students to transfer from urban districts to schools in surrounding suburban districts to achieve greater racial equity. Perhaps the most well-known is Boston's METCO program, which began in 1966 and served 3,336 primarily minority students in 2010, or approximately 6 percent of Boston's enrollment. Even though the $3,132 per pupil paid to receiving districts is far below the 2010 statewide average per pupil cost of $12,500, thirty-seven suburban districts chose to participate.[75] While the program is highly regarded, it does not begin to meet the demand, as more than 12,000 students remain on the METCO waitlist.[76]

Cooperative race-based programs involving multiple districts also exist in Rochester, St. Louis, Indianapolis, East Palo Alto, and San Diego, among other locations. These programs tend to show an initial pattern of suburban opposition, then growing suburban support, with the most significant support coming from students themselves.[77] The overwhelming levels of participant interest testify to the demand for expanded school choice options.

Regional Magnet Schools. Magnet schools attempt to reverse the flow of cross-district transfers by attracting white, largely higher-income students to low-income areas.[78] San Diego Unified School District instituted an interdistrict magnet school program as a result of a 1977 court-ordered desegregation ruling. While the state legislature outlawed the preferential use of race as an admissions criterion in 1996, students from certain geographic areas have their applications weighted, which indirectly encourages integration.[79]

Bergen County, New Jersey's multidistrict magnet school programs, established in 2002, have been "successful in creating competitive academic programs, attracting students from throughout Bergen County and creating a racial/ethnic mix much more diverse than many of the districts from which its students are drawn."[80] Although limited in scope and restricted to students who can meet selective admissions requirements, Bergen County's success suggests the potential of utilizing interdistrict magnet school programs to increase diversity.

Dual Race-based Models. The race-based Chapter 220 program in Milwaukee attempts to facilitate transfers both from the city to the suburbs and from the suburbs to the city. Enacted in 1976, the program enables minority students who attend schools where they constitute more than 30 percent of the population to transfer to schools with less than 30 percent minority students. Similarly, nonminority students are eligible to transfer when they attend schools where 30 percent of the population is nonminority. In the 2008–09 school year, 2,525 Milwaukee students, or roughly 3 percent of the district's enrollment, transferred to suburban schools and 400 suburban students transferred to Milwaukee schools.[81] State aid covers transportation and average per pupil costs in the receiving districts and provides city schools with state equalization aid.[82]

The Hartford metropolitan area also uses a two-way plan to reduce racial segregation. In the 1996 *Sheff v. O'Neill* case, the state Supreme Court ruled that current levels of segregation violated the Connecticut Constitution. This ruling ultimately resulted in the establishment of a ceiling for integrated schools in which minority student attendance would "not exceed 30% of the regional minority enrollment."[83] As a result, the Hartford area is now home to twenty-two new magnet schools, and more than one thousand minority students from Hartford attend suburban schools through Project Choice.[84] However, the demand for Project Choice far exceeds the number of seats available, as none of the twenty-seven receiving districts provide more than 3 percent of their seats to Hartford students.[85]

Interdistrict Choice

Most states currently allow students to transfer across district boundaries, subject to various procedural constraints. The number of states with interdistrict choice laws expanded from fourteen to forty-four between 1993 and 2000, and by the start of the new century, more students nationally were enrolled in interdistrict choice than in charter schools and voucher programs combined.[86] However, while interdistrict choice programs offer the potential to reduce socioeconomic segregation, they are not currently designed to achieve this end.

In fact, uncontrolled interdistrict choice may even have a detrimental impact on socioeconomic school segregation, as those with the most access to information about the program and the means of transportation are most likely to participate.[87] A recent study specific to San Diego's interdistrict choice policy echoed these results, concluding that programs without transportation provisions and quotas do little to enhance diversity.[88] If interdistrict transfer programs are to affect segregation, they must be accompanied by transportation accommodations, parental outreach, and preferential admissions in order to target the students who will most advance the cause of diverse schools.

District Consolidation

Another option that might be used to reduce the number of high-poverty schools is district consolidation, a process that has recently gained impetus as a cost-saving measure.[89] A 2007 Maine law established a minimum school district size of 2,500, or 1,200 if geographic or similar obstacles made the larger number impractical.[90] In Massachusetts, the governor's office has provided both incentives and pressure for districts with fewer than 1,500 students to regionalize or consolidate.[91] Given research supporting the cost efficiencies of district consolidation up to a district size of around 3,000 students,[92] the interest in district consolidation may continue to grow. Such initiatives could also increase socioeconomic diversity if mergers are strategically designed between low- and high-poverty school districts, although political opposition is likely to be intense in such cases.

Independent of such political considerations, no real projections regarding the potential impact of cross-district integration efforts exist. This study attempts to provide this data by developing initial estimates of the demographic viability of interdistrict integration in six states.

TABLE 5.12. States Selected for Interdistrict Analysis—
District Elementary Schools

	Enrollment	Median District Size	Population Density [i] Per Square Mile	State Low-Income Percentage	% Black	% Latino	% White
Massachusetts	447,569	1,119	810	31%	7%	14%	70%
Virginia	589,022	2,028	179	36%	25%	10%	56%
Colorado	370,911	176	42	40%	6%	31%	58%
Nebraska	144,260	172	22	42%	9%	15%	73%
Missouri	435,959	521	81	45%	17%	4%	77%
Florida	1,215,200	5,774	296	53%	22%	26%	44%

Sources: U.S. Census Bureau, Census 2000 Summary File 1, "GCT-PH1. Population, Housing Units, Area, and Density: 2000"; authors' compilations from National Center for Education Statistics Common Core of Data (CCD) for the 2007–08 school year.

Sample for Interdistrict Study

Given that interdistrict strategies can involve many possible district combinations, our viability assessment was necessarily more exploratory than the preceding intradistrict analysis. This section of the study is based on a sample of six states, selected to represent a diverse cross-section in terms of enrollment, district size, population density, and student demographics, as shown in Table 5.12.

This sample is slightly skewed in that it includes only one high-poverty state, Florida. Our hypothesis was that states with more than 50 percent low-income students would have a limited ability to reduce their percentage of high-poverty schools, and the sample would yield more information if focused on states with greater socioeconomic diversity. The data bore out this assumption, as discussed below.

Viability Measures

As with the intradistrict analysis, we developed our interdistrict viability measures based on the goal of bringing all schools in a given district below 50 percent low-income. Our interdistrict assessment is based on two criteria: *geographic viability,* which looks at whether a district with high-poverty schools actually borders one or more low-poverty districts; and *demographic viability,* which then factors in the size and low-income percentage of these neighboring districts to determine whether high-poverty schools could, at least in theory, be entirely eliminated. While additional issues like the distances between schools, political resistance, impact on private school enrollment, insufficient facilities, and the availability of transportation funding are all clearly salient, they are too complex to be analyzed at the national level and are not addressed in this analysis.

Geographic Viability. We began our assessment by mapping each state by the percentage of low-income students in each district. Districts were then sorted as follows:

- *low-poverty partners*—districts with less than 40 percent low-income students;
- *higher-poverty partners*—districts with more than 40 percent low-income students and at least one high-poverty school; and
- *borderline districts*—districts with 40 percent–50 percent low-income students and no high-poverty schools.

Mapping districts by these three categories conveys an immediate sense of where interdistrict strategies may be viable. For example, in Virginia (see Map 5.2), we can see that the low-poverty district of Arlington County borders higher-poverty Alexandria City, thus making possible the consideration of an interdistrict strategy. Conversely, Scott County, a higher-poverty district bordering only other higher-poverty districts, has no ability to leverage the socioeconomic diversity of a neighboring district. Note that our definition of geographic viability is restrictive, in that a district's only potential partners are limited to those districts it actually borders. In areas with a proliferation of small districts, this limitation means that geographic viability is probably understated.

Giles County illustrates the situation of borderline poverty districts, which are not viable for interdistrict strategies. Lacking both high-poverty schools and an FRL percentage below 40 percent, this district has neither the need to ally with a low-poverty district, nor the capacity to assist a higher-poverty one. Such borderline districts are not uncommon, but are shaded out on the map to reflect their exclusion from potential partnerships in this study.

Demographic Viability. While geographic viability indicates which districts might explore collaboration with a neighboring district, it overstates the percentage of districts that could actually eliminate all their high-poverty schools using such a strategy. Florida's Monroe County and Dade County, for example, meet the geographic viability standard because low-poverty

MAP 5.2. Virginia, by Percentage of Low-Income Students

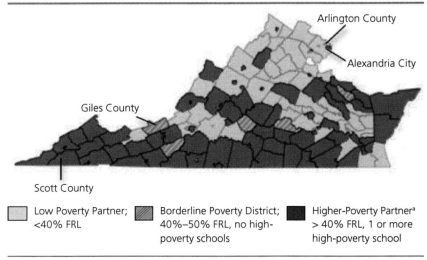

	Low Poverty Partner; <40% FRL		Borderline Poverty District; 40%–50% FRL, no high- poverty schools		Higher-Poverty Partner[a] > 40% FRL, 1 or more high-poverty school

Source: Authors' compilations from National Center for Education Statistics Common Core of Data (CCD) for the 2007–08 school year.
[a]Unshaded district is Department of Defense schools, not in study.

Monroe borders higher-poverty Dade. However, Monroe has just 4,500 elementary school students, while neighboring Dade, which includes the city of Miami, has 161,300. An interdistrict partnership between the two districts would thus have little impact on concentrations of poverty in Dade County schools, and the districts fail the demographic viability test.

Our second, more stringent measure of interdistrict viability therefore incorporates demographic analysis. For this measure, we calculated the overall low-income percentage that would result if we combined the enrollments of neighboring low-poverty and higher-poverty districts. Only pairings with a combined low-income percentage of 40 percent or less[93] are considered demographically viable.

Table 5.13 depicts three examples of possible interdistrict partnerships. The Florida example and the second Massachusetts example are viable in terms of demographics; the first Massachusetts example is not, because the combined low-income percentage exceeds 40 percent. Note that our viability measure allows higher-poverty partners such as Lowell to combine with more than one bordering low-poverty partner. When low-poverty districts border more than one higher-poverty district, we give priority to the district with the greatest number of high-poverty schools.

TABLE 5.13. Sample Interdistrict Pairings

State	Low-Poverty Partner(s)	Adjacent Higher-Poverty Partner(s)	Combined Low-income %	High-Poverty Schools Affected
FL	Leon	Wakulla, Jefferson	40%	2
MA	Everett	Medford	53%	6
MA	Billerica, Chelmsford, Tewksbury, Tyngsborough	Lowell	30%	15

Source: Authors' compilations from National Center for Education Statistics Common Core of Data (CCD) for the 2007–08 school year.

Interdistrict Viability. The final step in determining interdistrict viability is to tally the number of high-poverty schools located in districts that have passed both the geographic and demographic screens. This sum is then expressed as a percentage of the total number of high-poverty schools located in higher-poverty districts. (High-poverty schools in low-poverty districts can be addressed through intradistrict strategies.) A state's interdistrict viability percentage can thus be seen as an answer to the question: What percentage of the state's high-poverty schools can be reduced through interdistrict strategies?

Findings

Our analysis of six sample states enabled us to identify broad differences and patterns that might impact the potential for integration strategies involving more than one district. While the findings below must be viewed as preliminary, they nonetheless constitute a significant step forward in determining the "true" viability of SES-based interdistrict strategies around the country.

Finding 1: In the six states we examined, the percentage of high-poverty schools with interdistrict solutions ranges from 7 percent in Florida to 52 percent in Nebraska.

As shown in Table 5.14, the percentage of high-poverty schools with interdistrict solutions ranges from 7 percent in Florida to a surprising 52 percent in Nebraska. The state with the largest number of students impacted is Virginia; the smallest, Missouri.

The numbers in Table 5.14 should be viewed with a few caveats in mind, as the measures chosen for this study potentially overstate

TABLE 5.14. Percent Reduction in High-Poverty Schools through Inter-district Strategies[a]

	% Low-income	High-Poverty Elementary Schools[b]	# with Viable Inter-district Strategies	% with Viable Inter-district Strategies	Elementary Students Affected
Nebraska	42%	163	85	52%	29,533
Virginia	36%	315	114	36%	47,363
Colorado	40%	296	101	34%	34,097
Massachusetts	31%	292	99	34%	41,755
Missouri	45%	577	96	17%	28,649
Florida	53%	1,001	74	7%	36,427

Source: Authors' compilations from National Center for Education Statistics Common Core of Data (CCD) for the 2007–08 school year.
[a]Based on demographic viability screen.
[b]Borderline and higher-poverty districts only. Intradistrict strategies used in low-poverty districts.

interdistrict viability in some ways and understate it in others. As noted earlier, transportation time and costs, facilities capacity, and political climate all affect the potential impact of interdistrict strategies. To the extent that these factors cannot be addressed through policy, they would clearly lower the viability percentages found above.

Other aspects of our measures have the reverse effect, and depress the percentages of interdistrict viability below what could be achieved in practice. The use of the 40 percent combined low-income enrollment criterion, for example, omits pairings that could reduce some but not all of the high-poverty schools in a district. For example, Florida's Martin school district is too small for a viable pairing with larger Palm Beach, but it does have enough capacity to reduce the number of high-poverty schools in Palm Beach by 5 percent, or roughly three schools. Though potentially beneficial, such pairings are not counted in our method as demographically viable. Our criterion that districts share a physical border can also result in an understatement of interdistrict viability, as previously discussed.

Finding 2: The percent of higher-poverty districts that could participate in interdistrict strategies generally tracks the overall state poverty level.

This study examined the district-level viability of inter-district strategies in addition to the school-level observations of Finding 1. As shown by Table 5.15, the geographic viability of higher-poverty districts is closely

TABLE 5.15. Interdistrict Viability—Higher-Poverty Districts

State	Low-Income Percentage	Geographic Viability	Demographic Viability
Massachusetts	31%	97%	62%
Virginia	36%	67%	35%
Colorado	40%	81%	33%
Nebraska	42%	87%	32%
Missouri	45%	35%	13%
Florida	53%	34%	7%

Source: Authors' compilations from National Center for Education Statistics Common Core of Data (CCD) for the 2007–08 school year.

related to a state's low-income percentage, with poorer states having fewer potential partnerships. Nonetheless, in all six states a large share of higher-poverty districts border at least one low-poverty district. Among higher-poverty districts, geographic viability ranges from 97 percent in Massachusetts to just over one-third in Florida and Missouri. Judging only by how districts border one another, interdistrict partnerships appear to be a viable policy alternative for education officials to consider in these six states.

Adding in the more stringent demographic test lowered the percentage of viable districts in each state by an average of thirty-six percentage points, with the greatest falloff being the fifty-five-point drop in Colorado. Once again, state viability levels were linked with their overall low-income percentages. In states with low or moderate poverty, the proportion of higher-poverty districts that could potentially eliminate all their high-poverty schools through interdistrict strategies remained high, ranging from 62 percent of districts in Massachusetts to roughly one-third in Virginia, Colorado, and Nebraska. Percentages in Missouri and Florida, the two poorest states, were 13 percent and 7 percent, respectively.

As the only high-poverty state in our interdistrict sample, Florida demonstrates the limits of interdistrict strategies in states where the majority of students are low-income. Only four of Florida's fifty-six higher-poverty districts border other districts with sufficient higher-income students to make an interdistrict strategy viable. (See Map 5.3.)

However, even within this high-poverty state, regional poverty variations make possible a larger reduction in high-poverty schools than one might expect. In Florida, 45 percent of public elementary school

MAP 5.3. Florida, by Percentage of Low-Income Students

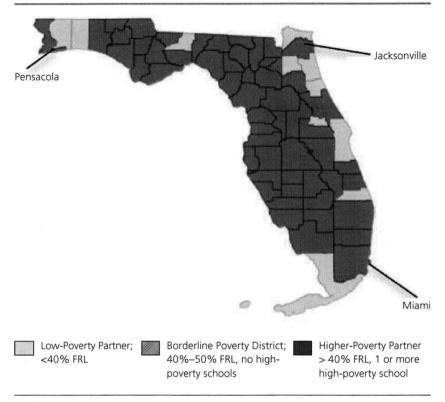

Low-Poverty Partner; <40% FRL	Borderline Poverty District; 40%–50% FRL, no high-poverty schools	Higher-Poverty Partner > 40% FRL, 1 or more high-poverty school

Source: Authors' compilations from National Center for Education Statistics Common Core of Data (CCD) for the 2007–08 school year.

students do not currently attend high-poverty schools, and interdistrict strategies could reduce the number of high-poverty schools by roughly another 7 percent. Although this overall percentage gain is small, Florida's large population means that interdistrict strategies could affect approximately 36,000 elementary school children who currently attend high-poverty schools.

Metropolitan Jacksonville demonstrates how regional variations make possible the reduction of high-poverty schools even in high-poverty states. Located in Duval County, Jacksonville's poorer urban center is surrounded by more affluent suburban districts: Clay, with 28 percent low-income students; Nassau, with 39 percent; and St. John's, with 22 percent. A strategy that linked Duval County with these three districts would bring the joint low-income percentage to 39 percent, thus making it possible to bring Jackson's sixty-one high-poverty schools down below the 50 percent low-income line.

As shown by the successful Jacksonville partnership, these pockets of interdistrict viability depend in part on the degree of poverty in the higher-poverty districts. Duval County, where Jacksonville is located, is 46 percent low-income. In contrast, the counties containing Pensacola and Miami, both viable at the geographic level, have a much higher 66 percent and 67 percent FRL respectively, thus making it infeasible for interdistrict strategies to bring all schools below 50 percent low-income.

Finding 3: Interdistrict strategies appear to be more viable in states where poverty is either dispersed or concentrated in cities and towns.

The states of Nebraska and Missouri appear statistically similar enough that one would anticipate their interdistrict viability percentages to be similar as well. Both states have low population densities; Nebraska's median district size is 173 elementary students, while in Missouri, 70 percent of the districts have only one elementary school. The two states have the highest percentages of white students in the six-state sample: 77 percent in Missouri and 73 percent in Nebraska. Lastly, their low-income percentages are nearly identical: 45 percent in Missouri and 42 percent in Nebraska.

And yet, interdistrict strategies enable Nebraska to reduce its number of high-poverty schools by 52 percent, while in Missouri, interdistrict viability is only 17 percent. The maps of the two states explain the difference (see Maps 5.4 and 5.5).

As can be seen by Missouri's state map, higher-poverty districts dominate the southern third of the state. This concentration of higher-poverty districts in one area effectively walls off the majority of them from the state's low-poverty districts. In fact, 65 percent of higher-poverty districts statewide, including Kansas City, do not border a single low-poverty district.

This regional pattern of higher-poverty districts is not evident on the Nebraska map. Instead, low- and higher-poverty districts are fairly evenly dispersed, with no significant regional concentrations of poverty. This pattern means that 87 percent of higher-poverty districts in Nebraska do border a low-poverty district, a stark contrast from Missouri.

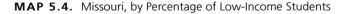

MAP 5.4. Missouri, by Percentage of Low-Income Students

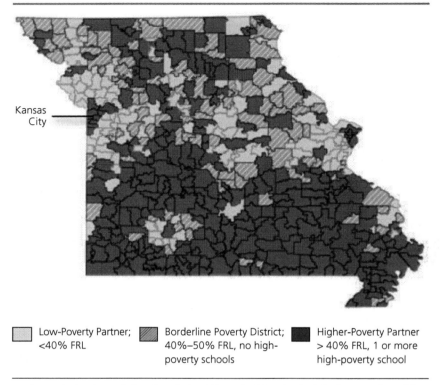

Kansas
City

| Low-Poverty Partner; <40% FRL | Borderline Poverty District; 40%–50% FRL, no high-poverty schools | Higher-Poverty Partner > 40% FRL, 1 or more high-poverty school |

Source: Authors' compilations from National Center for Education Statistics Common Core of Data (CCD) for the 2007–08 school year.

Nebraska's patchwork pattern of low- and higher-poverty districts is more amenable to interdistrict partnerships than the regionalized poverty in southern Missouri. So too are urban patterns of poverty concentration, as they effectively place poorer urban districts in proximity to more-affluent suburban schools. Nebraska serves as an example here again. Though hardly considered an urbanized state, Nebraska has fully one-third of its high-poverty schools in the population centers of Lincoln and Omaha; since these two districts are viable, the numbers for the entire state are strong.

The state of Virginia offers another example of urban patterns of poverty concentration. As shown in Map 5.6, the state is a mix of both urban and regional concentrations of poverty. Virginia's district map reveals

MAP 5.5. Nebraska, by Percentage of Low-Income Students

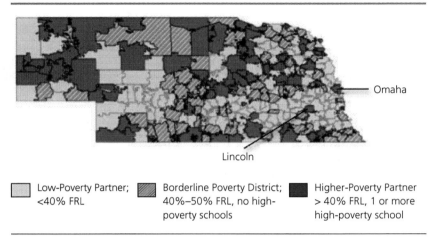

| Low-Poverty Partner; <40% FRL | Borderline Poverty District; 40%–50% FRL, no high-poverty schools | Higher-Poverty Partner > 40% FRL, 1 or more high-poverty school |

Source: Authors' compilations from National Center for Education Statistics Common Core of Data (CCD) for the 2007–08 school year.

pronounced regional disparities in income distribution, with concentrations of poverty in Appalachia and along the southern border. One-third of higher-poverty districts are geographically isolated, with little possibility of an interdistrict partnership; this is the dark swath along the bottom of the state map. However, many other higher-poverty districts correspond to small cities and towns inside a more affluent county; these areas show up as dark dots surrounded by lighter-colored regions, mostly in the upper part of the map. Such areas are much better candidates for inter-district integration, choice, or consolidation.

Finding 4: Interdistrict viability is higher for urban areas if nearby but nonadjacent low-poverty districts are considered as potential partners.

In regions with geographically small districts and/or effective transportation systems, policies linking nonadjacent districts are often feasible. In metropolitan regions, then, our geographic viability standard excludes some potential partners and thereby understates the viability of interdistrict integration.

Colorado and Massachusetts are both examples of states where our interdistrict viability measure is depressed because of urban district geography, rather than an actual lack of low-poverty partners. For example,

MAP 5.6. Virginia, by Percentage of Low-Income Students

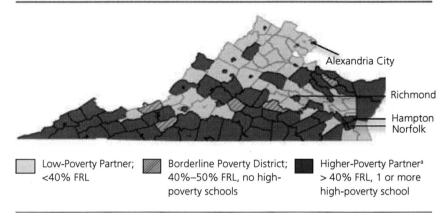

Low-Poverty Partner; <40% FRL	Borderline Poverty District; 40%–50% FRL, no high-poverty schools	Higher-Poverty Partner[a] > 40% FRL, 1 or more high-poverty school

Source: Authors' compilations from National Center for Education Statistics Common Core of Data (CCD) for the 2007–08 school year.
[a]Unshaded district is Department of Defense schools, not in study.

in the Colorado Springs area, there are two higher-poverty districts, Colorado Springs 11 and Harrison 2, surrounded by more-affluent suburbs. If potential partnerships are restricted to adjacent districts, only Colorado Springs is viable. But if all seven districts in the metropolitan region participated, the overall low-income percentage would be comfortably below 40 percent; all schools in both Colorado Springs and Harrison could exit high-poverty status. (See Map 5.7.)

A similar situation occurs in Boston. Massachusetts' 31 percent low-income percentage—the lowest in the sample—seems favorable to inter-district strategies, and 97 percent of the state's higher-poverty districts border a low-poverty district. Yet the state's 34 percent interdistrict viability percentage ranks below that of both Nebraska and Virginia, both of whom have higher FRL percentages than Massachusetts. A major reason is that Boston would be unable to bring all its schools below the 50 percent low-income line through alliances with its adjacent districts. (See Map 5.8.)

Boston, however, is unusual in that it has a voluntary integration program that brings city children to suburban schools. Thirty-three districts, some more than twenty miles away, accept transfer students through METCO,[94] thus demonstrating that it is possible for children from Boston to attend schools in districts that do not share a border with the city.

MAP 5.7. Colorado, by Percentage of Low-Income Students

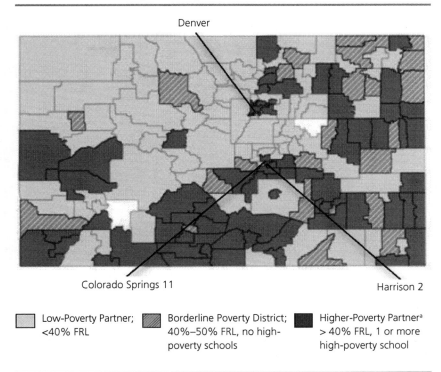

Denver

Colorado Springs 11   Harrison 2

| | Low-Poverty Partner; <40% FRL | | Borderline Poverty District; 40%–50% FRL, no high-poverty schools | | Higher-Poverty Partner[a] > 40% FRL, 1 or more high-poverty school |

Source: Authors' compilations from National Center for Education Statistics Common Core of Data (CCD) for the 2007–08 school year.

Including these METCO districts as viable partners for Boston would bring the joint low-income percentage well below 40 percent.

With Boston included as a viable district, the percentage of Massachusetts high-poverty schools that can be reduced through interdistrict strategies would rise from the 34 percent shown on Tables 5.14 and 5.16 to 59 percent, which would rank highest in the sample.

Finding 5: In all six states studied, interdistrict strategies carry more potential for reducing the number of high-poverty schools than intradistrict strategies.

In all six states, interdistrict strategies were more effective in reducing the numbers of high-poverty schools than intra-district approaches. The

MAP 5.8. Massachusetts, by Percentage of Low-Income Students

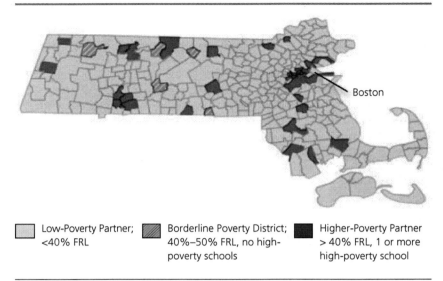

Low-Poverty Partner; <40% FRL	Borderline Poverty District; 40%–50% FRL, no high-poverty schools	Higher-Poverty Partner > 40% FRL, 1 or more high-poverty school

Source: Authors' compilations from National Center for Education Statistics Common Core of Data (CCD) for the 2007–08 school year.

smallest difference was in Florida, where each county is a single school district. The largest difference was in Nebraska, whose intradistrict viability of 6 percent is dwarfed by the 52 percent reduction in high-poverty schools possible through interdistrict strategies. Table 5.16 shows the viability of both intra- and interdistrict strategies for the six states in our sample.

With a combination of intra- and interdistrict strategies, our data indicates that high-poverty schools in both Nebraska and Virginia could be reduced by more than one-half, in Massachusetts and Colorado by more than one-third. Even in high-poverty Florida, the 13 percent reduction is significant in terms of numbers, with 70,000 elementary school children benefiting from a combination of intra- and interdistrict strategies.

Conclusion

While a state's overall poverty level and internal patterns of poverty both impact interdistrict viability, a number of other factors do not seem as important. For instance, racial demographics do not appear to be related to viability; the states with the highest and lowest percentages of nonwhite

TABLE 5.16. Viability of Intra- and Interdistrict Strategies

State	% Low-Income	Percent Reduction in High-Poverty Schools		
		Intradistrict	*Interdistrict*	*TOTAL*
Virginia	36%	24%	36%	60%
Nebraska	42%	6%	52%	58%
Colorado	40%	18%	34%	52%
Massachusetts	31%	4%	34%	37%
Missouri	45%	2%	17%	37%
Florida	53%	6%	7%	13%

Source: Authors' compilations from National Center for Education Statistics Common Core of Data (CCD) for the 2007–08 school year.

students, Florida and Missouri, are both quite poor and have the lowest viability estimates among the six states. Of course, more states need to be examined to test this conclusion. Population density and median district enrollment also do not seem to affect the geographic and demographic viability measures used here, although the distance between schools and the capacity of districts to accept more students would certainly determine whether the transportation of students across current boundaries could work in practice.

Looking at the interdistrict findings as a whole, we see that in no state, even the most affluent, is it possible to eliminate all high-poverty schools. Nonetheless, in four of the six states studied, interdistrict strategies could reduce the number of high-poverty schools by more than one-third. Even in Florida, with its 7 percent interdistrict viability, roughly 35,000 children stand to benefit from SES integration strategies. A combination of intra- and interdistrict strategies could yield even greater reductions in high-poverty schools. The following section explores a range of policy approaches that could be used to translate this finding from possibility to actuality.

Policy Implications

Our results suggest that a combination of intra- and interdistrict integration strategies based on SES could substantially reduce the number of high-poverty schools across the United States. The question that logically follows, then, is how to implement these strategies in the parts of the country where they could make the most difference.

In the preceding two sections, we outlined a wide variety of models for both intra- and interdistrict student assignment policies, which are being utilized in locations as diverse as Minneapolis, Louisville, Berkeley, and La Crosse, Wisconsin. The problem is therefore not a lack of innovative ideas on how to reduce socioeconomic isolation at the district and regional levels.

Rather, the main barrier is the assumption that school segregation is an ugly but unchanging reality, impermeable to policy intervention. This reality has led Americans to watch with a feeling of helplessness as our schools become ever more segregated, leaving ever more students behind. The current silence on the stratification of our educational system prevents us from achieving the goal of equitable outcomes for all children.

The prospect of community resistance and the difficulty of implementing any policy across existing district lines stand as real and formidable obstacles in the path of large-scale socioeconomic integration efforts. However, instead of relegating integration efforts to the past, we should be talking about policy efforts that address these challenges by breaking up concentrations of school poverty.[95] The following implications provide initial guidance on how to proactively support strategies that reduce socioeconomic isolation.

Implication 1: Federal and state governments must provide the political cover needed for districts to pursue politically contentious integration plans.

The long history of efforts to achieve greater equity in education is one of local-level inertia and resistance, overcome by pressure from above. For example, it took the seminal 1954 *Brown v. Board of Education* decision[96] and the 1964 Civil Rights Act to surmount school boards' resistance to racial desegregation. Similarly, advocacy to secure more resources for low-income students resulted in the 1965 Elementary and Secondary Education Act, which directed federal education dollars to schools serving poor children. Such actions recognized the failure of local control mechanisms to protect children of low SES and minority status, and compelled even the most unwilling districts to enact more equitable student assignment policies and resource allocations.

Today's school board officials are still democratically elected by local voters, who may view any student reassignment as a potential threat: "Voters in well-off (predominantly white) districts usually perceive direct costs and perhaps even a zero-sum game in the prospect of sharing their resources with children in poor (disproportionately non-white) districts."[97] History suggests that state and federal action must provide the political cover necessary for districts to challenge this resistance and disrupt the status quo.

Implication 2: The federal government can contribute to reductions in the number of high-poverty schools through three major policy interventions.

Leveraging Existing Competitive Grant Programs. States and districts are currently in desperate need of additional revenue streams to support their education funding. Current budgetary crises mean that financial incentives may work to induce changes that might be politically unpalatable in more abundant times.

The 2009–10 Race to the Top funding competition was a remarkable demonstration of how federal policy levers can induce radical reforms at the state and local levels of education, even in the face of entrenched opposition. The offer of $4.35 billion in competitive grant money to states meeting certain eligibility criteria incentivized thirty-four states to change laws or policies to bolster their applications.[98] These changes included lifting charter school caps and changing contract provisions on teacher evaluation, ideas that previously had been considered politically untouchable. Given this precedent, it is likely that states or districts would voluntarily pursue new socioeconomic strategies if the next rounds of federal grant funding rewarded them for doing so.

Reworking the Student Transfer Provision in the Reauthorization of ESEA. Title I of the current Elementary and Secondary Education Act (ESEA), which has been up for reauthorization since 2007, authorizes students in districts identified for corrective action to transfer to a better-performing school in another district. The law requires that the state cover transportation costs, but not that other districts must accept such students. Moreover, ESEA offers no compensation to schools losing students or schools receiving them under this transfer provision.[99] What this has meant in practice is that nationally, only 1 percent of students eligible to transfer actually do so.[100] ESEA revisions could target low-income students for transfer requests,[101] provide transportation support,[102] offer financial incentives for receiving districts, institute a grace period during which transfer students would not be counted in the receiving district's AYP calculation,[103] or include a combination of these strategies.

Providing Greater Support for Regional Magnet Schools. Inter-district choice allows students in low-performing schools, which are often high-poverty, to attend a higher-performing school in a nearby community. However, if successful, such programs would result in a one-way movement of students from higher-poverty to low-poverty districts. Since all low-income students cannot possibly transfer, the necessary implication is that those who are left behind become trapped in increasingly hyper-segregated schools; meanwhile, more-affluent districts balloon in size as their enrollments swell with transfer students. In contrast, high-quality regional magnet schools help ensure that the flow of students across district lines is bi-directional.

Title V of the current ESEA, "Promoting Informed Parent Choice and Innovative Programs," includes competitive funding for magnet schools designed to promote voluntary racial desegregation. Currently, such schools must be in a district or local consortium with a desegregation plan, approved either by a court or the U.S. Department of Education (ESEA, Section 5304). A revised version of this program could make funding available more broadly to consortia of districts for regional magnet schools designed to promote socioeconomic as well as racial desegregation.

Implication 3: State governments also can promote the adoption of integration strategies through a variety of mechanisms.

Revising Existing Interdistrict Choice. Research on interdistrict choice programs at the state level reveals that, while students exercising choice are usually moving from higher- to low-poverty districts, these students are more frequently from middle-class backgrounds. A study focused on the Denver area found that interdistrict choice has actually exacerbated socioeconomic segregation across districts.[104]

Evidence from existing programs offers concrete guidance for how to ensure that interdistrict choice actually improves integration. One key area of focus is transportation costs; if these are not covered, most low-income families are effectively barred from participating. But of the forty-three states (including Puerto Rico) with interdistrict choice laws that were not designed specifically for desegregation purposes, only seven currently fund the transportation costs of low-income families.[105]Additionally, states can improve existing laws by increasing parental education about choice options, establishing expectations for participation of more affluent districts, and mandating that SES is a diversity factor to ensure the program targets low-income students.[106]

Funding Intensive Local-level Feasibility Studies. While our study provides estimates of the potential impact of intra- and interdistrict strategies, such issues as facility capacity, distances and transportation alternatives between schools, demographic trends in enrollment, financing, and programmatic shifts that create incentives both for urban students to attend schools in suburban areas and for suburban students to attend schools in urban areas would all need to be considered. Particularly in areas where such arrangements have never been explored in the past, funding a feasibility study is a vital first step with which the state could assist.

Massachusetts' support of regional planning solutions, in which districts explored potential consolidation alternatives, provides an example of how other states might proceed. The Massachusetts Department of Elementary and Secondary Education funded two types of regional planning studies in 2008–09: one for districts throughout the state that expressed interest voluntarily, and one in Franklin County, which contained a proliferation of very small and perennially cash-strapped districts.[107] Other states might adopt a similar "carrot-and-stick" approach that encompasses those districts amenable to integration strategies and those where financial realities virtually compel a different administrative structure.

Providing Financial Incentives such as Transportation Support. As part of the race-based Chapter 220 program in Milwaukee, the state pays the transportation costs for students to travel from Milwaukee to suburban schools. It also provides the receiving suburban districts with the average cost per pupil from the state, and the sending urban district with state equalization aid.[108]

While not quite as generous, Massachusetts' METCO and interdistrict choice programs have high rates of district participation despite reimbursements well below the average district per pupil cost. In the 2010 fiscal year, the statewide average per pupil cost was $12,500. However, METCO averaged $4,900 per student, while the reimbursement for interdistrict choice students was $5,000.[109] Even minimal levels of financial support, then, may encourage participation in cross-district partnerships.

Imposing Financial Penalties to Compel District Policy Changes. For example, the 2007 Maine School District Consolidation Law included financial penalties for any district that failed to comply, including a reduction in the district's "system administration allocation" and less favorable consideration for school construction.[110] As a result of these consequences, within two years, 98 small school districts had merged into 26, and 84 percent of districts were in compliance with the new law.[111] While states would need to be careful using such an approach for interdistrict integration,[112] the idea of withholding or reducing state funds for districts that refuse to participate in such plans might hold promise.

To summarize, our objective here is not to prescribe a policy agenda around SES-based integration, but rather to refute the idea that nothing can be done to achieve it. Prioritization and incentives at the state and federal levels could very well create traction around this reform and induce participation by school districts around the country. A number of existing policy levers can be utilized to motivate communities and local districts to pursue more socioeconomically balanced schools. Our conclusion lays out an argument for why policymakers should choose to focus on this goal among a host of competing education reform priorities.

Conclusion

Our findings address two broad issues: patterns of existing school segregation by income and the viability of intra- and interdistrict integration strategies to reduce the number of high-poverty schools. In line with previous studies, we find that U.S. schools are increasingly segregated on socioeconomic lines, with nearly half of public elementary students now attending high-poverty schools. However, our data indicate that SES-based integration strategies could dramatically reduce the national number of high-poverty schools, although most of the change would have to come across existing district boundary lines. Given the focus on closing the achievement gap and the plethora of evidence linking high-poverty schools to low academic performance, intra- and interdistrict integration strategies therefore appear to merit serious consideration.

However, the typical reaction to arguments for increasing school diversity has been skepticism, if not outright dismissal. Concerns over socioeconomic integration as a potential strategy focus on the politically charged, protracted debate that usually occurs over any change in student assignment policies. Districts are better off bowing to political realities, the argument runs, and embracing other types of reform that are more easily implemented. As Education Sector co-founder Andrew J. Rotherham notes:

> No one in the mainstream of the education debate wants segregated schools. But while such schools are not an immutable condition, they are an unfortunate fact of life. That's why so many in the reform community see issues such as improving teacher effectiveness, providing a better curriculum and expanding high performing charters in underserved communities as more impactful and immediate steps than grand schemes.[113]

It is not that the reforms on the above list are without merit. Rather, *none of these reforms is as clearly linked to increased student achievement as the opportunity to attend a low-poverty school*. In the twenty-six-year wake of the *Nation at Risk* report,[114] reformers have adopted and spent heavily on a raft of education reforms designed to turn around the lowest performing schools, which are virtually always high-poverty. None has been successful at scale.

To be clear, SES-based integration should not be viewed as a silver bullet. Our study demonstrates its limitations:

- It is not a universal solution—in many areas, geography and demographic constraints would preclude even the most willing communities from undertaking SES-based student reassignments.
- It is not a stand-alone reform—socioeconomic integration would need to be accompanied by efforts to minimize tracking and improve the overall quality of classroom instruction.
- It is not a quick fix—student assignment policies generally cannot be implemented by a stroke of the pen from the district superintendent.

However, the past few decades of school reform attempts have surely shown that no single initiative can be any of these things. SES-based integration cannot be the sole component of the reform agenda, but it ought to be near the top of the list by virtue of what it is:

- It is firmly grounded in research—high-poverty schools are demonstrably bad for students, and we now know that low-income students achieve more in middle-class schools even when they are tracked.[115]
- It is a reform that offers benefits for all children and families within the system, such as more school choice and the opportunity to learn

and interact in diverse environments that mimic the twenty-first-century workplace.

- It can reduce substantial inequities across racial/ethnic and SES groups in different states.
- It can be implemented through multiple routes and leverage points—there are numerous variations on intra- and interdistrict models that can be explored at the local level, and many ways to incentivize these models at the state and federal levels.
- It leverages existing resources within the educational system to narrow the achievement gap—poor academic outcomes for low-income students are a national challenge, and addressing them should be the work of all U.S. schools and educators, not just those in the poorest areas.

The policy context of American public education today stresses high-stakes accountability; schools are expected to deliver uniformly high results, regardless of their student demographics. However, the research is clear: most high-poverty schools yield poorer achievement by all the students who attend them. Given this evidence and the increasing prevalence of such schools, strategies to reduce their numbers should be an explicit goal of federal and state policy.

Our hope is that the data presented here about the state-level viability of such approaches will advance the debate over high poverty schools beyond simplistic "no excuses" rhetoric and turnaround strategies that ignore fundamental imbalances in school composition. Many high-poverty schools exist because of arbitrary school assignment policies that can be changed if the political will exists to do so; potentially millions of children who are currently in low-performing, high-poverty schools stand to benefit.

Appendix 5.1
Prevalence of High-Poverty Elementary Schools

State	State Low-Income Percentage	High-Poverty Elementary Schools	High-Poverty School Enrollment	High-Poverty School Enrollment as a Percentage of Total Enrollment
Mississippi	72%	442	204,097	85%
Louisiana	69%	642	277,085	78%
New Mexico	69%	346	116,747	74%
Arkansas	61%	458	178,045	71%
Oklahoma	61%	761	240,667	69%
West Virginia	54%	309	86,982	63%
California	58%	3,289	1,779,914	62%
Kentucky	55%	510	210,361	62%
Tennessee	55%	673	294,667	61%
Alabama	56%	506	208,490	60%
Georgia	55%	819	478,047	60%
Texas	51%	2,515	1,340,516	57%
South Carolina	55%	422	200,893	56%
Florida	53%	1,062	673,996	55%
Oregon	48%	351	129,700	49%
Arizona	47%	451	257,263	48%
New York	49%	1,017	589,315	47%
Illinois	48%	1,044	491,117	46%
Kansas	45%	326	97,434	41%
Missouri	45%	588	180,490	41%
Nevada	46%	143	84,510	41%
Maryland	40%	349	147,787	37%
Washington	43%	434	173,919	36%
Indiana	44%	443	183,157	36%
Rhode Island	41%	62	22,987	36%
Michigan	41%	721	252,876	36%
Colorado	40%	360	132,654	36%
Maine	41%	160	32,417	35%
Delaware	41%	38	18,529	34%
Nebraska	42%	175	48,440	34%
Montana	42%	124	22,124	32%
New Jersey	32%	404	200,962	30%
Virginia	36%	412	174,942	30%

(continued)

State	State Low-Income Percentage	High-Poverty Elementary Schools	High-Poverty School Enrollment	High-Poverty School Enrollment as a Percentage of Total Enrollment
Pennsylvania	38%	501	226,610	29%
Connecticut	34%	170	77,290	28%
Idaho	40%	98	35,319	27%
Massachusetts	31%	303	117,881	26%
Utah	37%	139	72,078	26%
Iowa	37%	188	56,887	25%
Wisconsin	36%	279	95,664	24%
South Dakota	35%	100	12,466	24%
Minnesota	34%	213	75,292	20%
Wyoming	36%	37	8,432	20%
Vermont	33%	39	7,704	17%
North Dakota	35%	49	7,128	15%
New Hampshire	19%	15	3,992	4%
TOTAL		22,487	10,327,873	48%

Source: Authors' compilations from National Center for Education Statistics Common Core of Data (CCD) for the 2007–08 school year.

Appendix 5.2
Socioeconomic Isolation of Low-Income Elementary School Students

State	Low-Income Percentage	Hyper-Segregation: % of FRL Students at Schools with > 90% FRL	Exposure Index: FRL % of School Attended by the Average FRL Student
New Mexico	69%	48%	79
Mississippi	72%	38%	78
Illinois	48%	38%	72
Connecticut	34%	35%	67
New York	49%	30%	72
Louisiana	69%	29%	76
Nevada	46%	27%	64
California	58%	25%	73
Arizona	47%	24%	69
Rhode Island	41%	20%	64
Alabama	56%	19%	67
Arkansas	61%	18%	69
Oklahoma	61%	18%	70
Tennessee	55%	17%	66
South Dakota	35%	17%	53
Georgia	55%	16%	68
Wisconsin	36%	16%	54
Texas	51%	15%	68
Pennsylvania	38%	13%	57
Michigan	41%	12%	58
Massachusetts	31%	11%	59
South Carolina	55%	10%	65
Utah	37%	10%	51
Kansas	45%	9%	60
Florida	53%	8%	64
Indiana	44%	7%	56
Washington	43%	7%	57
Minnesota	34%	7%	48
New Jersey	32%	7%	60
Maryland	40%	6%	58
Missouri	45%	5%	57
Nebraska	42%	5%	57
Colorado	40%	5%	59
Oregon	48%	4%	59

(continued)

State	Low-Income Percentage	Hyper-Segregation: % of FRL Students at Schools with > 90% FRL	Exposure Index: FRL % of School Attended by the Average FRL Student
Montana	42%	3%	52
Virginia	36%	3%	51
Vermont	33%	3%	42
Kentucky	55%	2%	62
Iowa	37%	2%	48
Wyoming	36%	2%	44
North Dakota	35%	2%	43
West Virginia	54%	1%	59
Maine	41%	1%	49
Delaware	41%	0%	51
Idaho	40%	0%	47
New Hampshire	19%	0%	31

Source: Authors' compilations from National Center for Education Statistics Common Core of Data (CCD) for the 2007–08 school year.

Appendix 5.3
Socioeconomic Isolation of Higher-Income
Elementary School Students

State	Low-Income Percentage	Hyper-Segregation: % of Non-FRL Students at Schools with < 10% FRL	Exposure Index: Non-FRL % of School Attended by the Average Non-FRL Student
Connecticut	34%	55%	83
Massachusetts	31%	50%	82
New Jersey	32%	47%	81
New Hampshire	19%	40%	83
Illinois	48%	34%	74
Arizona	47%	33%	72
New York	49%	32%	73
Texas	51%	28%	67
Colorado	40%	28%	73
Rhode Island	41%	27%	75
Maryland	40%	24%	72
Virginia	36%	24%	72
South Dakota	35%	24%	75
Pennsylvania	38%	23%	73
California	58%	22%	64
Michigan	41%	19%	71
Kansas	45%	18%	67
Wisconsin	36%	18%	74
Washington	43%	16%	68
Nebraska	42%	16%	69
Delaware	41%	15%	66
Missouri	45%	14%	65
Minnesota	34%	14%	73
Georgia	55%	13%	60
Utah	37%	12%	72
Oregon	48%	10%	62
Indiana	44%	10%	66
Tennessee	55%	9%	58
Nevada	46%	9%	69
Maine	41%	9%	49
Iowa	37%	9%	70
Florida	53%	8%	60

(continued)

State	Low-Income Percentage	Hyper-Segregation: % of Non-FRL Students at Schools with < 10% FRL	Exposure Index: Non-FRL % of School Attended by the Average Non-FRL Student
Alabama	56%	7%	58
North Dakota	35%	7%	70
Vermont	33%	7%	71
Idaho	40%	6%	64
South Carolina	55%	5%	56
Montana	42%	5%	65
New Mexico	69%	4%	54
Kentucky	55%	4%	54
Wyoming	36%	4%	69
Oklahoma	61%	3%	53
Louisiana	69%	2%	47
Mississippi	72%	1%	45
Arkansas	61%	1%	50
West Virginia	54%	0%	51

Source: Authors' compilations from National Center for Education Statistics Common Core of Data (CCD) for the 2007–08 school year.

Appendix 5.4
High-Poverty School Enrollment by Race

State	% of White Students at High-Poverty Schools	% of Black Students at High-Poverty Schools	% of Latino Students at High-Poverty Schools	% of Asian Students at High-Poverty Schools	% of Native Americans at High-Poverty Schools
Alabama	45%	81%	65%	30%	53%
Arizona	27%	44%	66%	26%	72%
Arkansas	63%	91%	83%	64%	68%
California	31%	73%	80%	43%	64%
Colorado	18%	57%	66%	24%	49%
Connecticut	9%	64%	67%	16%	24%
Delaware	22%	44%	62%	20%	28%
Florida	38%	77%	69%	36%	53%
Georgia	44%	81%	76%	34%	51%
Idaho	22%	33%	50%	16%	59%
Illinois	19%	83%	75%	26%	40%
Indiana	25%	80%	68%	23%	38%
Iowa	19%	59%	61%	30%	47%
Kansas	30%	70%	79%	37%	55%
Kentucky	61%	74%	68%	36%	64%
Louisiana	64%	92%	82%	74%	87%
Maine	33%	66%	42%	32%	77%
Maryland	15%	60%	58%	18%	33%
Massachusetts	12%	69%	73%	33%	36%
Michigan	23%	79%	63%	19%	45%
Minnesota	12%	49%	46%	36%	57%
Mississippi	76%	93%	84%	66%	89%
Missouri	34%	71%	60%	27%	53%
Montana	25%	36%	36%	23%	75%
Nebraska	21%	68%	71%	29%	72%
Nevada	20%	47%	64%	24%	42%
New Hampshire	3%	21%	30%	4%	11%
New Jersey	7%	63%	65%	12%	46%
New Mexico	53%	65%	82%	50%	89%
New York	17%	82%	78%	62%	59%
North Dakota	10%	16%	28%	13%	63%
Oklahoma	61%	81%	82%	47%	80%
Oregon	41%	70%	75%	42%	66%
Pennsylvania	15%	74%	70%	27%	28%

(continued)

State	% of White Students at High-Poverty Schools	% of Black Students at High-Poverty Schools	% of Latino Students at High-Poverty Schools	% of Asian Students at High-Poverty Schools	% of Native Americans at High-Poverty Schools
Rhode Island	16%	78%	86%	49%	44%
South Carolina	43%	75%	61%	32%	58%
South Dakota	16%	12%	18%	17%	72%
Tennessee	54%	83%	76%	36%	56%
Texas	37%	74%	68%	31%	48%
Utah	17%	46%	59%	40%	51%
Vermont	17%	32%	26%	16%	16%
Virginia	19%	55%	37%	13%	21%
Washington	26%	56%	68%	33%	54%
West Virginia	63%	72%	52%	34%	50%
Wisconsin	12%	75%	58%	32%	45%
Wyoming	16%	33%	32%	16%	58%
NATIONAL AVERAGE	29%	75%	72%	36%	67%

Source: Authors' compilations from National Center for Education Statistics Common Core of Data (CCD) for the 2007–08 school year.

6

Can NCLB Choice Work?

Modeling the Effects of Interdistrict Choice on Student Access to Higher-Performing Schools

MEREDITH P. RICHARDS, KORI J. STROUB, and JENNIFER JELLISON HOLME

The Policy Context

Under current No Child Left Behind (NCLB) legislation, a Title I school is deemed "in need of improvement" if it fails to make Adequate Yearly Progress (AYP) for at least two consecutive years. Moreover, students attending schools in need of improvement are eligible to transfer, at the cost of the district, to another public school within their home district that is not in need of improvement. Despite skyrocketing numbers of schools identified as in need of improvement, the number of students taking advantage of choice under NCLB has been extremely low.[1] As Figure 6.1 reveals, between 2003 and 2005, fewer than 2 percent of the students eligible to transfer to other schools in their district actually took advantage of this option. Moreover, while the number of students enrolled in schools labeled in need of improvement increased by approximately 300 percent between

FIGURE 6.1. Number of Students Eligible to Participate in NCLB Choice and Percent Participating, 2003–05

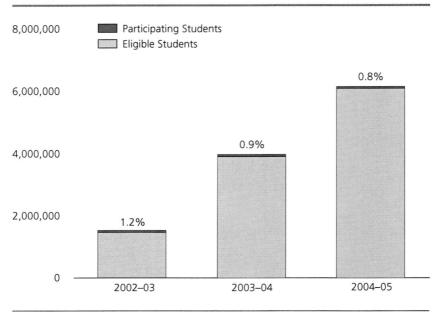

Source: State and Local Implementation of the No Child Left Behind Act, Volume IV—Title I School Choice and Supplemental Educational Services: Interim Report (Santa Monica, Calif.: RAND Corporation, 2008), http://www.rand.org/pubs/reprints/RP1332/.

2003 and 2005 (from 1.5 million to 6.1 million), actual rates of participation in NCLB choice declined over this period.

What makes these participation rates even more troublesome is the fact that, despite NCLB's emphasis on reducing the achievement gap and targeting students in high-poverty and high-minority schools, participation rates for racial and ethnic minorities lag behind those for white students. In 2005, 1.1 percent of eligible white students took advantage of the NCLB choice option, while only 0.9 percent of African Americans and 0.4 percent of Hispanics chose to transfer to a higher-performing school.[2]

While some have argued that low participation rates are a result of parental preferences for neighborhood schools,[3] others suggest that the NCLB school choice program has failed because it does not provide high-quality options to most students in failing schools. By limiting the options of students in failing schools to allow them to choose among

FIGURE 6.2. Percent of Schools in Need of Improvement

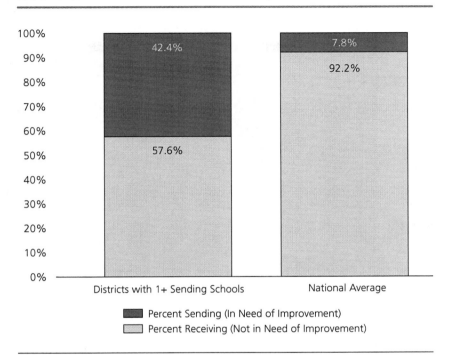

Source: National AYP and Identification (NAYPI) database, 2004-05, http://www.air.org/focus-area/education/index.cfm?fa=viewContent&content_id=860.

only the other schools in their districts, NCLB choice suffers from a fundamental problem of inadequate supply of schools eligible to receive transfer students (that is, schools not in need of improvement, known as "receiving schools").[4]

Supporting this argument of inadequate supply, schools eligible to send transfer students under NCLB choice (that is, schools in need of improvement, known as "sending schools") are often situated in districts that have few, if any, eligible receiving schools, resulting in few to no intra-district choice options available to eligible students. Figure 6.2 demonstrates that districts with at least one eligible sending school have higher proportions of schools in need of improvement than the national average. In 2005, the most recent year for which national data are available, 42.4 percent of campuses in districts with at least one eligible sending school

FIGURE 6.3. Average Quality of Receiving Schools

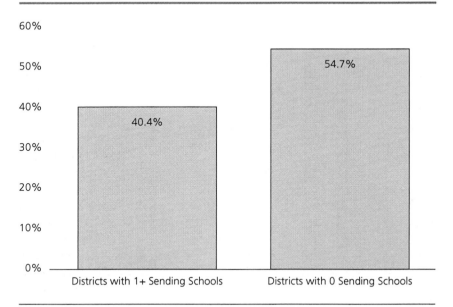

Source: National AYP and Identification (NAYPI) database, 2004-05, http://www.air.org/focus-area/education/index.cfm?fa=viewContent&content_id=860; National Longitudinal School-Level State Assessment Score Database (NLSLSASD), 2004-05, http://www.schooldata.org/.

are also in need of improvement. This stands in stark contrast to the national average for districts; on average, only 7.8 percent of campuses are deemed in need of improvement.

Exacerbating the scarcity of supply of eligible receiving schools in districts that have schools in need of improvement is the fact that those receiving schools that are available tend to perform only marginally better, at least in terms of test scores, than the schools from which students might transfer.[5] When compared to districts without schools in need of improvement, the receiving schools in districts with schools in need of improvement are substantially lower quality in terms of the proportions of students passing NCLB assessments in both math and English (see Figure 6.3). Specifically, receiving schools in districts with one or more eligible sending schools have a combined math/English pass rate nearly 15 percentage points lower than receiving schools in districts with no eligible sending schools.

Expanding Options through Interdistrict Choice

Citing the de facto limitation on intradistrict NCLB choice imposed by the limited supply of high-quality receiving schools in the districts of schools labeled as in need of improvement, a number of reformers have proposed redesigning rather than abolishing the policy, so that students could transfer to schools *outside* their home district.[6] Such an interdistrict NCLB choice policy could theoretically provide students trapped in failing schools and districts with greater access to higher-performing schools by allowing them to cross district boundaries. Available data show that, compared to the average non-failing school, schools in need of improvement are far more likely to be located in districts with large clusters of relatively low-performing schools. Consequently, allowing students to attend schools in other districts in their metropolitan area would, on average, allow them to access schools of substantially higher quality. Indeed, as Figure 6.3 reveals, the combined math/English pass rate of receiving schools under conditions of interdistrict choice would be 20 percentage points higher than under conditions of intradistrict choice.

Consistent with this emphasis on interdistrict choice, the Obama administration's blueprint for reform would seek to expand meaningful NCLB choice through the dissemination of competitive grants that give priority to districts or consortia of districts that enact interdistrict choice policies. Under existing NCLB choice regulations, districts with numerous failing schools and few viable choice options are encouraged to enter into cooperative agreements with surrounding districts "to the extent practicable."[7] However, these arrangements are voluntary and are rare in practice.[8] The blueprint would increase the federal commitment to interdistrict choice by offering monetary incentives for districts to enter into cooperative interdistrict arrangements.[9] At the same time, the Obama proposal dilutes the current law's intradistrict choice provisions by eliminating the requirement that districts offer any choice to students in schools identified as in need of improvement.

The Obama administration's proposal constitutes one of the many possible formulations a federal interdistrict choice policy might take. An interdistrict choice policy may be mandatory, like the current NCLB intradistrict choice policy, or it may be voluntary, with participation encouraged via the provision of financial incentives for participating districts. It may be universal, whereby all eligible students are equally eligible to transfer, or it may be targeted at certain disadvantaged subgroups, such as low-performing students, or non-white or low-income student populations. Likewise, choice may be equally available to students in all eligible sending schools or it may be targeted at students in the lowest-performing schools. In addition, interdistrict arrangements may vary in scale, ranging from cooperative agreements between two or more districts to a more regional solution incorporating all districts in a metropolitan area.

Can NCLB Interdistrict Choice Succeed?

Despite the burgeoning federal emphasis on interdistrict choice, there has been surprisingly little research evaluating whether an NCLB interdistrict choice program holds the potential to meaningfully expand choice beyond existing NCLB intradistrict choice provisions. Two recent reports by Education Sector policy analyst Erin Dillon have attempted to model the effects of NCLB interdistrict choice.[10] Using an innovative geographic information system-based (GIS) approach that counted the number of higher-performing schools within a fixed drive distance, Dillon evaluated the extent to which students could potentially benefit from interdistrict choice. On the basis of this analysis, Dillon concluded that "permitting students to move further, beyond school system boundaries, is unlikely to increase most students' educational opportunities significantly," owing largely to prohibitive increases in travel time to higher-performing schools and capacity limitation of eligible receiving schools.[11] In a subsequent study examining the potential effects of targeting choice to lowest-performing schools and students, however, Dillon concluded that tailored interdistrict choice programs may yield "more robust results" than would more generic programs.[12]

The validity of both reports' conclusions, however, is undermined by the problematic method of modeling interdistrict choice.[13] Specifically, the method of quantifying choice is premised on a number of arbitrary assumptions regarding student eligibility for choice, school capacity, and the time students are willing to travel to attend a higher-performing school.[14] First, the reports define students eligible to transfer as "students in the bottom 40 percent of schools," as measured by Reading and Math Proficiency (RAMP) scores. This lacks validity as a measure of student eligibility for NCLB choice, as it is inconsistent with the NCLB eligibility criterion of failing to make AYP for two or more consecutive years. Additionally, the reports impose a 10 percent cap on capacity beyond current enrollment for all receiving schools, despite a lack of empirical evidence regarding actual school capacity. Likewise, the reports limit travel time to twenty minutes, based on the average commute time reported in a 2001 travel survey. Anecdotal evidence from existing choice programs (for example, Boston's Metco program), however, suggests that this figure may dramatically underestimate the time students are willing to travel to a higher-performing school.[15]

Moreover, instead of focusing on schools in metropolitan areas—which have higher levels of school density, where proponents believe interdistrict choice would be most effective, and where more than 90 percent of all students reside[16]—Dillon's analysis examined schools in remote and rural areas. Evidence on eligibility rates for NCLB choice has demonstrated that students in schools in more sparsely populated areas are generally less likely to be eligible to participate in NCLB choice than students in suburban and, in particular, urban areas. Indeed, in 2005, Title I schools in rural areas were half as likely to be required to offer NCLB choice as suburban schools, and a third as likely as schools in urban areas.[17] Dillon's inclusion of rural schools may have downwardly biased her findings about the potential for interdistrict choice to increase options for students in low-performing schools, because of the prohibitive driving time within rural areas.[18] While Dillon's follow-up analysis[19] does focus on a single urban metropolitan area (Chicago), it relies on similar problematic assumptions regarding eligibility for NCLB choice.[20]

Taken together, both reports fail to examine the effects of NCLB systematically across different types of metropolitan areas with different geopolitical configurations.[21]As a result, they provide policymakers with little useful information about the impact of expanding choice in those areas where policymakers believe it most necessary: densely populated metropolitan areas.

Modeling the Effects of NCLB Interdistrict Choice

This chapter presents a study that examines the potential for an NCLB interdistrict choice policy to expand student access to higher-performing schools beyond the existing intradistrict choice policy using a modeling technique adapted from the human geography literature. This study corrects for a number of the limitations of the reports outlined above, by examining NCLB interdistrict choice in a national context and attending to the metropolitan contexts in which it is most likely to be effective. Toward this end, the study addresses the following primary research question:

Would an NCLB interdistrict choice policy increase student access to
higher-performing schools beyond NCLB intradistrict choice?

It should be noted that the proposed policy being tested in this study assumes an NCLB interdistrict choice policy that is parallel in structure to the current NCLB intradistrict choice policy, with transfer eligibility based on whether a school failed to make AYP for two or more years. Specifically, the policy being tested is mandatory inasmuch as it assumes that students would have the automatic right to transfer from low-performing schools to higher-performing schools in nearby districts. It is universal, in that all students at all schools in need of improvement are equally eligible to transfer. And it is large-scale, in that it assumes that students in schools in need of improvement would be permitted to transfer to any eligible receiving school in their metropolitan area.

It is also important to note that the purpose of the study is to assess the potential availability of higher-performing options to students under interdistrict choice, not to determine whether students will actually take advantage of these options. It is acknowledged that systematic differences in parental and student school preferences, and capital to realize these preferences, will ultimately influence actual choice behaviors. However, access to higher-performing schools is a necessary precondition to allow parents to exercise their choice preferences.

Contextual Effects

In addition to determining the overall change in accessibility to higher-performing schools that students would experience under interdistrict choice, the study also seeks to identify those school and metropolitan contexts under which such a policy would be more or less effective. At the school level, this study evaluates the extent to which an interdistrict choice policy would specifically benefit students in high-poverty and high-minority schools. Given the federal emphasis on improving the performance of students in high-poverty, high-minority schools and on prioritizing choice programs that promote diversity, these populations are of particular concern. As such, the current study addresses the following research question:

Would the effect of an NCLB interdistrict choice policy depend on a
school's proportion of low-income and non-white students?

At the metropolitan level, this study examines the role of the prolifera-tion of school districts in a metropolitan area,[22] known as metropolitan fragmentation, in expanding and limiting the choices available to stu-dents under NCLB. Metropolitan statistical areas (MSA) vary signifi-cantly in terms of the number and size of their school districts, with met-ropolitan areas with larger numbers of districts having higher levels of fragmentation than metropolitan areas with smaller numbers of districts, holding the total number of students constant. Map 6.1 illustrates the difference between the highly fragmented Milwaukee metropolitan area, where 239,912 students are distributed across 68 school districts, and the less fragmented Jacksonville metropolitan area, which accommodates a similar-sized student population of 206,414 in only 7 districts.[23]

Fragmentation may be calculated as the probability that two students in the same MSA will attend schools in different districts, controlling for the metropolitan population.[24] Fragmentation values range from 0 to 1, where 0 indicates that all students in an MSA attend the same district (that is, zero fragmentation) and 1 indicates that all students in an MSA attend different districts (that is, perfect fragmentation). For example, using this formula, the fragmentation value for Milwaukee is 0.83, while the value for Jacksonville is 0.55. This means that two students in Mil-waukee have an 83 percent chance of attending different districts, while students in Jacksonville have a 53 percent chance of attending different districts. The formula for fragmentation is presented in Appendix 6.1.[25]

Because metropolitan fragmentation is related to the probability that students will reside in the same district, on average, highly fragmented MSAs tend to have fewer students per district than less fragmented MSAs (for example, Milwaukee has 3,528 students per district, while Jacksonville has 29,488 students per district). Thus, holding school size constant, highly fragmented MSAs will have fewer schools per district than less fragmented MSAs. For example, Milwaukee has an average of 77 schools per district, while Jacksonville has 104 schools per district. District boundaries thus impose a limit on the supply of available receiv-ing schools, whereby highly fragmented MSAs may have fewer viable transfer options under intradistrict choice. As such, highly fragmented metropolitan areas may be expected to experience the greatest gains in choice under an NCLB interdistrict school choice policy.

The phenomenon of metropolitan fragmentation is especially salient given that, after nearly a century of school district consolidation result-ing in dramatic declines in the number of school districts in the United

MAP 6.1. Metropolitan School District Fragmentation

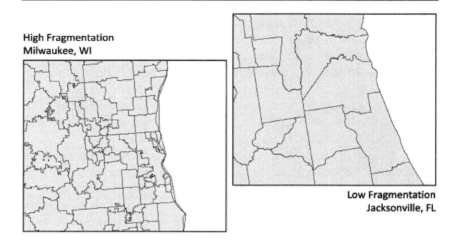

High Fragmentation
Milwaukee, WI

Low Fragmentation
Jacksonville, FL

States, the past three decades have witnessed substantial increases in the total number of school districts and associated measures of metropolitan fragmentation.[26] This growth in metropolitan fragmentation highlights the potential for educational policies that transcend district boundaries and underscores the importance of understanding how fragmentation would influence the effectiveness of an NCLB interdistrict choice policy. Toward these ends, this study addresses the following research queston:

Would the effect of an NCLB interdistrict choice policy depend on a metropolitan area's level of school district fragmentation?

Accessibility Model

Student access to higher-performing schools was calculated using a gravity model of accessibility, of the type used in the study of human geography. Gravity models have been consistently shown to accurately predict travel behavior[27] and have been used extensively in the urban planning, transportation, and public health literatures to model accessibility of resources such as grocery stores, bus stops, and health clinics.[28]

In a traditional gravity model, accessibility of a set of destinations to a given origin is computed as a function of the travel time between the origin and each destination as well as the attractiveness of each destination.

Specifically, the attractiveness of each destination is discounted by the time required to reach that destination, such that as the travel time between an origin and destination increases, accessibility decreases, holding constant the level of attractiveness between the origin-destination pair. Similarly, as the attractiveness of a destination increases, accessibility increases, holding constant the travel time between the origin and destination. The formula for a simple gravity model of accessibility is presented in Appendix 6.2.

Accessibility models have not yet been applied to the realm of education; however, school choice presents an ideal opportunity to leverage such an approach. Dillon identified[29] three factors that influence the choices available to students: (1) the quality of schools to which students might transfer, (2) the drive time to higher-performing schools, and (3) the capacity of receiving schools to accommodate transfer students. The first two of these factors generally correspond with the components of the traditional accessibility model: school quality is a measure of the attractiveness of receiving schools, while student travel time to school serves as a constraint to students' ability to access higher-performing receiving schools.

Although traditional gravity models do not contain a capacity constraint on accessibility comparable to that identified by Dillon, this constraint is critical in the school choice context, as schools do not have an infinite capacity to accept new students. As such, the traditional model was modified for the school context, constraining accessibility by the capacity of receiving schools to accommodate transfer students. Thus, as the capacity of a receiving school increases, accessibility increases, holding constant the quality of the receiving school and the travel time between the sending-receiving pair. The formula for the modified gravity model of accessibility used in this analysis is presented in Appendix 6.2.

It should be noted that, because it is a composite of attractiveness and drive time, the gravity-based accessibility index is not as readily interpretable in an absolute sense as more simplistic accessibility measures, such as those produced by "cumulative opportunities" models. Such models, like those used by Dillon,[30] essentially count the number of destinations available to each point of origin, resulting in metrics that are easily interpretable. However, such measures weigh all opportunities equally, providing a rather crude conceptualization of accessibility. For example, under a cumulative opportunities model, a school located in a district with five eligible receiving schools, each with a combined math/English pass rate of below 50 percent, would have the same accessibility score as a school located in a district with five eligible receiving schools, each with a combined math/English pass rate of above 80 percent. Likewise, a school in a district with five eligible receiving schools, all of which are more than ten miles away, would have the same accessibility score as a school in a district with five eligible receiving schools within a three-mile radius. A gravity-based accessibility model, however, would take into account both the quality and distance to each receiving school, and weigh their accessibility accordingly.

The theoretical shortcomings of the cumulative opportunities approach are evident in its lack of predictive power. A cumulative opportunities model, for example, would fail to provide insight into the disparity between rates of eligibility and rates of participation in NCLB intradistrict choice, presented in Figure 6.1. A gravity-based accessibility model, however, which takes into account factors related to individual preferences, would predict that participation would be low on the basis of the low quality of eligible receiving schools in the districts with schools in need of improvement (see Figure 6.3).

Model Components

Relative School Quality. Because the attractiveness of a receiving school to students at a sending school is a function of the quality of both schools, the quality component of the accessibility model was computed in terms of the quality of each receiving school relative to the quality of each sending school. Specifically, the quality, q, of each sending and receiving school was operationalized as the probability of a student at that school passing both the math and English assessments used by the state for calculating AYP.[31] These measures of quality were then compared for each sending-receiving pair to determine how much more likely a student at each receiving school was to pass both math and English than at the sending school. This approach allows for a direct comparison of the relative attractiveness of a set of eligible receiving schools to a given sending school.

For example, if a sending school has a math pass rate of 50 percent and an English pass rate of 50 percent, the probability of a student at that school passing both math and English assessments is 0.25. If an eligible receiving school has a math pass rate of 75 percent and an English pass rate of 95 percent, the probability of a student at that school passing both math and English is 0.71. Thus, the relative quality of the sending-receiving pair is 0.71–0.25, or 0.46, meaning that 46 percent more students at the receiving school passed both math and English than students at the sending school. If a second eligible receiving school has an overall quality of 0.50, the relative quality of that receiving school to the sending school above is 0.50–0.25, or 0.25. While students at both eligible receiving schools outperform students at the sending school, the first receiving school has a higher relative quality than the second receiving school (0.46 versus 0.25) and can be considered, all else being equal, nearly twice as attractive to eligible transfer students.

Receiving School Capacity. Because schools do not have an infinite capacity to accept new students, accessibility must be constrained by the receiving school's capacity, c. Unfortunately, there is no existing standard for measuring or reporting school capacity. Limited data on physical capacity are available; however, physical capacity may not reflect the actual capacity of a school to take on additional students. While not a traditional measure of capacity, student-teacher ratios (STRs) provide insight into a school's capacity to accommodate more students. Based on the assumption that the 75th percentile of the distribution of student-teacher ratios in the state in which the school is located reflects a reasonable STR (where schools in the 1st percentile have the lowest STRs and schools in the 99th percentile have the highest STRs), the STR of each receiving school was compared to this figure to determine the total residual capacity of all eligible receiving schools.[32] For example, if an eligible receiving school has an STR of 15.6, and the state's 75th percentile of STRs for schools of that level is 18.1, the receiving school has 16.0 percent residual capacity to accommodate transfers. Conversely, if an eligible receiving school has an STR of 18.2 or higher, it is assumed to have zero residual capacity to accommodate transfers.

Since receiving schools must share their residual capacity among multiple competing eligible sending schools, the residual capacity of each receiving school will be constrained by the number of eligible sending schools, weighted by the number of students in each sending school. Accounting for school population ensures that the model does not overestimate the accessibility of relatively small sending schools or underestimate the accessibility of relatively large sending schools. For example, suppose the receiving school above, with an STR of 15.6 and residual capacity of 16.0 percent, is located in a district with three sending schools in need of improvement, with 200, 100, and 150 students. The residual capacity of the receiving school (16.0 percent) is proportionally divided among these three sending schools, such that the sending school with 200 students will be allowed to fill 44.4 percent of the receiving school's residual capacity (that is, 7.1 percent), while the sending schools with 100 students and 150 students will be allowed to fill 22.2 percent and 33.3 percent of the receiving school's residual capacity (that is, 3.6 percent and 5.33 percent), respectively.

It should be noted that, because interdistrict choice may increase the competition for slots in receiving schools, it is theoretically possible that some schools could have lower accessibility to higher-performing schools under interdistrict choice than under intradistrict choice. For example, if sending school A is located in a district with no other eligible sending schools and one eligible receiving school with a capacity of 10 percent, all the residual capacity of that school is available to students in that sending school under intradistrict choice. If an adjacent district contains another sending school B of equal size, but no eligible receiving schools, the residual capacity allotted to each sending school under an interdistrict choice policy would be 5 percent. As such, sending school A's accessibility to a higher-performing receiving school would be higher under intradistrict choice than interdistrict choice (although, in this case, the accessibility of school B would increase).

Our model also assumes that students in schools inside and outside a given receiving school's district will have an equal opportunity to transfer to that receiving school under an interdistrict choice policy. This may or may not reflect the actual implementation of an NCLB interdistrict choice policy, which might prioritize intradistrict transfers over interdistrict transfers. On the whole, however, because so few eligible receiving schools are located in districts with schools in need of improvement, it is unlikely that available receiving slots would be filled by intradistrict transfers.

While relying on STR as a proxy for school capacity is yet to be validated, it has one important advantage over Dillon's fixed measure of capacity (10 percent across all schools). The assumption that all eligible receiving schools have identical capacity to accept transfer students is problematic in that it fails to account for variation in capacity and how capacity may vary systematically across contexts. The measure of capacity used in the current study, while imperfect, provides a relative measure of capacity that is sensitive to differences across schools, as compared to a national standard.

Travel Time between Sending and Receiving Schools. Drive times were calculated between all eligible sending and receiving schools in each MSA using Freeway 2009 spatial analysis software. All travel times were estimated under "normal" traffic conditions.

School quality and capacity were discounted by the travel time in hours, d, from sending school i to receiving school j to compute the accessibility between each sending-receiving pair. Thus, as the travel time between a sending school and an eligible receiving school gets larger, the accessibility of the receiving school decreases, regardless of its relative quality.

The functional form of the gravity model (which discounts accessibility by the square of the drive time between each sending-receiving pair) results in accessibility values that are highly sensitive to changes in drive time, and thus highly conservative. This sensitivity ensures that, for any given sending-receiving pair, if drive time is very high, the accessibility to that receiving school will be very low (even if that receiving school is highly attractive in terms of its relative quality). Consequently, a distant receiving school will contribute very little to a sending school's cumulative accessibility score.

This sensitivity constitutes one of the advantages of an accessibility-type model as it does not require an upper bound on drive time because it already penalizes receiving schools that are temporally distant from a sending school. Moreover, it does not require any a priori assumptions about the travel time preferences of parents. Thus, all eligible sending-receiving pairs were included in accessibility calculations, regardless of the distance between the schools, as long as a potential receiving school was located within the same MSA as an eligible sending school. The only exceptions to this rule were areas where receiving schools were inaccessible to sending schools via car (for example, Hawaii).

To illustrate how drive time influences the accessibility of receiving schools, suppose an eligible sending school with a combined pass rate of 20 percent is five minutes away from an eligible receiving school with a combined pass rate of 25 percent. Holding capacity constant, the receiving school has an accessibility value of 0.002. For a receiving school that is ten minutes away from the sending school to have an equivalent level of accessibility, it must have a combined pass rate of 40 percent.

Identifying Eligible Sending and Receiving Schools

To identify all schools eligible to send or receive transfer students under NCLB choice, a number of exclusion and categorization criteria were applied to data on the full population of U.S. schools for the 2004–05 school year, the most recent year for which all required data were available. At the state level, schools in the District of Columbia and Hawaii were excluded from analysis because they have only one school district; as such, an interdistrict choice policy would be logistically unfeasible in these states. At the metropolitan level, schools located in metropolitan and micropolitan areas, as defined by the U.S. Census, were included (hereafter collectively as "metropolitan areas"). At the school level, because alternative and magnet schools operate under different standards for student admissions and are not required, under current NCLB policy, to accept transfer students (thought they may accept students voluntarily), such schools were excluded from the analysis.[33] Because they are subject to NCLB intradistrict charter provisions, charter schools were retained in the analysis.

The remaining schools were categorized as either sending or receiving, depending on their AYP status.[34] Title I schools that failed to make AYP for two or more consecutive years and were, therefore, classified as in need of improvement, were categorized as eligible sending schools. Consistent with NCLB regulations, schools that either made AYP or had failed to make AYP for only one year were categorized as eligible receiving schools.

Study Sample. After applying these exclusion and categorization criteria, 6,085 (9.9 percent) schools were classified as eligible sending schools and 55,477 (90.1 percent) schools were classified as eligible receiving schools. Combined, these schools represent 60.3 percent of all U.S. public schools, and serve 65.0 percent of the nation's students in 45 states. As noted previously, schools in Hawaii and Washington, D.C., were excluded from analysis because an intradistrict choice policy would not be feasible in those contexts. In addition, schools in New Jersey, Tennessee, North Dakota, and Utah were ultimately excluded from analysis owing to lack of data to compute accessibility. Schools in the sample were located in 272 metropolitan areas and 182 micropolitan areas. The average level of fragmentation for metropolitan areas was 0.84, meaning that two students in the average metropolitan area have an 84 percent chance of attending different schools, while the average level of fragmentation for micropolitan areas was 0.61.

Examination of the demographic characteristics of the sending and receiving samples revealed systematic differences in student populations consistent with the robust associations between student characteristics and achievement. On average, 70.8 percent of the student population at eligible sending schools was eligible for free- or reduced-price lunch (FRL), nearly twice the proportion in eligible receiving schools (38.5 percent). Likewise, while 75.4 percent of the population at eligible sending schools was classified as non-white, only 34.7 percent of students at eligible receiving schools were non-white.

Computation of Accessibility Indices

To determine how much NCLB interdistrict choice would increase access to higher-performing schools beyond the current intradistrict choice policy, two accessibility values were computed for each eligible sending school: (1) intradistrict accessibility, weighing the quality, capacity, and drive time of all eligible receiving schools in the sending school's district; and (2) interdistrict accessibility, weighing the quality, capacity, and drive time of all eligible receiving schools in the sending school's MSA, but not in the sending school's district. Appendix 6.3 provides a detailed example of how intra- and interdistrict accessibility indices were calculated and compared.

Findings

Would an NCLB interdistrict choice policy increase student access to higher-performing schools beyond NCLB intradistrict choice?

To assess the overall effects of an NCLB interdistrict choice policy as well as the effects of school and metropolitan contextual factors on the change in accessibility under interdistrict choice, a hierarchical longitudinal model was used to predict the increase in accessibility under interdistrict choice as a function of school percent FRL and non-white and metropolitan fragmentation. Because our sample contained larger metropolitan areas as well as smaller micropolitan areas, we also added a categorical variable reflecting whether an area was metropolitan or micropolitan to evaluate whether the predicted change in accessibility under interdistrict choice varied by the type of urban area. However, since type of urban area was not related to changes in accessibility, this variable was dropped in the final analysis.

The results of the model are depicted in Table 6.1. Each of the results will be discussed and interpreted in light of the study's research questions at length below.

TABLE 6.1. Effects of School and Metropolitan Characteristics on the Change in Accessibility to Higher-Performing Schools Under Intra- and Interdistrict Choice

	Coefficient	SE
Intercept	3.97*	1.55
Level 1		
Choice (Inter vs. Intra)	13.99*	1.40
Level 2		
% FRL	0.04	0.05
% Non-white	0.09*	0.05
Choice X % FRL	0.21*	0.06
Choice X % Non-white	0.14*	0.06
Level 3		
Fragmentation	−0.24*	0.08
Choice X Fragmentation	0.36*	0.08

*$p < 0.05$

Contrary to the findings of previous research, the current study finds that an NCLB interdistrict choice policy, if implemented nationally, has the potential to meaningfully expand access to higher-performing schools for students in over 80 percent of eligible sending schools. Under the current intradistrict policy, the model estimates that an average sending school (that is, average proportion of non-white and free- and reduced-price lunch-eligible students in a metropolitan area of average fragmentation) has an accessibility value of 3.97. If, however, NCLB choice was expanded to include interdistrict options, the average sending school's accessibility value would increase fivefold, to 17.96.

Consistent with the argument that low participation in current NCLB intradistrict choice may be attributed to a paucity of eligible receiving schools, analysis revealed that an overwhelming 94.5 percent of eligible sending schools have no meaningful access to higher-performing schools under intradistrict choice (5,749 of 6,085). As such, the vast majority of eligible sending schools are currently located in districts that either: (1) have no eligible receiving schools under NCLB's criteria, (2) have no eligible receiving schools that performed better than the sending schools, and/or (3) have eligible receiving schools with no capacity to accommodate transfers (see Table 6.2).

Specifically, of the sending schools with no intradistrict accessibility, 1,651 (28.7 percent) are located in districts with no eligible receiving

TABLE 6.2. Intradistrict Accessibility Breakdown

	n
No Intradistrict Accessibility	**5,749**
No Eligible Receiving Schools	1,651
Some Eligible Receiving Schools	4,098
No Higher-Performing Receiving Schools	*3,629*
No Capacity at Receiving Schools	*100*
No Higher-Performing Schools or Schools with Capacity	*369*
Some Intradistrict Accessibility	**336**
Total	**6,085**

schools under NCLB's definition. Thus, nearly a third of eligible sending schools are located in districts in which all other schools have failed to make AYP for at least two consecutive years. The remaining 4,098 (71.3 percent) are located in districts that have eligible receiving schools under NCLB, but these schools are of a lower quality than the sending school and/or lack the capacity to accept transfer students.

With regard to quality, 3,629 (63.1 percent of 5,749) schools have no eligible receiving schools that performed better than the school from which students might transfer (in terms of the likelihood of a student passing both math and reading). With regard to capacity, 100 schools (1.7 percent of 5,749) have no eligible receiving schools that have capacity to accept transfers (based on the 75th percentile of state STRs). Three hundred and sixty-nine schools lack any eligible sending schools of higher quality than the school from which they might transfer or with any capacity to accept transfers. This finding suggests that the problem of access to higher-performing schools under existing NCLB policy is primarily attributable to a lack of higher-quality receiving options.

Of these schools that have no access to higher-performing schools under intradistrict choice, 84.8 percent would experience gains under an interdistrict choice policy (4,874 of 5,749), while 15.2 percent would not benefit from the ability to transfer across district boundaries (876 of 5,749).

For the remaining 5.5 percent of schools that already have some access to higher-performing schools under NCLB intradistrict choice, the effects of an interdistrict choice policy would be somewhat more equivocal. Of the 336 schools with non-zero intradistrict accessibility, 50 would experience increases in access under interdistrict choice (14.9 percent), while 18 would experience no change in access (5.4 percent), and 268 schools would actually experience decreases owing to increased competition for receiving slots for nearby higher-quality schools (79.8 percent). However, it must be emphasized that the overall proportion of schools that would experience reductions in access to higher-performing choice is extremely low—comprising only 4.4 percent of all eligible sending schools; the vast majority of schools would experience increases in access to higher-performing schools in nearby districts.

These increases in access to higher-performing schools may be attributed to the greater supply and higher quality of eligible receiving schools outside sending schools' districts, even after accounting for increases in travel time required to reach these schools and competition among students for slots in eligible receiving schools. Specifically, interdistrict choice would dramatically increase the pool of eligible receiving schools available to students in schools in need of improvement. On average, the number of eligible receiving schools available to each sending school would increase from 11 under intradistrict choice to 117 under interdistrict choice. It should be reiterated, however, that this is the number of schools technically eligible to receive under NCLB requirements—as discussed previously, these schools may have lower quality than the sending schools from which students might transfer or may not have any capacity to accept transfer students. Moreover, even after controlling for competition effects of other sending schools, the number of receiving slots available to students from each sending school would increase under interdistrict choice. Sending schools have an average of 117 slots available to their students under intradistrict choice, but 267 slots under interdistrict choice, an increase of 128 percent.

Even more importantly, sending schools would have access to substantially higher-quality schools if they were permitted to cross district boundaries. Under intradistrict choice, sending schools would have access to receiving schools with an average quality of 33 percent (that is, 33 percent of students pass both reading and math assessments required for AYP). Under interdistrict choice, however, sending schools would have access to receiving schools with an average quality of 43 percent, reflecting a 30 percent increase in the overall quality of receiving schools.

State Effects

Because responsibility for most educational policy decisions rests with states, it is important to identify how an interdistrict choice policy would play out in the state context. Appendix 6.4 enumerates state-level

MAP 6.2. Projected Change in Accessibility (Inter- vs. Intra-) by State

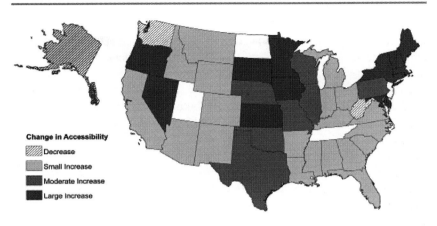

accessibility values under conditions of intra- and interdistrict choice, as well as the characteristics of schools in the sample of sending schools.

Aggregate state-level measures of accessibility confirm school-level findings regarding the lack of available intradistrict transfer options. Indeed, fully fifteen states had an average of zero intradistrict accessibility, meaning that none of the state's schools in need of improvement currently have meaningful access to any higher-performing schools under current NCLB intradistrict choice policy (Connecticut, Delaware, Iowa, Kansas, Maine, Maryland, Massachusetts, Minnesota, Nevada, New Hampshire, New York, Oregon, Rhode Island, South Dakota, and Vermont).

Moreover, in all but six of the states studied, schools would, on average, experience increases in accessibility under an interdistrict choice policy. Among the six states that would not benefit, schools in three states (Alaska, West Virginia, and Washington) would experience decreases in accessibility under interdistrict choice (owing to increased competition for available receiving slots), while three others would experience no gains (Nevada, New Hampshire, and Rhode Island). It should be noted that, in the three states that would experience decreases under interdistrict choice, students in failing schools already have high rates of intradistrict accessibility, and that accessibility would still remain relatively high even after accounting for decreases from competition effects.

To evaluate the geographic distribution of the magnitude of the change in accessibility under an NCLB interdistrict choice policy, Map 6.2

244 | CAN NCLB CHOICE WORK?

depicts the expected change in accessibility by state. The map reveals that although interdistrict choice would improve access to higher-performing schools in all but three states in the analysis, the effects of such a policy would likely vary by geographic region. Schools in states in the Northeast and Midwest would exhibit relatively large increments in accessibility under an interdistrict choice policy, while metropolitan areas in the South and, to a lesser extent, the West would likely experience more marginal increases. As will be discussed at length below, this finding may be attributable to differences in rates of metropolitan fragmentation among these geographic regions.

Would the effect of an NCLB interdistrict choice policy depend on a school's proportion of low-income and non-white students?

At the school level, changes in accessibility under interdistrict choice were positively related to a sending school's percentage of FRL and non-white students. Figure 6.4 depicts the linear relationship between a school's student characteristics and the predicted change in access under interdistrict choice, controlling for the level of metropolitan fragmentation. The figure reveals that schools with higher proportions of low-income and non-white students would experience relatively larger gains in access than students in schools with lower proportions of these students. As such, students in schools with higher proportions of low-income and non-white students should experience the greatest gains in access to higher-performing schools under an NCLB interdistrict choice policy.

As the figure reveals, schools with higher proportions of FRL and non-white students have higher levels of accessibility under intradistrict choice and interdistrict choice than schools with less disadvantaged populations. Moreover, schools with higher proportions of FRL and non-white students would experience larger gains in accessibility from an interdistrict choice policy than schools with less disadvantaged populations.

For example, a school with 95 percent FRL students would experience gains in access under interdistrict choice more than twice as large as those of a school with only 45 percent FRL students. Similarly, a school with 95 percent non-white enrollment would experience gains in accessibility under interdistrict choice nearly twice as large as those of a school with only 45 percent non-white enrollment. Taken together, these findings suggest that, if implemented nationally, an NCLB interdistrict choice

FIGURE 6.4. Estimated Change in Access by School Percent Free/Reduced Priced Lunch and Non-white Students

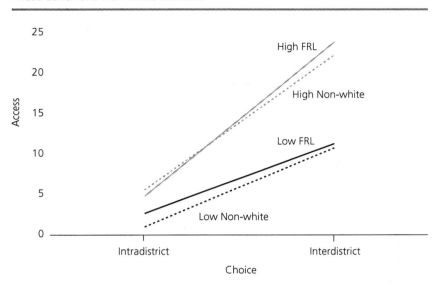

policy has the potential to specifically benefit students in high-poverty and high-minority schools.

Would the effect of an NCLB interdistrict choice policy depend on a metropolitan area's level of school district fragmentation?

Consistent with expectations, metropolitan school district fragmentation was positively related to the change in accessibility under conditions of interdistrict choice. As such, schools in highly fragmented MSAs would experience much larger gains in access to higher-performing schools than less fragmented MSAs. Figure 6.5 depicts the linear relationship between metropolitan fragmentation and accessibility under intra- and interdistrict choice, after controlling for school-level contextual effects.

Figure 6.5 reveals that, although highly fragmented metropolitan areas have *lower* access to higher-performing schools under conditions of intradistrict choice, they would have *higher* access to higher-performing schools under an NCLB interdistrict choice policy. Specifically, under an interdistrict choice policy, schools in metropolitan areas with low

FIGURE 6.5. Estimated Change in Access by Metropolitan School District Fragmentation

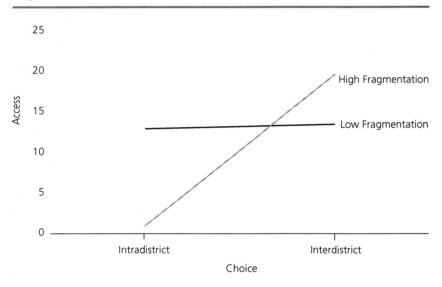

fragmentation values would experience virtually no increase in accessibility under an interdistrict choice policy, while schools in highly fragmented metropolitan areas would experience large gains in accessibility. For example, an MSA with a fragmentation value of 95 percent would experience a gain in accessibility nearly thirty times as high as that of an MSA with a fragmentation value of 45 percent.

Returning to the example discussed above, the predicted accessibility gains in the highly fragmented MSA of Milwaukee, Wisconsin, (fragmentation = 0.83) would be significantly higher than those in the less fragmented areas of Jacksonville, Florida (fragmentation = 0.55). The model estimates that Milwaukee schools, under interdistrict choice, would experience accessibility gains nearly twice as large as schools in Jacksonville.[35]

Summary of Findings

Since its inception, the NCLB school choice program has suffered from consistently low student participation rates, despite high rates of school failure to make AYP. Consistent with arguments that these low participation rates are a function of the limited supply of higher-performing schools, this study finds that students in the vast majority of eligible sending schools have little to no access to eligible higher-performing schools within their district. Moreover, owing to the supply of higher-quality eligible receiving schools in nearby districts, an NCLB interdistrict choice policy has the potential to meaningfully expand students' access to higher-performing schools beyond the existing intradistrict choice policy, even after controlling for the effect of competition among sending schools for transfer slots and increases in travel time to schools.

The potential effectiveness of an NCLB interdistrict choice policy, however, would vary depending upon the characteristics of schools and the metropolitan and regional contexts in which they are embedded. At the school level, we find that gains in accessibility under interdistrict choice would be higher for students in schools with a high proportion of FRL and non-white students. These findings are encouraging, especially in light of the current federal education policy emphasis on students in high-poverty and high-minority schools.

At the metropolitan level, an interdistrict choice policy would be more effective in highly fragmented metropolitan and micropolitan areas than in metropolitan areas with fewer school districts per capita. In addition, results suggest that the benefits of an interdistrict choice policy would be especially large for students in schools in the Northeast and Midwest—a finding that may be attributable, in part, to the higher levels of school district fragmentation in these regions.

Policy Constraints

The accessibility model employed in this study holds considerable promise for exploring geographic issues in education, especially the inherently spatial issue of school choice. It provides an empirically validated tool for assessing the opportunities available to students, which are necessary, albeit not sufficient, to ensure that students actually take advantage of choice opportunities and gain access to higher-performing schools. However, because the goal of the model is to identify the opportunities available to students and not to predict actual student behaviors, the model is relatively parsimonious, and thus neglects several important considerations that may constrain the effectiveness of the implementation of an NCLB interdistrict choice policy, namely: (1) Who will take advantage of choice? (2) Where will they choose to transfer? (3) How will they get there?

Who will take advantage of interdistrict choice?

While the present findings suggest that students in schools in need of improvement will largely benefit from increased access to high-performing schools under interdistrict choice, they do not address the critically important issue of which students will actually take advantage of these options. Prior research on participation rates by race and socioeconomic status has found that non-white and low-income students are less likely to take advantage of available interdistrict choice options.[36] Moreover, the higher-performing students in the sending schools may be more likely to take advantage of interdistrict choice than the other eligible students, leaving sending schools with even larger proportions of low-performing students.[37]

Where will they choose to transfer?

This study's model of accessibility quantified the attractiveness of schools in terms of school quality, as measured via student performance on state assessments used for AYP. While such a measure provides a valid test of NCLB policy, it may not be an accurate measure of parental preferences. Indeed, research suggests that parental preferences are relatively heterogeneous, as parents attend to a variety of factors in addition to academic quality in decisions regarding whether or where to transfer (for example, racial diversity, special programs, safety).[38] There is also some evidence that parental school choice preferences may be influenced by parents' race and socioeconomic status as well as the racial and socioeconomic composition of schools.[39]

How will they get there?

This study's model of accessibility discounted school quality by the drive time between a student's sending school and the receiving school of choice. Such a measure, however, fails to account for important differences in access to transportation by race and socioeconomic status. A growing body of research highlights the importance of transportation inequities, finding that transportation is a significant barrier to accessibility, particularly for non-white and low-income individuals, who are less likely to own personal vehicles and more likely to rely on public transportation.[40] As such, drive time estimates may systematically underestimate the actual travel time for non-white and low-income students.

This problem may be mitigated, however, if transportation is provided equitably to all eligible students.

Policy Design Recommendations

NCLB interdistrict choice policy has the potential to expand student access meaningfully to higher-performing schools beyond existing intra-district choice, especially for non-white and low-income students and students in highly fragmented metropolitan areas. However, while inter-district choice may be a necessary condition for increasing access to higher-performing schools, it is not sufficient. Coupled with the afore-mentioned evidence that non-white, low-income, and lower-performing students may be less likely to take advantage of choice and may have more limited access to transportation to higher-performing schools, poorly designed interdistrict school choice policies have the potential to exacerbate, rather than ameliorate, existing inequities by race and socio-economic status if implemented in an uncontrolled fashion. As such, a federal NCLB interdistrict choice policy should adopt a controlled, tar-geted approach designed to maximize access to higher-performing schools without exacerbating existing racial and socioeconomic inequalities.

Perhaps the most direct means of ensuring that NCLB interdistrict choice provides equitable access to higher-performing schools is to give priority to students in high-poverty and high-minority schools and/or low-income and non-white students when allocating available receiv-ing slots and transportation funds. Under current NCLB policy, districts are to give priority to low-achieving, low-income students in consider-ing transfer requests. This policy should be retained and strengthened to include students in schools with the highest concentrations of poor and minority students. Any federal interdistrict choice policy should be for-mulated to target low-income and minority students specifically to ensure that the policy helps those populations it is designed to benefit.

Transportation is another essential consideration in the design of any equitable and meaningful school choice program. Schools participating in NCLB intradistrict choice are required to provide transportation; to be successful, an NCLB interdistrict choice program must also compel districts to provide transportation for eligible transfer students. Without such a provision, additional transportation costs would have to be shoul-dered by the families of those children eligible to transfer, often those who can least afford the burden and who already face significant barriers to equitable transportation.[41]

Finally, to be successful, interdistrict choice requires the cooperation of multiple districts. The political obstacles associated with establishing and maintaining such polices can be difficult to surmount, particularly in jurisdictionally complex areas. As such, federal policy should provide meaningful incentives and support for districts interested in implementing interdistrict choice.

Conclusion

The present study finds that NCLB interdistrict choice has the potential to increase students' access to higher-performing schools meaningfully beyond intradistrict choice. Indeed, estimates suggest that, on average, students would experience a fivefold increase in access to higher-performing schools under an interdistrict choice policy, even after accounting for travel time to receiving schools and increased student competition for available transfer slots. Such a policy would be especially beneficial for the overwhelming majority of students who attend schools that currently have no meaningful access to higher-performing schools under the existing NCLB intradistrict choice policy. In addition, students in highly fragmented metropolitan areas and in northeastern and midwestern states would experience particularly large gains under an NCLB interdistrict choice policy. Even more encouraging, consistent with the federal policy goal of effectively targeting schools in high-poverty and high-minority schools, this study finds that gains in access to higher-performing schools under interdistrict choice would be particularly pronounced for non-white and low-income students.

Two important caveats should be acknowledged when drawing inferences from this study. First, it is important to note that the number of schools in need of improvement has increased substantially since the 2004-05 school year. While only 18 percent of schools failed to make AYP in 2004-05, 37 percent of schools failed to make AYP in 2009–10. Indeed, Secretary of Education Duncan recently estimated that 82 percent of schools could fail to make AYP this year.

Although it is unlikely that the current AYP criteria will be retained under the reauthorization of NCLB, these increasing rates of school failure have clearly increased the number of eligible sending schools and reduced the number of eligible receiving schools, resulting in more students eligible to transfer and fewer transfer options for students in schools in need of improvement. However, the effect of these changes on interdistrict choice vis-à-vis intradistrict choice is unclear. If schools failing to make AYP continue to be clustered in districts with other low-performing schools, it is likely that sending schools will have even fewer intradistrict choice options. This reduction in intradistrict choice may mean that an NCLB interdistrict choice policy would have an even more dramatic positive effect on student access to higher-performing schools. However, if the increase in failure rates has resulted in a more even distribution of schools in need of improvement across districts, it is possible that increases in rates of school failure would reduce interdistrict choice as much as or more than intradistrict choice, thus attenuating the potential benefits of interdistrict choice.

Second, for an interdistrict choice policy to be effective in practice, it must overcome the documented barriers to the equitable implementation of choice often faced by non-white and low-income students. As such, it is argued that such a policy must be sensitive to both the geographic contexts within which the choice programs operate and the differential effects such programs may have on families. Toward that end, any federal interdistrict choice policy should include provisions specifically targeting students in high-poverty, high-minority schools and subsidizing the transportation costs associated with interdistrict choice to ensure that the imperative for meaningful choice is balanced with a concern for equity. In addition, incentives should be provided to encourage district participation, particularly in highly fragmented metropolitan areas.

Appendix 6.1
Fragmentation Formula

Fragmentation was quantified as the probability that two students in the same metropolitan area will attend schools in different districts, controlling for the metropolitan population.[41] Specifically, metropolitan fragmentation was operationalized as:

$$F_m = \sum_{d=1}^{k} p_d (1 - p_d)$$

where p is the proportion of students in the MSA m enrolled in district d. Fragmentation values range from 0 to 1, where 0 indicates that all students in an MSA attend the same district (that is, zero fragmentation) and 1 indicates that all students in an MSA attend different districts (that is, perfect fragmentation).

Appendix 6.2
Accessibility Formulae

Traditional Gravity Model of Accessibility

In their traditional formulation, gravity models compute the accessibility of a set of destinations as a function of the travel time between the origin and each destination and the attractiveness of each destination. Gravity models have the following general functional form:

$$A_i = \sum_{j=1}^{n} \frac{a_j}{d_{ij}^2}$$

where A_i is the accessibility of the origin, a is the attractiveness of destination j, and d is the drive time from origin i to destination j. In a gravity model, the attractiveness of each destination is discounted by the time required to reach that destination.

Modified Gravity Model of Accessibility

To adapt the functional form of gravity models to the educational context, the formulation presented above was modified slightly. Since schools do not have an infinite capacity to accept new students, an additional term was included in the model constraining accessibility by the capacity of receiving schools to accommodate transfer students as follows:

$$A_i = \sum_{j=1}^{n} \frac{q_{ij} c_j}{d_{ij}^2}$$

where A_i is the accessibility of a given sending school, q is the quality of a receiving school j (which is used as a proxy for the attractiveness of the school), d is the drive time from school i to school j, and c is the capacity of school j.

Appendix 6.3
Example Accessibility Calculation

Map of Districts within MSA

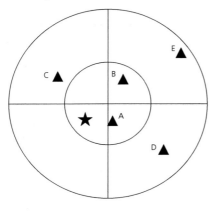

Characteristics of Eligible Receiving Schools

School	Δ Quality	Capacity	Drive Time
A[1]	1%	2%	2 mins
B[1]	3%	1.5%	3 mins.
C[1,2]	5%	1.75%	4 mins.
D[1,2]	10%	1%	5 mins.
E[1,2]	6%	2.5%	6 mins.

1. Schools eligible to receive under intradistrict choice.
2. Schools eligible to receive under interdistrict choice.

Intradistrict Accessibility	Interdistrict Accessibility
$$A_{Intra} = \sum_{j=1}^{2} \frac{q_{ij}c_j}{d_{ij}^2}$$	$$A_{Inter} = \sum_{j=1}^{5} \frac{q_{ij}c_j}{d_{ij}^2}$$
$$A_{Intra} = \frac{1(2)}{2^2} + \frac{3(1.5)}{3^2}$$	$$A_{Inter} = \frac{1(2)}{2^2} + \frac{3(1.5)}{3^2} + \frac{5(1.75)}{4^2} + \frac{10(1)}{5^2} + \frac{6(2.5)}{6^2}$$
$A_{Intra} = 2.4$	$A_{Inter} = 2.4$

Interpretation

As shown above, under conditions of intradistrict choice (2 eligible receiving schools), the sending school has an accessibility value of 1. However, under conditions of interdistrict choice (5 eligible receiving schools, with the addition of 3 eligible receiving schools outside its district), the sending school has an increment in accessibility of 1.4, resulting in a total accessibility value of 2.4. As such, this school's accessibility to higher-performing schools would be 2.4 times higher under an NCLB interdistrict choice policy than under the existing intradistrict policy.

N.B.: Because the metropolitan area above contains only one sending district, the capacity index is not adjusted for competition effects.

Appendix 6.4
State-level Accessibility Results

State	Accessibility Intra	Inter	N Schools	Districts	MSAs	% Min	% FRL	Frag
Alabama	.09	1.51	119	39	16	79.6	77.9	0.53
Alaska	30.95	23.13	20	3	2	54.8	63.0	0.28
Arizona	0.34	10.88	87	43	8	87.4	88.5	0.78
Arkansas	2.16	4.67	100	49	13	54.9	69.8	0.73
California	0.23	7.83	1,367	301	33	86.4	77.7	0.84
Colorado	0.67	11.12	92	16	5	87.1	77.8	0.66
Connecticut	0.0	14.69	104	21	5	81.9	70.9	0.92
Delaware	0.0	1.75	10	7	2	64.5	48.0	0.81
Florida	5.90	12.16	506	27	9	75.4	78.6	0.52
Georgia	1.27	1.55	162	57	24	76.4	73.4	0.49
Idaho	0.53	1.18	27	22	10	26.9	53.6	0.62
Illinois	0.01	3.46	513	162	25	76.4	70.0	0.76
Indiana	1.32	20.17	77	35	18	50.8	63.6	0.68
Iowa	0.0	14.16	10	6	5	53.0	72.0	0.72
Kansas	0.0	2.61	14	4	2	70.8	82.9	0.77
Kentucky	3.16	19.09	74	24	11	31.0	—	0.53
Louisiana	9.65	17.48	130	21	11	96.7	88.6	0.40
Maine	0.0	1.42	23	18	5	8.8	40.9	0.89
Maryland	0.0	6.32	85	6	1	95.2	80.0	0.81
Massachusetts	0.0	91.03	295	104	4	54.2	59.2	0.90
Michigan	3.73	26.75	183	35	11	88.4	80.1	0.88
Minnesota	0.0	13.23	61	15	3	82.2	80.9	0.77
Mississippi	1.03	6.69	46	26	15	86.2	82.1	0.65
Missouri	0.12	29.49	94	22	9	82.0	79.2	0.84
Montana	0.07	0.38	12	12	6	42.4	54.4	0.72
Nebraska	0.12	8.1	3	3	3	65.2	67.5	0.63
Nevada	0.0	0.0	8	2	2	—	24.4	0.01
New Hampshire	0.0	0.0	20	14	4	11.5	30.7	0.88
New Mexico	6.37	9.30	195	44	15	83.6	78.4	0.42
New York	0.0	4.87	332	74	19	77.3	24.3	0.86
North Carolina	0.08	0.23	40	15	9	34.8	59.9	0.40

(continued)

Appendix 6.4
State-level Accessibility Results (*continued*)

State	Accessibility		N			% Min	% FRL	Frag
	Intra	Inter	Schools	Districts	MSAs			
Ohio	1.38	18.58	381	110	22	64.1	68.7	0.84
Oklahoma	0.14	5.34	76	26	12	72.2	86.8	0.76
Oregon	0.0	13.25	36	15	8	45.1	67.9	0.63
Pennsylvania	0.01	68.99	218	61	17	77.3	63.7	0.82
Rhode Island	0.0	0.0	17	4	1	81.1	76.8	0.97
South Carolina	2.47	7.40	85	28	12	65.2	75.0	0.60
South Dakota	0.0	6.57	19	11	7	23.9	43.0	0.46
Texas	0.02	6.48	135	70	24	89.1	66.2	0.70
Vermont	0.0	0.06	8	7	3	7.2	40.3	0.89
Virginia	2.09	4.24	75	33	11	69.7	66.7	0.67
Washington	7.64	7.17	81	32	11	65.6	69.3	0.82
West Virginia	19.13	14.19	17	13	9	9.2	68.4	0.60
Wisconsin	0.01	14.89	29	3	2	90.6	76.4	0.88
Wyoming	0.31	11.69	3	3	3	51.4	58.4	0.45

Note: No shading indicates that state would, on average, experience increases in accessibility under NCLB interdistrict choice versus intradistrict choice; medium shading indicates no change under interdistrict choice; light shading indicates decreases under interdistrict choice. Excluded from analysis: District of Columbia, Hawaii (feasibility of policy), New Jersey, Tennessee, North Dakota, Utah (lack of data).

7

The Politics of Maintaining Balanced Schools:

An Examination of Three Districts

SHENEKA M. WILLIAMS

The Supreme Court's 2007 decision in *Parents Involved in Community Schools v. Seattle School District #1* (or *PICS*) sparked a firestorm in many school districts across the nation.[1] Given that the 5–4 Court ruling determined that race can no longer be the sole factor in assigning students to schools, several districts have developed and implemented student assignment plans that focus on variables such as socioeconomic status (SES), geography, and parental educational attainment. As school board members analyze student assignment options that best meet the needs of their respective constituents, community leaders and parents voice their opinions by supporting and electing school board members who share their sentiments. The development and implementation of student assignment plans, juxtaposed against school board elections, highlights potential tensions between policy and politics in student assignment. Such tensions are visible not only on the local stage but also at state-level politics. The present-day political press given to student assignment resembles the time before the landmark *Brown v. Board of Education* decision.[2] As a result, it is worth investigating again the politics-policy dichotomy of student assignment.

Student assignment remains as salient today as it was before and during the desegregation of the nation's schools. Research suggests that schools are resegregating along racial and social class lines;[3] therefore, twenty-first-century student assignment debates question whether or not students receive equal educational opportunities when assigned to certain schools. Evidence from the Coleman Report[4] as well as more recent studies show that deep inequality exists, negatively affecting those in schools that have more low-income non-white students.[5] Additionally, racially isolated schools tend to have more limited curricula and more exposure to crime and violence in the school's neighborhood.[6] These factors, along with myriad others, enhance the achievement and opportunity gaps that persist between high-income and low-income students and between white students and students of color.[7] This situation is particularly problematic for low-income students of color. Scholar H. Richard Milner notes that there are stark differences between and among students regarding their exposure and experiences—economic resources, qualification of teachers, rigor of the curriculum, expectations of teachers, and parental involvement.[8] Thus, it is widely known and documented that racially isolated schools fail to provide students with equal learning opportunities in terms of teacher quality and resource allocation, thereby signaling a need for integrating schools along social class lines.

Studies show that both black[9] and white children who attended desegregated schools before they graduated from high school were more likely to attend desegregated colleges, have friends from other races, work in desegregated workplaces, and live in desegregated neighborhoods.[10] Racially integrated schools and classrooms are beneficial for both African-American and white students. For instance, white students in integrated settings report that they value interracial experiences and report that their school experiences better prepared them to live and work and participate in public life in their multiracial communities.[11] In addition, studies have shown that African-American students who attend desegregated schools perform better academically in school. The negative consequences of racially isolated schools run deeply through educational outcomes, thus highlighting the importance of studying student assignment policies that might remedy racial and social class segregation.

While present-day student assignment concerns abound, the issues, however, are not merely about race, but also about socioeconomic status. Socioeconomic status, which is related to parental income and parents' social and cultural capital, determines the neighborhood in which students might live. As higher-income parents have more options in neighborhood choice, they often choose to live in neighborhoods that reflect their socio-economic status. This, in turn, leads to residential segregation that persists along social class lines as well as racial lines. Racially segregated neighbor-hoods, in most instances, lead to racially and socioeconomically segregated neighborhood schools. Sociologist Camille Z. Charles writes, "Whether voluntary or involuntary, living in racially segregated neighborhoods has serious implications for the present and future mobility opportunities of those who are excluded from desirable areas."[12] Additional research on residential patterns demonstrates that whites actually continue to move to predominately or all-white neighborhoods in order to avoid living with African Americans.[13] While clear gains have been made in residential seg-regation patterns over the years, neighborhoods across the nation continue to be highly segregated by race and socioeconomic status today.

Given that schools are funded primarily through local taxes, funding streams vary greatly from neighborhood to neighborhood, thus impact-ing resources available to students within the same district. Students who live in low-income neighborhoods, regardless of race, tend to receive an inferior education when schooling occurs closer to home. Politically, however, neighborhood schools remain popular. A more recent study by Goldring, Cohen-Vogel, Smrekar, and Taylor notes that "the return to neighborhood schools has in general been met with public enthusiasm; parents, Black and White, have expressed the desire for their children to be schooled closer to home even if it means they attend more segregated schools."[14] As school boards vote to educate students closer to home, resegregation has occurred in public schools, and low-income and minor-ity students are denied equal educational opportunities. Given these cir-cumstances, it is essential that school boards develop and implement cre-ative and politically viable student assignment policies that offer students an opportunity to succeed both academically and socially.

The student assignment debate has returned to the educational policy agenda with increased momentum; therefore, the purpose of this chapter is to examine the interaction of policy and politics in developing, imple-menting, and evaluating student assignment plans. The three districts that will be examined include Wake County Public School System, North

Carolina; Jefferson County Public Schools, Kentucky; and Champaign Unit 4 Schools, Illinois.

The Reality behind Today's Student Assignment

Recent student assignment debates reflect concerns similar to those raised in *Brown v. Board of Education*. The core issues of *Brown* were about racially balancing schools so that all students, regardless of race, might have equal educational opportunities. The justices in *Brown* declared that segregated schools would never be equal, which supposedly ended the *Plessy* era of "separate but equal."[15] It now appears that after decades of battling to provide equal educational opportunities to our nation's students, the clock stands still, and perhaps moves backward in terms of how students are assigned to schools.

There are many reasons why schools of today look almost as segregated as they did forty years ago. Some scholars argue that neither the federal government nor the courts have done enough to curtail the issues of housing segregation, which is problematic because public schools tend to mirror the neighborhoods in which students live. In 1990, residential segregation was so high that almost 70 percent of all African Americans or whites living in metropolitan areas within the United States would have to move to new neighborhoods in order to achieve integration.[16] Twenty years later, national trends show that residential segregation between whites and nonwhites has declined, offering a glimmer of hope in terms of racially mixed neighborhood schools.[17]

The continued resistance to integrated neighborhoods on the part of all races is critical to note because it goes directly to the heart of recent court decisions that have ended desegregation plans. Many civil rights activists argue that residential segregation is often created by more than simply preference and instead reflects discriminatory real estate and zoning practices. They argue that, accordingly, there is some obligation on the part of the courts to implement policies designed to reduce the level of residential segregation as well. In any case, assuming that the racial climate in the United States has changed significantly enough to believe that fully integrated neighborhoods, and by extension, integrated schools will become the norm in the near future is naïve at best.[18] Despite evidence that indicates that there has been a positive change in attitudes toward living in integrated neighborhoods, the vast majority of neighborhoods throughout the nation are not integrated, and much of the American public still would prefer to have their children attend neighborhood schools. As legal scholar Erwin Chemerinsky notes, "In a country deeply committed to the ideal of the neighborhood school, residential segregation often produces school segregation. But decades have passed since the enactment of the most recent law to deal with housing discrimination, and efforts to enhance residential integration seem to have vanished."[19] Given that the courts and legislatures have done very little to eradicate residential segregation, the onus is on local school boards and community activists to address issues of student assignment. This, in turn, depends on the political will of local communities to integrate.

The politics of school integration are complicated by the fact that the reputation of a neighborhood school often serves as the driving force for potential homebuyers. Quality neighborhood schools often predict property values. In the context of student assignment and persistent residential segregation, how then do community members coalesce to ensure quality schools for all students? This chapter examines three case studies to determine the role of politics in the development and formulation of student assignment policies.

Selecting and Analyzing the Three Case Studies

The analysis in this chapter is based on qualitative data collected in three school districts: Wake County Public School System, North Carolina; Jefferson County Public Schools, Kentucky; and Champaign Unit 4 Schools, Illinois. The districts were selected based on their potential for political conflict as they reformulated student assignment plans post-*PICS*. Districts were purposefully selected based on their rich student assignment history.

The qualitative research design includes semi-structured interviews, focus groups, and document review. A total of ten semi-structured interviews were conducted with policy elites of the Wake County community; three interviews and one focus group were conducted with district officials in Jefferson County; and six interviews were conducted with district stakeholders in Champaign. Such policy elites and district officials include former school superintendents, former school board members, members of the Chamber of Commerce, employees of nonpartisan educational organizations, and district consultants. Most interviews conducted in Wake County and Champaign Unit 4 Schools were conducted face-to-face, while all Jefferson County interviews were conducted via teleconference. During the interviews, participants described district demographics and political histories that enabled the interviewer to better understand community context in the districts. Additionally, perspectives of policy elites and district stakeholders include both recollections of policy formulation as well as longitudinal perspectives on how the policy has been implemented over time.

Qualitative data analysis focused on recognizing themes and patterns that emerged based on the study's conceptual framework and interview protocol. The analysis was organized according to two drivers: (1) questions that were generated during the conceptual and design phases of the study and (2) analytic insights and interpretations that emerged during data collection. Interview questions clustered around three major themes and were intentionally nondirective to trigger broad, comprehensive responses.[20] The core clusters include (a) political tensions during the development of student assignment plan, (b) political tensions during the implementation of student assignment plan, and (c) political tensions that led to an evaluation of student assignment in the district.

Reviews of the (Raleigh) *News and Observer,* the (Louisville) *Courier-Journal,* the (Champaign) *News-Gazette,* weblogs, and district public records serve as data sources to capture the formulation and implementation phases of student assignment policies in each district. These documents also led researchers to purposefully sample interview participants for the study. Although document review is utilized in this study, the primary source of data for the study is semi-structured interviews and focus groups conducted with local policy elites and district officials who designed and passed student assignment policies in each district.

While all three districts selected for study face student assignment challenges, district demographics and politics determine how each district responds to such challenges. The profiles of each district are presented as a means to offer possible solutions to other districts that face similar student assignment challenges in the post-*PICS* era.

Wake County Public School System, North Carolina

The Wake County Public School System is the eighteenth-largest district in the nation. With an approximate enrollment of 140,000 students for the 2009–10 school year, the district spans more than 800 square miles. Encompassing a portion of the Research Triangle area, Wake County is not only one of the largest school districts in the nation, but also one of the fastest growing.

Eleven years ago, fearing that the federal circuit court might interfere with the district's means of achieving racially balanced schools, school officials in Wake County voted to implement a student assignment plan based on socioeconomic status. Few districts had implemented such a plan at the time, thus Wake County has been a leader in its efforts to maintain socioeconomically balanced schools based on geographical "nodes"—small, demographically cohesive areas.

The node system was established during the district's racial integration plan that was implemented after the 1976 merger of Wake County Schools and Raleigh City Schools. Although the board later struck down the racial plan, it held on to the node system as a useful tool that emanated from the plan. The node, which is defined as a group of households in the same geographic area, was used as the primary tool for ensuring racial integration.[21] To date, the node is at risk of being deactivated as a means of balancing schools along social class lines.

Commitment to Diversity

The Wake County Public School System has been hailed as a district with a commitment to diverse schools. Born from a merger of two racially segregated districts—Raleigh City Schools, a majority African-American district, and Wake County Schools, a predominantly white district—Wake officials have worked zealously to maintain racially desegregated schools. One district stakeholder commented, "African American and White [leaders] were committed 100% to having balanced school across the county. Nobody said, 'That is a bad idea.'"

Once merged, district officials sought to racially balance the schools by implementing a "15/45" student assignment policy. The policy mandated that no school could fall below an African-American population of 15 percent or rise above an African-American student population of 45 percent.[22] This policy remained effective until the late 1990s, when Wake County became cognizant of the judicial rulings of the Fourth Circuit Court of Appeals and sought to preserve balance in its schools instead by socioeconomic status.

Changed Policy Option, Unchanged Policy Goal

Wake County officials began considering a move toward a class-based definition of diversity in the late 1990s, when its board reviewed research showing the strong link between family income and achievement. On January 10, 2000, the Wake County Board of Education officially altered its student assignment policy, shifting from race-based to socioeconomic and performance-based criteria. This move has been acknowledged by some scholars as a reaction to a decision by the Fourth Circuit Court of Appeals striking down race-based student assignment in nearby Charlotte.[23] A former school board member noted, "It was our observation that the Fourth Circuit, which governs the area we are in, was particularly unsympathetic to the use of race in creating and supporting diversity in schools. I was elected to the Board in 1999, and that was almost literally the first thing we did was to change that policy."

In place of the 15/45 racial balance plan, the board adopted a goal that no school should have more than 40 percent of students eligible for free or reduced-price lunch, or more than 25 percent of students achieving below grade level. Thus, this policy shift placed Wake County at the forefront of districts using socioeconomic status as a means of diversifying its student population.

The Will to Maintain or Abolish

Although the SES-based plan remained intact for ten years, it faced much scrutiny over time. While the plan was implemented to minimize travel distances, make efficient use of school facilities, and maintain stability in assignment,[24] those factors have played a major role in school board members' decisions to alter the policy. District growth, as evidenced by the number of new schools opening yearly, made it difficult to maintain balance within the district's schools and forced repeated reassignment of students to fill new schools. New residents also lacked an understanding of why the integration plan had been adopted. One member of the business community noted, "The reality is that as many people as we've had moving in and the growth we've had, you're dealing in an environment in which you're playing to a parade and not a crowd." Newcomers from smaller, independent districts complained about long bus rides and reassignments, particularly to year-round schools that were used to maximize the use of space and accommodate growth.

A recent study has found that there was diminishing community support and a seeming lack of political will for the SES-based student policy.[25] The study noted not only that new residents did not understand the history of desegregation in the community, but also that such newcomers to the district did not support the way in which district officials sought to maintain balance within the schools. A member of Wake County's business community commented,

The public conversation on the subject of balance winds up being more intense because there are substantially more movements simply because of balancing schools from the standpoint of new schools coming on board and having enough students in the new schools and populating those schools by bringing some students who are new and some from other existing facilities. . . . That movement creates a discontent in some instances because people have patterns built up and they don't want to be disrupted.

A second concern with the policy's effectiveness was the number of schools out of compliance with the policy. In the past ten years, the district experienced significant growth in the number of low-income students, which resulted in a higher number of low-income schools than previously situated within the district. The rise in number of low-income students can be attributed to an increased Latino population in the area; given these two occurrences, the district policy became difficult to implement over time.[26]

Charting a New Course

The school board election on October 6, 2009, set the stage for sweeping changes in the Wake County student assignment policy as four opponents of the integration plan joined an incumbent opponent to form a new 5–4 majority. Immediately following the election, board members began discussing whether to maintain the current SES-based policy. Shortly thereafter, a vote was taken, and the board voted by a 5–4 majority to alter the student assignment policy in an effort to educate students closer to home. Some students were reassigned in a spring 2010 board vote in order to move students closer to their homes. This vote is viewed by many as a twenty-first-century mechanism of resegregating the district's schools.[27] Many residents fear that educating students closer to home not only will resegregate the district, but also might impede the achievement gains of minority students throughout the district.

In response to the initial board vote, the NAACP Legal Defense Fund filed a complaint with the Office for Civil Rights in the U.S. Department of Education. The superintendent, Del Burns, resigned in protest of the new school board's efforts. A new superintendent, Anthony Tata, former chief operating officer of Washington, D.C., Public Schools assumed the reins of the district on January 31, 2011.

A growing coalition of civil rights activists, teachers, education researchers, parents, and business leaders has geared up to fight the resegregation of Wake County schools. The NAACP has engaged in pro-tests at board meetings, and the turmoil drew national attention, includ-ing a January 2011 front-page story in the *Washington Post*. The story prompted a comment from U.S. Education Department secretary Arne Duncan in support of Wake County's diversity plan, and television come-dian Stephen Colbert parodied Tea Party supporters of resegregation, asking "What's the use of living in a gated community if my kids go to school and get poor all over them?" Meanwhile, highly vocal squabbling among conservative school board members prompted an investigation from a school accreditation agency. Public opinion appeared to be mov-ing against the new anti-integration school board. A January 2011 Public Policy Polling survey of local residents found that 51 percent viewed the school board unfavorably, while 29 percent viewed it favorably.[28]

In February 2011, the Chamber of Commerce of Greater Raleigh, and the Wake Education Partnership, an education foundation, released a third-way plan to try to preserve diversity in Wake County schools through public school choice rather than mandatory assignment. The "controlled choice" plan is meant to better manage Wake County's explosive growth by filling new schools through choice. And it would allocate seats in schools to ensure a balance of students by achievement level. Because kindergartners do not have test score results, elementary placements would examine factors that place students at risk of low achievement, such as low parental income or education levels.

The Chamber of Commerce's proposal, which was authored by educa-tion consultant Michael Alves, must be approved by the school board, but the early signs suggest that it could draw broad support. A February 2011 *Education Week* story on the plan suggested, "Debate over Busing in Wake County Shows Signs of Cooling."[29] In fall 2011, Democratic candidates supportive of school diversity swept into office with a 5–4 voting majority. A plan to marry integration and choice was the starting point for the new board's discussion.

Lessons Learned from Wake County Public School System

There are several political lessons that other districts might learn from watching the Wake County Public School System. First, its plan to han-dle district growth angered parents to a point that it became ineffective. Wake County, which at one point was growing by one hundred people per day, saw an increased student population in the suburban outer ring of the district. Such population bursts caused district officials to implement year-round schools—schools that operate on a staggered rotating calendar with different groups of students so as to maximize the use of space. The district did its best to keep siblings in the same year-round track, but it proved inefficient and costly to parents who needed child-care options during school breaks. Annual reassignment of students in order to accommodate growth was chaotic, so the school district went to a three-year rotation for student assignment. Politically, however, this proved toxic, as three times as many parents were potentially upset by each round of reassignment, fueling greater unrest. Reassignments are annoying because they are disruptive and because many parents purchased homes based on the fact that their children might be able to attend the neighborhood schools for a number of years. When parents were assigned outside their neighborhood or a nearby neighborhood, they again protested to the school board. Thus, the district's response to growth became a major impetus in the school board's decision to over-turn the SES-based policy.

While it seemed that the school board had significant support in reversing the SES-based policy in the fall of 2009, it is clear in Wake County that groups forming a coalition in support of integration have been energized. On the left, the Great Schools in Wake coalition, which included the NAACP and other activist groups, supported maintaining diversity within the district's schools. Leaders for Great Schools in Wake adamantly support the SES-based policy, and they propose that diversity must be a component of a new student assignment plan. Their position is that regardless of where a child lives, he/she should have the opportunity to attend a good school. Supporters of Great Schools in Wake, including the NAACP president, Reverend Barber, argued that a return to neigh-borhood schools will return the district to de facto segregation. In other words, leaders of this coalition are fighting against the reemergence of a "separate but equal" school system.

Supplementing the Great Schools in Wake Coalition in support of diversity, as we noted above, is the more centrist Chamber of Commerce, which represents the interests of the business community. Their decision to advocate a third way on integration sought to avoid the constant reassignments involved in the old diversity plan and also to avoid resegregation under the new conservative majority's plan for neighbor-hood schools. The main purpose of a controlled choice plan is to provide parents with some choice while also maintaining integrated schools. The Chamber supports diversity in schools because business leaders realize that concentrations of low-income, at-risk students are bad educational policy. In addition, employers know that it is important for employees to be able to get along with people of all backgrounds.

In Wake County, the activism of liberals also created an environment in which the business community wanted a way to get beyond the negative publicity associated with protests over resegregation. Being the subject of an Office of Civil Rights investigation and the butt of jokes hurts the image of the community and makes it harder to recruit new businesses and employees to the area.

Increasingly, in Wake County, the liberal-centrist coalition left the more conservative members of the community isolated. Sitting on the right end of the political continuum is the school board majority and their constituents. The constituents, who live in more affluent neighborhoods in Wake County, argue that they want their children schooled closer to home. While their argument has a basis for the sake of proximity, there is little racial or socioeconomic diversity in their areas of town. Opponents of that position suggest that the more-affluent residents want to keep the schools to themselves and not admit a more diverse student population. At first, with a 5–4 majority, it seemed that this coalition would use its power to return to neighborhood schools. One of the new board members, however, has resisted a full resegregation of schools and has squabbled with her conservative allies on the board.

The fight in Wake County is ongoing, but as this book goes to press, it appears that the district will move forward with a plan that emphasizes choice, stability, and integration. It may be that Wake County will find a politically acceptable way to promote integrated schools through choice rather than compulsion.

Jefferson County Public Schools, Kentucky

The Jefferson County Public Schools system is comprised of approximately 96,000 students. Of the 96,000 students, a majority are either black or white. Over 50 percent of students enrolled receive free or reduced-price lunch. Although Jefferson County exhibits a white/black dichotomy, the district is one of the most successfully desegregated districts in the nation.[30] Similar to Wake County, Jefferson County came into existence by way of a merger between Louisville Public Schools and Jefferson County Public

Schools on April 1, 1975. The newly created school district developed a student assignment plan that required a 12 percent to 40 percent black population for elementary schools and a 12.5 percent to 35 percent black population for secondary schools.[31] Widespread busing was implemented to achieve the new desegregation goals, but African-American students bore the brunt of the forced commute. To be more precise, black students were to be bused for ten of their school years whereas white students were bused two of their twelve school years. The discrepancy in treatment among students led to protests and political uprisings.

As the politics of student assignment heated in the mid- to late 1970s, the district found hope in its magnet school program. Magnet schools, which were born out of the desegregation movement, provided a way of achieving racial balance in schools while also offering strong academic programs. Both white and black parents vied for seats in the district's magnet schools. A senior district official commented, "The magnet program developed and bloomed in that time period. In a community that's very political, magnets were a way of letting out the air. Magnet programs allowed parents to apply, and they were accepted into magnet programs that specialized in some particular area of study." By 1978, the district court had stopped closely monitoring JCPS's progress toward desegregation; however, the district remained committed to truly integrating its schools.

Commitment to Diversity

By the early 1990s, the district abandoned its busing policy for Project Renaissance, a program designed to desegregate elementary schools by giving parents a choice of schools. A district official explained, "At the elementary level, we had twelve elementary clusters, and the smallest one paired five schools together and the largest one paired ten schools together. The choice was in and among the elementary school clusters." Middle school students could attend either their neighborhood school or a magnet school, while high school students could apply to any high school in the district. In 1996, still under the auspices of Project Renaissance, Jefferson County implemented a plan that stated no school was allowed to have an enrollment of black students less than 15 percent or greater than 50 percent of its student population.

Jefferson County achieved unitary status in 2000, and the school board developed and implemented a student assignment plan to maintain substantial racial integration. Students were given a choice of schools, but not all schools could accommodate all applicants. In those cases, student enrollment was decided on the basis of several factors, including place of residence, school capacity, and random chance, as well as race. Race, as a sole factor, created judicial problems for the district.

In 2002, Crystal Meredith and other parents sued the school district, arguing that the plan's racial classifications violated students' Fourteenth Amendment right to equal protection of the laws. Meredith's argument lost in circuit court; however, the United States Supreme Court agreed to hear the case. On June 28, 2007, in conjunction with a similar case from Seattle (*PICS*), the Supreme Court ruled in favor of Meredith.

Upon the decision rendered by the U.S. Supreme Court, the Jefferson County Board of Education was forced to develop a new student assignment plan. With the assistance of the Kirwin Institute of Ohio State University, the school board approved a plan in 2008 and began implementing the plan in Fall 2009.

Moving Forward, Trying Not to Look Back

There are several differences in the district's approach post-*PICS*. However, the major difference is that the district no longer divides groups primarily by race and instead looks also at parental income and education. The most recent student assignment plan organizes the district into two geographic areas: Geographic Area A and Geographic Area B. Geographic Area A is an area of the entire county where residents are below the district median income per household member, below the district average in educational attainment for adults age 25 and above, but above the district average for minority populations that live there. Geographic Area B is basically the residents that Geographic Area A does not cover.

The plan arranges elementary schools into six contiguous clusters to provide a more equitable distribution of the multiple criteria across the clusters. A district official explained,

> The biggest difference here is making the decision to construct a multiple-criteria plan and develop a new diversity guideline. We did keep our diversity guidelines, and it is that the school will have enrollment of no less than 15 percent and no more than 50 percent of students living in geography area "A". All students, regardless of their race, SES, or parents' educational attainment . . . if you live in geography area "A" all students are treated the same. And

no matter what, if you live in geography area "B" all students are treated the same.

The student assignment policy, which is currently being implemented in elementary schools, will not begin implementation in middle schools and high schools until school year 2011–12. However, new middle school and high school magnet programs and magnet schools opened this school year. The resurgence of magnet programs might ease some of the tensions that plague parents within the district. A district official stated,

> Our community is kind of racially divided in terms of where people live and that has played a big part in how we implement the plan. We've been able to hold on to certain aspects of the plan because we wanted to make sure we provided visibility, predictability, quality, choice, diversity, and equity in the plan. So keeping all those things in mind, we tried not to uproot kids who were following in the old plan and through them in the new plan.

Implementation of the new student assignment policy has been challenging, and required long bus rides when the plan was first implemented. A student assignment official stated,

> Since it's a geography plan, some of our exchanges from urban areas to our suburban areas, are pretty far apart geographically. They could be 15 to 20 miles. So we've got kids with really long bus rides. They [parents] accept it better for their older kids, but for five- and six-year-olds we're getting a lot of pushback, and we've had a lot of problems the first day of school the last couple of years with kids not getting home until 9 o'clock at night.

District officials will continue to work on bus routes and other challenges as they move forward with the final stage of implementation.

Political Play and the Road Ahead

Similar to Wake County, Jefferson County officials will move forward on implementation with a new district leader at the helm. While the former superintendent in Wake County resigned in the midst of political turmoil, the Jefferson County school board did not seek to renew its superintendent's contract. That will leave implementation leadership in the hands of other district stakeholders.

272 | THE POLITICS OF MAINTAINING BALANCED SCHOOLS

Not only will district officials have to contend with a new leader, but they also will have to work alongside a mayor's office that has newfound interest in the district's schools. Although the mayor's office has no governance over the school district, it became a part of each candidate's platform in the last mayoral election. One district official noted, "By the end of the race, the Democratic candidate, who won the election, was saying, 'I'm going to work with the district to fix some of this stuff.'" Additionally, poll numbers showed political divisiveness along school district geography areas. Most parents who live in Geographic Area A voted for the Democratic candidate, and those who live in Geographic Area B voted for the Republican candidate.

In addition to local politics, Jefferson County school officials have had to contend with state-level politics. At the beginning of the 2010–11 school year, a group of parents tried to get an injunction under state law related to school mergers and enrollment. The parents based their case on an old law that stated that, when schools merged, students had to enroll in the nearest school. The state judge ruled in favor of Jefferson County Public Schools because the law was from the mid-1970s, and it was amended when the Kentucky Educational Reform Act became law.

Although the judge ruled in favor of the school system, a state representative and state senate president filed pre-legislation for the assembly that will change the language back to what it stated in the 1970s. The house of representatives in Kentucky is controlled by Democrats, and the senate is controlled by Republicans. District officials hypothesized that the bill may pass through the state senate, but they are unsure of what the outcome might yield from the state house. Regardless, district officials feel they are in a political quagmire. One district official stated, "I've been with the school district for 27, almost 28 years, and mostly been involved with student assignment during that time in one aspect or the other. This is the first time I can remember the school system becoming a political issue in a mayoral race and now at the gubernatorial level." In addition to that political tension, the most recent mayor of Louisville has become the state's lieutenant governor. The former mayor was a major supporter of the district's student assignment plan during his tenure. The perfect political storm is brewing along the lines of student assignment in Jefferson County. To further explain, there is a Republican state senate president running for governor who introduced legislation that runs counter to the district's student assignment policy, and there is a Democratic lieutenant governor who has supported the district's commitment to diversity. The state legislature meets from January through April, and if student assignment gets on the political agenda in the general assembly, then it will have an impact on primaries that will be held in May. As a result, student assignment in Jefferson County might ultimately affect the next governor's race in Kentucky. Given the recent political events in Kentucky as a state and Louisville as a city, the future of student assignment in Jefferson County Public Schools might be determined by stakeholders external to the district. This will call for a resurgence of local political will within the Jefferson County community.

Lessons Learned from Jefferson County Public Schools

Both local residents and national education policy analysts watched closely as school board election results were announced for Jefferson County Public Schools in November 2010. School board elections often go unnoticed, but those who favored the district's revised student assignment policy were afraid that a new school board majority might follow in the footsteps of Wake County and dismantle attempts for diverse schools. To many that possibility was an alarming thought. Unlike in Wake County, however, incumbents in Jefferson County who supported integration were able to hold on to their school board seats and maintain a board majority that favored the district's geography-based plan.

How did Jefferson County Schools dodge the blow that hit Wake? One answer rests in the fact that, whereas the Republican Party played an important role in opposing the diversity policy in Wake County, the school board elections in Jefferson County have remained nonpartisan. Additionally, individuals in Jefferson County can contribute only up to $100 to school board candidates; therefore, crucial candidate endorsements must come from businesses and teacher unions. In Louisville, the teachers' union supports the socioeconomic and racial diversity policy. A school board member noted, "Teacher unions are allowed to spend up to $50,000 on a candidate." Given the financial backing provided by businesses and teacher unions, most candidates who are supported by the business community or a teacher union normally win.

Although four incumbents won reelection in Jefferson County, some community members continue to complain about the geography-based plan. The district currently is being advised by UCLA education professor Gary Orfield to devise a plan that will be more suitable for district needs. A district survey reported that 80 percent of the district's parents favor a plan that includes a diversity component.

Champaign Unit 4 Schools, Illinois

In comparison to Wake County and Jefferson County, Champaign Unit 4 Schools is a relatively small district. Nestled in the college town of Champaign, Illinois, the district student population is approximately 10,000. A majority of the students in the district are either African American or white; however, 9 percent of students classify as Asian/Pacific Islander population, and 6 percent represent the Hispanic population. Approximately 42 percent of the district's students receive free or reduced-price lunch.

Commitment to Diversity

The history of school desegregation litigation in Champaign dates back to the 1970s; however, the most recent litigation dates to the 1990s. With Champaign divided between the North End and the South End, most black residents live in the North End. Champaign Centennial High School, which is located in the North End, had no black teachers teaching core subjects as late as twenty years ago. However, there were more black teachers teaching in elementary schools. This led black parents to believe that the district was not concerned about equal education for black students, especially in preparing black students to attend college. Because of these issues, John Lee Johnson brought in the Office of Civil Rights in the 1994–95 school year to address issues concerning black students and teachers. A district stakeholder explained, "We started out with a race-based assignment. What happened was that African Americans had been bused from the north to the south in order to integrate schools. An EEO complaint was filed; then another complaint was filed by John Lee Johnson, who was an African American advocate in the community."

After the complaints were filed, an equity audit was conducted in the district, and the audit found that there were disparities between black and white students in terms of special education, gifted education, and discipline referrals. More specifically, the audit determined that there was an overrepresentation of African-American students placed in special education; an underrepresentation of African-American students placed in gifted education; and a disproportionate number of African-American students with discipline infractions. The school board was strongly advised not to go to court over these issues; therefore, a consent decree was signed. The consent decree served as a binding agreement to address articulated issues in a positive, sustainable way. As a result, the board agreed to achieve results by working with parents who brought forth complaints. This agreement was entered into initially in 1998 and then the second revised consent decree was completed in January 2002. District personnel agree that educational improvements have been made in the district since the consent decree. One district official stated, "It's not anywhere near where we'd like it [student achievement] to be, but we've done a lot in terms of eliminating lower-level classes. . . . We've probably more than tripled the numbers of African American students in honors courses." The consent decree was initially implemented in elementary schools, and three years later it was implemented in middle schools.

The consent decree expired in June 2009 and, in order to comply with the *PICS* decision, district officials were faced with developing and implementing a student assignment plan that did not use race. Under the advisement of consultant Michael Alves, the district decided to continue using its controlled choice plan, but it decided to base the plan on socioeconomic status instead of race. Alves concluded that a socioeconomic controlled choice assignment lottery would continue to accommodate a high degree of rank-ordered school choices and that an SES lottery that was based on the actual percentage of low-income and non-low-income students in the lottery applicant pool would likely produce the results that are most similar to the district's race-conscious kindergarten controlled choice assignment lottery. Alves also concluded that a socioeconomic controlled choice lottery would prevent the resegregation of black and non-black students in the district's elementary schools. The key factors that appear to support this hypothesis are the distribution of black and non-black rank-ordered school choices and the fact that over three-quarters of the district's black kindergarten applicants were low-income.[32] As a result of Alves's consultation, the district began implementing a controlled choice plan based on socioeconomic status in fall 2009.

A More Perfect Union

While district stakeholders for Champaign Unit 4 Schools acknowledge that they are not a completely healed district, they indicate that their continued efforts to fight for better, more inclusive schools have improved relationships within the district. When asked if race relations have improved in the district, a stakeholder replied, "My opinion is to a degree, yes. You can integrate the schools themselves but if in fact your heart's not right when it comes to the children, then it does not help. I think most teachers' hearts are in the right place." Another district stake-holder did not seem as hopeful. He commented,

> Trust is at the crux of the matter. Having a Black superintendent does not change the trust issue. Is the progress sustainable? If Blacks continue to see a string of progress, then the trust factor may no longer be an issue. Most media stories show that Blacks are still skeptical. . . . A new "normal" is needed in Champaign. People often take disparities for granted. They tend to see disparities as "normal." Can citizens see and feel the "new normal"? That is the question to be answered.

Even though Champaign residents, for the most part, are still learning to trust each other, community members have accepted the controlled choice plan with fewer political tensions than either Wake County or Jefferson County. It is possible that the district's size has played a role in its being able to heal sooner than later.

Pressing toward the Future

As district officials move forward with their controlled-choice student assignment plan, they have noted progress in racial isolation and student achievement as well. A district leader commented, "I can say that we've had really good progress with our K–8 programs. Middle school, elementary, and middle schools and high schools are still a challenge, as it relates to achievement. But as you look at grade rate distributions for African American kids, we're making progress. The most frequent grade is not an F in math, so you know it's improving."

In addition to improved student achievement and less racial isolation, the district will offer magnets as an additional student achievement and integration option. According to a district leader, three elementary school magnets will open in 2011. They will be purposefully located in a poorer section of Champaign so that students in that area will have access to the schools. Booker T. Washington Elementary School's magnet program will adopt a science, technology, engineering, and mathematics (STEM) theme while Stratton Elementary School's magnet program will adopt a MicroSociety-esque theme. Garden Hills Elementary will implement the Primary Years Programme, an International Baccalaureate program for primary grades. A district leader commented on the schools' location:

We are not going to do anything that would keep the neighborhood kids out of the school. They had a magnet years ago at Booker T. Washington, but it was, before implementation of controlled choice, where neighborhood kids were not able to get in. That was something that was really a sensitive issue in the African American community. All of that, including transportation and programming issues also led to the consent decree.

Champaign Unit 4 Schools is a recipient of the Magnet Schools Assistance Program, or MSAP, grant from the U.S. government for the 2010–11 and 2012–13 school years. The award will grant the district $2.5 million each year for three years to support the implementation of the elementary magnet programs. According to school district officials, the grant will aid the district in its voluntary desegregation efforts to eliminate, reduce, and prevent the isolation of minority groups in educational programs while enabling them to meet challenging academic content and student academic achievement standards.

It appears that Champaign Unit 4 Schools residents saw their change in student assignment as nothing new. They began using socioeconomic status instead of race, and many residents did not notice the difference. This notion might mean that race and socioeconomic status in Champaign are highly correlated; thereby community members accept one as well as the other. This also might mean that fewer political tensions arose because community members recognize that they are segregated by income as well as by race.

Lessons Learned from Champaign Unit 4 Schools

As mentioned earlier, Champaign faced fewer political tensions than did Wake County or Jefferson County. One of the main reasons for such political cohesiveness might be district size. The district is much smaller; therefore, there are fewer people to resist change. Additionally, Champaign did not have to develop a new student assignment policy; they simply revised one that was already being implemented. This brought little attention to the process. Not only did Champaign make adjustments to a plan they already had in place, but also the fact that the plan provides some form of choice makes it more palatable to district residents. A major lesson that might be learned from Champaign, regardless of district size, is that providing parents with a modicum of choice might lessen political fallout later in the process.

Lessons for Policymakers

What can policymakers learn about the politics of socioeconomic school integration from the experiences in Wake County, Jefferson County, and Champaign? Several lessons emerge.

First, public school choice is generally a more politically sustainable way of promoting socioeconomic school integration than compulsory reassignment. Public school choice appears to offer a few advantages. For one thing, choice is politically popular and gives parents a feeling of ownership in a way that mandatory reassignment does not. Parents want some say in where their children attend school; when choice is combined with magnet school offerings, parents have a positive incentive to participate in integrated schooling above and beyond the benefits of having a child educated in a diverse environment. In Champaign, for example, the system of universal choice has faced little of the opposition found by integration policies in other communities.

For another, in school districts experiencing large growth in the student population, choice can better manage the influx of students into a district. In Wake County, for example, most reassignment of students was due to growth, not the socioeconomic diversity plan, yet opponents of diversity were able to conflate the issues by blaming instability and reassignment of students on the diversity policy. Programs that fill new schools through voluntary choice, not mandatory reassignment, can accommodate growth more easily than plans based on residential assignment.

Second, districts need to constantly communicate to members of the public about the rationale for socioeconomic school integration policies. Especially in districts that experience growth, such as Wake County, it is important to communicate with the ever-changing parade of new families. It cannot be assumed that parents are long-time residents who know the history of and the rationale for diversity policies.

Third, natural supporters of school integration, such as members of civil rights organizations, will be more likely to succeed if they strongly ally with other groups, including teachers and the business community. In Jefferson County and Wake County, for example, teachers have been strong supporters of diversity policies because they know they can do a better job if schools avoid concentrations of poverty. In Jefferson County, in particular, teachers have provided strong financial support for school board candidates who favored the diversity policy. Likewise, the role of the Chamber of Commerce in Wake County has been especially important in offering a way forward on diversity given the business community's strong interest in having a work force that is well educated and knows how to interact with people of all different backgrounds.

Fourth, national leaders can play an important role in providing political support for school integration efforts. For some time, supporters of diversity policies, including those in Jefferson County, have expressed concern that members of the Obama administration have not provided "bully pulpit" support for diversity and that the emphasis on charter schools instead suggests that addressing segregation is not a priority. By contrast, support for Wake County's integration plan, from such disparate national voices as television comedian Stephen Colbert and U.S. education secretary Arne Duncan, appears to have had a positive impact in Wake County. Business leaders and members of the public have expressed embarrassment at the critical national attention directed at the Wake County school board's efforts to resegregate the schools. The board is now viewed negatively by an almost two-to-one margin among local residents.

Future Directions in Student Assignment

As a result of the *PICS* decision and districts being granted unitary status, school districts will be challenged to maintain diverse schools. While it seems that diversity matters less to some school boards, research indicates that balanced schools provide a win-win environment for all student populations. Moreover, research indicates society as a whole benefits when schools are balanced along racial and social class lines.

The districts profiled in this study each developed, implemented, and evaluated student assignment policies in the face of some community opposition. While the policies were met with varying levels of community resistance and political tension, district officials show evidence of having developed seemingly inclusive policies. Whether or not these policies will endure will depend on communities' political will—the desire to support and maintain diversity. These examples suggest that intelligently designed policies can create the political will to allow school district stakeholders to promote integrated schooling that is aimed at serving the interests of students. That, in the end, is the key to successful student assignment policy.

Socioeconomic Integration and the Washington Education Policy Debate

8

Turnaround Schools and Charter Schools That Work:

Moving Beyond Separate but Equal

RICHARD D. KAHLENBERG

Education Secretary Arne Duncan courageously has taken on the most important—and most difficult—problem in American education: turning around America's lowest-performing schools. Duncan has noted that for years districts allowed failing schools to slide and has called, instead, for "far-reaching reforms" that fundamentally change the culture in the country's worst five thousand schools.[1] Seeking to transform these poorly performing schools into successful ones—creating what is known as "turnaround schools"—is indeed an ambitious challenge. Ironically, Duncan's approach, which focuses almost entirely on changing the faculty and school governance, is itself too timid.

In *Education Week,* Duncan wrote that, in Chicago, "We moved the adults out of the building, kept the children there, and brought in new adults."[2] But the exclusive focus on achieving performance gains through changing the principal and teachers misses the important role played by the two other big groups in a school community: students and parents. There is ample research showing that having an economic mix in that larger community can have a beneficial result.[3]

The turnaround approach taken in Chicago was a partial one, and, as education consultant Bryan Hassel told the *New York Times,* it achieved only "mixed" results.[4] The Civic Committee of the Commercial Club of Chicago noted in a recent report that "most students in Chicago Public Schools continue to fail."[5] Nationally, turnaround schools have seen "lackluster" results.[6] While there have been "scattered, individual successes," according to a widely cited 2007 report by Mass Insight Education and Research Institute, research finds "very little enduring progress at scale."[7] Citing extensive research in California, Ohio, Maryland, and elsewhere, Andrew Smarick writes in *Education Next,* "overall, school turnaround efforts have consistently fallen short of hopes and expectations."[8] Likewise, as we shall see below, while some charter schools such as Knowledge Is Power Program (KIPP) schools and the Harlem Children's Zone (HCZ) Promise Academies have been highly successful with low-income students, those models have limited applicability to the nation's five thousand lowest-performing public schools.

Why Current Turnaround Approaches Are Inadequate

The most discussed plans for turning schools around—firing the principal and teachers in a school, or adopting a charter school governance structure—fail to recognize that school quality is driven by three sets of actors in a school community: students, parents, and faculty (teachers and principals).

Classmates

Many years of research have confirmed what all parents know: kids learn from one another as well as from the teacher. In high-poverty schools, a child is surrounded by classmates who are less likely to have big dreams, and, accordingly, are less academically engaged and more likely to act out and cut class. In such schools, peers are less likely to do homework and graduate, and more likely to watch television and cut class—all of which have been found to influence the behavior of classmates. Low-income schools have widespread disorder problems three times as often as middle-class schools, so less learning goes on. Classmates in high-poverty schools also are more likely to move in the middle of the year, creating disruption in the classroom. (By third grade, 60 percent of

FIGURE 8.1. Classmate Characteristics, by Socioeconomic Status

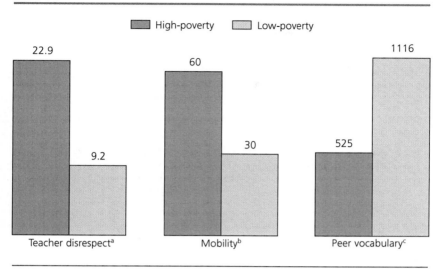

Notes:
[a]*Teacher disrespect* is the percentage of schools reporting student acts of disrespect for teachers in classrooms at least once per week. *High-poverty* refers to schools with 50 percent or more of their students eligible for free or reduced-price lunch; and *low-poverty* refers to schools with 20 percent or less of their students eligible for free or reduced-price lunch.
[b]*Mobility* is the percentage of students who have attended two or more schools between first and third grades. *High-poverty* refers to the study's lowest family income group (family income is less than $10,000). *Low-poverty* refers to the study's highest family income group (family income is $50,000 or more).
[c]*Peer vocabulary* is the number of words in a student's vocabulary by thirty-six months of age. *High-poverty* means child is part of a family receiving welfare, and *low-poverty* means child is part of a professional family.
Source: Rachel Dinkes, Emily Forrest Cataldi, and Wendy Lin-Kelly, *Indicators of School Crime and Safety: 2008* (Washington, D.C.: National Center for Education Statistics, U.S. Department of Education and U.S. Department of Justice, December 2008), 99, Table 7.2 (teacher disrespect); *Elementary School Children: Many Change Schools Frequently, Harming Their Education* (Washington, D.C.: U.S. General Accounting Office, 1994) (mobility); and Paul Barton and Richard Coley, *Windows on Achievement and Inequality* (Princeton, N.J.: Educational Testing Service, 2008), 9, Figure 2 (vocabulary).

very-low-income students have attended two schools, compared with 30 percent of more affluent third graders.) Research finds that it is an advantage to have high-achieving peers, whose knowledge is shared informally with classmates all day long; but low-income peers come to school with half the vocabulary of more-advantaged children, for example, so any given child is less likely in a high-poverty school to expand his vocabulary through informal interaction.[9] (See Figure 8.1.)

Parents

Parents also are an important part of a school community. Students benefit when parents regularly volunteer in the classroom and know how to hold school officials accountable when things go wrong. Low-income parents, who may be working several jobs, may not own a car, and may have had a bad experience themselves as students, are four times less likely than more-affluent parents to be members of a PTA.[10] They are only half as likely to volunteer in the classroom or serve on a school committee.[11] Finally, low-income parents are less likely to have the political power to push for adequate resources, which helps explain why even within school districts, spending disparities exist, generally to the disadvantage of low-income students.[12] (See Figure 8.2.)

Teachers and Principals

The makeup of a school in terms of students and parents profoundly affects the type of teachers who typically can be recruited. Research consistently finds that the best teachers, on average, avoid high-poverty and high-minority schools.[13] Teachers in disadvantaged schools are less likely to be licensed, to be teaching in their field of expertise, to have high teacher test scores, to have considerable teaching experience, and to have extensive formal education. Principal turnover also is higher in high-poverty schools.[14]

School leaders employing traditional turnaround efforts try to fix the maldistribution of high-quality teachers by firing existing teachers in high-poverty schools and hiring new ones, citing data on the seminal role that teachers play in raising student achievement.[15] But without changing the student and parent mix, this effort is usually an uphill battle. Teachers generally consider it a promotion to move from poor to middle-class schools, and many of the best teachers transfer into middle-income schools at the first opportunity. Research consistently finds that teachers care at least as much about work environment as they do about salary.[16] Teachers care about school safety, whether they will have to spend large portions of their time on classroom management, and whether parents will make sure kids do their homework. (In urban schools, teachers are more likely to say parents do not support teachers.[17]) The departure of some good teachers sets off a vicious cycle, as younger teachers seek schools with colleagues who will help them perfect their craft. (See Figure 8.3.)

FIGURE 8.2. Parental Involvement, by Family Socioeconomic Status

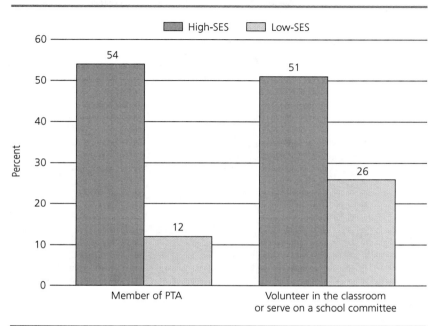

Source: 1988 National Educational Longitudinal Study data on PTA membership, cited in Richard D. Kahlenberg, *All Together Now: Creating Middle-Class Schools through Public School Choice* (Washington, D.C.: Brookings Institution Press, 2001), 62; *Parent and Family Involvement in Education, 2006–07 School Year* (Washington, D.C.,: National Center for Education Statistics, August 2008), 9, Table 3 (volunteer and committee service). NCES considers students living in households with incomes below the poverty threshold to be poor, or low-SES. Both studies gauge parental involvement based on the socioeconomic status of students—not schools.

Accordingly, it is very difficult to attract and keep great teachers in high-poverty schools, even when bonuses are offered. In other sectors (such as the military and health care), salary premiums of 10–30 percent are common in filling hard-to-staff positions.[18] In education, Eric Hanushek of Stanford, John Kain of the University of Texas at Dallas, and Steven Rivkin of Amherst estimated that, in order to get nonminority female teachers to stay in urban schools, school officials would have to offer a salary premium of between 25 percent and 43 percent for teachers with zero to five years experience.[19] Given the significance of labor costs in overall school spending, a 25–43 percent salary premium would require an extraordinary expenditure unlikely to be sustainable under current political and economic conditions. (See Figure 8.4.)

FIGURE 8.3. Teaching Quality, by School Socioeconomic Status

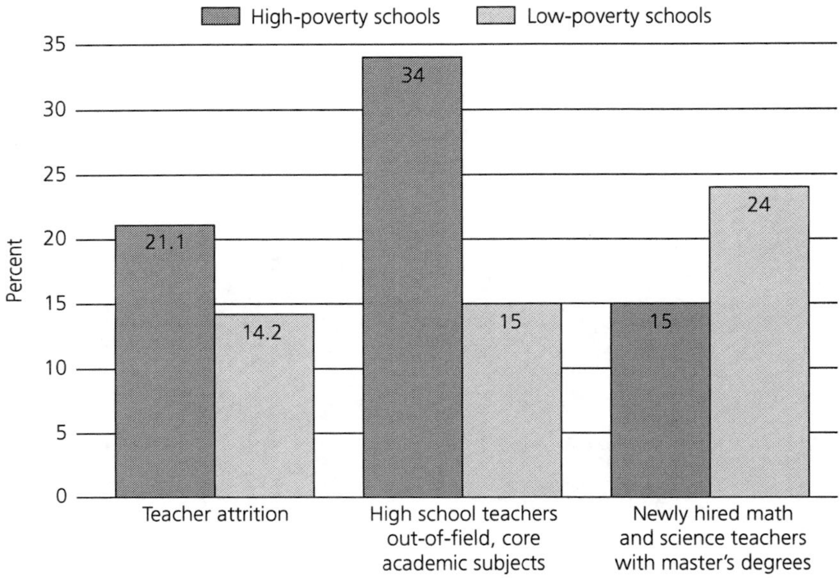

Source: U.S. Department of Education, *The Condition of Education 2008* (Washington, D.C.: Government Printing Office, 2008), 51; Richard M. Ingersoll, cited in "Parsing the Achievement Gap," Educational Testing Service, 2003, 11; Linda Darling-Hammond, "Doing What Matters Most: Investing in Quality Teaching," National Commission on Teaching and America's Future, 1997, 25–27.

In discussing the difficulties of making high-poverty schools work, it is important to draw a distinction between the problems associated with concentrations of school poverty and beliefs about the ability of poor children to learn. Many people confuse the first with the second. Evidence suggests that children from all socioeconomic groups can learn to high levels if given the right environment. High-poverty schools, however, do not normally provide the positive learning environment that children need and deserve.

A Better Approach: Turning Around Schools with Magnet Approaches that Integrate Students by Socioeconomic Status

The most promising turnaround model is one that seeks to turn high-poverty schools into magnet schools that change not only the faculty

FIGURE 8.4. Salary Increase Needed to Counteract Turnover Effects Caused by Differences in Student Characteristics between Large Urban and Suburban Districts, by Experience Class of Teacher (for Female, Non-minority Teachers)

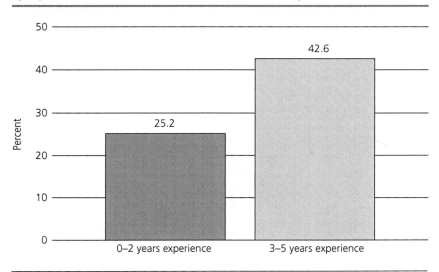

Source: Eric A. Hanushek, John F. Kain, and Steven G. Rivkin, "Why Public Schools Lose Teachers," *Journal of Human Resources* 39, no. 2 (2004): 326–54.

but also the student and parent mix in the school. Failing schools can be shuttered, reinvented, and reopened with new themes and pedagogical approaches that attract new teachers and a mix of middle-class and low-income students. Some low-income students from the old school would be given the opportunity to fill the spots in more-affluent schools vacated by middle-income children who were transferring to the magnet school.

Examples of Magnet Schools as Turnarounds

Nationally, there were 2,736 magnet schools educating roughly 2 million students in the 2005–06 school year, according the National Center for Education Statistics Common Core of Data. (By comparison, in that year, there were 4,000 charter schools educating about 1 million students.)[20] Like charter schools, there are good magnet schools and bad ones—and not all, by any means, are able to attract middle-class students into schools located in disadvantaged areas.[21] But the best ones can serve as models for turning around failing schools. In well-designed plans, school leaders poll parents ahead of time and find out what sort of programs would be attractive to them and then place attractive magnet themes in previously failing schools. Consider these examples:

- *Wexford Elementary, Lansing, Michigan.* Wexford Elementary School struggled for many years, failing to make Adequate Yearly Progress and in the 2003-04 school year was facing reconstitution. In the 2004-05 school year, it began to transition to a Montessori magnet school. In 2005-06, Wexford was still high-poverty (81.5 percent low income) and racially isolated (69 percent African American, and 8 percent Hispanic). By 2008-09, the middle-class student population had grown to 33.6 percent (from 18.5 percent) and the white population to 40 percent (from 17 percent). A school that was underutilized is now oversubscribed and even draws students from the suburbs surrounding Lansing. The number of suspensions has declined from 173 to under 10. Today, Wexford is a nicely integrated school (44.2 percent African American, 39.5 percent white, and 11.6 percent Hispanic), and the school makes Adequate Yearly Progress overall and for all subgroups (including low-income and racial and ethnic minority categories). In grades 3-7 reading, 84.6 percent of African Americans at Wexford are proficient or advanced (compared with a 59 percent statewide target), and 85.6 percent of economically disadvantaged students are proficient or advanced (compared with a 59 percent statewide target). White students also outperform students statewide in reading. In math, African Americans, economically disadvantaged students, and whites outperform comparable groups statewide.[22]
- *Wake County (Raleigh), North Carolina Magnet Schools.* Wake County, which includes the city of Raleigh and its surrounding suburbs, made a critical decision in the early 1980s to avoid the problems associated with concentrated poverty in neighboring Durham schools and provided virtually every Raleigh school with special magnet themes such as science and technology, arts and theater, and International Baccalaureate. As Gerald Grant notes in his important new book, *Hope and Despair in the American City: Why There Are No Bad Schools in Raleigh,* Raleigh's inner-city schools, which had been marked by white flight, were soon filled with economically and racially diverse student bodies. Many of the schools now have waiting lists.[23] To prevent the creation of enclaves

of privilege, the Raleigh magnets do not require tests for admission. And to avoid legal problems associated with using race in assigning students, the schools look to establish a mix of pupils based on who is eligible for subsidized lunch (with a goal of limiting low-income students to 40 percent in any school). The results have been very promising, with Wake's low-income, minority, and white students generally outperforming comparable students in other large North Carolina districts that do not break up concentrations of school poverty.[24] Although Wake County voters in 2009 elected a conservative school board that is opposed to socioeconomic diversity through mandatory reassignment of students, 2011 elections brought renewed support for diversity.[25]

- *The Tobin School, Cambridge, Massachusetts.* In Cambridge, which has a system of universal choice and seeks an economic balance among schools, officials recently turned the struggling, predominantly low-income Tobin School, located near a large low-income housing complex, into a Montessori. In 2006-07, Tobin had attracted only 12 first-choice applicants to fill 60 pre-kindergarten and kindergarten seats. The next year, when it reopened as a Montessori, Tobin attracted 145 applicants, with twice as many middle-class as low-income students applying, says Michael Alves, who administers the student lottery.[26]

These types of successful magnet school turnaround efforts appear, finally, to have caught the attention of Washington policymakers. In October 2011, a major proposal in the U.S. Senate would include magnet schools as a turnaround school option.[27]

Evidence that Turnaround Magnet Schools with an Economic Mix Can Raise Student Achievement

A number of studies over the past quarter-century have found that magnet schools have higher levels of achievement than do other schools, and produce faster achievement gains in most subjects. Several of these studies account for self-selection bias by examining gains in over-subscribed magnet schools and regular public schools, comparing lottery winners and losers, and continue to find advantages to attending magnet schools.[28] For example, comparing lottery winners and losers in interdistrict magnet schools in Connecticut, a 2008 study by Robert Bifulco of Syracuse

University, Casey Cobb of the University of Connecticut, and Courtney Bell of the Educational Testing Service found positive effects on math and reading scores in high school and on reading scores in middle school.[29]

Moreover, the magnet school turnaround model—in which schools seek to improve the performance of low-income students by drawing into a high-poverty school a contingent of middle-class students—is backed up by four decades of research finding that the socioeconomic composition of a school profoundly affects the achievement of any given student in the school. This research dates back to the landmark 1966 Coleman Report, which found that the most important predictor of academic achievement is the socioeconomic status of the family a child comes from, and the second most important predictor is the socioeconomic makeup of the school she attends.[30] More recently, a growing number of studies have linked a school's socioeconomic status with student achievement, after controlling for the individual socioeconomic status of a student's family.[31] Indeed, a new analysis of Coleman's data using a more sophisticated statistical technique (hierarchical linear modeling, or HLM) finds that the social class of the school matters even more to student achievement than does the socioeconomic status of the family. Geoffrey Borman and Maritza Dowling of the University of Wisconsin at Madison concluded that "the achievement difference between a school attended by students of average wealth and a school with a student body composed of students 1 standard deviation below the mean level of wealth was nearly 1¾ times greater than the achievement difference between a student of average wealth and a student who was 1 standard deviation less wealthy."[32]

- In 2002, researcher David Rusk's study of public schools in Madison-Dane County, Wisconsin, found that among fourth-grade students, for every 1 percent increase in middle-class classmates, the test scores of low-income students improved 0.64 percentage points in reading and 0.72 percentage points in math. Any given low-income student attending an 85 percent middle-class school rather than a 45 percent middle-class school saw "a 20 to 32 percentage point improvement in that low income pupil's test scores."[33]
- In 2005, University of California professor Russell Rumberger and his colleague Gregory J. Palardy, examining a large data set, found that a school's socioeconomic status had as much impact on the achievement growth of high school students in math, science, reading, and history as a student's individual economic status.[34]

- Data from the 2006 Programme for International Student Assessment (PISA) for fifteen-year-olds in science showed a "clear advantage in attending a school whose students are, on average, from more advantaged socioeconomic backgrounds." The report continued, "Regardless of their own socio-economic background, students attending schools in which the average socio-economic background is high tend to perform better than when they are enrolled in a school with a below-average socioeconomic intake."[35] Analyzing PISA data, researchers Laura Perry and Andrew McConney recently concluded that the academic success of nations like Finland and Canada appears to be related in part to their greater degrees of socioeconomic school integration.[36] Likewise, J. Douglas Willms, examining PISA data, found that schools with higher levels of socioeconomic segregation had lower mean scores on average and noted that Finland—often held out as a remarkable education success story—had the very lowest degree of socioeconomic segregation of 57 countries participating in PISA.[37]
- In 2006, the University of Wisconsin's Douglas Harris published what may be the largest study analyzing school integration and achievement. Using math exams required under the No Child Left Behind Act, Harris examined data from 22,000 schools enrolling 18 million students. He found that minority students have greater gains in racially integrated schools, and that "a substantial portion of the 'racial composition' effect is really due to poverty and peer achievement."[38]
- Data from the 2007 National Assessment of Educational Progress (NAEP) given to fourth graders in math show that low-income students attending more-affluent schools scored almost two years ahead of low-income students in high-poverty schools. Indeed, *low-income* students given a chance to attend more-affluent schools performed more than half a year better, on average, than *middle-income* students who attend high-poverty schools.[39] (See Figure 8.5.)

Today, more than eighty school districts have acted on this research and employ explicit policies seeking to reduce concentrations of school poverty. As outlined at length elsewhere, these districts generally have seen strong achievement gains and other positive academic outcomes.[40] In Cambridge, Massachusetts, for example, a longstanding policy of universal magnet schools to balance student populations, originally by race and

FIGURE 8.5. National Assessment of Educational Progress 2007, Fourth Grade Math Results

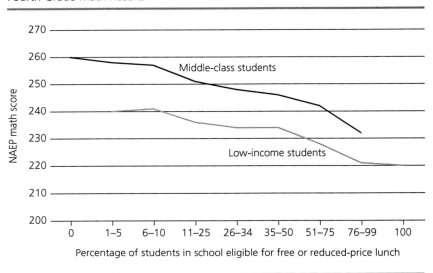

Percentage of students in school eligible for free or reduced-price lunch

Source: U.S. Department of Education, Institute of Education Sciences, National Center for Education Statistics, National Assessments of Educational Progress (NAEP), 2007 Math Assessment, Grade 4.

more recently by socioeconomic status, has yielded very positive benefits. In 2008, Cambridge graduated 88.8 percent of its low-income students in four years compared with 64.8 percent of low-income students statewide and 59.1 percent of low-income students in Boston. As can be seen in Figure 8.6, Cambridge's black and Hispanic students also far surpassed blacks and Hispanics in Boston and statewide in graduation rates, while whites in Cambridge graduate at the same level as whites statewide, and far ahead of whites in Boston.

Further evidence of the importance of economic school integration comes from research on the effects of concentrated residential poverty. For years, researchers consistently have found that living in a low-income neighborhood stunts the opportunities of children.[41] For example, a 2008 study by Robert Sampson of Harvard, Patrick Sharkey of New York University, and Stephen W. Raudenbush of the University of Chicago found that growing up in high-poverty neighborhoods had the effect for African-American children of reducing verbal ability later in life on the order of one year of schooling.[42]

FIGURE 8.6. Cambridge, Massachusetts, and Boston Four-Year Cohort Graduation Rates, 2008

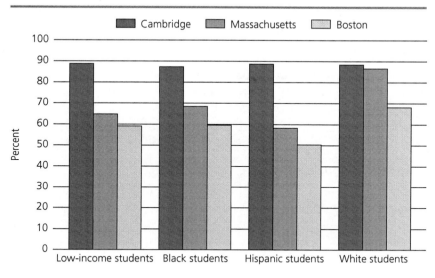

Source: Massachusetts Department of Elementary and Secondary Education, Cohort 2008 Four-Year Graduation Rates—State Results, http://www.doe.mass.edu/infoservices/reports/gradrates/08_4yr.html.

Well-designed efforts to deconcentrate neighborhood poverty have had broad success. As a remedy to housing discrimination, under the *Hills* v. *Gautreaux* Supreme Court case, almost 25,000 African Americans in public housing in the Chicago metropolitan area were given a chance to live in mostly white affluent suburbs.[43] Because the program was oversubscribed, researchers could compare families who wished to move to the suburbs but were instead assigned to housing in the city with suburban movers. James Rosenbaum and other scholars at Northwestern University found that children of those who moved to the suburbs were four times more likely to finish high school and twice as likely to attend college as those who remained in the city.[44] A more recent experiment aimed at replicating *Gautreaux*—the federal Moving to Opportunity (MTO) program—found few benefits, but it was a poor test of poverty deconcentration strategies, as students in the treatment group attended schools with a mean subsidized lunch population of 67.5 percent, compared to 73.9 percent in the control group. This looked more like moving to mediocrity than to opportunity.[45] The evidence from Montgomery

County, Maryland's housing integration program, outlined in chapter 2 of this volume, provides strong confirmation of the success in Chicago.

While well-run socioeconomic school integration and housing mobility programs such as under *Gautreaux* have been highly successful, most efforts to improve high-poverty neighborhoods and schools have proven disappointing over the years. Billions of dollars have been invested in Community Development Corporations (CDCs), but as researcher David Rusk notes, even the nation's best CDCs "are losing the war against poverty."[46] Likewise, numerous evaluations of the federal Title I program for high-poverty schools consistently have found that the many billions of dollars expended have failed to produce significant academic gains.[47]

Integration by Class versus Integration by Race

Importantly, school districts today are emphasizing integration by economic status, as opposed to race, in magnet and other programs because doing so avoids the constitutional problems associated with racial integration plans. Also, pursuing integration by economic status is consistent with the social science research that has long found that the socioeconomic makeup of a school matters more to academic achievement than its racial mix. (There are other reasons to want schools to be racially integrated per se, whatever the effects on academic achievement.)

As a legal matter, school districts are wary about using race to guide admissions after the U.S. Supreme Court's decision striking down racial integration plans in Louisville, Kentucky, and Seattle, Washington, in *Parents Involved in Community Schools* v. *Seattle School District No. 1* (decided jointly with *Meredith* v. *Jefferson County Board of Education*).[48] Unlike voluntary racial integration plans, socioeconomic integration programs are on very sound legal footing.[49]

But the emphasis on socioeconomic integration also comports with a long line of social science research on the relatively greater importance of socioeconomic status in producing better academic outcomes. Racial desegregation raised the achievement of black students in certain areas (such as Charlotte, North Carolina, where middle-class whites and low-income blacks were integrated) but not in others (such as Boston, where low-income whites and low-income blacks were integrated). Research found that the academic benefits of racial desegregation came not from giving African-American students a chance to sit next to whites, but from giving poor students of all races a chance to attend predominantly middle-class institutions.[50] The well-regarded Coleman Report, for example, found that the "beneficial effect of a student body with a high proportion of white students comes not from racial composition *per se* but from the better educational background and higher educational aspirations that are, on the average, found among whites."[51] More recent research confirms this notion.[52] Indeed, UCLA professor Gary Orfield, a strong proponent of racial desegregation, notes that "educational research suggests that the basic damage inflicted by segregated education comes not from racial concentration but the concentration of children from poor families."[53]

Considering why it is important to avoid concentrations of school poverty underlines the economic rather than racial dimension of the issue. To take one example, it is a disadvantage to be in a school where classmates exhibit a high level of antisocial behavior, but that problem is far more closely associated with class than race. One study finds that, while blacks scored 13 points higher on an antisocial index than whites, when one controls for social class, the black/white difference is reduced to 3 points. Meanwhile, poor students of all races scored 21 points higher than advantaged students.[54]

While school quality is tied to concentrations of poverty, not concentrations of racial minorities, it is also important to point out that, because of discrimination in the housing markets, it is unmistakably black and Latino students who overwhelmingly bear the brunt of attending high-poverty schools. As Figure 8.7 demonstrates, almost two-thirds of black and Hispanic public school students attend schools in which more than 50 percent of students are eligible for subsidized meals, compared with just one in five white students—a difference that helps explain why low-income whites tend to outperform low-income African Americans and Latinos.[55]

Overcoming Political Obstacles

Some argue that economically integrated schools are a nice idea in theory but will never fly politically. If there is a broad social science consensus that economic segregation impedes equality of opportunity, there is also a durable political assumption that housing integration and "busing" for school integration programs are politically toxic. The concern is understandable, but dated, for three reasons.

First, turning around failing schools through magnet programs relies on positive incentives rather than compulsory busing. Thirty years ago, districts shipped kids across town and parents had no say in the matter, a practice that fueled white flight. Today, however, most districts

FIGURE 8.7. Percentage of Students in High-Poverty Schools, by Race, 2008–09

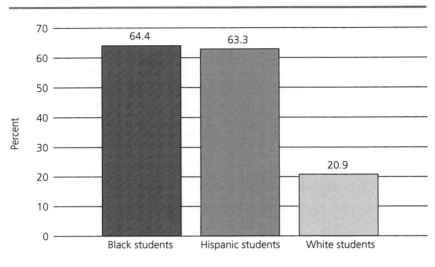

Note: *High-poverty* is defined as at least 50 percent of students eligible for free or reduced-price lunch.
Source: S. Aud et al, *The Condition of Education 2011* (Washington, D.C.: U.S. Department of Education, National Center for Education Statistics, May 2011), 240, Table A-28-1.

seeking integration rely primarily on systems of magnet schools and public school choice. In Cambridge, Massachusetts, for example, all schools have been designated magnet schools, each with something distinctive to offer. Parents rank their preferences among schools, and the district honors choices in a way to ensure that all schools are within plus or minus ten percentage points of the system's average eligibility for free and reduced-price lunch.

The most sophisticated plans poll parents ahead of time, asking them what sort of themes or pedagogical approaches would attract them to attend a school farther away. In Hartford, Connecticut, for example, a Montessori school, located in a tough neighborhood, has a long waiting list of white, middle-class suburban families because what is at the end of the bus ride is attractive to them. Likewise, a number of metropolitan communities, such as St. Louis, Missouri, provide extra funds to suburban schools that accept urban transfer students. This approach is likely to be especially attractive to suburban districts at a time when they are desperately seeking ways to balance their books.

Second, the "neighborhood school" does not have the same resonance it did three decades ago. Although Americans are divided on private school vouchers, they overwhelmingly support giving greater choice and options to students within the public school system.[56] The share of families choosing a non-neighborhood public school increased by 45 percent between 1993 and 2007.[57]

Third, a growing share of Americans now recognize that diversity is a good thing for all students. Research has long found that integration is not a zero-sum game: low-income students can benefit from economically integrated schools and middle-class achievement does not decline so long as a strong core of middle-class children are present. This is true in part because the majority sets the tone in a school, and because research finds that middle-class children are less affected by school influences (for good or ill) than low-income children.[58] Moreover, many families now believe that racial, ethnic, and income diversity enriches the classroom, noting that students cannot learn how to live in a multicultural society while in a segregated white school.

The number of districts using socioeconomic status in student assignment has increased dramatically over the past decade; notably, the list includes districts from "red" states and "blue" states, from Omaha, Nebraska, to San Francisco, California; from La Crosse, Wisconsin, to McKinney, Texas. While conventional wisdom declares school integration a thing of the past, in all, some 4 million students live in school districts with some form of socioeconomic integration plan in place. (See Appendix.)

Current Emphasis on "Fixing" High-Poverty Schools Is Not Scalable

In recent years, some observers have claimed to have cracked the safe and figured out how to make "separate but equal" work, citing high-poverty public schools that have "beaten the odds" or highly successful high-poverty charter schools such as KIPP, and the HCZ package of pre-kindergarten programs, social services, and charter schools. To some, the existence of these successful models suggests that segregation is just an "excuse" for failure. Because high-poverty public school and charter school successes raise different issues, we address them in turn.

High-Poverty Public Schools

Successful high-poverty public schools that beat the odds paint a heartening story that often attracts considerable media attention. In 2000, the conservative Heritage Foundation published a report, entitled *No Excuses,* meant to show that high-poverty schools can work well. The author proudly declared that he "found not one or two [but] twenty-one high-poverty high performing schools." Unfortunately, these twenty-one schools were dwarfed by the seven thousand high-poverty schools identified by the U.S. Department of Education as low-performing.[59]

Subsequently, the liberal Education Trust purported to find 3,592 high-poverty schools with test scores in the top one-third of their states.[60] The study was useful to the extent that it exposed the myth that poor children cannot learn, but a follow-up study by University of Wisconsin professor Douglas Harris found that Education Trust included in its total many flukes—schools that performed well in just one grade, or on just one test (math or reading), or in just one year. Examining the Education Trust's data, Harris found that, when schools had to perform well in more than one grade and more than one subject and for more than one year, the number of high-poverty high flyers was reduced by 93 percent, from 15.6 percent of high-poverty schools to just 1.1 percent. Using this more rigorous definition of flying high, Harris reported in a 2006 paper that high-poverty schools (those with 50 percent or more students eligible for free and reduced price lunch) were falling short when compared to middle-class schools (those with fewer than 50 percent of students eligible for subsidized lunch). Indeed, low-poverty schools were twenty-two times more likely to be high-performing compared to high-poverty schools.[61] (See Figure 8.8.)

High-Poverty Charter Schools

In response to the paucity of successful high-poverty public schools, some have argued that a change in governance—charter schools—can take successful high-poverty schools to scale. Because most charter schools are nonunionized, some make the profoundly conservative assertion that teacher unions are the primary impediment to equal opportunity.[62] Some go further and argue that the success of high-poverty charter schools suggests not only that separate can be equal, but also that separate schools for low-income students are perhaps *superior* because they can focus on the special needs of low-income students.

FIGURE 8.8. Percentage of Schools That Are Persistently High-Performing, by Socioeconomic Status

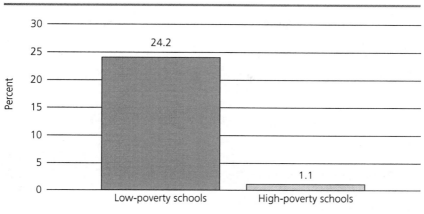

Note: High-poverty is defined as at least 50 percent of students eligible for free or reduced-price lunch; *low-poverty* is defined as fewer than 50 percent eligible. *High-performing* is defined as being in the top third in the state in two subjects, in two grades, and over a two-year period.
Source: Douglas N. Harris, "Ending the Blame Game on Educational Inequity: A Study of 'High Flying' Schools and NCLB," Educational Policy Studies Laboratory, Arizona State University, March 2006, 20.

But on closer examination, these high-poverty charter school success stories are very difficult to take to scale nationally because the three key sets of players in schools such as KIPP and HCZ's Promise Academies—the parents, students, and teachers—are not representative of those typically found in high-poverty public schools.

KIPP Schools. KIPP is a chain of 109 schools educating more than 32,000 students in twenty states and the District of Columbia.[63] Founded by David Levin and Mike Feinberg, the school program emphasizes "tough love": a longer school day and school year, more homework, and the explicit teaching of middle-class habits and norms. In his excellent book on KIPP, the *Washington Post*'s Jay Mathews says that test scores in KIPP have risen faster for more low-income students than anywhere else.[64] The results are very impressive, but it seems unlikely that KIPP can translate its success to help turn around a significant number of the nation's five thousand low-performing schools.

KIPP does not educate the typical low-income student, but rather a subset fortunate enough to have striving parents who take the initiative to apply to a KIPP school and sign a contract to read to their children at night.[65] KIPP also educates a disproportionate share of girls.[66] Most importantly, according to a 2008 SRI International study of San Francisco Bay-area KIPP middle schools, of students who begin KIPP, 60 percent leave, many because they find the program too rigorous.[67] While some subsequent research finds that KIPP has attrition rates similar to other high-poverty schools, the difference is that KIPP students who leave generally are not replaced by new students, as happens in regular public schools.[68] Columbia University researcher Jeffrey Henig described the attrition rate as jaw dropping.[69] KIPP is successful, then, with a motivated and determined group of students, a cohort that is surrounded by classmates who are likely to provide positive peer influences. It is not surprising, therefore, that KIPP's one effort to turn around an existing school's student population failed after two years.[70] A KIPP spokesperson said, "our core competency is starting and running new schools."[71]

Nor are the teachers typical of those attracted to regular high-poverty public schools. The dedication of KIPP teachers is legendary—they work from 7:15 a.m. to 5:00 p.m. and then go home to plan for the next day, as they take phone calls to help students with home work—but may not translate into an effective model for three million teachers nationally, many of whom have family obligations that make a KIPP-style existence hard to sustain. Indeed, the SRI International study of five San Francisco-area KIPP schools, nearly half (49 percent) of teachers who taught in the 2006–07 school year had left before the beginning of the 2007–08 school year. This compares with a 20 percent turnover rate in high-poverty schools generally.[72] Moreover, as KIPP's reputation grew, it could select among prospective teachers who wished to be part of an exciting program and be surrounded by high-performing colleagues, an applicant pool not typical of high-poverty public schools.

Nor are KIPP schools funded at levels typical of high-poverty schools. KIPP has won the backing of some of the richest individuals in the country who have helped fund the program at levels more likely to be found in middle-class schools than high-poverty public schools.[73] With at least $50 million to $60 million in funding from the founders of Gap Inc., KIPP spends an estimated $1,100–$1,500 more per pupil than do regular public schools.[74]

HCZ Promise Academies. To its credit, the Harlem Children's Zone, founded by Geoffrey Canada, consciously set out to educate an entire ninety-seven-block region of the Harlem community—not just the most motivated subset. Unlike KIPP, HCZ supplements its Promise Academy charter schools with a comprehensive system of parenting classes, pre-kindergarten programs, and extra social services. A preliminary study by Harvard's Will Dobbie and Roland G. Fryer, Jr., was highly lauda-tory. As David Brooks wrote in a *New York Times* column, "Harlem Miracle," Dobbie and Fryer found that by eighth grade, on the New York State math test, the Promise Academy "eliminated the achievement gap between its black students and the city average for white students."[75]

To date, however, HCZ runs only three charter schools (two elemen-tary and one middle school), educating 1,300 students—pupils whose parents must apply for a lottery to participate.[76] (By comparison, there are about 70 public and 30 private schools in the Harlem neighbor-hood.)[77] Moreover, HCZ's elementary school students increasingly are drawn from a group whose parents are particularly motivated, having given up four to five hours every Saturday for two rounds of nine-week "Baby College" parenting classes.[78]

Even with this self-selected population, the results have been over-blown. Columbia University professor Aaron Pallas, in a piece entitled "Just How Gullible Is David Brooks?" points out that, while students did well on the New York State high-stakes exam on a different assess-ment—the Iowa Test of Basic Skills—eighth-grade Promise Academy students scored at the thirty-third percentile for a national sample in math. These disappointing results on the Iowa test are significant, Pallas notes, because "if proficiency in English and math are to mean any-thing, these skills have to be able to generalize to contexts other than a particular high-stakes test."[79] Others have noted that New York State tests are considered weak compared with the National Assessment for Educational Progress.[80]

Moreover, like KIPP, HCZ's results come not from the entire entering cohort of students but rather from the subset who survive a longer school day and school year. In the case of HCZ's middle school, more than one-third of students left between sixth and eighth grade, and, unlike with public schools, no new students entered.[81]

Other questions arise about how easily HCZ can be taken to scale. The founder, Geoffrey Canada, is a highly charismatic figure, who has been profiled in the *New Yorker* and the *New York Times Magazine* and was able to convince former president Bill Clinton to attend a building opening. Canada also has won the backing of hedge fund billionaires such as Stanley Druckenmiller and Kenneth Langone, who helped found Home Depot.[82] (Druckenmiller alone has contributed more than $100 million to the HCZ.)[83] Canada's fame and resources, in turn, help recruit excellent teachers who put in extraordinary hours, something hard to sustain at scale.[84]

None of this should diminish the success of HCZ and KIPP. There are very important lessons to learn from both programs. Giving students a longer school day and year may be a productive (if expensive) idea. HCZ's Baby College and well funded pre-kindergarten programs (at $13,000 a student, double the cost of a Head Start program) seem especially beneficial.[85]

It would be a mistake, however, to think that KIPP and HCZ suggest that "separate but equal" can be taken to scale. Indeed, although both programs take place in economically and racially isolated settings, the theory behind the programs is completely consistent with the theory of socioeconomic school integration. Besides having good teachers, sufficient funding, and motivated families—of the type more often found in middle-class schools than high-poverty schools—the thrust of both programs is to teach what Canada calls "middle class cultural values" and "middle class aspirations."[86] Moreover, Canada continually returns to the importance of peer influences. His goal is to attain 60 percent participation in HCZ programs, so that middle-class values—a sense of responsibility and hopefulness about the future—"would come to seem normal." Writes HCZ chronicler Paul Tough, "Canada's theory was that each child would do better if all the children around him were doing better."[87] As an example, Canada said, "If you are surrounded by people who are always talking about going to college, you're going to end up thinking, 'Hey, maybe this is something I could do, too.'"[88]

Canada's theory—strong parenting and pre-kindergarten programs on the one hand; and positive peer environments on the other—is consistent with the Coleman Report's famous conclusion that the socioeconomic status of the family and the socioeconomic status of the school are the two most important determinants of academic achievement. Taking Canada's success to scale, however, would seem far more likely if low-income families received a combination of parenting classes, pre-kindergarten, and access to middle-class public schools, where their peers will be "talking about going to college" and where hopefulness is "normal"—the sorts of schools, in fact, that administrators in HCZ send their own children to attend.[89]

FIGURE 8.9. Chance of Adult Poverty, by School Socioeconomic Status

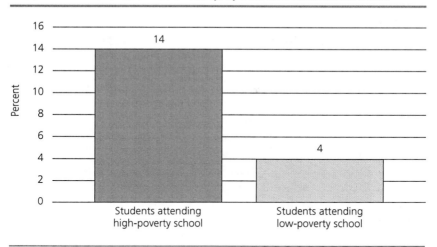

Source: Claude S. Fischer et al., *Inequality by Design: Cracking the Bell Curve Myth* (Princeton, N.J.: Princeton University Press, 1996), 84. The authors of the study controlled for individual ability and family home environment.

Even if academic success were scalable in segregated high-poverty schools, there are other reasons to be unsatisfied with segregation. When students graduate and search for jobs, those in high-poverty schools may be cut off from valuable networks that facilitate employment. Research confirms the adage that who you know matters as much as what you know, and studies find that one of the greatest benefits to blacks of attending desegregated schools came when seeking employment.[90] Indeed, University of California–Berkeley researcher Claude Fischer and colleagues found that, even after controlling for individual ability and family home environment, attending a middle-class school reduced the chances of adult poverty by more than two-thirds (4 percent versus 14 percent).[91] (See Figure 8.9.)

Likewise, separate but equal approaches reduce the racial understanding and tolerance that comes from integration. In his book on HCZ, Tough quotes from a poem posted in the school hallway written by a middle-school student, Julien Coutourier: "When I see myself I see/a black man trying to make it in the world. Trying to dodge what the white man says about us."[92] In an integrated environment, where Coutourier had white classmates, some racially sensitive, others not, he might be less likely to make universal statements about "the white man." Likewise, white students attending segregated white schools suffer from not getting to know students like Coutourier.

Other Charter Schools. Charter school supporters correctly point out that KIPP and HCZ are not the only successful charter schools. For example, in a 2009 report for the Boston Foundation, Harvard economist Thomas Kane and colleagues revealed that students who applied for and won the lottery to attend charter schools in Boston significantly outperformed students who lost the lottery and attended regular public schools.[93] (The comparison of lottery winners and losers is meant to control for self-selection bias.) But critics pointed out that the only charter schools included in the study were the 26 percent that were popular and oversubscribed, so the finding of superior performance compared with public schools generally was unsurprising. Moreover, self-selected students in sought-after charter schools were surrounded by peers who also were highly motivated, a school-level effect for which the study did not control.[94] Likewise, a 2009 study of New York City charter schools by Stanford University's Caroline Hoxby, which claimed to find a significant closing of the Scarsdale-Harlem gap, relied on a set of methodologically questionable assumptions. As Hoxby's colleague Sean Reardon found, the methodologically sound gains mentioned in the study were substantially smaller.[95]

Recent research raises serious questions about whether charter schools in fact can help turn around the nation's worst performing schools. Particularly devastating was the landmark study of the generally pro-charter Center for Research on Education Outcomes at Stanford University, examining fifteen states and the District of Columbia, which together educate roughly 70 percent of the nation's charter school students. Looking at gains in math over time, the study found that only 17 percent of charter schools outperform regular public schools.[96] (See Figure 8.10.) The finding underlines the fact that high-flying charter schools such as KIPP and HCZ's Promise Academies are the exception, and rely on a model—self-selected students, high rates of attrition, generous funding from philanthropists, and super-human efforts by young teachers without families—that is not scalable generally to high-poverty schools.

The degree to which charter schools such as KIPP rely upon self-selected students and high rates of attrition for success was underlined by the charter school community's reaction to Education Secretary Arne Duncan's call that they get involved in the business of turning around

FIGURE 8.10. Impact of Charter Schools on Math Gains in Fifteen States and Washington, D.C.

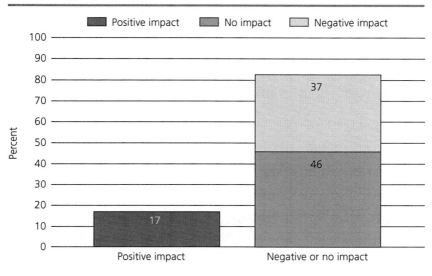

Source: *Multiple Choice: Charter School Performance in 16 States* (Stanford, Calif.: Center for Research on Educational Outcomes, Stanford University, June 2009), 44, Table 9.

failing schools. In an extraordinary June 2009 speech to the National Alliance for Public Charter Schools, Duncan challenged charter school leaders to "get into the game" of turning around failing schools. "I know this is tough work," he said, "but there is an upside. You start with a school full of kids so there is no student recruiting."[97] But as former Bush education official Andy Smarick has argued, charter schools are much better at fresh starts, building a school from scratch, rather than turn-arounds, which inherit schools with large populations of disadvantaged students.[98] By the time the U.S. Department of Education released guide-lines for funding in August 2009, a new option had emerged—a "restart" model—in which charter school operators do not automatically take the same set of students who had been attending a failing school but instead require students to apply (with a preference for those who were already there).[99] It is understandable that KIPP and other charter school opera-tors do not want to have to educate the large blocs of disadvantaged students who are automatically assigned to some public schools, but it suggests their role is limited in reaching traditional student populations in high-poverty schools. KIPP does a wonderful job at the important task of rescuing the Cedric Jenningses of the world—the aspiring, hard-working student hero of Ron Suskind's book *Hope in the Unseen*. But that is a far different job than trying to educate all low-income students, including those whose parents do not apply, and the 60 percent who did not survive KIPP's rigorous regimen in the San Francisco Bay area.

Identifying the Root Problem in Failing Schools: Segregation and Poverty, not Teacher Unions

Fundamentally, it is time to rethink the basic theory of turning around failing schools. One unspoken assumption of many current approaches is that teachers in high-poverty schools (and their union protectors) are to blame; and that if we could fire those teachers, and bring in union-free charter schools, we could fix the problem. This approach is mistaken. Teacher unions are hardly perfect, but there is no solid research suggesting that they are on balance damaging to the education of children. The American South, and America's charter schools, both of which have weak teacher unions or none at all, generally have lower student performance than schools in states, such as New Jersey and Massachusetts, that have strong unions.[100] Moreover, there is ample research to suggest that teacher unions produce very positive educational benefits: they reduce teacher turnover, boost salaries, and reduce class size.[101] (In charter schools, most of which are not unionized, the teacher turnover rate is 25 percent, compared with 14 percent for traditional public schools.)[102]

Instead, mountains of research suggest that the reason high-poverty schools fail so often is that economic segregation drives failure: it congregates the children with the smallest dreams, the parents who are the most pressed, and burnt-out teachers who often cannot get hired elsewhere. There is a strange quality to the turnaround debate, in which we stand in awe of the impressive efforts of a few schools and ignore the larger reality that economic segregation normally perpetuates failure. As James Foreman, Jr., has written, "As much as it thrills us to read about extraordinary people succeeding with poor children, I want to see how ordinary people can do the same."[103] Using magnet themes to turn around failing high-poverty schools will not work everywhere, but high-quality economically integrated schools should be the first turnaround option explored, with efforts to improve economically segregated schools—always an uphill battle—reserved only as a fallback.

Appendix

Local Education Agencies Employing Socioeconomic Status in Some Fashion in Student Assignment, with Corresponding Student Populations in Parentheses

Local education agencies listed below are school districts, except for two charter schools indicated by a †.

Local Education Agency	Student Population
Alachua County Public Schools, FL[1]	29,533
Allen Independent School District, TX[2]	18,715
Amherst Regional Public Schools, MA[3]	4,000
Beaumont Independent School District, TX[4]	19,534
Berkeley Unified School District, CA[5]	8,954
Bloomington Public Schools, MN[6]	10,070
Boulder Valley School District, CO[7]	28,660
Brandywine Public School District, DE[8]	10,321
Bryan Independent School District, TX[9]	13,401
Brunswick School Department, ME[10]	2,962
Burlington School District, IA[11]	4,266
Burlington School District, VT[12]	3,590
Burnsville-Eagan-Savage Independent School District 191, MN[13]	9,897
Cambridge Public School District, MA[14]	5,861
Champaign Community Unit School District Number 4, IL[15]	9,244
Chapel Hill-Carrboro City Schools, NC[16]	11,626
Charles County School District, MD[17]	25,903
Chicago Public Schools, IL[18]	435,000
Christina School District, Wilmington, DE[19]	17,116
Clark County (Las Vegas) Public School District, NV[20]	308,554
Davenport Community Schools, IA[21]	15,921
Denver School of Sciences and Technology, Denver, CO[22]†	728

Local Education Agency	Student Population
Des Moines Independent Community School District, IA[23]	30,683
Duval County (Jacksonville) Public School District, FL[24]	125,176
East Baton Rouge Parish School System, LA[25]	49,197
Eden Prairie Schools, MN[26]	9,700
Eugene School District 4J, OR[27]	17,896
Fairfax County Public Schools, VA[28]	168,384
Farmington Public Schools, MI[29]	12,000
Fresno Unified School District, CA[30]	82,906
Greenville County Public School District, SC[31]	67,537
Guilford County Public School District, NC[32]	71,176
Hamilton County (Chattanooga) Public Schools, TN[33]	40,922
Hernando County Schools, FL[34]	22,450
High Tech High, San Diego, CA[35]†	3,500
Hillsborough County (Tampa) Public Schools, FL[36]	193,517
Jefferson County (Louisville) Public Schools, KY[37]	91,425
Kalamazoo Public Schools, MI[38]	11,588
La Crosse School District, WI[39]	7,215
Lafayette Parish School District, LA[40]	30,255
Lee County (Fort Myers) Public Schools, FL[41]	78,981
Lee County Schools, NC[42]	9,527
Little Rock School District, AR[43]	25,899
Madison Metropolitan School District, WI[44]	24,755
Manatee County School District, FL[45]	42,235
McKinney Independent School District, TX[46]	21,073
Miami-Dade Public School District, FL[47]	353,790
Minneapolis Public Schools, MN[48]	34,570
Montclair Public Schools, NJ[49]	6,600
Montgomery County Public School District, MD[50]	139,000
Moorpark Unified School District, CA[51]	7,200
Napa Valley Unified School District, CA[52]	17,418
New York City Public Schools: Community School Districts 13, 14, 15, 20 and 21, NY[53]	206,151
Omaha Public School District, NE[54]	47,044
Palm Beach County School District, FL[55]	171,431
Pitt County School District, NC[56]	22,763
Pittsburgh Public Schools, PA[57]	26,649
Portland Public Schools, OR[58]	41,409
Postville Community Schools, IA[59]	530
Proviso Township High Schools, IL[60]	5,020
Redlands Unified School District, CA[61]	21,482
Rochester City School District, NY[62]	32,000

Local Education Agency	Student Population
Rock Hill Public School District of York County, SC[63]	17,653
Rockford School District, IL[64]	29,515
Rosemont-Apple Valley-Eagan Public Schools, MN[65]	27,700
Salina Public Schools, KS[66]	7,267
San Diego Unified School District, CA[67]	131,577
San Francisco Unified School District, CA[68]	55,497
San José Unified School District, CA[69]	31,230
Seattle Public Schools, WA[70]	45,581
Seminole County Public Schools, FL[71]	65,299
South Orange-Maplewood School District, NJ[72]	6,090
South Washington County Schools, MN[73]	16,800
Springdale Public School District, AR[74]	17,429
St. Lucie County Public School District, FL[75]	38,793
Stamford School District, CT[76]	15,036
Topeka Public School District, KS[77]	13,262
Troup County School District, GA[78]	12,381
Tucson Unified School District, AZ[79]	54,907
University Place School District, WA[80]	5,472
Waterloo Community Schools, IA[81]	10,590
West Liberty Community School District, IA[82]	1,188
Williamsburg-James County Public Schools, VA[83]	10,410
TOTAL: 83 districts	3,978,587 students

Notes

Chapter 1

1. David J. Hoff, "Echoes of the Coleman Report," *Education Week,* March 24, 1999, 33.

2. See chapter 5, 345–46.

3. *Parents Involved in Community Schools v. Seattle School District No. 1,* 551 U.S. 701 (2007).

4. Emily Bazelon, "The Next Kind of Integration," *New York Times Magazine,* July 20, 2008.

5. Douglas N. Harris, "Ending the Blame Game on Educational Inequity: A Study of 'High Flying' Schools and NCLB," Great Lakes Center for Education Research and Practice, 2006, http://greatlakescenter.org/docs/Policy_Briefs/Ending%20the%20 Blame%20Game-%20Doug%20Harris.pdf.

6. See chapter 5, 158, figure 5.1.

7. See chapter 8, 286–90.

8. See chapter 4.

9. See Ulrich Boser, "Return on Educational Investment: A District-by-District Evaluation of U.S. Educational Productivity," Center for American Progress, January 19, 2011, http://www. americanprogress.org/issues/2011/01/educational_productivity/ report.html.

10. Susan Aud et al., *The Condition of Education 2011* (Washington, D.C.: U.S. Government Printing Office, 2011), Table A-28-1, 87.

11. Elizabeth Kneebone and Emily Garr, "The Suburbanization of Poverty: Trends in Metropolitan America, 2000 to 2008," Brookings Institution, January 20, 2010.

12. The Century Foundation has long been interested in this issue and supported *All Together Now: Creating Middle-Class Schools through Public School Choice* (Washington, D.C.: Brookings, 2001); and *Divided We Fail: Coming Together through Public School Choice* (New York: The Century Foundation Press, 2002).

13. See Stephanie McCrummen and Michael Birnbaum, "Study of Montgomery County Schools Shows Benefits of Economic Integration," *Washington Post,* October 15, 2010, A1; and Bob Herbert, "Separate and Unequal," *New York Times,* March 22, 2011, A23.

14. This section draws upon Richard D. Kahlenberg, "Lifting Student Performance: Housing Policy Is School Policy," *Education Week,* October 20, 2010, 24.

15. Stacey M. Childress, Denis P. Doyle, and David A. Thomas, *Leading for Equity: The Pursuit of Excellence in Montgomery County Public Schools* (Cambridge, Mass.: Harvard Education Press, 2009), 3.

16. Personal e-mail communication with author, August 30, 2010.

17. See Lisa Sanbonmatsu, Jeffrey R. Kling, Greg J. Duncan, Jeanne Brooks-Gunn, "Neighborhoods and Academic Achievement: Results from the Moving to Opportunity Experiment," NBER Working Paper 11909, January 2006, 18 and 45, Table 2; and Alexander Polikoff, *Waiting for Gautreaux: A Story of Segregation, Housing and the Black Ghetto* (Evanston, Ill: Northwestern University Press, 2006).

18. Chapter 2, 42.

19. Ibid., 50.

20. Edward Zigler and Sally J. Styfo, *The Hidden History of Head Start* (New York: Oxford University Press, 2010), 126-127.

21. Chapter 3, 73–74.

22. Ibid., 107–08.

23. Ibid.

24. Ibid., 106.

25. Ibid., 92.

26. Ibid., 114.

27. Chapter 4, 128.

28. Ibid., 127.

29. Ibid., 131, 136 n. 20.

30. Ibid., 131.

31. Ibid., 134.

32. Ibid., 135–39.

33. Ibid., 139.

34. Ibid., 141–44. For recent support for the connection between segregation and high school graduation rates, see Russell W. Rumberger, *Dropping Out: Why Students Drop Out of High School and What Can Be Done about It* (Cambridge, Mass.: Harvard University Press, 2011).

35. Chapter 4, 139–40.

36. Ibid., 144–46.

37. Ibid., 147–48.

38. Ibid., 149–50.

39. Ibid., 143–50.

40. Ibid., 130.

41. Ibid., 128, 140–41.

42. Chapter 5, 156.

43. Susan Aud et al., *The Condition of Education 2011* (Washington, D.C.: U.S. Government Printing Office, 2011). Note that this figure differs somewhat from that in the author's study because of the more recent school year and larger sample size.

44. Chapter 5, 156.

45. Ibid., 162–63.

46. Ibid., 165–66.

47. Ibid., 172.

48. Ibid., 175.

49. Ibid., 181–82.

50. See, e.g., McKinsey & Company, *The Economic Impact of the Achievement Gap in America's Schools,* April 2009, 14 (pointing to different levels of performance in Texas and California and crediting policies surrounding teachers and leaders as potential factors).

51. Chapter 5, 183–89. Note that these percentages are based solely on district demographics and should be viewed as a ceiling on what intradistrict integration could accomplish given the realities associated with actual implementation.

52. Ibid., 190–92.

53. Ibid., 194.

54. Ibid., 194–95.

55. Ibid., 197–98.

56. Ibid., 207.

57. Ibid., 212.

58. Portions of this discussion are drawn from Richard D. Kahlenberg, "The Potential of Interdistrict School Choice," *Education Week,* June 8, 2011.

59. Chapter 6, 223.

60. Arne Duncan, "School Reform: A Chance for Bipartisan Governing," *Washington Post,* January 3, 2011.

61. Erin Dillon, "Plotting School Choice: The Challenges of Crossing School District Lines," Education Sector, 2008.

62. Chapter 6, 232–37.

63. Ibid., 240.

64. Ibid., 240–42.

65. Ibid., 244.

66. Chapter 7, 264–65.

67. Wake County Public Schools website, http://www.wcpss.net/demographics/. Data are for 2010–11.

68. Chapter 7, 265–66.

69. For example, a 2005 effort to eliminate the diversity policy was turned back. See Richard Kahlenberg, "Best and Worst in Education," Taking Note Blog, The Century Foundation, December 25, 2005, http://tcf.org/commentary/2005/nc1169.

70. Chapter 7, 266.

71. Ibid., 267.

72. Andy Kroll, "How the Koch Brothers Backed Public-School Segregation," *Mother Jones,* August 15, 2011.

73. Chapter 7, 267–68.

74. Richard D. Kahlenberg, "A Tea Party Defeat on Schools in North Carolina," Blog of The Century, The Century Foundation, October 14, 2011.

75. Chapter 7, 270–72.

76. Ibid., 274–75.

77. Ibid., 276.

78. See Jodi Heckel, "Income to Be Factor in Champaign School Assignments," *Champaign News-Gazette*, January 9, 2009; and Champaign Community School District #4—Elementary Student Registration Form, http://www.champaignschools.org/FIC/forms/Elementary%20Registration%20packet.pdf.

79. Chapter 7, 279.

80. See William Freivogel, "St. Louis: Desegregation and School Choice in the Land of Dred Scott," in *Divided We Fail: Coming Together through Public School Choice* (New York: Century Foundation Press, 2002), 209–31.

81. This section draws upon Richard D. Kahlenberg, "Turnaround Schools that Work," *Education Week*, September 2, 2009, 32.

82. Arne Duncan, "Education Reform's Moon Shot," *Washington Post*, July 24, 2009, A21.

83. Arne Duncan, "Start Over: Turnarounds Should Be the First Option for Low-performing Schools," *Education Week*, June 17, 2009.

84. Sam Dillon, "U.S. Effort to Reshape Schools Faces Challenges," *New York Times*, June 2, 2009.

85. *Still Left Behind: Student Learning in Chicago's Public Schools* (Chicago: Civic Committee of the Commercial Club of Chicago, June 2009), 1.

86. Gerald Grant, *Hope and Despair in the American City: Why There Are No Bad Schools in Raleigh* (Cambridge, Mass.: Harvard University Press, 2009), 98–99.

87. Ibid., 92.

88. E-mail correspondence with Michael Alves to the author, July 28, 2009.

89. Magnet Schools of America, "MASA Supports Senate Draft Reauthorization Bill," October 14, 2011.

90. Erica Frankenberg, Genevieve Siegel-Hawley, and Jia Wang, *Choice without Equity: Charter School Segregation and the Need for Civil Rights Standards* (Los Angeles: Civil Rights Project/Proyecto Derechos Civiles at UCLA, January 2010), 72, Table 30. Data are from the 2007–08 NCES Common Core of Data.

91. *Multiple Choice: Charter School Performance in 16 States* (Stanford, Calif.: Center for Research on Educational Outcomes, Stanford University, June 2009), 44, Table 9.

92. See Richard D. Kahlenberg, "Do Self-selection and Attrition Matter in KIPP Schools?" Washington Post Answer Sheet Blog, June 14, 2011, http://www.washingtonpost.com/blogs/answer-sheet/post/do-self-selection-and-attrition-matter-in-kipp-schools/2011/06/13/AG1sQeTH_blog.html.

Chapter 2

1. David Rusk, "Trends in School Segregation," in *Divided We Fail: Coming Together through School Choice: The Report of The Century Foundation Task Force on The Common School* (New York: The Century Foundation Press, 2002).

2. Stacy Childress, Denis Doyle, and David Thomas, *Leading for Equity: The Pursuit of Excellence in Montgomery County Public Schools* (Cambridge, Mass.: Harvard Education Press, 2009).

3. Michael Birnbaum, "Montgomery Schools Add to their A+ Reputation; System Will Be Paid to Create Curriculum, which Firm Will Sell," *Washington Post*, June 9, 2010, A1.

4. Digest of Education Statistics, Table 42, Institute of Education Statistics, U.S. Department of Education, 2009, http://nces.ed.gov/programs/digest/d09/tables/dt09_042.asp.

5. Heather Schwartz, "Inclusionary Zoning and Schools," Report for the MacArthur Foundation (ongoing).

6. High-poverty schools are here defined as those with 75 percent or higher concentrations of students who qualify for a free or reduced-price meal (those who come from families making less than 185 percent of the poverty line). Fifty-five percent of fourth graders and 47 percent of eighth graders scored "below basic" on the National Assessment of Educational Progress in 2009 in high-poverty schools, whereas 17 percent of fourth graders and 13 percent of eighth graders scored "below basic" from schools where less than 20 percent of students qualified for a free or reduced-price meal. Susan Aud, William Hussar, Michael Planty, Thomas Snyder, Kevin Bianco, Mary Ann Fox, Lauren Frohlich, Jana Kemp, and Lauren Drake, *The Condition of Education 2010*, NCES 2010-028 (Washington, D.C.: National Center for Education Statistics, 2010).

7. Ibid.

8. See Leonard S. Rubinowitz and James E. Rosenbaum, *Crossing the Class and Color Lines* (Chicago: University of Chicago Press, 2000) for details of the *Gautreaux* case. In a 1989 survey that compared families in public housing who had moved eight to thirteen years earlier to white Chicago neighborhoods, versus families in public housing who had moved around the same time to white neighborhoods in Chicago's suburbs, children of African-American suburban movers were more likely to have not dropped out of school (20 percent versus 5 percent), were more likely to be in college-track classes (24 percent versus 40 percent), were more likely to attend college (21 percent versus 54 percent), and more likely to attend a four-year college (4 percent versus 27 percent).

9. For a full evaluation of Moving to Opportunity, see Larry Orr, Judith Feins, Robin Jacob, Eric Beecroft, Lisa Sanbonmatsu, Lawrence F. Katz, Jeffrey B. Liebman, and Jeffrey R. Kling, *Moving to Opportunity Interim Impacts Evaluation* (Washington, D.C.: U.S. Department of Housing and Urban Development, 2003), http://www.huduser.org/Publications/pdf/MTOFullReport.pdf. For further research regarding schools and Moving to Opportunity, see Lisa Sanbonmatsu, Jeffrey R. Kling, Greg J. Duncan, and Jeanne Brooks-Gunn, "Neighborhoods and Academic Achievement: Results from the Moving to Opportunity Experiment," NBER Working Paper 11909, National Bureau of Economic Research, Cambridge, Mass., January 2006, 18 and 45, Table 2.

10. David J. Harding, Lisa Gennetian, Christopher Winship, Lisa Sanbonmatsu, and Jeffrey R Kling, "Unpacking Neighborhood Influences on Education Outcomes: Setting the Stage for Future Research," Working Paper 16055, National Bureau of Economic Research, Cambridge, Mass., June 2010; Greg J. Duncan and Katherine A. Magnuson, "Can Family Socioeconomic Resources Account for Racial and Ethnic Test Score Gaps?" *The Future of Children* 15, no. 1 (2005): 35–54; Greg J. Duncan and Jeanne Brooks-Gunn, "The Effects of Poverty on Children," *The Future of Children* 7, no. 2 (1997): 55–71; Christopher Jencks and Susan E. Mayer, "The Social Consequences of Growing Up in a Poor Neighborhood, in *Inner-City Poverty in the United States,* ed. Laurence E. Lynn, Jr., and Michael G. H. McGeary (Washington, D.C.: National Academy Press, 1990), 111–86.

11. For studies on teacher sorting, see Brian A. Jacob, "The Challenges of Staffing Urban Schools with Effective Teachers," *The Future of Children* 17, no. 1 (2007):

129–53; Eric A. Hanushek, John F. Kain, and Steven G. Rivkin, "Why Public Schools Lose Teachers," *The Journal of Human Resources* 39, no. 2 (2004): 326–54; Eric A. Hanushek, John F. Kain, and Steven G. Rivkin, "Teachers, Schools, and Academic Achievement," *Econometrica* 73, no. 2 (2005): 417–58; Donald Boyd, Hamilton Lankford, Susanna Loeb, and James Wyckoff, "The Draw of Home: How Teachers' Preferences for Proximity Disadvantage Urban Schools," *Journal of Policy Analysis and Management* 24, no. 1 (2005): 113–32; Donald Boyd, Hamilton Lankford, Susanna Loeb, and James Wyckoff, "Explaining the Short Careers of High-achieving Teachers in Schools with Low-performing Students," *American Economic Review* 95, no. 2 (2005): 166–71; Benjamin Scafidi, David L. Sjoquist, and Todd R. Stinebrickner, "Race, Poverty, and Teacher Mobility," *Economics of Education Review* 26 (2007): 145–59; and Robert P. Strauss, Lori L. Bowes, Mindy S. Marks, and Mark S. Plesko, "Improving Teacher Preparation and Selection: Lessons from the Pennsylvania Experience," *Economics of Education Review* 19, no. 4 (2000): 387–415. For studies on student absenteeism and mobility, see Committee on the Impact of Mobility and Change on the Lives of Young Children, Schools, and Neighborhoods, "Student Mobility: Exploring the Impact of Frequent Moves on Achievement: Summary of a Workshop," National Academies Press, 2010, http://www.nap.edu/catalog/12853.html (accessed on July 12, 2010); Hanushek, Kain, and Rivkin, "Why Public Schools Lose Teachers"; Russell W. Rumberger and Katherine A. Larson, "Student Mobility and the Increased Risk of High School Dropout," *American Journal of Education* 107, no. 1 (1998): 1–35; Christopher A. Kearney, "School Absenteeism and School Refusal Behavior in Youth: A Contemporary Review," *Clinical Psychology Review* 28, no. 3 (2008): 451–71. For ethnographic studies about high-poverty school environments, see Judith M. Parr and Michael A. R. Townsend, "Environments, Processes, and Mechanisms in Peer Learning," *International Journal of Educational Research* 37 (2002): 403–23; Martin Thrupp, "A Decade of Reform in New Zealand Education: Where to Now? Introduction," *New Zealand Journal of Educational Studies* 34, no. 1 (1999): 5–7; Martin Thrupp, "Education Policy and Social Change," *British Journal of Sociology of Education* 23, no. 2 (2002): 321–32. For studies about parental interactions with schools, see Annette Lareau and Erin M. Horvat, "Moments of Social Inclusion and Exclusion: Race, Class, and Social Capital in Family-School Relationships," *Sociology of Education* 72, no. 1 (1999): 37–53; Erin M. Horvat, Elliot B. Weininger, and Annette Lareau, "From Social Ties to Social Capital: Class Differences in the Relations between Schools and Parent Networks," *American Educational Research Journal* 40, no. 2 (2003): 319–51. For studies about *teacher expectations* and *student-teacher interactions,* see Annette Lareau, "Social Class Differences in Family-School Relationships: The Importance of Cultural Capital," *Sociology of Education* 60, no. 2 (1987): 73–85; Susan Lasky, "The Cultural and Emotional Politics of Teacher-Parent Interactions," *Teaching and Teacher Education* 16, no. 8 (2000): 843–60; P. Penny Hauser-Cram, Selcuk R. Sirin, and Deborah Stipek, "When Teachers' and Parents' Values Differ: Teachers' Ratings of Academic Competence in Children from Low-income Families," *Journal of Educational Psychology* 95, no. 4 (2003): 813–20; Ian A. G. Wilkinson, "Introduction: Peer Influences on Learning: Where Are They?" *International Journal of Educational Research* 37 (2002): 395–401; Matthew L. Pittinsky, "Smart by (Perceived) Association: Cognitive Social Networks and Teacher Academic Judgments," Ph.D. dissertation, Columbia University, 2008; and Barbara F. Chorzempa and Steven Graham, "Primary-grade Teachers' Use of Within-class Ability Grouping in Reading," *Journal of Educational Psychology* 98, no. 3 (2006): 529–41.

12. Frederick M. Hess, *Spinning Wheels: The Politics of Urban School Reform* (Washington, D.C.: Brookings Institution Press, 1999).

13. A number of studies find a link between achievement levels and school socioeconomic status above and beyond the effect of family socioeconomic status. For a summary, see, for example, Richard D. Kahlenberg, *All Together Now: Creating Middle Class Schools through Public School Choice* (Washington, D.C.: Brookings Institution Press, 2001), 25–42, and Richard D. Kahlenberg, "Turnaround Schools that Work: Moving beyond Separate but Equal," Agenda Brief, The Century Foundation, 2009, 7–10. Some of these studies attempt to control for self-selection. But studies of specific interventions for socioeconomic (as opposed to racial) integration are rare.

14. Approximately sixty school districts that collectively educate four million students have adopted some form of economic integration policy, up from two districts in 2000 (Kahlenberg, "Turnaround Schools that Work").

15. This has proved a challenge to researching the impacts of optional inter-district enrollment programs such as Boston's Metco program and the Voluntary Interdistrict Choice Corporation in St. Louis, Missouri.

16. Jim Mann and Kirk Sharfenberg, "Montgomery Eyes Methods to Solve Housing Crisis," *Washington Post,* March 11, 1971, F1.

17. Neighborhoods are defined in this study as census block groups, which respectively house about 500 households per block group and are approximately 0.25 square miles each.

18. Note that the maximum rate of poverty in any given school that a public housing student attended varied by school year. In 2001, public housing students attended five elementary schools where the percent of students who qualified for a free or reduced price meal exceeded 65 percent. In 2002, 2004, and 2005, four schools met this criterion, while in 2003, students in public housing attended three such schools. In 2006, students in public housing attended one school that met this criterion, and then two schools in 2007. For consistency, and to keep every possible school in the analysis, the graphs below show school poverty ranges up to 85 percent, which is the highest poverty rate in any single elementary school that a public housing child attended in any year from 2001 to 2007. It should be noted, however, that only one school out of 114 attended had a poverty rate in excess of 80 percent, and up to three schools in any given year had a poverty rate of 70 percent to 80 percent.

19. *Our Call to Action* (Rockville, Md.: Montgomery County Public Schools, 1999).

20. *Early Success Performance Plan: Educational Reform in Montgomery County Public Schools* (Rockville, Md.: Montgomery County Public Schools, May 2003), http://www.montgomeryschoolsmd.org/info/CTBS2003/PDF/EarlySuccessPerformance Plan.pdf.

21. For a history and description of inclusionary zoning, see David Rusk, *Inside Game/Outside Game: Winning Strategies for Saving Urban America* (Washington, D.C.: Brookings Institution Press, 2001), and Robert Burchell, et al., "Inclusionary Zoning: A Viable Solution to the Affordable Housing Crisis?" *New Century Housing* 1, no. 2 (2000).

22. Since the housing authority does not track rejected offers, this statistic was derived from six months of offers made during 2008.

23. To validate findings, the study also examined a second set of low-income children: 3,200 children whose families used a federally-subsidized housing voucher to rent an apartment in Montgomery County during 2001–07. Unlike public housing, however, these families were not randomly assigned to neighborhoods or schools, so

their results are not discussed here. However, these children's outcomes were consistent with those described for public housing children.

24. Since children were not tested until the second grade in Montgomery County, too few public housing children had test scores prior to two years enrollment in the district (that is, only those who first ported into the district at grade levels higher than kindergarten) to derive estimates.

25. For example, having a teacher with less than two full years of experience was associated with a reduction of student test score gains in math and reading of approximately 0.1 of a standard deviation (Hanushek, Kain, and Rivkin, "Teachers, Schools, and Academic Achievement," for children in Texas; Thomas J. Kane and Douglas O. Staiger, "Using Imperfect Information to Identify Effective Teachers," unpublished paper, School of Public Affairs, University of California–Los Angeles, 2005, for children in Los Angeles; and Jonah E. Rockoff, "The Impact of Individual Teachers on Student Achievement: Evidence from Panel Data," *American Economic Review* 94, no. 2 [2004]: 247–52 for children in two New Jersey districts). A teacher's cognitive ability (as measured by performance on teacher exams or standardized tests like ACT or SAT) positively impacted student performance; having a teacher whose test score on the state's teacher test was at the top or bottom of the distribution of teachers' scores had a modest effect (+/- 0.06 of a standard deviation) (see also Jacob, "The Challenges of Staffing Urban Schools with Effective Teachers"; Charles T. Clotfelter, Helen F. Ladd, and Jacob L. Vigdor. "Teacher Credentials and Student Achievement: Longitudinal Analysis with Student Fixed Effects," *Economics of Education Review* 26, no. 6 [2007]: 673–82).

26. Aud et al., *The Condition of Education 2010*; Kahlenberg, *All Together Now*, 39–40, citing Jonathan Crane, "The Epidemic Theory of Ghettos and Neighborhood Effects on Dropping Out and Teenage Childbearing," *American Journal of Sociology* 96, no. 5 (1991): 1226–59, and Dennis P. Hogan and Evelyn M. Kitagawa, "The Impact of Social Status, Family Structure, and Neighborhood on the Fertility of Black Adolescents," *American Journal of Sociology* 90, no. 4 (1985): 825–55.

27. Two studies of Texas and Georgia teachers suggest that the percentage of black students within the school and students' academic performance are respectively the two most important predictors of teacher mobility, followed by the economic composition of the student body (Hanushek, Kain, and Rivkin, "Why Public Schools Lose Teachers"; Scafidi, Sjoquist, and Stinebrickner, "Race, Poverty, and Teacher Mobility").

28. During the study period, the school district had a global gifted and talented screening process for all second graders as well as for students who ported into the district in third through fifth grades.

29. Initial gaps in public housing students' reading and math scores between green and red zone schools are not statistically significant at the p<.20 level.

30. As described in the technical appendix, public housing children's test scores were regressed on their prior school year's status (in this case, attendance at a red zone or green zone school). Thus, for children who had seven years of data, children's sixth grade scores (which was the first year of middle school) were regressed on their fifth grade red zone status, which was the last grade level in their elementary school.

31. *Our Call to Action.*

32. Paul Jargowsky and Mohamed El Komi, "Before or After the Bell? School Context and Neighborhood Effects on Student Achievement," Working Paper 28, National Center for Analysis of Longitudinal Data in Education Research, Urban Institute, 2009.

33. For example, Montgomery County has the highest proportion of three-bedroom public housing apartments among the trio of Prince Georges and Washington, D.C., public housing portfolios. This makes Montgomery County a draw for larger-sized households, which may or may not have a preference for Montgomery County's public school system.

34. For information about the expansion of inclusionary zoning, see David Rusk, "Nine Lessons for Inclusionary Zoning," keynote remarks, National Inclusionary Housing Conference, Washington, D.C., 2005, http://www.gamaliel.org/DavidRusk/keynote%2010-5-05.pdf.

35. Kahlenberg, *All Together Now*, 114, citing Gary Orfield and Susan E. Eaton, *Dismantling Desegregation: The Quiet Reversal of Brown v. Board of Education* (New York: New Press, 1996), 93, and Nina S. Mounts and Laurence Steinberg, "An Ecological Analysis of Peer Influence on Adolescent Grade Point Average and Drug Use," *Developmental Psychology* 31, no. 6 (November 1995): 915–22.

36. Aud et al., *The Condition of Education 2010*.

37. For information about the expansion of inclusionary zoning, see Rusk, "Nine Lessons for Inclusionary Zoning."

38. Jewel Bellush and Murray Hausknecht, "Public Housing: The Contexts of Failure," in *Housing Urban America*, ed. Jon Pynoos, Robert Schafer, and Chester Hartman (Chicago, Ill.: Aldine Publishing Company, 1967), 116.

39. Children in public housing were so widely spread across schools throughout the school district that they were infrequently clustered within the same classrooms in schools. For example, in 2006, 56 percent of students in public housing were the only students in public housing within their respective homerooms, 29 percent of students in public housing were in homerooms with one other student in public housing, 9 percent of students in public housing were enrolled in homerooms with three students in public housing, and the remaining 6 percent of students in public housing were enrolled in homerooms where anywhere from four to seven students in public housing were enrolled.

40. Students in public housing who lived in a single census block group attended as many as three different elementary schools. But students in public housing who attended the same school in a given year were drawn from as many as sixteen census block groups.

41. It is assumed that the variance terms from levels 2A, 3, and 2B are uncorrelated with each other, and that they have a mean of 0 and unrestricted covariance matrices of $\Sigma\varepsilon_i$, $\Sigma\varepsilon_s$, and $\Sigma\varepsilon_j$.

Chapter 3

1. W. S. Barnett, K. B. Robin, J. T. Hustedt, and K. L. Schulman, *The State of Preschool: 2003 State Preschool Yearbook* (New Brunswick, N.J.: NIEER, 2003).

2. I. V. Sawhill and R. Haskins, "The Future of Head Start: The Nation's Dual System of Child Care and Preschool Education," Brookings Center on Children and Families Briefs 27, Brookings Institution, 2003.

3. D. Stipek, "No Child Left Behind Comes to Preschool," *Elementary School Journal*, 106, no. 5 (2006): 455–65.

4. G. J. Duncan and K. Magnuson, "Can Family Socioeconomic Resources Account for Racial and Ethnic Test Score Gaps?" *The Future of Children* 15, no. 1 (2005): 35–54; S. F. Reardon, "The Widening Academic-Achievement Gap between the Rich and the

Poor: New Evidence and Possible Explanations," in *Whither Opportunity? Rising Inequality, Schools, and Children's Life Chances,* ed. G. Duncan and R. M. Murnane (New York: Russell Sage Foundation, 2011), 91–115.

5. V. E. Lee and D. T. Burkam, *Inequality at the Starting Gate: Social Background Differences in Achievement as Children Begin School* (Washington, D.C.: Economic Policy Institute, 2002).

6. *Head Start Impact Study: First Year Findings* (Washington, D.C.: U.S. Department of Health and Human Services, Administration for Children and Families, 2005).

7. S. Barnett, *Change We Need: Responding Responsibly to the Results of the Head Start Impact Study* (New Brunswick, N.J.: NIEER, 2010); *Investing in Young Children: New Directions in Federal Preschool and Early Childhood Policy,* ed. R. Haskins and W. S. Barnett (Washington, D.C.: Center on Children and Families at Brookings, 2010); S. Mead, "An Evolving Debate on Pre-k Quality?" *Education Week,* October 21, 2010, http://blogs.edweek.org/edweek/sarameads_policy_notebook/2010/10/an_evolving_debate_on_Pre-k_quality.html; C. T. Ramey and S. L. Ramey, "Head Start: Strategies to Improve Outcomes for Children Living in Poverty," in *Investing in Young Children,* 59–67 ; I. V. Sawhill and J. Baron, "We Need a New Start for Head Start," *Education Week* 29, no. 23 (2010): 22–23.

8. N. Aikens, L. Tarullo, L. Hulsey, C. Ross, J. West, and Y. Xue, *ACF-OPRE Report: A Year in Head Start: Children, Families and Programs* (Washington, D.C.: U.S. Department of Health and Human Services, Administration for Children and Families, Office of Planning, Research, and Evaluation, 2010).

9. W. S. Barnett, "Effectiveness of Early Educational Intervention," *Science* 333, no. 6045 (August 19, 2011): 975–78; W. T. Gormley, D. Phillips, S. Adelstein, and C. Shaw, "Head Start's Comparative Advantage: Myth or Reality?" *Policy Studies Journal* 38, no. 3 (2010): 397–418; G. T. Henry, C. S. Gordon, and D. K. Rickman, "Early Education Policy Alternatives: Comparing Quality and Outcomes of Head Start and State Pre-kindergarten," *Educational Evaluation and Policy Analysis* 28, no. 1 (2006): 77–99; F. Zhai, J. Brooks-Gunn, and J. Waldfogel, "Head Start and Urban Children's School Readiness: A Birth Cohort Study in 18 Cities," *Developmental Psychology* 47, no. 1 (2011): 134–52.

10. Henry, Gordon, and Rickman, "Early Education Policy Alternatives."

11. *Head Start Reauthorization,* Public Law 110-134, 110th Cong., 1st sess. (December 12, 2007).

12. L. Guernsey, "Proposed Rules Will Shake Up Head Start," Early Ed Watch blog, New American Foundation, September 23, 2010.

13. R. Pianta et al., "Features of Pre-kindergarten Programs, Classrooms and Teachers: Do They Predict Observed Classroom Quality and Child–Teacher Interactions?" *Applied Developmental Science* 9, no. 3 (2005):144–59.

14. E. D. Cahan, *Past Caring: A History of U.S. Preschool Care and Education for the Poor, 1820–1965* (New York: National Center for Children in Poverty, 1989); A. J. Cohen, "A Brief History of Federal Financing for Child Care in the U.S.," *The Future of Children* 6, no. 2 (1996): 26–40; M. A. Vinovskis, *The Birth of Head Start: Preschool Education Policies in the Kennedy and Johnson Administrations* (Chicago: University of Chicago Press, 2005).

15. *Parents Involved in Community Schools v. Seattle School District No. 1,* et al., 05-908 U.S. (2007).

16. G. Borman and M. Dowling, "Schools and Inequality: A Multilevel Analysis of Coleman's Equality of Educational Opportunity Data," *Teachers College Record*

112, no. 5 (2010): 1201–46; S. Konstantopoulos, "Trends of School Effects on Student Achievement: Evidence from NLS:72, HSB:82, and NELS:92," *Teachers College Record* 108, no. 12 (2006): 2550–81; S. Konstantopoulos and G. Borman, "Family Background and School Effects on Student Achievement: A Multilevel Analysis of the Coleman Data," *Teachers College Record* 113, no. 1 (2011): 97–132; R. W. Rumberger and G. J. Palardy, "Does Segregation Still Matter? The Impact of Student Composition on Academic Achievement in High School," *Teachers College Record* 107, no. 9 (2005): 1999–2045.

17. N. L. Aikens and O. Barbarin, "Socioeconomic Differences in Reading Trajectories: The Contribution of Family, Neighborhood, and School Contexts," *Journal of Educational Psychology* 100, no. 2 (2008): 235–51.

18. Ibid., 249.

19. J. G. Benson and G. Borman, "Family, Neighborhood, and School Settings across Seasons: When Do Socioeconomic Context and Racial Composition Matter for Reading Achievement Growth of Young Children," *Teachers College Record* 112, no. 5 (2010): 1338–90; K. Kainz and L. Vernon-Feagans, "The Ecology of Early Reading Development for Children in Poverty," *Elementary School Journal* 107, no. 5 (2007): 407–27.

20. C. Schechter and B. Bye, "Preliminary Evidence for the Impact of Mixed-Income Preschool on Low-Income Children's Language Growth," *Early Childhood Research Quarterly* 22 (2007): 137–46.

21. *From Neurons to Neighborhoods: The Science of Early Childhood Development,* ed. J. Shonkoff and D. Phillips (Washington, D.C.: National Academy Press, 2000); D. Kirp, *The Sandbox Investment: The Preschool Movement and Kids-First Politics* (Cambridge, Mass.: Harvard University Press, 2007).

22. W. S. Barnett, D. J. Epstein, M. E. Carolan, J. Fitzgerald, D. J. Ackerman, and A. H. Friedman, *The State of Preschool 2010* (New Brunswick, N.J.: NIEER, 2010).

23. M. Burchinal, L. Nelson, M. Carlson, and J. Brooks-Gunn, "Neighborhood Characteristics and Child Care Type and Quality," *Early Education and Development,* 19, no. 5 (2008): 702–25; B. Fuller, S. L. Kagan, S. Loeb, and Y. W. Chang, "Child Care Quality: Centers and Home Settings That Serve Poor Families," *Early Childhood Research Quarterly* 19 (2004): 505–27.

24. W. S. Barnett and D. J. Yarosz, *Who Goes to Preschool and Why Does It Matter?* (New Brunswick, N.J.: NIEER, November 2007).

25. H. Levin and H. L. Schwartz, "Educational Vouchers for Universal Preschools," *Economics of Education* 26 (2007): 3–16.

26. W. S. Barnett, D. J. Epstein, A. H. Friedman, R. A. Sansanelli, and J. T. Hustedt, *The State of Preschool 2009* (New Brunswick, N.J.: NIEER, 2009).

27. A. M. Dotterer, M. Burchinal, D. Bryant, D. Early, and R. C. Pianta, "Comparing Universal and Targeted Pre-Kindergarten Programs," in *The Promise of Pre-K,* ed. R. C. Pianta and C. Howes (Baltimore, Md.: Brookes Publishing, 2009), 65–76 .

28. *Eager to Learn: Educating Our Preschoolers,* ed. B. T. Bowman, M. S. Donovan, and M. S. Burns (Washington, D.C.: National Academy Press, 2001); M. Burchinal et al., "Predicting Child Outcomes at the End of Kindergarten from the Quality of Pre-Kindergarten Teacher-Child Interactions and Instruction," *Applied Developmental Science* 12, no. 3 (2008): 140–53; G. Camilli, S. Vargas, S. Ryan, and W. S. Barnett, "A Meta-Analysis of the Effects of Early Education Intervention on Cognitive and Social Development," *Teachers College Record* 112, no. 3 (2010): 579–620; D. M. Early et al., "Teachers' Education, Classroom Quality, and Young Children's Academic Skills:

Results from Seven Studies of Preschool Programs," *Child Development* 78, no. 2 (2007): 558–80; Mashburn et al., "Measures of Classroom Quality in Prekindergarten and Children's Development of Academic, Language, and Social Skills," *Child Development* 79, no. 3 (2008): 732–49; Pianta et al., "Features of Pre-Kindergarten Programs, Classrooms and Teachers"; Preschool Curriculum Evaluation Research Consortium, *Effects of Preschool Curriculum Programs on School Readiness* (Washington, D.C.: Institute of Education Sciences, U.S. Deptartment of Education, 2008).

29. W. S. Barnett and C. R. Belfield, "Early Childhood Development and Social Mobility," *The Future of Children* 16, no. 2 (2006): 73–98; Camilli et al., "A Meta-Analysis of the Effects of Early Education Intervention on Cognitive and Social Development."

30. D. Boyd, H. Lankford, S. Loeb, and J. Wyckoff, "Explaining the Short Careers of High-Achieving Teachers in Schools with Low-Performing Students," *American Economic Review* 95, no. 2 (2005): 166–71; Education Trust, *Out-of-field Teaching Persists in Key Academic Courses and High Poverty Schools* (Washington, D.C.: U.S. Deptartment of Education, National Center for Education Statistics, 2006); *The Condition of Education, 2006* (Washington, D.C.: U.S. Government Printing Office, 2006).

31. E. A. Hanushek, J. F. Kain, and S. G. Rivkin, "Why Public Schools Lose Teachers," *Journal of Human Resources* 39, no. 2 (2004): 326–54; C. K. Jackson, "Student Demographics, Teacher Sorting, and Teacher Quality: Evidence from the End of School Desegregation," *Journal of Labor Economics* 27, no. 2 (2009): 213–56.

32. Konstantopoulos, "Trends of School Effects on Student Achievement"; S. W. Raudenbush, R. P. Fotiu, and Y. F. Cheong, "Inequality of Access to Educational Resources: A National Report Card for Eighth-Grade Math," *Educational Evaluation and Policy Analysis* 20, no. 4 (1998): 253–67; Rumberger and Palardy, "Does Segregation Still Matter?"

33. R. M. Clifford et al., "What Is Pre-Kindergarten? Characteristics of Public Pre-Kindergarten Programs," *Applied Developmental Science* 9, no. 3 (2005): 126–43; L. M. Justice, A. J. Mashburn, B. K. Hamre, and R. C. Pianta, "Quality of Language and Literacy Instruction in Preschool Classrooms Serving At-Risk Pupils," *Early Childhood Research Quarterly* 23 (2008): 51–68; R. Pianta et al., "Features of Pre-kindergarten Programs, Classrooms and Teachers."

34. D. M. Early et al., "How Do Pre-Kindergartners Spend Their Time? Gender, Ethnicity, and Income as Predictors of Experiences in Pre-kindergarten Classrooms," *Early Childhood Research Quality* 25 (2010): 177–93; D. Stipek, "Teaching Practices in Kindergarten and First Grade: Different Strokes for Different Folks," *Early Childhood Research Quarterly* 19 (2004): 548–68.

35. D. Stipek, "No Child Left Behind Comes to Preschool," *The Elementary School Journal* 106, no. 5 (2006): 455–65; for a contrary view, see L. Delpit, *Other People's Children: Cultural Conflict in the Classroom* (New York: New Press, 1995).

36. G. Camilli, S. Vargas, S. Ryan, and W. S. Barnett, "A Meta-analysis of the Effects of Early Education Intervention on Cognitive and Social Development," *Teachers College Record* 112, no. 3 (2010): 579–620; R. DeVries, H. Reese-Learned, and P. Morgan, "Socio-moral Development in Direct-Instruction, Eclectic, and Constructivist Kindergartens: A Study of Children's Enacted Interpersonal Understanding," *Early Childhood Research Quarterly* 6 (1991): 473–517; D. Stipek, R. Feiler, D. Daniels, and S. Milburn, "Effects of Different Instructional Approaches on Young Children's Achievement and Motivation," *Child Development* 66 (1995): 209–23.

37. Stipek, Feiler, Daniels, and Milburn, "Effects of Different Instructional Approaches on Young Children's Achievement and Motivation."

38. S. J. Holochwost, K. DeMott, M. Buell, K. Yannetta, and D. Amsden, "Retention of Staff in the Early Childhood Education Workforce," *Child Youth Care Forum* 38 (2009): 227–37.

39. S. L. Kagan, *American Early Childhood Education: Preventing or Perpetuating Inequity?* (New York: Teachers College at Columbia University, April 2009); K. Magnuson and J. Waldfogel, "Early Childhood Care and Education: Effects on Ethnic and Racial Gaps in School Readiness," *The Future of Children* 15, no. 1 (2005): 169–96.

40. P. E. Barton and R. J. Coley, *The Family: America's Smallest School* (Princeton, N.J.: Educational Testing Service, 2007); J. Brooks-Gunn and G. J. Duncan, "The Effects of Poverty on Children," *Future of Children* 7 (1997): 55–71; W. J. Yeung, M. R. Linver, and J. Brooks-Gunn, "How Money Matters for Young Children's Development: Parental Investment and Family Processes," *Child Development* 73, no. 6 (2002): 1861–79.

41. A. Lareau, *Unequal Childhoods: Class, Race, and Family Life* (Berkeley: University of California Press, 2003).

42. R. D. Kahlenberg, *All Together Now: Creating Middle-class Schools through Public School Choice* (Washington, D.C.: Brookings Institution Press, 2001).

43. G. T. Henry and D. K. Rickman, "Do Peers Influence Children's Skill Development in Preschool?" *Economics of Education Review* 26 (2007): 100–12.

44. A. J. Mashburn, L. M. Justice, J. T. Downer, and R. C. Pianta, "Peer Effects on Children's Language Achievement during Pre-Kindergarten," *Child Development* 80, no. 3 (2009): 686–701.

45. Henry and Rickman, "Do Peers Influence Children's Skill Development in Preschool?"

46. L. M. Justice, Y. Petscher, C. Schatschneider, and A. Mashburn, "Peer Effects in Preschool Classrooms: Is Children's Language Growth Associated with Their Classmates' Skills?" *Child Development* 82, no. 6 (2011): 1768–77.

47. A. Lareau, *Unequal Childhoods: Class, Race, and Family Life.*

48. Henry and Rickman, "Do Peers Influence Children's Skill Development in Preschool?"; *From Neurons to Neighborhoods: The Science of Early Childhood Development,* ed. J. Shonkoff and D. Phillips (Washington, D.C.: National Academy Press, 2000).

49. A. Buttaro, S. Catsambis, L. M. Mulkey, and L. C. Steelman, "An Organizational Perspective on the Origins of Instructional Segregation: School Composition and Use of Within-class Ability Grouping in American Kindergarten," *Teachers College Record,* 112, no. 5 (2010): 1300–37.

50. *Beginning Literacy with Language,* ed. D. K. Dickinson and P. O. Tabors (Baltimore, Md.: Brookes Publishing, 2001).

51. B. Hart and T. R. Risley, *Meaningful Differences in the Everyday Experience of Young American Children* (Baltimore, Md.: Brookes Publishing, 1995); Justice, Mashburn, Hamre, and Pianta, "Quality of Language and Literacy Instruction in Preschool Classrooms Serving At-Risk Pupils."

52. R. Grant, "Meeting the Needs of Young Second Language Learners," in *Meeting the Challenge of Linguistic and Cultural Diversity in Early Childhood Education,* ed. E. E. Garcia and B. McLaughlin (New York: Teachers College Press, 1995), 1–17; F. Genesee and E. Nicoladis, "Language Development in Bilingual Preschool Children," in *Meeting the Challenge of Linguistic and Cultural Diversity in Early Childhood Education,* 18–33.

53. W. G. Bowen and D. Bok, *The Shape of the River: Long-Term Consequences of Considering Race in College and University Admissions* (Princeton, N. J.: Princeton University Press, 1998); J. H. Braddock and A. D. C. Gonzalez, "Social Isolation and Social Cohesion: The Effects of K–12 Neighborhood and School Segregation on Intergroup Orientations," *Teachers College Record* 112, no. 6 (2010): 4–5; P. L. Carter, "Race and Cultural Flexibility among Students in Different Multiracial Schools," *Teachers College Record* 112, no. 6 (2010): 1–2; P. R. Goldsmith, "Learning Apart, Living Apart: How the Racial and Ethnic Segregation of Schools and Colleges Perpetuates Residential Segregation," *Teachers College Record* 112, no. 6 (2010): 3–4; *Race-Conscious Policies for Assigning Students to Schools: Social Science Research and the Supreme Court Cases,* ed. R. L. Linn and K. G. Welner (Washington, D.C.: National Academy of Education, 2007); E. Stearns, "Long-term Correlates of High School Racial Composition: Perpetuation Theory Reexamined," *Teachers College Record,* 112, no. 6 (2010): 5–6, www.tcrecord.org; A. S. Wells, J. Duran, and T. White, "Refusing to Leave Desegregation Behind: From Graduates of Racially Diverse Schools to the Supreme Court," *Teachers College Record* 110, no. 12 (2008): 2532–70; A. S. Wells, J. J. Holme, A. T. Revilla, and A. K. Atanda, *Both Sides Now: The Story of School Desegregation's Graduates* (Berkeley: University of California Press, 2009).

54. P. Gurin, E. Dey, S. Hurtado, and G. Gurin, "Diversity in Higher Education: Theory and Impact on Educational Outcomes," *Harvard Educational Review* 72, no. 3 (2002): 330–66.

55. R. S. Bigler and L. S. Liben, "Developmental Intergroup Theory: Explaining and Reducing Children's Social Stereotyping and Prejudice," *Current Directions in Psychological Science* 16, no. 3 (2007): 162–66; J. A. Chafel and C. Neitzel, "Young Children's Ideas about the Nature, Causes, Justification, and Alleviation of Poverty," *Early Childhood Research Quarterly* 20 (2005): 433–50; N. W. Finkelstein and R. Haskins, "Kindergarten Children Prefer Same-color Peers," *Child Development* 54 (1983): 502–08; P. R. Goldsmith, "Learning Apart, Living Apart: How the Racial and Ethnic Segregation of Schools and Colleges Perpetuates Residential Segregation," *Teachers College Record* 112, no. 6 (2010): 3–4; C. Howes, K. H. Rubin, H. S. Ross, and D. C. French, "Peer Interaction of Young Children," *Monographs of the Society for Research in Child Development* 53, no. 1 (1988): 1–78; R. L. Leahy, "The Development of the Conception of Economic Inequality: Descriptions of Rich and Poor People," *Child Development* 52 (1981): 523–32; P. G. Ramsey, "Growing Up with the Contradictions of Race and Class," *Young Children* 50, no. 6 (September 1995): 18–22; M. B. Spencer and C. Markstrom-Adams, "Identity Processes among Racial and Ethnic Minority Children in America," *Child Development* 61 (1990): 290–310.

56. C. Howes and F. Wu, "Peer Interactions and Friendships in an Ethnically Diverse School Setting," *Child Development* 61 (1990): 537–41.

57. J. Piaget and B. Inhelder, *The Psychology of the Child* (New York: Basic Books, 1969).

58. Justice, Schatschneider, and Mashburn, "Peer Effects in Preschool Classrooms."

59. Mashburn, Justice, Downer, and Pianta, "Peer Effects on Children's Language Achievement during Pre-Kindergarten."

60. *Eager to Learn: Educating Our Preschoolers,* ed. B. T. Bowman, M. S. Donovan, and M. S. Burns (Washington, D.C.: National Academy Press, 2001).

61. Y. Xue and S. J. Meisels, "Early Literacy Instruction and Learning in Kindergarten: Evidence from the Early Childhood Longitudinal Study—Kindergarten Class of 1998–1999," *American Educational Research Journal* 41, no. 1 (2004): 191–229.

62. Borman and Dowling, "Schools and Inequality"; C. C. Burris, E. Wiley, K. G. Welner, and J. Murphy, "Accountability, Rigor, and Detracking: Achievement Effects of Embracing a Challenging Curriculum as a Universal Good for All Students," *Teachers College Record* 110, no. 3 (2008): 571–607; J. Oakes, A. S. Wells, M. Jones, and A. Datnow, "Detracking: The Social Construction of Ability, Cultural Politics, and Resistance to Reform," *Teachers College Record* 98 (1997): 482–510; M. J. Petrilli, "All Together Now? Educating High and Low-Achievers in the Same Classroom," *Education Next* (Winter 2011): 49–55. Research on racial desegregation policies has also not found academic detriment to white students, although most of the white students were low-income as well. See *Race-Conscious Policies for Assigning Students to Schools: Social Science Research and the Supreme Court Cases,* ed. R. L. Linn and K. G. Welner (Washington, D.C.: National Academy of Education, 2007); A. Saatcioglu, "Disentangling School- and Student-Level Effects of Desegregation on the Dropout Problem in Urban High Schools: Evidence from the Cleveland Municipal School District, 1997–1998," *Teachers College Record* 112, no. 5 (2010): 6–7.

63. M. R. Burchinal and D. Cryer, "Diversity, Child Care Quality, and Developmental Outcomes," *Early Childhood Research Quarterly* 18 (2003): 401–26; C. Howes et al., "Ready to Learn? Children's Pre-academic Achievement in Pre-kindergarten Programs," *Early Childhood Research Quarterly* 23 (2008): 27–50.

64. K. E. Sanders, A. Deihl, and A. Kyler, "DAP in the 'Hood: Perceptions of Child Care Practices by African American Child Care Directors Caring for Children of Color," *Early Childhood Research Quarterly* 22 (2007): 396.

65. L. Delpit, *Other People's Children: Cultural Conflict in the Classroom* (New York: New Press, 1995); O. A. Barbarin et al., "Parental Conceptions of School Readiness: Relation to Ethnicity, Socioeconomic Status, and Children's Skills," *Early Education and Development* 19, no. 5 (2008): 671–701.

66. C. S. Huntsinger and P. E. Jose, "Parental Involvement in Children's Schooling: Different Meanings in Different Cultures," *Early Childhood Research Quarterly* 24 (2009): 398–410.

67. C. B. Day, "Leveraging Diversity to Benefit Children's Social-Emotional Development and School Readiness," in *School Readiness and Social-Emotional Development: Perspectives on Cultural Diversity,* ed. B. Bowman and E. K. Moore (Washington, D.C.: National Black Child Development Institute, 2006), 23–32; L. M. Espinosa, "Assessment of Young English Language Learners," in *Young English Language Learners: Current Research and Emerging Directions for Practice and Policy,* ed. E. E. Garcia and E. C. Frede (New York: Teachers College Press, 2010), 119–42.

68. J. B. Hinnant, M. O'Brien, and S. R. Ghazarian, "The Longitudinal Relations of Teacher Expectations to Achievement in the Early School Years," *Journal of Educational Psychology* 101, no. 3 (2009): 662–70; S. R. Sirin, P. Ryce, and M. Mir, "How Teachers' Values Affect Their Evaluation of Children of Immigrants: Findings from Islamic and Public Schools," *Early Childhood Research Quarterly* 24 (2009), 463–73.

69. V. Buysse, B. D. Goldman, and M. L. Skinner, "Friendship Formation in Inclusive Early Childhood Classrooms: What Is the Teacher's Role?" *Early Childhood Research Quarterly* 18 (2003): 485–501; C. J. Dowsett, A. C. Huston, A. E. Imes, and L. Gennetian, "Structural and Process Features in 3 Types of Child Care for Children from High and Low Income Families," *Early Childhood Research Quarterly* 23 (2008): 69–93; F. Palermo, L. D. Hanish, C. L. Martin, R. Fabes, and M. Reiser, "Preschoolers' Academic Readiness: What Role Does the Teacher-Child Relationship Play?" *Early Childhood Research Quarterly* 22 (2007): 407–22.

70. B. Fuller and R. F. Elmore, "Empirical Research on Educational Choice: What Are the Implications for Policymakers?" in *Who Chooses? Who Loses?* ed. B. Fuller and R. F. Elmore (New York: Teachers College Press, 1996), 196.

71. Duncan and Magnuson, "Can Family Socioeconomic Resources Account for Racial and Ethnic Test Score Gaps?"

72. "Census Bureau Estimates Nearly Half of Children under Age 5 Are Minorities: Estimates Find Nation's Population Growing Older, More Diverse," press release, U.S. Census Bureau, May 14, 2009.

73. V. E. Lee, "Using Hierarchical Linear Modeling to Study Social Contexts: The Case of School Effects," *Educational Psychologist* 35, no. 2 (2000): 125–41; S. W. Raudenbush and A. S. Bryk, *Hierarchical Linear Models: Applications and Data Analysis Methods* (Thousand Oaks, Calif.: Sage Publications, 2002).

74. J. S. Coleman et al., *Equality of Educational Opportunity* (Washington, D.C.: U.S. Department of Health, Education, and Welfare, Office of Education, 1966).

75. D. Early et al., "Pre-Kindergarten in Eleven States: NCEDL's Multi-state Study of Pre-kindergarten and Study of State-Wide Early Education Programs (SWEEP): Preliminary Descriptive Report," National Center for Early Development and Learning, May 2005.

76. "2003 HHS Poverty Guidelines," U.S. Dept. of Health and Human Services, Office of the Assistant Secretary for Planning and Evaluation, *Federal Register* 68 (26), (2003): 6456–58, http://aspe.hhs.gov/poverty/03poverty.htm.

77. "Income Stable, Poverty Up, Numbers of Americans with and without Health Insurance Rise, Census Bureau Reports," press release, U.S. Census Bureau, Washington, D.C., 2004, http://www.census.gov/PressRelease/www/releases/archives/income_wealth/002484.html.

78. When data is normally distributed, about two-thirds of the data points (family income in this example) lie within one standard deviation above or below the sample mean and about one-third lie below or above those boundaries.

79. D. Ready, "Socioeconomic Disadvantage: School Attendance and Early Cognitive Development: The Differential Effects of School Exposure," *Sociology of Education* 83, no. 4 (2010): 271–86.

80. Magnuson and Waldfogel, "Early Childhood Care and Education."

81. J. Brooks-Gunn and L. B. Markman, "The Contribution of Parenting to Ethnic and Racial Gaps in School Readiness," *The Future of Children* 15, no. 1 (2005): 139–57.

82. R. Chetty et al., "How Does Your kindergarten Classroom Affect Your Earnings? Evidence from Project STAR," NBER Working Paper No. 16381, Cambridge, Mass., National Bureau for Economic Research, 2010; E. Dearing, K. McCartney, and B. A. Taylor, "Does Higher Quality Early Childhood Care Promote Low-income Children's Math and Reading Achievement in Middle Childhood? *Child Development* 80, no. 5 (2009): 1329–49; G. J. Duncan, J. Ludwig, and K. A. Magnuson, "Reducing Poverty through Preschool Interventions," *The Future of Children* 17, no. 2 (2007): 143–60; A. J. Reynolds, J. A. Temple, and S.-R. Ou, "School-based Early Intervention and Child Well-being in the Chicago Longitudinal Study," *Child Welfare* 82, no. 5 (2003): 633–56; A. J. Reynolds et al., "Effects of a School-based, Early Childhood Intervention on Adult Health and Well-being," *Archives of Pediatrics and Adolescent Medicine* 161, no. 8 (2007): 730–39.

83. J. J. Heckman, J. Stixrud, and S. Urzua, "The Effects of Cognitive and Noncognitive Abilities on Labor Market Outcomes and Social Behavior," *Journal of Labor Economics* 24, no. 3 (2006): 411–82.

84. J. Piaget, *The Construction of Reality in the Child* (New York: Ballantine Books, 1954).

85. C. S. Reichardt, "The Statistical Analysis of Data from Nonequivalent Group Designs," in *Quasi-experimental Design and Analysis Issues for Field Settings*, ed. T. D. Cook and D. T. Campbell (Chicago: Rand McNally College Publishing, 1979), 147–205.

86. G. J. Duncan and C. M. Gibson-Davis, "Connecting Child Care Quality to Child Outcomes: Drawing Policy Lessons from Non-experimental Data," *Evaluation Review* 30, no. 5 (2006): 611–30; B. Schneider, M. Carnoy, J. Kilpatrick, W. H. Schmidt, and R. J. Shavelson, *Estimating Causal Effects Using Experimental and Observational Designs* (Washington, D.C.: American Education Research Association, 2007).

87. Duncan and Gibson-Davis, "Connecting Child Care Quality to Child Outcomes."

88. Reichardt, "The Statistical Analysis of Data from Nonequivalent Group Designs."

89. Dearing, McCartney, and Taylor, "Does Higher Quality Early Childhood Care Promote Low-income Children's Math and Reading Achievement in Middle Childhood?"

90. See chapter 2 in this volume.

91. B. K. Hamre and R. C. Pianta, "Learning Opportunities in Preschool and Early Elementary Classrooms," in *School Readiness and the Transition to Kindergarten in the Era of Accountability*, ed. R. C. Pianta, M. J. Cox, and K. L. Snow (Baltimore: Brookes Publishing, 2007), 49–83.

92. L. M. Desimone and D. Long, "Teacher Effects and the Achievement Gap: Do Teacher and Teaching Quality Influence the Achievement Gap between Black and White and High- and Low-SES Students in the Early Grades?" *Teachers College Record* 112, no. 12 (2010): 3024–73.

93. Burchinal and Cryer, "Diversity, Child Care Quality, and Developmental Outcomes"; Burchinal et al., "Predicting Child Outcomes at the End of Kindergarten from the Quality of Pre-Kindergarten Teacher-Child Interactions and Instruction"; Howes et al., "Ready to Learn?"; Justice, Mashburn, Hamre, and Pianta, "Quality of Language and Literacy Instruction in Preschool Classrooms Serving At-Risk Pupils"; Mashburn et al., "Measures of Classroom Quality in Prekindergarten and Children's Development of Academic, Language, and Social Skills"; E. S. Peisner-Feinberg et al., "The Relation of Preschool Child-care Quality to Children's Cognitive and Social Developmental Trajectories through Second Grade," *Child Development* 72, no. 5 (2001): 1534–53.

94. C. J. Hill, H. S. Bloom, A. R. Black, and M. W. Lipsey, *Empirical Benchmarks for Interpreting Effect Sizes in Research* (New York: Manpower Development Research Council, 2007).

95. D. N. Harris, "Toward Policy-relevant Benchmarks for Interpreting Effect Sizes: Combining Effects with Costs," *Educational Evaluation and Policy Analysis* 31, no. 1 (2009): 3–29.

96. *Head Start Impact Study: First Year Findings* (Washington, D.C.: U.S. Dept. of Health and Human Services, Administration for Children and Families, 2005). The Head Start Impact Study found an effect of 0.12 standard deviations for three-year-olds; no effect was found for four-year-olds.

97. Coleman et al., *Equality of Educational Opportunity*.

98. Borman and Dowling, "Schools and Inequality."

99. Indeed, I do not mean to imply that schools matter more than families or neighborhoods in a child's academic trajectory. After finding comparable estimates for high school socioeconomic composition and children's own SES, Rumberger and Palardy nevertheless concluded, "Most of the variability in student achievement overall, as opposed to achievement growth during high school, is associated with students (and their families and communities), not the schools they attend." Rumberger and G. J. Palardy, "Does Segregation Still Matter?" 2023.

100. Henry and Rickman, "Do Peers Influence Children's Skill Development in Preschool?"

101. Duncan and Magnuson, "Can Family Socioeconomic Resources Account for Racial and Ethnic Test Score Gaps?"; J. R. Smith, J. Brooks-Gunn, and P. K. Klebanov, "Consequences of Living in Poverty for Young Children's Cognitive and Verbal Ability and Early School Achievement," in *Consequences of Growing Up Poor*, ed. G. J. Duncan and J. Brooks-Gunn (New York: Russell Sage Foundation, 1997), 132–67.

102. Duncan and Magnuson, "Can Family Socioeconomic Resources Account for Racial and Ethnic Test Score Gaps?"; Brooks-Gunn and Markman, "The Contribution of Parenting to Ethnic and Racial Gaps in School Readiness"; I. N. Sandler, E. N. Schoenfelder, S. A. Wolchik, and D. P. MacKinnon, "Long-term Impact of Prevention Programs to Promote Effective Parenting: Lasting Effects but Uncertain Processes," *Annual Review of Psychology* 62 (2010): 299–329.

103. C. V. Willie, R. Edwards, and M. J. Alves, *Student Diversity, Choice, and School Improvement* (Westport, Conn.: Bergin and Garvey, 2002).

104. Lee and Burkam, *Inequality at the Starting Gate*.

105. Henry and Rickman, "Do Peers Influence Children's Skill Development in Preschool?"

106. Ibid.

107. D. M. Early et al., "Teachers' Education, Classroom Quality, and Young Children's Academic Skills: Results from Seven Studies of Preschool Programs," *Child Development* 78, no. 2 (2007): 558–80; Howes et al., "Ready to Learn?"; Mashburn et al., "Measures of Classroom Quality in PreKindergarten and Children's Development of Academic, Language, and Social Skills."

108. Early et al., "Teachers' Education, Classroom Quality, and Young Children's Academic Skills"; B. J. Hardin et al., "Teachers, Families, and Communities Supporting English Language Learners in Inclusive Pre-Kindergartens: An Evaluation of a Professional Development Model," *Journal of Early Childhood Teacher Education* 31, no. 1 (2010): 20–36; S. L. Kagan, K. Kauerz, and K. Tarrant, *The Early Care and Education Teaching Workforce: An Agenda for Reform* (New York: Teachers College Press, 2008); C. Rothstein-Fisch, E. Trumbull, and S. G. Garcia, "Making the Implicit Explicit: Supporting Teachers to Bridge Cultures," *Early Childhood Research Quarterly* 24 (2009): 474–86.

109. *Eager to Learn: Educating Our Preschoolers*, ed. B. T. Bowman, M. S. Donovan, and M. S. Burns (Washington, D.C.: National Academy Press, 2001); W. S. Barnett and C. R. Belfield, "Early Childhood Development and Social Mobility," *The Future of Children* 16, no. 2 (2006): 73–98; Magnuson and Waldfogel, "Early Childhood Care and Education"; M. Malakoff, "The Need for Universal Preschool Access for Children Not Living in Poverty," in *A Vision for Universal Preschool Education*, ed. E. Zigler, W. A. Gilliam, and S. M. Jones (New York: Cambridge University Press, 2006), 89–106.

110. Henry and Rickman, "Do Peers Influence Children's Skill Development in Preschool?"

111. H. Levin and H. L. Schwartz, "Educational Vouchers for Universal Preschools," *Economics of Education* 26 (2007): 3–16.

112. J. J. Holmes and A. S. Wells, "School Choice beyond District Borders: Lessons for the Reauthorization of NCLB from Interdistrict Desegregation and Open Enrollment Plans," in *Improving on No Child Left Behind*, ed. R. D. Kahlenberg (New York: The Century Foundation Press, 2008), 139–215: C. L. McAllister, T. L. Thomas, P. C. Wilson, and B. L. Green, "Root Shock Revisited: Perspectives of Early Head Start Mothers on Community and Policy Environments and Their Effects on Child Health, Development, and School Readiness," *American Journal of Public Health* 99, no. 2 (2009): 205–10; *Head Start: Progress and Challenges in Implementing Transportation Regulations* (Washington, D.C.: U.S. Government Accountability Office, July 27, 2006).

113. *NAEYC QRIS Toolkit* (Washington, D.C.: National Association for the Education of Young Children, 2008); A. Shlay, M. Weinraub, and M. Harmon, *Racial and Ethnic Differences in Welfare Leavers' Child Care Preferences: A Factorial Survey Analysis*, Report Prepared for the William Penn Foundation and the Claneil Foundation by the Family and Children's Policy Collaborative (Philadelphia: Temple University, April 2007).

114. Barbarin et al., "Parental Conceptions of School Readiness."

115. Y. E. Chang, A. C. Huston, D. A. Crosby, and L. A. Gennetian, "The Effects of Welfare and Employment Programs on Children's Participation in Head Start," *Economics of Education Review* 26 (2007): 17–32; McAllister et al., "Root Shock Revisited."

116. G. J. Duncan, J. Ludwig, and K. A. Magnuson, "Reducing Poverty through Preschool Interventions," *The Future of Children* 17, no. 2 (2007): 143–60; E. Zigler, W. S. Gilliam, and S. Jones, *A Vision for Universal Preschool Education* (New York: Cambridge University Press, 2006).

117. M. Chau and A. Douglas-Hall, *Low-income Children in the U.S.: National and State Trend Data, 1997–2007* (New York: National Center for Children in Poverty, November 2008); B. Western, D. Bloome, and C. Percheski, "Inequality among American Families with Children, 1975 to 2005," *American Sociological Review* 73 (2008): 903–20.

118. Malakoff, "The Need for Universal Preschool Access for Children Not Living in Poverty"; S. J. Styfco, "A Place for Head Start in a World of Universal Preschool," in *A Vision for Universal Preschool Education*, ed. E. Zigler, W. A. Gilliam, and S. M. Jones (New York: Cambridge University Press, 2006), 216–40.

119. Barnett, *Change We Need*; R. Haskins and W. S. Barnett, *Investing in Young Children: New Directions in Federal Preschool and Early Childhood Policy* (Washington, D.C.: Center on Children and Families at Brookings, 2010); S. Mead, "An Evolving Debate on Pre-K Quality? *Education Week*, October 21, 2010, http://blogs.edweek.org/edweek/sarameads_policy_notebook/2010/10/an_evolving_debate_on_Pre-k_quality.html; Sawhill and Baron, "We Need a New Start for Head Start."

120. Styfco, "A Place for Head Start in a World of Universal Preschool."

121. Ibid.

122. R. C. Pianta, K. M. LaParo, and B. K. Hamre, *Classroom Assessment Scoring System—CLASS* (Baltimore: Brookes Publishing, 2007).

123. T. Harms, R. M. Clifford, and D. Cryer, *The Early Childhood Environment Rating Scale,* rev. ed. (New York: Teachers College Press, 1998).

124. L. M. Dunn and L. M. Dunn, *Peabody Picture Vocabulary Test,* rev. 3d. ed. (Circle Pines, Minn.: American Guidance Services, 1997).

125. R. Woodcock, K. McGrew, and N. Mather, *Woodcock-Johnson III* (Itasca, Ill.: Riverside, 2001).

126. A. D. Hightower et al., "The Teacher-Rating Scale: A Brief Objective Measure of Elementary Children's School Problem Behaviors and Competencies," *School Psychology Review* 15, no. 3 (1986): 393–409.

Chapter 4

1. On the value for education policymakers of cost-effectiveness studies, see Henry Levin, "Waiting for Godot: Cost-Effectiveness Analysis in Education," *New Directions for Evaluation* 90 (Summer 2001): 55–68. Despite their value, earlier cost-effectiveness studies of education interventions have wisely cautioned readers about the "rough," assumption-heavy nature of these types of studies. See, e.g., Sarah J. Reber, "School Desegregation and Educational Attainment for Blacks," National Bureau of Economic Research, NBER Working Paper 13193, June 2007, 27–28.

2. McKinsey and Company, "The Economic Impact of the Achievement Gap in America's Schools," Summary of Findings, April 2009, 9.

3. Christopher B. Swanson, "Who Graduates in the South?" a policy bulletin from the Education Policy Center at the Urban Institute, May 2005.

4. *The Price We Pay: Economic and Social Consequences of Inadequate Education,* ed. Clive R. Belfield and Henry M. Levin (Washington, D.C.: Brookings Institution Press, 2007); Mark A. Cohen and Alex R. Piquero, "New Evidence on the Monetary Value of Saving a High Risk Youth," Vanderbilt University Law School, Law and Economics Research Paper No. 08-07, December 2007; Andrew Sum, Ishwar Khatiwada, and Joseph McLaughlin, "The Consequences of Dropping Out of High School: Joblessness and Jailing for High School Dropouts and the High Cost for Taxpayers," Center for Labor Market Studies, Northeastern University, October 2009.

5. The case for socioeconomically integrated schools is made most comprehensively in Richard D. Kahlenberg, *All Together Now: Creating Middle-Class Schools through Public School Choice* (Washington, D.C.: Brookings Institution Press, 2001). For a summary of the literature comparing students, parents, and teachers in middle-class and high-poverty schools, see Richard D. Kahlenberg, "Turnaround Schools That Work: Moving Beyond Separate but Equal," The Century Foundation, November 11, 2009, 2–5, http://www.tcf.org/publications/education/turnaround.pdf.

6. U.S. Department of Education, *The Condition of Education 2008* (Washington, D.C.: Government Printing Office, 2008), 51; Richard M. Ingersoll, cited in "Parsing the Achievement Gap: Baselines for Tracking Progress," Educational Testing Service, October 2003, 11; Linda Darling-Hammond, *Doing What Matters Most: Investing in Quality Teaching* (New York: National Commission on Teaching and America's Future, 1997), 25–27.

7. Kahlenberg, *All Together Now,* 62 (PTA membership); Kathleen Herrold and Kevin O'Donnell, *Parent and Family Involvement in Education, 2006–07 School Year* (Washington, D.C.: National Center for Education Statistics, August 2008), 9, Table 3 (parent volunteer and committee service).

8. *Elementary School Children: Many Change Schools Frequently, Harming Their Education* (Washington, D.C.: U.S. General Accounting Office, 1994) (student

mobility); Rachel Dinkes, Emily Forrest Cataldi, and Wendy Lin-Kelly, *Indicators of School Crime and Safety: 2008* (Washington, D.C.: National Center for Education Statistics, December 2008), 99, Table 7.2 (disruption, as measured by incidents of teacher disrespect); William Elliott III and Sondra Beverly, "The Role of Savings and Wealth in Reducing 'Wilt' between Expectations and College Attendance," Center for Social Development, George Warren Brown School of Social Work, CSD Working Paper No. 10-01, 2010 (correlation between student savings and college aspiration and attendance).

9. Douglas N. Harris, "Ending the Blame Game on Educational Inequity: A Study of 'High Flying' Schools and NCLB," Education Policy Research Unit, Arizona State University, March 2006. High-poverty schools denotes schools with at least 50 percent of their student bodies eligible for free or reduced-price lunch; middle-class schools are those with fewer than 50 percent of their student body eligible for free or reduced-price lunch.

10. See this book's appendix for the list of school districts (which includes other local education agencies employing socioeconomic diversification in some fashion).

11. *Parents Involved in Community Schools v. Seattle School District No. 1*, 551 U.S. 701 (2007).

12. On legal strategies in support of socioeconomic school integration, see Kahlenberg, *All Together Now*, chapter 7, 167–84. On research comparing socioeconomic integration's effect on raising academic achievement to racial integration's effect, see: James S. Coleman et al., *Equality of Educational Opportunity*, U.S. Government Printing Office, Washington D.C., 1966, 307; Richard D. Kahlenberg, "A New Way on School Integration," The Century Foundation, November 2006, 4–6, http://www.tcf.org/publications/education/schoolintegration.pdf; Kahlenberg, *All Together Now*, 36, n. 61; Gary Orfield, *Must We Bus? Segregated Schools and National Policy* (Washington, D.C.: Brookings Institution Press, 1978), 69; Gary Orfield and Chungmei Lee, "Why Segregation Matters: Poverty and Educational Inequality," Harvard Civil Rights Project, January 2005; and Russell W. Rumberger and Gregory J. Palardy, "Does Resegregation Matter?" in *School Resegregation: Must the South Turn Back?* ed. John Charles Boger and Gary Orfield (Chapel Hill: University of North Carolina Press, 2005), 137.

13. St. Louis's integration model is nominally race-based, but its effect is socioeconomic integration because it centers on an exchange of students between low-income urban areas and more affluent suburban jurisdictions.

14. "CPS Announces New Policy for Admission to Selective Enrollment and Magnet Schools: Socio-Economic Data Will Be Used Instead of Race-Based Criteria," Chicago Public Schools Press Release, November 10, 2009, http://www.cps.edu/News/Press_releases/2009/Pages/11_10_2009_PR!.aspx.

15. On controlled choice, see Charles V. Willie, Ralph Edwards, and Michael J. Alves, *Student Diversity, Choice, and School Improvement* (Westport, Conn.: Praeger, 1998).

16. On the recent growth of poverty in the suburbs, see Elizabeth Kneebone and Emily Garr, "The Suburbanization of Poverty: Trends in Metropolitan America, 2000 to 2008," Metropolitan Policy Program, Brookings Institution, January 2010.

17. "Integrating Schools: John Edwards Has Interesting Ideas about How to Do It," Editorial, *Washington Post*, July 23, 2007, A16, http://www.washingtonpost.com/wp-dyn/content/article/2007/07/22/AR2007072200879.html, and Mike Allen, "Edwards

Has Plan to Diversify Schools," *Politico*, July 17, 2007, http://www.politico.com/news/stories/0707/4957.html.

18. See Duncan Chaplin, "Estimating the Impact of Economic Integration of Schools on Racial Integration," in *Divided We Fail: Coming Together through Public School Choice: The Report of the Century Foundation Task Force on the Common School* (New York: The Century Foundation Press, 2002), 87–113, especially Table 1 on 96; Charles T. Clotfelter, *After Brown: The Rise and Retreat of School Desegregation* (Princeton: Princeton University Press, 2004), 61–67; and Jennifer Jellison Holme and Amy Stuart Wells, "School Choice beyond District Borders: Lessons from the Reauthorization of NCLB from Interdistrict Desegregation and Open Enrollment Plans," in *Improving on No Child Left Behind: Getting Education Reform Back on Track*, ed. Richard D. Kahlenberg (New York: The Century Foundation Press, 2008), 145–48.

19. For an introduction to these benefits and the research literature illuminating them, see Erica Frankenberg and Genevieve Siegel-Hawley, "The Forgotten Choice? Rethinking Magnet Schools in a Changing Landscape," the Civil Rights Project at the University of California, 2008.

20. These index numbers, from 2005–06 data, are on file with the Editorial Projects in Education Research Center, 2009. Data from 2001–02 indicate that the national average socioeconomic segregation index level during that year was 0.40, suggesting that socioeconomic segregation has trended upward during the past decade. There are school districts currently at a socioeconomic segregation index level of 0.24, and at even lower levels, according to an Editorial Projects in Education survey of high schools in fifteen southern states and the District of Columbia. See Swanson, "Who Graduates in the South?" especially the graph "Graduation Rates and Economic Segregation" on 2.

21. The formula for the segregation index is $xP^*x = \sum (x_i/X)(x_i/t_i)$ where xP^*x is the segregation index level for a particular school district, x_i is the number of FRL students in school i, X is the total number of FRL students in the district, and t_i is the total number of students in school i. For the Editorial Projects in Education's presentation of the formula, see Christopher B. Swanson, "Who Graduates? Who Doesn't? A Statistical Portrait of Public High School Graduation, Class of 2001," The Education Policy Center at the Urban Institute, 2004, 10. For more on measuring segregation with an isolation index, see Douglas Massey and Nancy Denton, "The Dimensions of Racial Segregation," *Social Forces* 67, no. 2 (1988): 281–315. The isolation index primarily measures the distribution of FRL students across the district. Although it is sensitive to the overall composition of the district, according to an *American Journal of Sociology* article by Stanley Lieberson and Donna Carter, claims about the extent of this sensitivity have been "misleading" (299). Lieberson and Carter explain that an isolation index is not reducible to composition and hence is "not merely a reflection of population composition" (300–03). Further, they argue that relative composition is an essential aspect of understanding the consequences of segregation in terms of the actual experience of minorities. Indeed, in my own study, although I am primarily interested in the pre- and post-distribution of students before and after integration, the fact that the intervention under investigation moves from two separate groups of homogenous populations to a single population with a more balanced composition is a key factor in the students' pre- and post-intervention experiences. Because the isolation index is asymmetrical (that is, its measurement of the minority's interaction with the majority group and its measurement of the majority's interaction with the minority

group do not add up to 1.0), it helps capture how a given population distribution "may appear radically different to the groups involved" (309). Hence it is an attractive option for problems involving understanding a minority group's actual interaction with a majority group, such as in school integration problems—an area of study for which Lieberson and Carter explicitly endorse its use (298). Stanley Lieberson and Donna K. Carter, "Temporal Changes and Urban Differences in Residential Segregation: A Reconsideration," *American Journal of Sociology* 88, no. 2 (1982): 296-310. Also see Stanley Lieberson, "An Asymmetrical Approach to Segregation," in *Ethnic Segregation in Cities,* ed. Ceri Peach, Vaughn Robinson, and Susan Smith (London: Croom Helm, 1981), 61–82.

22. An isolation index and a dissimilarity index define and measure segregation differently, but both metrics seek to understand the same multifaceted phenomenon of segregation. I am not equating the two indices (indeed, any numerical similarity between their national averages is purely coincidental); rather, I seek to measure the same general phenomenon in two different ways, each of which says something different about a particular dimension of the phenomenon. The dissimilarity metric results in a better model of student spatial geography and movement, and the isolation metric allows us to understand segregation's association with graduation because of a study, discussed below, that links the two. Taken together, the two metrics help offer a bird's eye view of segregation.

23. Chaplin, "Estimating the Impact of Economic Integration," especially see Table 1 on 96.

24. In this chapter's thought experiment, all of the urban schools are magnetized. In practice, only a subset of urban schools would likely be magnetized in larger districts. This would reduce the scale of benefits of integration; but it would also reduce the costs.

25. This, of course, leads to a slightly higher cost estimate.

26. One study finds that fringe benefits are three percentage points higher in nonmagnets. Rolf K. Blank, Robert A. Dentler, D. Catherine Baltzell, and Kent Chabotar, "Survey of Magnet Schools: Analyzing a Model for Quality Integrated Education: Final Report of a National Study," prepared by James H. Lowry and Associates and Abt. Associates, Inc., U.S. Department of Education, 1983, 124–25.

27. Kent John Chabotar, "Measuring the Costs of Magnet Schools," *Economics of Education Review* 8, no. 2 (1989): 169.

28. Blank et al., "Survey of Magnet Schools," 115.

29. Chabotar, "Measuring the Costs of Magnet Schools," 169.

30. Vernay Mitchell et al., "Exemplary Urban Career-Oriented Secondary School Programs," National Center for Research in Vocational Education, Office of Vocational and Adult Education, 1989, 2.

31. Lorraine M. McDonnell, "Restructuring American Schools: The Promise and the Pitfalls," Conference Paper No. 10, Institute on Education and the Economy at Columbia University, 1989, 25–26; William Snider, "The Call for Choice: Competition in the Educational Marketplace," Special Report, *Education Week,* June 24, 1987, C1–C24.

32. Frankenberg and Siegel-Hawley, "The Forgotten Choice?" 51.

33. Holme and Wells, "School Choice beyond District Borders," 167–71. Also see Amy Stuart Wells et al., "Boundary Crossing for Diversity, Equity and Achievement: Inter-District School Desegregation and Educational Opportunity," Charles Hamilton Houston Institute for Race and Justice, November 2009, 17–19.

34. As Wells and her colleagues note, the Indianapolis court-ordered plan is currently being phased out. The authors cite the lack of reciprocity in the suburban transfer program as a main cause of the plan's termination. Wells et al., "Boundary Crossing," 18.

35. "Stipulation for Proposed Order on Voluntary Majority to Minority Transfers," *Little Rock School District v. Pulaski County Special School District No. 1,* U.S. District Court, Eastern District of Arkansas, Western Division, 5–7. Except for Little Rock's program, all of the above funding schemes are discussed and grouped in Holme and Wells, "School Choice beyond District Borders," 167–71 and Wells et al., "Boundary Crossing," 17–19.

36. William H. Freivogel, "St. Louis: Desegregation and School Choice in the Land of Dred Scott," in *Divided We Fail,* 214.

37. Research has long suggested that the cost curve of education is U-shaped. See William Fox's definitive review of the evidence of education's economies of scale in William F. Fox, "Reviewing Economies of Size in Education," *Journal of Education Finance* 6, no. 3 (Winter 1981): 273–96.

38. Holme and Wells, "School Choice beyond District Borders," 171 and Wells et al., "Boundary Crossing," 18.

39. Holme and Wells, "School Choice beyond District Borders," 169–70 and Wells et al., "Boundary Crossing," 18–19.

40. Elizabeth Cascio et al., "Paying for Progress: Conditional Grants and the Desegregation of Southern Schools," National Bureau of Economic Research, NBER Working Paper 14869, 2009, 25. As a more recent example, from the 1970s through the 1990s Massachusetts provided state funds to pay for 90 percent of new construction costs in school districts with approved voluntary racial desegregation plans. As even the program's critic, Governor Argeo Paul Cellucci, acknowledged, this program proved to offer "an enormous incentive" to encourage voluntary desegregation, and dozens of school districts adopted desegregation programs voluntarily as a result. Argeo Paul Cellucci, Jane Swift, and Andrew S. Natsios, "Policy Report: Reconstructing the School Building Assistance Program," Executive Office for Administration and Finance, Policy Report Series, No. 3, January 2000, 72. However, financial pressures led to the program's discontinuation in the 2000s, despite "huge support" from state officials who were very reluctant to scrap the program. Robert Preer, "Rush to Build Schools Puts Strain on State Funds," *The Boston Globe,* January 2, 2000.

41. See Wells et al., "Boundary Crossing," 19–20.

42. Blank et al., "Survey of Magnet Schools," 115.

43. Albeit Blank and colleagues' transportation cost ratio represents the cost of intradistrict transportation, rather than interdistrict transportation. Because of this difference, I walk through the calculation of an estimate for interdistrict transportation below.

44. "Table 175. Students Transported at Public Expense and Current Expenditures for Transportation: Selected Years, 1929–30 through 2005–06," Digest of Educational Statistics, IES National Center for Education Statistics, U.S. Department of Education; Holme and Wells, "School Choice beyond District Borders," 170.

45. According to the U.S. Department of Education, 55.1 percent of students were transported at public expense in 2005–06. See ibid.

46. "Table 181. Total and Current Expenditures per Pupil in Public Elementary and Secondary Schools: Selected Years, 1919–20 through 2005–06," Digest of Educational Statistics, IES National Center for Education Statistics, U.S. Department of Education.

47. In cases where parents opt to drive their children to their non-neighborhood schools (both in the case of students transferring to suburbs as well as for those commuting to magnet schools), these unmeasured private transportation costs offset some of the unmeasured private benefits of going to these schools that are evident in parents' revealed preference for these schools. In other words, said parents like the school enough to justify the private cost. Per spatial mismatch theory, one can expect that a considerable number of low-income parents commute to more affluent areas to work—and thus could drive their children to schools in these areas at no, or little, additional cost.

48. Although the research literature pertaining to the cost of socioeconomic school diversity is scant, it is worth noting that the 10 percent figure seems to be a relatively higher bound cost estimate. A recent paper that measured the social cost of integration related to San Diego Unified School District's Voluntary Ethnic Enrollment Program and magnet program found that the programs cost—at most—approximately $10.45 million in 1999–2000 dollars, or less than 1 percent of the school district's operating budget of roughly $1.4 billion. Cory Koedel et al., "The Social Cost of Open Enrollment as a School Choice Policy," working paper, April 2010, http://economics.missouri.edu/working-papers/2009/wp0910_koedel.pdf. It also bears emphasis that the 10 percent premium captures the increased costs as distributed across all students in the school system. If these costs were assigned to only the low-income students, then the intervention's premium would be reported as higher. Therefore, estimates from Rhode Island and Maryland that suggest it costs an additional 40 percent to educate low-income students are not incompatible with this chapter's 10 percent figure, because these estimates distribute the additional costs amongst the low-income students, not the student body at large. For more on the Rhode Island and Maryland estimates, see Augenblick & Myers, Inc., "Calculation of the Cost of an Adequate Education in Maryland in 1999–2000 Using Two Different Analytic Approaches," Maryland Commission on Education Finance, Equity, and Excellence, September 2001, 2, http://www.stateinnovation.org/Research/Education/Adequacy-Based-School-Funding/MarylandAdequacyStudysummary.aspx; Kenneth K. Wong, "The Design of the Rhode Island School Funding Formula: Toward a Coherent System of Allocating State Aid to Public Schools," Center for American Progress, August 2011, 14, http://www.americanprogress.org/issues/2011/08/pdf/rhode_island_reform.pdf.

49. This estimate also represents the projected cost of integrated middle school and high school (that is, seven years). The per-pupil cost of the intervention over thirteen years (that is, the duration of a student's entire K–12 tenure) is estimated at $11,400, and the four-year-cost for integrated high school is estimated at $3,690. Past costs are inflated to present value at the annual rate of 3.5 percent, which captures inflation and opportunity cost. The national average per-pupil expenditures for each year used in these calculations are included in Appendix 4.1. The 2005–06 school year is the most recent year for which these data are available, but the most recent benefit data (discussed below) are from 2004; expenditure from the 2004–05 school year (and so on for any given t) is used for cost estimates, rather than from the 2003–04 school year, in order to yield the more conservative cost estimates.

50. See "Education Pays: Education Pays in Higher Earnings and Lower Unemployment Rates," Current Population Survey, Bureau of Labor Statistics, U.S. Department of Labor, May 27, 2010, http://www.bls.gov/emp/ep_chart_001.htm.

51. On this correlation, see Belfield and Levin, *The Price We Pay*, 9–10, and James J. Heckman and Lance Lochner, "Rethinking Education and Training Policy: Understanding the Sources of Skill Formation in a Modern Economy," in *Securing the*

Future: Investing in Children from Birth to College, ed. S. Danziger and J. Waldfogel (New York: Russell Sage Foundation, 2000), 47–83, especially Figure 3.

52. Claude S. Fischer et al., *Inequality by Design: Cracking the Bell Curve Myth* (Princeton: Princeton University Press, 1996), 86. The authors cite Thomas A. DiPrete and David B. Grusky, "Structure and Trend in the Process of Social Stratification," *American Journal of Sociology* 96 (July): 107–44 and Christopher Jencks et al., *Inequality: A Reassessment of the Effect of Family and Schooling in America* (New York: Basic Books, 1972).

53. Swanson, "Who Graduates? Who Doesn't?" v.

54. Barack Obama, "Remarks of President Barack Obama: Address to Joint Session of Congress," February 24, 2009, Washington, D.C., http://www.whitehouse. gov/the_press_office/remarks-of-president-barack-obama-address-to-joint-session-of-congress/. Also see President Barack Obama's March 2009 speech on education reform: Barack Obama, "Remarks by the President to the Hispanic Chamber of Commerce on a Complete and Competitive American Education," March 10, 2009, Washington, D.C., http://www.whitehouse.gov/the_press_office/Remarks-of-the-President-to-the-United-States-Hispanic-Chamber-of-Commerce.

55. See Orfield and Lee, "Why Segregation Matters," 37, and *Difficult Choices: Do Magnet Schools Serve Children in Need? Report of the Citizens' Commission on Civil Rights,* ed. Corrine M. Yu and William L. Taylor (Washington, D.C.: Citizens' Commission on Civil Rights and Vanderbilt Institute for Public Policy Studies, 1997), 21.

56. Although this is not to say that how high school graduation rates are measured is not a source of controversy. See Joydeep Roy and Lawrence Mishel, "Using Administrative Data to Estimate Graduation Rates: Challenges, Proposed Solutions and Their Pitfalls," *Education Policy Analysis Archives* 16, no. 11 (2008): 1–34; Christine O. Wolfe, "The Great Graduation-Rate Debate," report by the Thomas B. Fordham Institute and the Thomas B. Fordham Foundation, July 2009; and "Understanding High School Graduation Rates in the United States," Alliance for Excellent Education, July 2009, http://www.all4ed.org/publication_material/understanding_HSgradrates.

57. Clive Belfield, "The Use of Cost-Benefit Analysis in Guiding Investments in Human Capital in Elementary and Secondary School," report prepared for Professor David Weimer, University of Wisconsin-Madison, 2006, http://www.cbcse.org/media/download_gallery/Guiding%20Investments%20in%20Human%20Capital.pdf, 15.

58. The need to avoid counting benefits through overlapping measures of success emerges from the expectation that improved graduation rates are partly based on improved test scores, so studies measuring the consequences of high school graduation capture the total impact of improving high school graduation and not just the impact while holding test scores constant. On the correlation between attainment and achievement, see Gordon Berlin and Andrew Sum, *Toward a More Perfect Union: Basic Skills, Poor Families, and Our Economic Future* (New York: Ford Foundation, 1988), especially Figure 7 on 31.

59. Henry M. Levin, "The Social Costs of Inadequate Education," summary by symposium chair, Teachers College Symposium on Educational Equity, Columbia University, October 24–25, 2005, http://www.mea.org/tef/pdf/social_costs_of_inadequate.pdf.

60. Barbara L. Wolfe and Robert H. Haveman, "Social and Nonmarket Benefits from Education in an Advanced Economy," *Education in the 21st Century: Meeting the Challenges of a Changing World,* proceedings of Conference Series 47 of the

Federal Reserve Bank of Boston, ed. Yolanda K. Kodrzycki (Boston: Federal Reserve Bank of Boston, June 2002), especially see 98–99.

61. Brief of 553 Social Scientists as Amici Curiae in Support of Respondents, *Parents Involved in Community Schools v. Seattle School District No. 1*, 2006, at 9, also see Appendix 24–5. On the benefits of better preparation for a diverse workforce, see Gary Orfield, "Schools More Separate: Consequences of a Decade of Resegregation," The Civil Rights Project at Harvard University, 2001; Orfield and Lee, "Why Segregation Matters"; Marguerite L. Spencer and Rebecca Reno, "The Benefits of Racial and Economic Integration in Our Education System: Why This Matters for Our Democracy," Kirwan Institute for the Study of Race and Ethnicity at Ohio State University, 2009, 14; and William T. Trent, "Outcomes of School Desegregation: Findings from Longitudinal Resarch," *Journal of Negro Education* 66, no. 3 (1997): 255–57.

62. Again, some gains from increased achievement are captured by increased attainment, because the two are closely linked. See note 58.

63. See Spencer and Reno's recent review of the relevant research literature in "Benefits of Racial and Economic Integration," 13–14. Also see: Douglas N. Harris, "Lost Learning, Forgotten Promises: A National Analysis of School Racial Segregation, Student Achievement, and 'Controlled Choice' Plans," Center for American Progress, November 24, 2006, 14, 18, and 22, http://www.americanprogress.org/issues/2006/11/pdf/lostlearning.pdf; Kahlenberg, *All Together Now*, 25–42; Laura B. Perry and Andrew McConney, "Does the SES of the School Matter? An Examination of Socioeconomic Status and Student Achievement Using PISA 2003," *Teachers College Record* 112, no. 4 (2010): 7–8; R. W. Rumberger and G. J. Palardy, "Does Segregation Still Matter? The Impact of Student Composition on Academic Achievement in High School," *Teachers College Record* 107, no. 9 (2005): 1999–2045; David Rusk, "Classmates Count: A Study of the Interrelationship between Socioeconomic Background and Standardized Test Scores of 4th Grade Pupils in the Madison-Dane County Public Schools," July 5, 2002, http://www.schoolinfosystem.org/archives/Unifiedfinal report.pdf; and J. Douglas Willms, "School Composition and Contextual Effects on Student Outcomes," *Teachers College Record* 112, no. 4 (2010): 3–4.

64. Eric A. Hanushek, "Alternative School Policies and the Benefits of General Cognitive Skills," *Economics of Education Review* 25 (2006): 447–62. Hanushek aggregates the findings from three studies: Edward P. Lazear, "Teacher Incentives," *Swedish Economic Policy Review* 10 (2003): 179–214; Casey B. Mulligan, "Galton Versus the Human Capital Approach to Inheritance," *Journal of Political Economy* 107, no. 6 (December 1999): S184–S224; and Richard J. Murnane, John B. Willett, Yves Duhaldeborde, and John H. Tyler, "How Important Are the Cognitive Skills of Teenagers in Predicting Subsequent Earnings?" *Journal of Policy Analysis and Management* 19, no. 4 (Fall 2000): 547–68.

65. James J. Heckman and Edward Vytlacil, "Identifying the Role of Cognitive Ability in Explaining the Level of and Change in the Return to Schooling," *Review of Economics and Statistics* 83 (2001): 1–12.

66. Heather Rose, "Do Gains in Test Scores Explain Labor Market Outcomes?" *Economics of Education Review* 25 (2006): 430–46.

67. Belfield, "Use of Cost-Benefit Analysis," 1–2. One recent study suggests that the magnitude might be very large. The Organisation for Economic Co-operation and Development projects that if the United States raised its average Program for International Student Assessment score by twenty-five points over twenty years, GDP would

grow by nearly $41 trillion in eighty years. And Laura Perry and Andrew McConney's study "Does the SES of the School Matter? An Examination of Socioeconomic Status and Student Achievement Using PISA 2003," published this year in *Teacher College Record* 112, no. 4 (2010), suggests that a school's mean socioeconomic status level is correlated with its students' academic achievement. See "The High Cost of Low Educational Performance: The Long-Run Economic Impact of Improving PISA Outcomes," the Organisation for Economic Co-operation and Development, 2010.

68. Swanson, "Who Graduates? Who Doesn't?" v. Swanson calculates graduation rates using the Cumulative Promotion Index (CPI), which "approximates the probability that a student entering the ninth grade will complete high school on time with a regular diploma" and counts only regular high school diploma recipients as graduates, a definition that "is consistent with the provisions of the federal No Child Left Behind Act" (7).

69. Swanson, "Who Graduates? Who Doesn't?" 31. I expect that the relationship between segregation and graduation will hold for segregation across districts as well as for segregation within districts, as is the case in Swanson's study. Indeed, the factors at the core of this relationship—different student, teacher, and parent populations—are altered by integration whether within or across districts.

70. Swanson, "Who Graduates in the South?" 2. On the link between racial segregation and graduation rates, also see Jonathan Guryan, "Desegregation and Black Dropout Rates," *American Economic Review* 94, no. 4 (2003): 919–43. Guryan's study of data from the 1970 and 1980 censuses found that racial desegregation in the 1970s reduced the black dropout rate by two to three percentage points, while observing no negative effects in white dropout rates (939–40). This accounted for half of the reduction in the dropout rate; the largest decline in dropout rates occurred in districts with the largest declines in school segregation (940). The two to three percentage point dropout rate reduction was associated with roughly a 0.1 change on a black-white exposure index. Very similar to an isolation index, an exposure index measures the exposure of a minority group to a majority group—that is, the converse of the minority group's isolation. If one assumes the relationship between segregation and graduation is linear, Guryan's finding would suggest that an intervention leading to a 0.24 change on a racial exposure or isolation index (that is, reducing the country's average racial segregation level by half) would result in a 4.8 to 7.2 percentage point graduation rate increase.

71. Swanson, "Who Graduates in the South?" 2. I assume midpoint graduation rates between the graduation rates listed for whites and blacks. Also see Christopher B. Swanson, "High School Graduation in Texas: Independent Research to Understand and Combat the Graduation Crisis," Editorial Projects in Education Research Center, October 2006. Swanson's work on the link between segregation and graduation is discussed in Brief of 553 Social Scientists, *Parents v. Seattle*, at 38. Given that Swanson assesses segregation within school districts, the use of a cohort of southern states is particularly informative for this chapter's interdistrict scenario because geographically larger southern school districts often include urban and suburban areas.

72. For further research illuminating this finding as well as theories of why this is the case, see: Kahlenberg, *All Together Now*, 38–42; Guryan, "Desegregation and Black Dropout Rates"; and Spencer and Reno, "Benefits of Racial and Economic Integration," 12–13.

73. Swanson, "Who Graduates in the South?" 2. Similarly, as a comparison to how housing segregation affects graduation rates, David Cutler and Edward Glaeser found

that a one standard deviation increase in housing segregation reduces graduation rates by just under ten percentage points. David M. Cutler and Edward L. Glaeser, "Are Ghettos Good or Bad?" *Quarterly Journal of Economics* 112, no. 3 (August 1997): 827–72, especially see Table IX on 864. On the relationship between housing segregation and graduation rates—which share several of the same factors as the relationship between school segregation and graduation, such as the type of peer influence a pupil experiences—also see Deborah L. McKoy and Jeffrey M. Vincent, "Housing and Education: The Inextricable Link," especially 137, and Margery Austin Turner, "Residential Segregation and Employment Inequality," especially 168, both in *Segregation: The Rising Costs for America,* ed. James H. Carr and Nandinee K. Kutty (New York: Routledge, 2008).

74. Again, Guryan found that decreasing racial segregation by only 0.1 on an exposure index increased the graduation rate by two to three percentage points. See note 70.

75. David J. Deming, Justine S. Hastings, Thomas J. Kane, and Douglas O. Staiger, "School Choice, School Quality and Postsecondary Attainment," National Bureau of Economic Research, NBER Working Paper 17438, September 2011, http://www.nber.org/papers/w17438, 19.

76. Yu and Taylor, "Difficult Choices," 21. Given that the transfer program and magnet school program required participating families to opt in, the St. Louis example involves a self-selected group of students.

77. Massachusetts Department of Elementary and Secondary Education, Cohort 2009 Four-Year Graduation Rates, http://profiles.doe.mass.edu/state_report/gradrates.aspx. However, there are no longitudinal data showing the change in Cambridge's graduation rates over the course of its integration efforts.

78. Robert L. Crain, Randi L. Miller, Jennifer A. Hawes, and Janet R. Peichert, "Finding Niches: Desegregated Students Sixteen Years Later: Final Report on the Educational Outcomes of Project Concern, Hartford, Connecticut," Institute for Urban and Minority Education, New York, June 1992. Because matriculation into the Hartford program requires expressing interest, it is uncertain how scalable this type of program would be for less motivated students and families.

79. Kahlenberg, *All Together Now,* 40–42.

80. *The Price We Pay.* For a summary of the findings, see chapter 9, "Educational Interventions to Raise High School Graduation Rates," 177–99, especially Table 9–5 on 189. The study uses consensus graduation rates between nine studies. The consensus rates correlate with the rates determined by Christopher Swanson. On desegregation's abating effect on crime in particular, see David A. Weiner, Byron F. Lutz, and Jens Ludwig, "The Effects of School Desegregation on Crime," National Bureau of Economic Research, NBER Working Paper 15380, September 2009, http://www.nber.org/papers/w15380.

81. Cohen and Piquero, "New Evidence," especially see Table 13. This study is a revision of an earlier paper by Cohen; see Mark A. Cohen, "The Monetary Value of Saving a High-Risk Youth," *Journal of Quantitative Criminology* 14, no. 1 (1998): 5–33.

82. Sum, Khatiwada, and McLaughlin, "The Consequences of Dropping Out of High School," 15. Discount rate not reported.

83. All inflation calculations in this paper are made using Consumer Price Index figures from the U.S. Bureau of Labor Statistics website, http://data.bls.gov/cgi-bin/cpicalc.pl. In general, recent research suggests a growing awareness of the long-term

public gains of reducing widespread poverty, either through education reform or other means. For example, see the recent Center for American Progress report on the long-term public costs of poverty: Harry J. Holzer, Diane Whitmore Schanzenbach, Greg J. Duncan, and Jens Ludwig, "The Economic Costs of Poverty in the United States: Subsequent Effects of Children Growing up Poor," Center for American Progress, January 24, 2007.

84. Pedro Manuel Carneiro and James J. Heckman, "Human Capital Policy," IZA Discussion Paper No. 821, Institute for the Study of Labor, July 2003, 148–49. Also see Belfield, "Use of Cost-Benefit Analysis," 1–2, and Spencer and Reno, "Benefits of Racial and Economic Integration," 12–14.

85. Cecilia Elena Rouse, "Consequences for the Labor Market," in *The Price We Pay,* ed. Belfield and Levin, 99–124.

86. Another recent study on the economic consequences of high school graduation measured the amalgamated benefit of additional private earnings and found that reducing the Class of 2008's dropout rate by half would result in $4.1 billion in increased earnings (and $536 million in increased tax revenue). "The Economic Benefits from Halving the Dropout Rate: A Boom to Businesses in the Nation's Largest Metropolitan Areas," Alliance for Excellent Education, January 2010.

87. The 2005–06 ninth grade population estimate, the most recent year for which student population data are available, is from U.S. Department of Education, "Table A-19-1. Averaged freshman graduation rate for public high school students and number of graduates, by state: School years 2000–02 through 2005–06," Student Effort and Educational Progress, IES National Center for Education Statistics.

88. In order not to double-count earnings (income, property, and sales) that generate tax revenues, I subtract $139,100, the expected gain in tax revenue, from the sum of the public and private gains. Thus, this sum per additional graduate is $330,100.

89. The estimated additional tax revenue (income, property, and sales) for a black male graduate ($157,600) is subtracted from the sum of average private earnings ($260,000) and black male public savings ($268,500) in order to avoid double counting. The total of this adjusted sum is $370,900. Again, note that a separate estimate for black male private earnings is not reported in Rouse's study.

90. The public benefit of $96,660 per student and total benefit of $133,520 are divided by the net present value cost of the intervention over thirteen years, or $11,400. Because the Hartford study measured the intervention's impact after an entire K–12 tenure, cost is calculated for thirteen years, rather than seven years.

91. See Clive Belfield, "The Prospects for Education Vouchers after the Supreme Court Ruling," Institute for Urban and Minority Education at Columbia University, 2002; William Howell and Paul Peterson, *The Education Gap: Vouchers and Urban Public Schools* (Washington, D.C.: Brookings Institution Press, 2002); and Henry Levin and Cyrus Driver, "Costs of an Educational Voucher System," *Education Economics* 5, no. 3 (1997): 265–83. Although, in theory, voucher programs would seem to decrease socioeconomic segregation, thus making them similar to large-scale socioeconomic diversity plans, in practice they have, in fact, increased such segregation, especially in Sweden, Chile, and the Netherlands. On this weakness of voucher programs as well as other possible shortcomings, see *Public School Choice vs. Private School Vouchers,* ed. Richard D. Kahlenberg (New York: Century Foundation Press, 2003).

92. On all of the aforementioned benefit-cost ratios, see *The Price We Pay,* ed. Belfield and Levin, 195.

93. The recent study of Head Start mandated by Congress found that Head Start produced small to moderate benefits—that is, results far smaller than those produced by the small-scale, specialized pre-school programs mentioned above. Further, the study found that these benefits began to wash out by the end of first grade. U.S. Department of Health and Human Services, "Head Start Impact Study: Final Report," Administration for Children and Families, January 2010.

94. See Richard Kahlenberg's review of this research literature in Kahlenberg, *All Together Now,* 115, and note 35 on 118–19. Also see W. Steven Barnett, Kirsty Brown, and Rima Shore, "The Universal vs. Targeted Debate: Should the United States Have Preschool for All?" *Preschool Policy Matters* 6 (April 2004): 10, and Carolyn Moureau, "Learning in Mixed Company: Study Shows Low-Income Preschoolers Learn Better, Faster Alongside More Affluent Peers," *Hartford Courant,* October 19, 2002, B1.

Chapter 5

1. James S. Coleman, *Equality and Educational Opportunity* (Washington, D.C.: U.S. Department of Health, Education, and Welfare, 1966); see also Christopher Jencks, "The Coleman Report and Conventional Wisdom," in *On Equality of Educational Opportunity: Non-Racial Approaches to Integration,* eds. Frederick Mosteller and Daniel P. Moynihan (New York: Vintage Books, 1972), 69–115; Kirk A. Johnson, *The Peer Effect on Academic Achievement among Public Elementary School Students* (Washington, D.C.: Heritage Foundation, 2000); David Rusk, "Classmates Count: A Study of the Interrelationship between Socioeconomic Background and Standardized Test Scores of 4th Grade Pupils in the Madison-Dane County Public Schools," unpublished manuscript (2002); U.S. Department of Education, National Center for Education Statistics, *The Condition of Education 2003* (Washington, D.C.: U.S. Government Printing Office, 2003); Russell Rumberger and Gregory Palardy, "Does Segregation Still Matter? The Impact of Student Composition on Academic Achievement in High School," *Teachers College Record* 107, no. 9 (2005): 1999–2045; Gregory J. Palardy, "Differential School Effects among Low, Middle, and High Social Class Composition Schools: A Multiple Group, Multilevel Latent Growth Curve Analysis," *School Effectiveness & School Improvement* 19, no. 1 (2008): 21–49; Laura B. Perry and Andrew McConney, "Does the SES of the School Matter? An Examination of Socioeconomic Status and Student Achievement using PISA 2003," *Teachers College Record* 112, no. 4 (2010): 1137. Moreover, the negative impact of high-poverty schools has been attracting increasing media attention. See, for example, the special section on high-poverty schools in Susan Aud et al., *The Condition of Education 2010* (Washington, D.C.: U.S. Government Printing Office, 2010); "Socioeconomics Replacing Race in School Assignments," *Education Week,* May 7, 2010; Andrew Rotherham, "Does Income-Based School Integration Work?" *Time,* October 28, 2010; and *The Economic Impact of the Achievement Gap in America's Schools* (McKinsey and Company, 2009).

2. Coleman, *Equality and Educational Opportunity;* see also Rumberger and Palardy, "Does Segregation Still Matter?" 1999–2045; Rusk, "Classmates Count."

3. While there is a consensus in the literature on the negative effects of high-poverty schools, there is no consensus on how to define a high-poverty school. A number of FRL percentage thresholds are used in different studies: 40 percent, in Laura Lippman, Shelley Burns, and Edith K. McArthur, *Urban Schools: The Challenge of Location*

and Poverty (Washington, D.C.: Office of Educational Research and Improvement, 1996); 50 percent, in Richard D. Kahlenberg, *All Together Now: Creating Middle-Class Schools through Public School Choice* (Washington, D.C.: Brookings Institution Press, 2001); Gary Orfield and Chungmei Lee, *Historic Reversals, Accelerating Resegregation, and the Need for New Integration Strategies* (Los Angeles: Civil Rights Project/Proyecto Derechos Civiles, UCLA, 2007); and Gary Orfield and Chungmei Lee, *Why Segregation Matters: Poverty and Educational Inequality* (Cambridge, Mass.: Civil Rights Project, Harvard University, 2005); 60 percent, in Julius Chambers et al., *The Socioeconomic Composition of the Public Schools: A Crucial Consideration in Student Assignment Policy* (Chapel Hill, N.C.: UNC Center for Civil Rights, 2005); and 75 percent in Russell W. Rumberger, "Parsing the Data on Student Achievement in High-Poverty Schools," *North Carolina Law Review* 85, no. 5 (2007): 101–19; Susan Aud et al., *The Condition of Education 2010.* Other researchers define high-poverty schools according to the distribution of their particular sample, for example, one or more standard deviations below the mean SES (Palardy, "Differential School Effects," 21–49; Rumberger and Palardy, "Does Segregation Still Matter?"), the poorest quartile of schools (Charles T. Clotfelter et al., "High Poverty Schools and the Distribution of Teachers and Principals," *North Carolina Law Review* 81, no. 4 [2007], 1345–79). This study uses the 50 percent low-income threshold, which falls between the 40 percent low-income threshold for Title I schools and the U.S. Department of Education's 75 percent threshold, a cap we rejected as too high, given the evidence of negative impact of poverty concentrations even less than 75 percent. See the Definitions section of this chapter for more discussion of this choice.

4. Susan Aud et al., *The Condition of Education 2011* (Washington, D.C.: U.S. Government Printing Office, 2011), Table A-28-1. Percentage is based on the percentage of students eligible for free or reduced-price lunch, commonly used as a proxy for poverty, during the 2008–09 school year, the most recent year for which data are available.

5. Ibid.; Aud et al., *The Condition of Education 2010,* Table A-24-2.

6. Analyzing the growth of high-poverty schools is challenging because of gaps in data in earlier years. While the 2008–09 NCES free or reduced-price lunch data are missing for only 2 percent of schools (either through failure to report data or to participate in school lunch program), 12 percent of the school FRL data is missing in 1999–2000 (including five states with no data at all), and 32 percent from 1998–99 (Aud et al., *The Condition of Education 2011,* Table A-27-1, and Aud et al., *The Condition of Education 2010,* Table A-24-2). Nonetheless, some observations can be made from the existing numbers. Overall, high-poverty schools are increasing faster than the number of low-income students, as measured by both Census data on the poverty rate for children ages 5 to 17 and data on enrollment in the free and reduced-price lunch program. Specifically, the percentage of majority low-income schools grew by roughly ten percentage points from 2000 to 2007, a period in which the percentage of students eligible for FRL grew by four points. This in turn outpaces the growth in child poverty as tracked by the Census, indicating increased participation by low-income families in the school lunch program. See U.S. Department of Education, National Center of Education Statistics, *The Condition of Education, 2002* (Washington, D.C.: U.S. Government Printing Office, 2002), Table 4-1; U.S. Census Bureau, Small Area Estimates Branch, "Table 1: 2007 Poverty and Median Income Estimates—States," 2008. We posit two possibilities. One is an increase in the socioeconomic segregation of U.S. schools. If this were the case, however, one would expect to see a growth in

the number of low-poverty schools to accompany that of high-poverty schools, with a widening trough in between. This does not seem to be the case, although the national data, which is kept by quartiles of low-income student percentages, may mask changes going on at the extreme low ends. The second possibility is a clustering of schools around the 50 percent low-income mark, such that an increase in the number of FRL students would be amplified into an even larger increase in the number of high-poverty schools. Future research is needed to better understand the causes behind the rise in the number of high-poverty schools.

7. Coleman, *Equality and Educational Opportunity;* Jencks, "The Coleman Report and Conventional Wisdom," 69–115; Mosteller and Moynihan, *On Equality of Educational Opportunity: Non-Racial Approaches to Integration;* Johnson, *The Peer Effect on Academic Achievement among Public Elementary School Students;* U.S. Department of Education, National Center for Education Statistics, *The Condition of Education 2003;* Palardy, "Differential School Effects among Low, Middle, and High Social Class Composition Schools,"; Perry and McConney, "Does the SES of the School Matter?"; Roslyn Arlin Mickelson and Martha Bottia, "Integrated Education and Mathematics Outcomes: A Synthesis of Social Science Research," *North Carolina Law Review* 88, no. 3 (2010): 993–1089.

8. One exception to this consensus is Rumberger, "Parsing the Data on Student Achievement in High-Poverty Schools," 101–19, whose study of longitudinal elementary school data found that when student background characteristics were controlled for, attending a high-poverty school did *not* appear to adversely affect student achievement. However, low-poverty schools with less than 25 percent FRL students did confer "a significant educational advantage" in terms of student learning, relative to schools with higher poverty levels.

9. Mickelson and Bottia, "Integrated Education and Mathematics Outcomes: A Synthesis of Social Science Research," 1043.

10. Mark C. Hogrebe and William F. Tate, "School Composition and Context Factors that Moderate and Predict 10th-Grade Science Proficiency," *Teachers College Record* 112 (2010): 1096; Perry and McConney, "Does the SES of the School Matter?"

11. Geoffrey D. Borman and Maritza Dowling, "Schools and Inequality: A Multilevel Analysis of Coleman's Equality of Educational Opportunity Data," *Teachers College Record* 112, no. 5 (2010): 1201–46.

12. See chapter 2 in this volume.

13. Palardy, "Differential School Effects among Low, Middle, and High Social Class Composition Schools," 21–49; Rumberger and Palardy, "Does Segregation Still Matter?"

14. Igor Ryabov and Jennifer Van Hook, "School Segregation and Academic Achievement among Hispanic Children," *Social Science Research* 36, no. 2 (2007): 784.

15. Coleman, *Equality and Educational Opportunity,* 5.

16. Jennifer Ehrle Macomber, Kristin Anderson Moore, and Brett V. Brown, *Children's Environment and Behavior: High Engagement in School* (Washington, D.C.: Urban Institute, 1999); Kahlenberg, *All Together Now;* Paul E. Barton and Richard J. Coley, *Windows on Achievement and Inequality* (Princeton, N.J.: Educational Testing Service, 2008).

17. Gary Orfield, *City-Suburban Desegregation: Parent and Student Perspectives in Metropolitan Boston* (Cambridge, Mass.: Civil Rights Project, 1997).

18. Kathleen Herrold, Kevin O'Donnell, and Gail Mulligan, *Parent and Family Involvement in Education, 2006–07 School Year, from the National Household*

Education Surveys Program of 2007 (Washington, D.C.: U.S. Department of Education, 2008).

19. Ellen Brantlinger, *Dividing Classes: How the Middle Class Negotiates and Rationalizes School Advantage* (New York: RoutledgeFalmer, 2003).

20. Rumberger and Palardy, "Does Segregation Still Matter?"; Palardy, "Differential School Effects among Low, Middle, and High Social Class Composition Schools"; Lippman, Burns, and McArthur, *Urban Schools: The Challenge of Location and Poverty.*

21. Aud et al., *The Condition of Education 2010;* Elaine Allensworth, Stephen Ponisciak, and Christopher Mazzeo, *The Schools Teachers Leave: Teacher Mobility in Chicago Public Schools* (Chicago: Chicago Consortium for School Research, 2009).

22. Aud et al., *The Condition of Education 2010;* Lippman, Burns, and McArthur, *Urban Schools.*

23. Rumberger and Palardy, "Does Segregation Still Matter?"; Stephen J. Caldas and Carl Bankston III, "Effect of School Population Socioeconomic Status on Individual Academic Achievement," *Journal of Educational Research* 90, no. 5 (May 1997): 269.

24. Douglas Harris, "Educational Outcomes of Disadvantaged Students: From Desegregation to Accountability," in *AEFA Handbook of Research in Education Finance and Policy,* ed. Helen F. Ladd and Edward B. Fiske (New York: Routledge, 2008), 30.

25. Perry and McConney, "Does the SES of the School Matter?"

26. Salvatore Saporito and Deenesh Sohoni, "Mapping Educational Inequality: Concentrations of Poverty among Poor and Minority Students in Public Schools," *Social Forces* 85, no. 3 (2007): 22.

27. *Parents Involved in Community Schools v. Seattle School District No. 1,* 551 U.S. 701 (2007).

28. Chambers et al., *The Socioeconomic Composition of the Public Schools,* 17.

29. The Wake County school board voted in April 2010 to revise its school assignment policy for a return to neighborhood schools, but this new plan has not been finalized and the current policy remains in place until at least 2012. See Dakarai Aarons, "Busing Fight Highlights Struggle with Diversity," *Education Week,* April 1, 2010.

30. Sean F. Reardon and Lori Rhodes, "The Effects of Socioeconomic School Integration Plans on Racial School Desegregation," in *Legal and Policy Options for Racially Integrated Education in the South and the Nation,* ed. Erica Frankenberg, Elizabeth DeBray-Pelot, and Gary Orfield (Chapel Hill, N.C.: University of North Carolina Press, forthcoming).

31. Mary Ann Zehr, "Socioeconomics Replacing Race in School Assignments," *Education Week,* May 7, 2010.

32. Richard D. Kahlenberg, *Turnaround Schools that Work: Moving Beyond Separate but Equal* (Washington, D.C.: Century Foundation, 2009).

33. Rusk, "Classmates Count"; James Campbell, "Closing Baltimore's Achievement Gap with Housing Policy," *Baltimore Sun,* May 30, 2011.

34. Sean F. Reardon, John T. Yun, and Michal Kurlaender, "Implications of Income-Based School Assignment Policies for Racial School Segregation," *Educational Evaluation and Policy Analysis* 28, no. 1 (2006): 49–75.

35. Rumberger and Palardy, "Does Segregation Still Matter?"; Mickelson and Bottia, "Integrated Education and Mathematics Outcomes"; Roslyn A. Mickelson, "Subverting *Swann:* First- and Second-Generation Segregation in the Charlotte-Mecklenburg

Schools," *American Educational Research Journal* 38, no. 2 (2001): 215; *Race-Conscious Policies for Assigning Students to Schools: Social Science Research and the Supreme Court Cases*, ed. Robert L. Linn and Kevin G. Welner (Washington, D.C.: National Academy of Research, 2007); Kahlenberg, *Turnaround Schools that Work*.

36. Tony Wagner, *The Global Achievement Gap: Why Even our Best Schools Don't Teach the New Survival Skills Our Children Need—and What We Can Do about It* (New York: Basic Books, 2008), 290.

37. Gary Orfield, Erica Frankenberg, and Liliana M. Garces, "Statement of American Social Scientists of Research on School Desegregation to the U.S. Supreme Court in *Parents v. Seattle School District* and *Meredith v. Jefferson County*," *Urban Review* 40 (2008): 96–136.

38. The large-scale reassignment of students required to eliminate high-poverty schools is extremely problematic in Alaska and Hawaii due to geographical constraints.

39. Federal Education Budget Project, "Federal School Nutrition Programs," http://febp.newamerica.net/background-analysis/federal-school-nutrition-programs (accessed August 25, 2010).

40. U.S. Department of Health and Human Services, "2009/2010 HHS Poverty Guidelines," http://liheap.ncat.org/profiles/povertytables/FY2010/popstate.htm (accessed December 5, 2010).

41. Leah Beth Curran et al., "Economic Well-being and Where We Live: Accounting for Geographical Cost-of-Living Differences in the U.S.," *Urban Studies* 43, no. 13 (2006): 2443–66.

42. Erica Frankenberg, Genevieve Siegel-Hawley, and Jia Wang, *Choice without Equity: Charter School Segregation and the Need for Civil Rights Standards* (Los Angeles: The Civil Rights Project/Proyecto Derechos Civiles, UCLA, 2010); Reardon and Rhodes, "The Effects of Socioeconomic School Integration Plans on Racial School Desegregation."

43. Selcuk R. Sirin, "Socioeconomic Status and Academic Achievement: A Meta-Analytic Review of Research," *Review of Educational Research* 75, no. 3 (2005): 417–53; Carol Pogash, "Free Lunch Isn't Cool, So Some Students Go Hungry," *New York Times*, March 8, 2010.

44. Donka M. Mirtcheva and Lisa M. Powell, "Participation in the National School Lunch Program: Importance of School-Level and Neighborhood Contextual Factors," *Journal of School Health* 79, no. 10 (2009): 485–94.

45. The study excludes schools whose grade spans begin with sixth grade or higher. Schools beginning in fifth grade are excluded if the ending grade is higher than seventh grade. Schools beginning in fourth grade are excluded if the ending grade is higher than ninth grade.

46. Frankenberg, Siegel-Hawley, and Wang, *Choice without Equity*.

47. Orfield and Lee, *Why Segregation Matters*.

48. Cambridge, Massachusetts, employs one of the most comprehensive controlled choice plans in the country, with a goal of ensuring that all schools are within 10 percent of the overall district low-income percentage; see Edward B. Fiske, "Controlled Choice in Cambridge, Massachusetts," in *Divided We Fail: Coming Together through Public School Choice: The Report of The Century Foundation Task Force on the Common School* (New York: Century Foundation Press, 2002), 167. Doubling this band to 20 percent and then measuring the percentage of schools that fell outside this larger band therefore seemed a reasonable gauge of extreme socioeconomic segregation.

49. Frankenberg, Siegel-Hawley, and Wang, *Choice without Equity.*

50. This study uses the five racial breakdowns of the National Center for Education Statistics, although we have modified the name of each group slightly. The term "whites" in this paper refers to non-Hispanic whites, "blacks" to non-Hispanic blacks, "Latinos" to Hispanics, "Asians" to Asian/Pacific Islanders, and "Native Americans" to American Indian/Alaskan Natives.

51. Orfield and Lee, *Historic Reversals, Accelerating Resegregation, and the Need for New Integration Strategies.*

52. Ibid.

53. U.S. Department of the Interior, "Education," http://www.doi.gov/tribes/education.cfm (accessed June 14, 2011).

54. Because NAEP is administered to a sample of students in each state, there are several states where the number of tested black and/or Latino students was too small for scores to be reported. For example, the 2009 fourth grade math data is missing for black students in Montana, Wyoming, Idaho, Vermont, New Hampshire, and North Dakota, and for Latino students in West Virginia, Maine, Mississippi, North Dakota, and Vermont. Such states do not contribute to the correlations, plots, or tables for which their data is missing.

55. Reardon and Rhodes, "The Effects of Socioeconomic School Integration Plans on Racial School Desegregation." These numbers do not mean that all students actively participate or are impacted by socioeconomic integration, but rather that there are at least some opportunities in the districts where they live.

56. Ibid.

57. Abbie Coffee and Erica Frankenberg, *Districts' Integration Efforts in a Changing Climate Two Years After the PICS Decision* (Los Angeles: The Civil Rights Project/Proyecto Derechos Civiles, 2009).

58. Dakarai Aarons, "Busing Fight Highlights Struggles with Diversity."

59. Kahlenberg, *All Together Now.*

60. Amherst Regional Public Schools, "Elementary Reorganization Committee," http://www.arps.org/node/977 (accessed August 25, 2010).

61. Danielle Holley-Walker, "After Unitary Status: Examining Voluntary Integration Strategies for Southern School Districts," *North Carolina Law Review* 88 (2010): 877.

62. Erica Frankenberg and Genevieve Siegel-Hawley, *Equity Overlooked: Charter Schools and Civil Rights Policy* (Los Angeles: The Civil Rights Project/Proyecto Derechos Civiles, 2009).

63. Zehr, "Socioeconomics Replacing Race in School Assignments."

64. The Wake County school board voted in April 2010 to revise its school assignment policy for a return to neighborhood schools, but the current policy remains in place until 2012. See Aarons, "Busing Fight Highlights Struggles with Diversity"; Robbie Brown, "District May End NC Economic Diversity Program," *New York Times,* February 7, 2010.

65. Reardon and Rhodes, "The Effects of Socioeconomic School Integration Plans on Racial School Desegregation."

66. Districts with three elementary schools were judged to be viable if the grade configurations overlapped (three K–5 schools, for example), but not viable if the grade configurations were sequential, such that students could not be assigned to different schools than the ones they already attended (PK–1, 2–3, 4–6).

67. Schools per district, percent high-poverty districts, percent low-poverty districts, and various segregation indices also had extremely weak correlations with intra-district viability.

68. Amy Stuart Wells et al., *Boundary Crossing for Diversity, Equity and Achievement: Inter District School Desegregation and Educational Opportunity* (Cambridge, Mass.: Charles Hamilton Houston Institute for Race and Justice, 2009).

69. Erin Dillon, *Plotting School Choice: The Challenges of Crossing District Lines* (Washington, D.C.: Education Sector, 2008).

70. Elizabeth A. Palmer, *The Choice Is Yours after Two Years: An Evaluation* (Minneapolis: Aspen Associates, 2003).

71. Erica Frankenberg, *Project Choice Campaign: Improving and Expanding Hartford's Project Choice Program* (Washington, D.C.: Poverty and Race Research Action Council, 2009).

72. Patrice Relerford, "Minneapolis to Table Plan to Leave Integration District," *Minneapolis Star Tribune*, March 10, 2009.

73. Richard D. Kahlenberg, *Rescuing Brown v. Board of Education: Profiles of Twelve School Districts Pursuing Socioeconomic School Integration* (Washington, D.C.: Century Foundation, 2007).

74. Learning Community of Douglas and Sarpy Counties, http://www.learningcommunityds.org/about/default.aspx (accessed August 25, 2010).

75. Massachusetts Department of Elementary and Secondary Education, "FY11 METCO Districts and Grant Allocations," http://www.doe.mass.edu/metco/funding.html (accessed December 6, 2010); Massachusetts Department of Elementary and Secondary Education, "FY09 Expenditures Per Pupil, District Comparisons Based upon Grade Structure, District Wealth, and Enrollment," http://finance1.doe.mass.edu/schfin/statistics/ppx09_comp.aspx?ID=001 (accessed December 6, 2010).

76. Dillon, *Plotting School Choice*.

77. Wells et al., *Boundary Crossing for Diversity, Equity and Achievement*.

78. Frankenberg, Siegel-Hawley, and Wang, *Choice without Equity*.

79. Julian R. Betts et al., *Does School Choice Work? Effects on Student Integration and Achievement* (San Francisco: Public Policy Institute of California, 2006).

80. Institute on Education Law and Policy, *New Jersey's Interdistrict Public School Choice Program: Program Evaluation and Policy Analysis* (Newark, N.J.: Rutgers University, 2006), 31.

81. Russ Kava, *School Integration (Chapter 220) Aid* (Madison: Wisconsin Legislative Financial Bureau, 2007).

82. John F. Witte and Christopher A. Thorn, "Who Chooses? Voucher and Interdistrict Choice Programs in Milwaukee," *American Journal of Education* 104, no. 3 (1996), 186–217.

83. Sheff Movement, "About *Sheff v. O'Neill*," http://www.sheffmovement.org/aboutsheffvoneill.shtml (accessed December 5, 2010).

84. Ibid.

85. Frankenberg, *Project Choice Campaign: Improving and Expanding Hartford's Project Choice Program*, 1.

86. Jennifer Jellison Holme and Meredith P. Richards, "School Choice and Stratification in a Regional Context: Examining the Role of Inter-District Choice," *Peabody Journal of Education* 84 (2009), 150–71.

87. Frances C. Fowler, "Meaningful Competition? A Study of Student Movement under Interdistrict Open Enrollment in Ohio" (paper presented at the annual meeting of the American Educational Research Association, New York, N.Y., 1996); Holme and Richards, "School Choice and Stratification in a Regional Context."

88. Betts et al., *Does School Choice Work?*

89. District consolidation has in fact been occurring across the country for the past eighty years. Since 1930, the number of U.S. school districts has dropped from 130,000 to 15,000; see Frederick M. Wirt and Michael W. Kirst, *The Political Dynamics of American Education*, 3rd ed. (Richmond, Calif.: McCutchan Pub. Corp., 2005).

90. Maine Department of Education, "Summary of the Reorganization Law," http://www.maine.gov/education/reorg/lawsummary.html (accessed May 7, 2010).

91. Peter Schworm, "Towns Turn to School Mergers," *Boston Globe*, July 19, 2010.

92. Standard & Poor's, *Study of Cost-Effectiveness of Consolidating Pennsylvania School Districts* (New York: Standard & Poor's, 2007).

93. This 40 percent district-wide threshold mirrors our intradistrict measure, since it allows individual schools to vary from the 40 percent combined district average by up to ten percentage points without exceeding the 50 percent high-poverty line.

94. Massachusetts Department of Elementary and Secondary Education, *FY11 METCO Districts and Grant Allocations.*

95. The following policy implications take the current landscape of neighborhoods segregated by income as a given. However, housing policy can effectively promote more integrated schools by reducing existing levels of residential segregation but that is not covered here; see Rusk, "Classmates Count," and chapter 2 in this volume.

96. *Brown v. Board of Education of Topeka*, 347 U.S. 483 (1954).

97. Jennifer Hochschild, "What School Boards Can and Cannot (Or Will Not) Accomplish," in *Besieged: Schools Boards and the Future of American Politics*, ed. W. Howell (Washington, D.C.: Brookings Institution Press, 2005), 351.

98. Sean Cavanagh, "Race to Top Now Faces Acid Test," *Education Week*, September 1, 2010.

99. Jane Dimyan-Ehrenfeld, "Making Lemonade: Restructuring the Transfer Provisions of the No Child Left Behind Act," *Georgetown Journal on Poverty Law and Policy* 16 (2009): 217.

100. Brian Gill et al., *Title I School Choice and Supplemental Educational Services Under No Child Left Behind* (Santa Monica, Calif.: RAND Corporation, 2008).

101. Holme and Richards, "School Choice and Stratification in a Regional Context."

102. Jennifer Jellison Holme and Amy Stuart Wells, "School Choice Beyond District Borders: Lessons for the Reauthorization of NCLB from Interdistrict Desegregation and Open Enrollment Plans," in *Improving on No Child Left Behind: Getting Education Reform Back on Track*, ed. Richard D. Kahlenberg (New York: Century Foundation Press, 2008), 139.

103. Ibid.

104. Holme and Richards, "School Choice and Stratification in a Regional Context."

105. Holme and Wells, "School Choice Beyond District Borders."

106. Frankenberg, *Project Choice Campaign.*

107. Sarah Carleton, Christine Lynch, and Robert O'Donnell, *School District Consolidation in Massachusetts: Opportunities and Obstacles* (Boston: Massachusetts Department of Elementary and Secondary Education, 2009).

108. Witte and Thorn, "Who Chooses?"

109. Massachusetts Department of Elementary and Secondary Education, *FY11 METCO Districts and Grant Allocations;* Massachusetts Department of Elementary and Secondary Education, "FY10 School Choice Tuition, June 2010," http://finance1.doe.mass.edu/schoice/choice10.html (accessed December 6, 2010); Massachusetts Department of Elementary and Secondary Education, *FY09 Expenditures Per Pupil, District Comparisons Based upon Grade Structure, District Wealth, and Enrollment.*

110. Maine Department of Education, *Summary of the Reorganization Law.*

111. David Sharp, "Maine Voters to Decide Fate of School District Merger Law," *Boston Globe,* October 17, 2009.

112. The Supreme Court's *Milliken v. Bradley* ruling declared that the planned busing of public school students across district lines among fifty-three school districts in metropolitan Detroit was unconstitutional, and that interdistrict integration remedies could be required only when there was actual evidence that multiple districts had deliberately engaged in a policy of segregation. *Milliken v. Bradley,* 418 U.S. 717 (1974).

113. Andrew Rotherham, "Does Income-Based School Integration Work?" *Time,* October 28, 2010.

114. *A Nation at Risk: The Imperative for Educational Reform* (Washington, D.C.: The National Commission on Excellence in Education, April 1983).

115. See chapter 2 in this volume.

Chapter 6

1. *State and Local Implementation of the No Child Left Behind Act, Volume IV—Title I School Choice and Supplemental Educational Services: Interim Report* (Santa Monica, Calif.: RAND Corporation, 2008), http://www.rand.org/pubs/reprints/RP1332/; Jennifer Jellison Holme and Meredith P. Richards, "Review of *Plotting School Choice* and *In Need of Improvement,*" Education and the Public Interest Center and Education Policy Research Unit, 2009, http://nepc.colorado.edu/thinktank/review-plotting-school-choice.

2. *State and Local Implementation of the No Child Left Behind Act, Volume IV.*

3. Diane Ravitch, *The Death and Life of the Great American School System: How Testing and Choice Are Undermining Education* (New York: Basic Books, 2010).

4. Jennifer Jellison Holme and Amy Stuart Wells, "School Choice beyond District Borders: How NCLB Could Provide Meaningful Choice to Children in Failing Schools," in *Improving on No Child Left Behind: Getting Education Reform Back on Track,* ed. Rick Kahlenberg (New York: The Century Foundation, 2008); Holme and Richards, "Review of *Plotting School Choice* and *In Need of Improvement.*"

5. Gail L. Sunderman, James S. Kim, and Gary Orfield, *NCLB Meets School Realities: Lessons from the Field* (Thousand Oaks, Calif.: Corwin Press, 2005).

6. Cynthia G. Brown, *Choosing Better Schools: A Report on Student Transfers under the No Child Left Behind Act* (Washington, D.C.: Citizens' Commission on Civil Rights, 2004); Richard D. Kahlenberg, "Helping Children Move from Bad Schools to Good Ones," Security and Opportunity Agenda Series, The Century Foundation, New York, June 15, 2006.

7. *Title I Accountability and School Improvement from 2001 to 2004* (Washington, D.C.: U.S. Department of Education, 2006), http://www.ed.gov/rschstat/eval/disadv/tassie3/tassie3.pdf.

8. Holme and Wells, "School Choice beyond District Borders."

9. *A Blueprint for Reform: The Reauthorization of the Elementary and Secondary Education Act* (Washington, D.C.: U.S. Department of Education, 2010), http://www2.ed.gov/policy/elsec/leg/blueprint/blueprint.pdf.

10. Erin Dillon, "Plotting School Choice: The Challenges of Crossing School District Lines," Education Sector, 2008, http://www.educationsector.org/research/research_show.htm?doc_id=702217; Erin Dillon, "In Need of Improvement: Revising NCLB's School Choice Provision," Education Sector, 2008, http://www.educationsector.org/analysis/analysis_show.htm?doc_id=727885.

11. Dillon, "Plotting School Choice," 1.

12. Dillon, "In Need of Improvement," 5.

13. Holme and Richards, "Review of *Plotting School Choice* and *In Need of Improvement.*"

14. Ibid.

15. Rosemary D'Amour, "METCO Supporters Fight Cutbacks," *MetroWest Daily News,* March 19, 2009, http://www.metrowestdailynews.com/state/x1555728763/METCO-supporters-fight-cutbacks; *METCO Newsletter,* Reading Public Schools, Mass., http://reading.k12.ma.us/coolidge/Metco.html.

16. National Center for Education Statistics Common Core of Data, Washington, D.C., 2005, http://nces.ed.gov/ccd/pubschuniv.asp.

17. *State and Local Implementation of the No Child Left Behind Act, Volume IV.*

18. Holme and Richards, "Review of *Plotting School Choice* and *In Need of Improvement.*"

19. Dillon, "In Need of Improvement."

20. Holme and Richards, "Review of *Plotting School Choice* and *In Need of Improvement.*"

21. Ibid.

22. Kendra Bischoff, "School District Fragmentation and Racial Residential Segregation: How Do Boundaries Matter?" *Urban Affairs Review* 44, no. 2 (2008): 182–217.

23. National Center for Education Statistics Common Core of Data, 2008.

24. Bischoff, "School District Fragmentation and Racial Residential Segregation."

25. National Center for Education Statistics Common Core of Data.

26. Bischoff, "School District Fragmentation and Racial Residential Segregation"; Thomas D. Snyder and Sally A. Dillow, *Digest of Education Statistics 2009* (Washington, D.C.: National Center for Education Statistics, Institute of Education Sciences, U.S. Department of Education, 2010); K. Stroub and Meredith P. Richards, "The Dynamics of Metropolitan School District Segregation and Fragmentation: A Longitudinal Time-Lag Analysis," manuscript in preparation, copy on file with author, 2010.

27. Jochen Albrecht, *Key Concepts and Techniques in GIS* (Thousand Oaks, Calif.: Sage Publications, 2007); S. L. Handy and D. A. Niemeier, "Measuring Accessibility: An Exploration of Issues and Alternatives," *Environment and Planning* 29, no. 7 (1997): 1175–94.

28. Handy and Niemeier, "Measuring Accessibility"; Karst T. Geurs and Bert van Wee, "Accessibility Evaluation of Land-use and Transport Strategies: Review and Research Directions," *Journal of Transport Geography* 12 (2004): 127–40.

29. Dillon, "Plotting School Choice."

30. Ibid.

31. National Longitudinal School-Level State Assessment Score Database (NLSL-SASD), http://www.schooldata.org/.

32. National Center for Education Statistics Common Core of Data.

33. "The Impact of the New Title I Requirement on Charter Schools: Non-Regulatory Guidance," U.S. Department of Education, July 2004, http://www2.ed.gov/policy/elsec/guid/charterguidance03.doc. Excluding alternative and magnet schools necessarily limits accessibility by reducing the number of eligible higher-performing schools. As such, excluding these schools provided a conservative estimate of the increment in accessibility students experience under interdistrict choice.

34. National AYP and Identification (NAYPI) database, http://www.air.org/focus-area/education/index.cfm?fa=viewContent&content_id=860. The NAYPI database contains AYP and school improvement status information on nearly 90,000 public schools in 15,000 districts across fifty states for the 2004–05 school year.

35. For a national map illustrating the relationship between metropolitan fragmentation and the increase in accessibility attributable to interdistrict choice across all MSAs in the study, see the version published on The Century Foundation website, http://tcf.org/publications/2011/5/can-nclb-work-modeling-the-effects-of-interdistrict-choice-on-student-access-to-higher-performing-schools.

36. David J. Armor and Brett M. Peiser, *Competition in Education: A Case Study of Interdistrict Choice* (Boston, Mass.: Pioneer Institute, 1997); Holme and Richards, "Review of *Plotting School Choice* and *In Need of Improvement*"; Rutgers Institute on Education Law and Policy, *New Jersey's Interdistrict Public School Choice Program* (Newark, N.J.: Rutgers University, 2006); *Open Enrollment Program: An Evaluation* (Madison, Wis.: Wisconsin Joint Legislative Audit Bureau, August 2002).

37. Armor and Peiser, *Competition in Education;* John F. Witte and Christopher A. Thorne, "Who Chooses? Voucher and Interdistrict Transfer Programs in Milwaukee," *American Journal of Education* 104, no. 3 (1996): 186–217.

38. Justine S. Hastings, Thomas J. Kane, and Douglas Staiger, "Parental Preferences and School Competition: Evidence from a Public School Choice Program," Yale Economic Applications and Policy Discussion Paper no. 10, Yale University Department of Economics, 2005.

39. Salvatore Saporito and Annette Lareau, "School Selection as a Process: The Multiple Dimensions of Race in Framing Educational Choice," *Social Problems* 46 (1999): 418–35.

40. Robert D. Bullard, Glenn S. Johnson, and Angel O. Torres, "Dismantling Transportation Apartheid: The Quest for Equity," in *Sprawl City: Race, Politics, and Planning in Atlanta,* ed. Robert D. Bullard et al. (Washington, D.C.: Island Press, 2000).

41. Ibid.; J. E. Ryan and M. Heise, "The Political Economy of School Choice," *Yale Law Journal* 111, no. 8 (2002): 2043–2136.

42. Bischoff, "School District Fragmentation and Racial Residential Segregation."

Chapter 7

1. *Parents Involved in Community Schools v. Seattle School District No. 1,* 551 U.S. 701 (2007).

2. *Brown v. Board of Education of Topeka,* 347 U.S. 483 (1954).

3. E. Frankenberg and C. Lee, *Race in American Public Schools: Rapidly Resegregating School Districts* (Cambridge, Mass.: Harvard Civil Rights Project, 2002).

4. James S. Coleman, *Equality of Educational Opportunity* (Washington, D.C.: Government Printing Office, 1966).

5. F. Mosteller, R. Light, and J. Sachs, "Sustained Inquiry in Education: Lessons from Skill Grouping and Class Size," *Harvard Educational Review* 66, no. 4 (1996): 797–842.

6. G. Orfield and C. Lee, *Racial Transformation and the Changing Nature of Segregation* (Cambridge, Mass.: Civil Rights Project, 2006).

7. Students of color in this instance refers to African-American and Latino students.

8. H. R. Milner, *Start Where You Are, but Don't Stay There* (Cambridge, Mass.: Harvard University Press, 2010).

9. The terms *black* and *African American* are used interchangeably in this paper.

10. J. H. Braddock, "The Perpetuation of Segregation across Levels of Education: A Behavioral Assessment of the Contact-hypothesis," *Sociology of Education* 53, no. 3 (1980): 178–86; J. H. Braddock, "Segregated High School Experiences and Black Students' College and Major Field Choices," paper presented at the National Conference on School Desegregation, Chicago, 1987; J. H. Braddock, R. L. Crain, and J. M. McPartland, "A Long-term View of School Desegregation: Some Recent Studies of Graduates as Adults," *Phi Delta Kappan* 66, no. 4 (1984): 259–64; J. E. Kaufman and J. Rosenbaum, "The Education and Employment of Low-Income Black Youth in White Suburbs," *Education Evaluation and Policy Analysis* 14 (1992): 229–40.

11. J. T. Yun and M. Kurlaender, "School Racial Composition and Student Educational Aspirations: A Question of Equity in a Multiracial Society," *Journal of Education for Students Placed At Risk* 9, no. 2 (2004): 143–68.

12. Camille Z. Charles, "The Dynamics of Racial Residential Segregation," *Annual Review of Sociology* 29 (2003): 167.

13. L. Quillian, "Why Is Black–White Residential Segregation So Persistent? Evidence on Three Theories from Migration Data," *Social Science Research* 31 (2002): 197–229; M. O. Emerson, K. J. Chai, and G. Yancey, "Does Race Matter in Residential Segregation? Exploring the Preferences of White Americans," *American Sociological Review* 66, no. 6 (2001): 922–35; S. Adair and S. M. Williams, "A Critical Race Theory Perspective of Student Assignment Policies," unpublished manuscript.

14. E. Goldring, L. Cohen-Vogel, C. Smrekar, and C. Taylor, "Schooling Closer to Home: Desegregation Policy and Neighborhood Contexts," *American Journal of Education* 112, no. 3 (2006): 335–62.

15. *Plessy v. Ferguson,* 163 U.S. 537 (1896).

16. L. J. Krivo and R. L. Kaufman, "How Low Can It Go? Declining Black-White Segregation in a Multiethnic Context," *Demography* 36 (1999): 93–109.

17. B. P. An and A. Gamoran, "Trends in School Racial Composition in the Era of Unitary Status," in *From the Courtroom to the Classroom: The Shifting Landscape of School Desegregation,* ed. C. Smrekar and E. Goldring (Cambridge: Harvard University Press, 2009).

18. Adair and Williams, unpublished manuscript.

19. E. Chemerinsky, "The Segregation and Resegregation of American Public Education: The Court's Role," in *School Resegregation: Must the South Turn Back?* ed. J. C. Boger and G. Orfield (Chapel Hill: University of North Carolina Chapel Hill Press, 2005), 30.

20. R. Yin, *Case Study Research: Design and Methods* (Thousand Oaks, Calif.: Sage Publications, 2003).

21. S. M. Williams and E. Frankenberg, "Using Geography to Further Racial Integration," in *Integrating Schools in a Changing Society: New Policies and Legal Options for a Multiracial Generation* (Chapel Hill: North Carolina Press, 2011).

22. *Making Choices: Diversity, Student Assignment and Quality in Wake's Schools* (Raleigh, N.C.: Wake Education Partnership, 2003), http://www.wakeedpartnership. org/publications/d/Making_Choices_report.pdf.

23. S. M. Williams and E. A. Houck, "Turning Back the Clock: Race, Class, and Student Assignment in Wake County Public Schools," unpublished manuscript.

24. R. Kahlenberg, "Rescuing *Brown v. Board of Education*: Profiles of Twelve School Districts Pursuing Socioeconomic School Integration," The Century Foundation, 2008.

25. Williams and Houck, "Turning Back the Clock."

26. Williams and Houck, unpublished manuscript.

27. Adair and Williams, unpublished manuscript.

28. "Statewide opinion on the Wake County School Board," Public Policy Polling survey, January 27, 2011, http://publicpolicypolling.blogspot.com/2011/01/statewide-opinion-on-wake-county-school.html.

29. Christina A. Samuels, "Debate over Busing in Wake County Shows Signs of Cooling," *Education Week*, February 23, 2011, http://www.edweek.org/ew/articles/2011/02/23/21wake_ep.h30.html.

30. Michael Winerip, "Seeking Integration, Whatever the Path," *New York Times*, February 27, 2011, http://www.nytimes.com/2011/02/28/education/28winerip.html?pagewanted=all.

31. K. J. R. Phillips, R. J. Rodosky, M. A. Munoz, and E. S. Larsen, "Integrated Schools, Integrated Futures? A Case Study of School Desegregation in Jefferson County, Kentucky," in *From the Courtroom to the Classroom*.

32. Ibid.

33. See the board meeting minutes from February 9, 2009, http://www.champaign schools.org/board/Minutes/Feb909RegMtgMinutes.pdf.

Chapter 8

1. Arne Duncan, "Education Reform's Moon Shot," *Washington Post*, July 24, 2009, A21.

2. Arne Duncan, "Start Over: Turnarounds Should Be the First Option for Low-Performing Schools," *Education Week*, June 17, 2009, 36.

3. Richard D. Kahlenberg, *All Together Now: Creating Middle-Class Schools through Public School Choice* (Washington, D.C.: Brookings Institution Press, 2001).

4. Sam Dillon, "U.S. Efforts to Reshape Schools Face Challenges," *New York Times*, June 2, 2009.

5. *Still Left Behind: Student Learning in Chicago's Public Schools* (Chicago: Civic Committee of the Commercial Club of Chicago, June 2009), 1.

6. Bryan C. Hassel and Lucy Steiner, *Starting Fresh: A New Strategy for Responding to Chronically Low Performing Schools* (Chapel Hill, N.C.: Public Impact, December 2003), 2.

7. Andrew Calkins, William Guenther, Grace Belfiore, and Dave Lash, *The Turnaround Challenge: Why America's Best Opportunity to Dramatically Improve Student Achievement Lies in Our Worst-Performing Schools* (Boston, Mass.: Mass Insight Education and Research Institute, 2007), 10.

8. See Andrew Smarick, "The Turnaround Fallacy," *Education Next*, Winter 2010.

9. See Richard D. Kahlenberg, *All Together Now: Creating Middle-Class Schools through Public School Choice* (Washington, D.C.: Brookings Institution Press, 2001), 50–58; E.D. Hirsch, Jr., *The Making of Americans: Democracy and Our Schools* (New Haven: Yale University Press, 2009), 59 (mobility rates); Eric A. Hanushek, John F. Kain and Steven G. Rivkin, "Why Public Schools Lose Teachers," *Journal of Human Resources* 39, no. 2 (2004): 326–54 (mobility hurts the achievement of stayers and newcomers); Rachel Dinkes, Emily Forrest Cataldi, and Wendy Lin-Kelly, *Indicators of School Crime and Safety: 2007* (Washington, D.C.: National Center for Education Statistics, U.S. Department of Education, and U.S. Department of Justice, December 2007), 82, Table 6.2 and Table 7.2 (disorder); Paul Barton and Richard Coley, *Windows on Achievement and Inequality* (Princeton, N.J.: Educational Testing Service, 2008), 9, Figure 2 (at thirty-six months of age, children from professional families have 1,116 words in their vocabularies, and children from welfare families have 525).

10. Kahlenberg, *All Together Now,* 62–64.

11. *Parent and Family Involvement in Education, 2006–07 School Year* (Washington, D.C.: National Center for Education Statistics, August 2008).

12. See Richard Rothstein, "Equalizing Education Resources on Behalf of Disadvantaged Children," in *A Notion at Risk: Preserving Public Education as an Engine for Social Mobility,* ed. Richard D. Kahlenberg (New York: Century Foundation Press, 2000), 79–85.

13. See, e.g., Debra Viadero, "Teacher Transfers Linked to Influx of Black Students," *Education Week,* June 10, 2009, 7 (citing research by Cornell's C. Kirabo Jackson, finding that, as Charlotte-Mecklenburg schools re-segregated, the best teachers tended to leave schools with an influx of black students).

14. Kahlenberg, *All Together Now,* 67–74.

15. See, e.g., Robert Gordon, Thomas J. Kane, and Douglas O. Staiger, *Identifying Effective Teachers Using Performance on the Job,* Hamilton Project Discussion Paper 2006-01 (Washington, D.C.: Brookings Institution, April 2006), 8 (suggesting that an average child assigned to a teacher in the top quartile of effectiveness will gain ten percentile points per year over the average child assigned to a teacher in the bottom quartile of effectiveness, and extrapolating that "if the effects were cumulative, having a top-quartile teacher rather than a bottom quartile teacher four years in a row would be enough to close the black-white test score gap").

16. Brian A. Jacob, "The Challenge of Staffing Urban Schools with Effective Teachers," *The Future of Children* 17, no. 1 (2007): 140; Eric A. Hanushek and Steven G. Rivkin, "Pay, Working Conditions, and Teacher Quality," *The Future of Children* 1, no. 1 (2007): 82.

17. Hanushek and Rivkin, "Pay, Working Conditions, and Teacher Quality," 73.

18. Julie Kowal, Bryan C. Hassel, and Emily Ayscue Hassel, *Financial Incentives for Hard-To-Staff Positions: Cross-Sector Lessons for Public Education* (Washington, D.C.: Center for American Progress, November 2008), 3, 18, and 23.

19. Hanushek, Kain, and Rivkin, "Why Public Schools Lose Teachers."

20. Erica Frankenberg and Genevieve Siegel-Hawley, *The Forgotten Choice? Rethinking Magnet Schools in a Changing Landscape* (Los Angeles: UCLA Civil Rights Project, November 2008), 15.

21. The most famous disappointment is probably a Kansas City high school, which featured a $5 million swimming pool, an indoor track, and a model United Nations wired for language translation, yet failed to draw white middle-class students. Stephan

Thernstrom and Abigail Thernstrom, *America in Black and White: One Nation, Indivisible* (New York: Simon and Schuster, 1997), 345–46.

22. See Nabila Boctor, "Introduction to Wexford & Montessori Education," (2009); and Wexford Montessori Magnet Program, *2008 Annual Report* (both on file with the author).

23. Gerald Grant, *Hope and Despair in the American City: Why There Are No Bad Schools in Raleigh* (Cambridge, Mass.: Harvard University Press, 2009), 98–99.

24. See, e.g., Richard D. Kahlenberg, *Rescuing* Brown *v.* Board of Education: *Profiles of Twelve School Districts Pursuing Socioeconomic School Integration* (New York: Century Foundation, 2007), 13.

25. Richard D. Kahlenberg, "A Tea Party Defeat on Schools in North Carolina," Blog of The Century, The Century Foundation, October 14, 2011.

26. E-mail correspondence from Michael Alves to author, July 28, 2009.

27. Magnet Schools of America, "MASA Supports Senate Draft Reauthorization Bill," October 14, 2011.

28. For a discussion of these studies, see Frankenberg and Siegel-Hawley, *The Forgotten Choice?* 13–14.

29. Robert Bifulco, Casey Cobb, and Courtney Bell, *Can Interdistrict Choice Boost Student Achievement? The Case of Connecticut's Interdistrict Magnet School Program* (New York: National Center for the Study of Privatization in Education, 2008).

30. See James S. Coleman et al., *Equality of Educational Opportunity* (Washington, D.C.: U.S. Government Printing Office, 1966).

31. For a summary of dozens of studies conducted from the 1960s through 2000, see Richard D. Kahlenberg, *All Together Now: Creating Middle-Class Schools through Public School Choice* (Washington, D.C.: Brookings Institution Press, 2001), 25–42 (reviewing numerous studies).

32. Geoffrey Borman and Maritza Dowling, "Schools and Inequality: A Multilevel Analysis of Coleman's Equality of Educational Opportunity Data," *Teachers College Record* 112, no. 5 (2010): 1–2.

33. David Rusk, "Classmates Count: A Study of the Interrelationship between Socioeconomic Background and Standardized Test Scores of 4th Grade Pupils in the Madison-Dane County Public Schools," July 5, 2002, http://www.schoolinfosystem.org/archives/Unifiedfinalreport.pdf

34. R. W. Rumberger and G. J. Palardy, "Does Segregation Still Matter? The Impact of Student Composition on Academic Achievement in High School," *Teachers College Record* 107, no. 9 (2005): 1999–2045.

35. *PISA 2006: Science Competencies for Tomorrow's World*, vol. 1 (Paris: Organisation for Economic Co-operation and Development, 2007), 194.

36. Laura B. Perry and Andrew McConney, "Does the SES of the School Matter? An Examination of Socioeconomic Status and Student Achievement Using PISA 2003," *Teachers College Record* 112, no. 4 (2010): 708.

37. J. Douglas Willms, "School Composition and Contextual Effects on Student Outcomes," *Teachers College Record* 112, no. 4 (2010): 3–4.

38. Douglas N. Harris, *Lost Learning, Forgotten Promises: A National Analysis of School Racial Segregation, Student Achievement, and 'Controlled Choice' Plans* (Washington, D.C.: Center for American Progress, November 24, 2006), 14, 18, and 22.

39. National Center for Education Statistics, NAEP Data Explorer, 2008 (on scores); and Christopher Lubienski and Sarah Theule Lubienski, *Charter, Private,*

Public Schools and Academic Achievement: New Evidence from NAEP Mathematics (New York: National Center for the Study of Privatization in Education, Teachers College, Columbia University, January 2006), 5 (that ten NAEP points corresponds roughly with a year of learning).

40. Kahlenberg, *Rescuing Brown*, 9–41.

41. Kahlenberg, *All Together Now*, 32–34.

42. Robert J. Sampson, Patrick Sharkey, and Stephen W. Raudenbusch, "Durable effects of concentrated disadvantage on verbal ability among African-American children," *PNAS* 105, no. 3 (January 22, 2008): 845–52.

43. Alexander Polikoff, *Waiting for Gautreaux: A Story of Segregation, Housing and the Black Ghetto* (Evanston, Ill.: Northwestern University Press, 2006), xiv.

44. James Rosenbaum et al., cited in Kahlenberg, *All Together Now*, 33.

45. Lisa Sanbonmatsu, Jeffrey R. Kling, Greg J. Duncan, Jeanne Brooks-Gunn, "Neighborhoods and Academic Achievement: Results from the Moving to Opportunity Experiment," NBER Working Paper 11909 (January 2006), 18 and 45, Table 2.

46. David Rusk, *Inside Game/Outside Game: Winning Strategies for Saving Urban America* (Washington, D.C.: Brookings Institution Press, 1999), p. 18. See also Alec MacGillis, "Obama Says He, Too, Is a Poverty Fighter; In D.C., He Offers Contrast with Edwards," *Washington Post*, July 19, 2007, A4 ("billions spent on jobs and housing through [Community Development Block] grants over the years have failed to turn around many areas").

47. Kahlenberg, *All Together Now*, 83 (regarding Title I); and, more recently, Richard D. Kahlenberg , "Introduction," in *Improving on No Child Left Behind*, ed. Richard D. Kahlenberg (New York: Century Foundation Press, 2008), 5 (on Title I funds under No Child Left Behind).

48. 127 S.Ct. 2738 (2007).

49. Under the U.S. Supreme Court's reading of the Fourteenth Amendment Equal Protection Clause, any use of race—even for the benign purpose of promoting integration—is subject to "strict scrutiny." This is a very exacting standard of review that requires government to offer a "compelling" interest and ensure that the means employed are "narrowly tailored." By contrast, the government's use of economic status need meet only the more relaxed "rational basis" test. See, e.g., *Gratz v. Bollinger*, 539 U.S. 244, 270 (1993) (all racial classifications subject to strict scrutiny); and *James v. Valtierra*, 402 U.S. 137, 141 (1971) (wealth classifications not subject to strict scrutiny). Even opponents of using race in student assignment—such as the George W. Bush administration, the conservative Pacific Legal Foundation, the American Civil Rights Institute, and the Center for Equal Opportunity—concede that using socioeconomic status in student assignment is perfectly legal. See, e.g., Brief for the United States as Amicus Curiae supporting Petitioner, *Parents Involved in Community Schools* v. *Seattle School District*, at 25–27 (citing socioeconomic considerations as a valid race-neutral alternative); Brief Amicus Curiae of the Pacific Legal Foundation, American Civil Rights Institute and Center for Equal Opportunity in support of the Petitioner, *Meredith* v. *Jefferson County Board of Education*, at 25 (same). A legal challenge to the socioeconomic integration program in Wake County, North Carolina—which alleged that economic status was just a proxy for race—was denied because Wake County had "legitimate nondiscriminatory reasons" for using socioeconomic status. See U.S. Department of Education Office of Civil Rights, Southern Division, letter to William R. McNeal, Superintendent, Wake County Public School System, August 29,

2003 (regarding OCR Complaint Nos. 11-02-1044, 11-02-1104, and 11-02-1111). And, in August 2008, the Department of Educations's Office for Civil Rights sent a letter to school districts saying it "strongly encourages" them to consider integration plans based on socioeconomic status. Stephanie J. Monroe, assistant secretary for civil rights, Dear Colleague Letter, August 28, 2008, http://www.ed.gov/about/offices/list/ocr/letters/raceassignmentese.pdf.

50. See Richard D. Kahlenberg, "A New Way on School Integration," The Century Foundation, November 2006, 4–6, available online at http://www.tcf.org/publications/education/schoolintegration.pdf.

51. Coleman et al., *Equality of Educational Opportunity*, 307.

52. For a survey of such studies, see Kahlenberg, *All Together Now*, 36, n. 61. See also Russell W. Rumberger and Gregory J. Palardy, "Does Resegregation Matter?" in *School Resegregation: Must the South Turn Back?* ed. John Charles Boger and Gary Orfield (Chapel Hill: University of North Carolina Press, 2005), 137 (socioeconomic status of the student body mattered more than the racial composition in affecting student achievement).

53. Gary Orfield, *Must We Bus? Segregated Schools and National Policy* (Washington, D.C.: Brookings Institution Press, 1978), 69. See also Gary Orfield and Chungmei Lee, "Why Segregation Matters: Poverty and Educational Inequality," Harvard Civil Rights Project, January 2005, pp. 8–9 ("The civil rights movement was never about sitting next to whites, it was about equalizing opportunity. If high poverty schools are systematically unequal and segregated minority schools are almost always high poverty schools, it is much easier to understand both the consequences of segregation and the conditions that create the possibility of substantial gains in desegregated classrooms.").

54. Richard Rothstein, *Class and Schools: Using Social, Economic, and Educational Reform to Close the Black-White Achievement Gap* (Washington, D.C.: Economic Policy Institute, 2004), 100, Figures 4A and 4B.

55. Michael Planty et al., *The Condition of Education 2009* (Washington, D.C.: U.S. Department of Education, National Center for Education Statistics, June 2009), 196, Table A-25-1.

56. See, e.g., *Phi Delta Kappan*, September 2007, 42 (74 percent say providing low-performing students the ability to enroll in any public school of choice would be somewhat or very effective, compared with 55 percent saying the same of providing low-performing students financial support to cover part or all of the tuition cost at a private school); *Phi Delta Kappan*, September 2006, p. 43.

57. Planty et al., *The Condition of Education 2009*, 78, Indicator 32 ("From 1993 to 2007, the percentage of children attending a 'chosen' public school [a public school other than their assigned public school] increased from 11 to 16 percent").

58. Kahlenberg, *All Together Now*, 37–42. Although the NAEP data contained in Figure 8.5 indicates a decline in middle-class student achievement even when moving from very-low-poverty schools (0–10 percent of students receiving free or reduced-price meals) to economically mixed schools (26–34 percent of students receiving free or reduced-price meals), research suggests that this decline is more likely due to differences in family environments within the very broad category of students defined as "middle class" rather than to differences in school environments. In his study of schools in Madison-Dane County, Wisconsin, researcher David Rusk found that "middle-class" students (those not eligible for free and reduced-price lunch) attending

very-low-poverty schools tended to be far wealthier than "middle-class" students attending economically mixed schools, and were expected to do better, irrespective of the school they attended. By contrast, the economic range within the low-income group (those eligible for free and reduced-price lunch) is much smaller and does not account for the differences in achievement between low-income students in high-poverty schools as compared with those in economically mixed schools. See David Rusk, "Classmates Count: A Study of the Interrelationship between Socioeconomic Background and Standardized Test Scores of 4th Grade Pupils in the Madison-Dane County Public Schools," July 5, 2002, available online at http://www.schoolinfosystem.org/archives/Unifiedfinalreport.pdf.

59. Samuel Casey Carter, *No Excuses: Lessons from 21 High-Performing High Poverty Schools* (Washington, D.C.: Heritage Foundation, 2000), 2; and Kenneth Cooper, "School Defies Its Demographics," *Washington Post,* June 7, 2000, A3 (on 7,000 low-performing, high-poverty schools).

60. Craig Jerald, *Dispelling the Myth Revisited: Preliminary Findings from a Nationwide Analysis of "High-Flying" Schools* (Washington, D.C.: Education Trust, 2001). See also Douglas N. Harris, *Ending the Blame Game on Educational Inequity: A Study of "High Flying" Schools and NCLB* (Tempe, Ariz.: Education Policy Research Unit, Arizona State University, March 2006), 5.

61. Harris, *Ending the Blame Game,* 20, Table 2. This reduced the number of high-flying, high-poverty schools to roughly 250.

62. See, e.g., Steven Greenhouse and Jennifer Medina, "Teachers at 2 Charter Schools Plan to Join Union, Despite Notion of Incompatibility," *New York Times,* January 14, 2009 (quoting Jeanne Allen, executive director of the Center for Education Reform: "A union contract is actually at odds with a charter school").

63. KIPP Web site, www.kipp.org.

64. Jay Mathews, *Work Hard. Be Nice: How Two Inspired Teachers Created the Most Promising Schools in America* (Chapel Hill, N.C.: Algonquin Books, 2009), 2.

65. Ibid., 89. Some research also finds that KIPP students begin school at more advanced levels than is typical of neighborhood peers; Martin Carnoy, Rebecca Jacobsen, Lawrence Mishel, and Richard Rothstein, *The Charter School Dust-Up: Examining the Evidence on Enrollment and Achievement* (Washington, D.C.: Economic Policy Institute, 2005), 51–65; Paul Tough, *Whatever It Takes: Geoffrey Canada's Quest to Change Harlem and America* (Boston: Houghton Mifflin, 2008), 161. But Jeffrey Henig's review of seven studies disputes the "creaming" charge. See Jeffrey R. Henig, "What Do We Know About the Outcomes of KIPP Schools?" Greater Lakes Center for Education Research and Practice, November 2008, p. 1.

66. Carnoy et al., *The Charter School Dust-Up,* 61, Table 5.

67. Katrina R. Woodworth, Jane K. David, Roneeta Guha, Haiwen Wang, and Alejandra Lopez-Torkos, *San Francisco Bay Area KIPP Schools: A Study of Early Implementation and Achievement, Final Report* (Eugene, Ore.: Center for Educational Policy and SRI International, 2008), ix and 13–14.

68. See Richard D. Kahlenberg, "Myths and Realities about KIPP," Answer Sheet Blog, *Washington Post,* January 4, 2011; and Richard D. Kahlenberg, "Do Self-Selection and Attrition Matter in KIPP Schools?" Answer Sheet Blog, *Washington Post,* June 14, 2011.

69. Erik W. Robelen, "KIPP Study Finds High Student Attrition Amid Big Learning Gains," *Education Week,* September 24, 2008, 10.

70. See Richard D. Kahlenberg, "Do Self-Selection and Attrition Matter in KIPP Schools?"

71. Smarick, "The Turnaround Fallacy."

72. Woodworth et al., *San Francisco Bay Area KIPP Schools*, 32. See also Robelen, "KIPP Study," 10; Nanette Asimov, "Students at KIPP Perform Better, Study Finds," *San Francisco Chronicle*, September 18, 2008.

73. Mathews, *Work Hard*, 263, 285, and 308.

74. Mathews, *Work Hard*, 263, 285 (per pupil expenditure), 308 (more than $50 million); and Chester Finn, *The Education Gadfly*, October 1, 2009 (more than $60 million).

75. Will Dobbie and Roland G. Fryer, "Are High-Quality Schools Enough to Close the Achievement Gap? Evidence from a Bold Social Experiment in Harlem" (April 2009); and David Brooks, "The Harlem Miracle," *New York Times*, May 8, 2009.

76. Tough, *Whatever It Takes*, 261 (1,200 students participated in the pre-k, elementary and middle schools. Another 6,000 participate in a more modest way, through after-school program and the like.) See also Dobbie and Fryer, "Are High-Quality Schools Enough" 5–6 (1,300 students attending three schools).

77. Javier C. Hernandez, "Charters Offer More Choices in Harlem, but Stir Concern for Public Schools," *New York Times*, March 1, 2009.

78. Tough, *Whatever It Takes*, 13 and 196.

79. Aaron Pallas, "Just How Gullible Is David Brooks?" GothamSchools.org, May 8, 2009.

80. Jennifer Medina, "U.S. Math Tests Find Scant Gains Across New York," *New York Times*, October 15, 2009.

81. Tough, *Whatever It Takes*, 254.

82. Ibid., 9–10, 134, and 153.

83. Mike Spector, "Bear Market for Charities," *Wall Street Journal*, January 24, 2009.

84. Tough, *Whatever It Takes*, 224–25.

85. David L. Kirp, "Audacity in Harlem," *American Prospect*, October 2008, 42.

86. Tough, *Whatever It Takes*, p. 108.

87. Ibid., 4.

88. Ibid., 125.

89. Ibid.,124, 212.

90. Kahlenberg, *All Together Now*, 61.

91. Claude S. Fischer et al., *Inequality by Design: Cracking the Bell Curve Myth* (Princeton: Princeton University Press, 1996), 84.

92. Tough, *Whatever It Takes*, 236.

93. Atila Abdulkadiroglu, Josh Angrist, Sarah Cohodes, Susan Dynarski, Jon Fullerton, Thomas Kane, and Parag Pathak, *Informing the Debate: Comparing Boston's Charter, Pilot and Traditional Schools* (Boston: Boston Foundation, 2009).

94. Dan French, "Lack of Clarity Seen in Study of Boston Charters," *Education Week*, February 11, 2009, 25.

95. See Caroline M. Hoxby, Sonali Murarka, and Jenny Kang, *How New York City's Charter Schools Affect Achievement* (Cambridge, Mass.: New York City Charter Schools Evaluation Project, September 2009), http://www.aeaweb.org/aea/conference/program/retrieve.php?pdfid=532; and Sean F. Reardon, "Review of 'How New York City's Charter Schools Affect Achievement,'" Education and the Public Interest Center and Education Policy Research Unit, November 2009.

96. *Multiple Choice: Charter School Performance in 16 States* (Stanford, Calif.: Center for Research on Educational Outcomes, Stanford University, June 2009), 1, 44, http://credo.stanford.edu/reports/MULTIPLE_CHOICE_CREDO.pdf.

97. See Arne Duncan, "Turning Around the Bottom Five Percent," Remarks at the National Alliance for Public Charter Schools Conference, June 22, 2009, http://www.ed.gov/print/news/speeches/2009/06/06222009.html.

98. Alyson Klein, "Expected Turnaround Aid Has Districts Eager, Wary," *Education Week,* September 22, 2009.

99. "Obama Administration Announces Historic Opportunity to Turn Around Nation's Lowest-Achieving Public Schools," U.S. Department of Education, August 26, 2009, http://www.ed.gov/print/news/pressreleases/2009/08/08262009.html

100. See Linda Darling Hammond, "What Are the Best Methods for School Improvement?" *National Journal,* September 4, 2009, http://education.nationaljournal.com/2009/08/what-are-the-best-methods-for.php. Critics correctly will note that performance is linked in large measure to the higher economic status of northerners, but that is precisely the point: addressing poverty (through programs like prekindergarten) is far more productive than focusing on teacher union density. Note also that some KIPP schools are unionized, as are the Green Dot charter schools that are widely lauded. See Steven Greenhouse and Jennifer Medina, "Teachers at 2 Charter Schools Plan to Join Union, Despite Notion of Incompatibility," *New York Times,* January 14, 2009; and Mathews, *Work Hard,* 284.

101. Richard D. Kahlenberg, *Tough Liberal: Albert Shanker and the Battles over Schools, Unions, Race, and Democracy* (New York: Columbia University Press, 2007), 369–70 (reviewing the research on teacher unions).

102. David A. Stuit and Thomas M. Smith, "Teacher Turnover in Charter Schools," National Center on School Choice, Vanderbilt University, 2009, 22–23.

103. James Foreman Jr., "No Ordinary Success," *Boston Review,* May/June 2009.

Appendix

1. Section 5120, titled "Assignment within District," of the School Board of Alachua County Bylaws & Policies: "It is the policy of the Board to make the most economical and practical use of its physical resources in the implementation of its educational programs consistent with the best interests of students. Toward this end, the Superintendent shall periodically review school enrollment and recommend to the Board such changes in attendance zones for the following school year as may be justified after consideration of all the following criteria, listed in descending order of significance: (a) school capacity; (b) convenience of access to schools; (c) sage and efficient student transportation and travel; (d) effective and appropriate instructional programs; (e) socioeconomic diversity in school enrollments; (f) financial and administrative efficiency." See < http://www.neola.com/alachua-fl/search/policies/po5200.htm>.

2. See "September 28, 2009 Board Meeting Summary," Allen Independent School District, http://www.allenisd.org/200610610121458713/cwp/view.asp?A=3&Q=288578&C=58824 (noting that "allowing for the continuation of economic parity between campuses in determining middle school boundaries" was one of the parameters for redistricting) and Mark Tarpley, Assistant Superintendent, Finance & Operations, Allen Independent School District, telephone interview with Halley Potter,

March 24, 2011 (confirming that maintaining similar percentages of "economically disadvantaged" students—defined as those receiving free or reduced-price lunch—across middle school campuses was a factor in the final boundary decisions).

3. See Diane Lederman, "Amherst OKs School Redistricting," *The Republican,* October 29, 2009 (describing redistricting of elementary schools so roughly 35 percent of students will be eligible for free and reduced price lunch at each school); and "Our Schools," Amherst Regional Public Schools, http://www.arps.org/OurSchools/.

4. See Emily Guevara, "BISD Replaces Race-Based Transfers with Policy Based on Students' Economic Status," *Beaumont Enterprise,* February 3, 2008 (describing program that allows students in schools with more than 65 percent of students eligible for free or reduced-price lunch to transfer to one in which fewer than 65 percent of students are eligible).

5. See Kahlenberg, *Rescuing* Brown *v.* Board of Education, 34 (describing public school choice plan to create socioeconomically and racially integrated schools within ten percentage points plus or minus of the district average using neighborhood rather than individual family factors).

6. See Les Fujitake, letter from the Superintendent of Schools, January 4, 2011, http://elementary.department.about.bloomington.k12.mn.us/modules/groups/home pagefiles/gwp/1630755/2018354/File/Elementary%20Neighborhood%20School%20 Renewal%20Project/New%20Elementary%20Boundaries%20Approved%202011- 12.pdf?sessionid=ea337c5635cbb6cf8c233063f32e6dd1, and "Elementary Neighborhood School Renewal Project, Minutes, November 29, 2010, Oak Grove Elementary School," Bloomington Public Schools, http://elementary.department.about.blooming- ton.k12.mn.us/modules/locker/files/get_group_file.phtml?gid=2018354&fid=93898 13&sessionid=ea337c5635cbb6cf8c233063f32e6dd1 (noting that "socio-economic percentage by school" was one of the factors in redrawing the boundaries).

7. John Ingold, "School Ahead in Race for Diversity: Boulder Valley's Community Montessori Elementary seeks students from different socioeconomic strata rather than from various races and may be a model for avoiding legal challenge," *Denver Post,* January 2, 2007, A1.

8. See Kahlenberg, *Rescuing* Brown *v.* Board of Education, 34–35 (describing student assignment plan designed to keep all schools between 16 percent and 47 percent low income).

9. See Laura Henslet, "Bryan Offers Third Plan for Schools" *Bryan Eagle,* December 12, 2006 (describing program under which magnet schools will seek socioeconomic balance).

10. See Beth Brogan, "Whither the Little Children? Brunswick School Board Sorts Through Elementary Redistricting Options," *The Times Record,* November 5, 2010 http://www.timesrecord.com/articles/2010/11/05/news/doc4cd433f31378d45 6050475.txt (describing the socioeconomic impact of the proposed redistricting maps) and Michelle Small, at-large school board member for the Brunswick School Department, telephone interview with Halley Potter, February 9, 2011 (discussing the school board's decision to approve the map resulting in the most equitable percentages of free and reduced-price lunch eligibility between the two affected schools).

11. See Craig T. Neises, "Book Hands Over Superintendent Post, Challenges," *Hawkeye,* July 1, 2007 (noting after the Supreme Court decision in PICS, superintendent indicated that racial balance factors could be replaced by socioeconomic factors); and Jane Evans, e-mail correspondence with Kristen Oshyn, March 9, 2009 (indicating

that "socioeconomic balance" was one of the factors used in redrawing elementary school district boundaries).

12. See Molly Walsh, "Board OKs Magnet Plan for Schools," *Burlington Free Press,* February 1, 2008 (describing plan to create magnet schools with the goal of socioeconomic integration). See also "Building Burlington's Future," Burlington Diversity Task Force, June 13, 2006, http://bsdweb.bsdvt.org/district/EquityExcellence/TaskForcefullreport.pdf.

13. At its March 18, 2010, school board meeting, the board voted unanimously "to adopt a resolution to attain [...] balanced enrollments through implementation of targeted incentives in Independent School District 191." See the approved minutes from the meeting: <https://v3.boardbook.org/Public/PublicItemDownload.aspx?mk=50002528&fn=minutes.pdf>.

14. See Kahlenberg, *Rescuing* Brown *v.* Board of Education, 28–34 (describing plan in which controlled public school choice is used to reach a goal of having all schools within plus or minus fifteen percentage points of the district-wide percentage of students eligible for free and reduced-price lunch).

15. See Jodi Heckel, "Income to Be Factor in Champaign School Assignments," *Champaign News-Gazette,* January 9, 2009; and Jodi Heckel, "Change in Unit 4 Assignment Plan Explained," *Champaign News-Gazette,* January 13, 2009 (describing shift in basis of school integration plan from race to socioeconomic status).

16. See Cheryl Johnston Sadgrove, "Board Poised to Consider Redistricting Plan," *Raleigh News and Observer,* April 7, 2007; and board meeting-amended minutes from May 3, 2007 (describing the drawing of attendance boundaries to achieve socioeconomic diversity).

17. Theola Labbe, "Charles Sets Meetings on Remapping," *Washington Post,* June 8, 2003 (redistricting committee considered the socioeconomic status of students in reviewing reassignments).

18. "CPS Announces New Policy for Admission to Selective Enrollment and Magnet Schools: Socio-Economic Data Will Be Used Instead of Race-Based Criteria," Chicago Public Schools Press Release, November 10, 2009, <http://www.cps.edu/News/Press_releases/2009/Pages/11_10_2009_PR!.aspx>.

19. See "School Choice Program Guidelines, Board Policy 3040," Christina School District, http://www.christina.k12.de.us/SchoolBoard/ChoiceProgramGuidelines.htm (one of the criteria for accepting or rejecting applications is the "Impact on the socioeconomic composition of the affected school[s]").

20. See Jhone M. Ebert, director of Magnet Schools for the Clark County School District, in panel, "How Socioeconomic Integration Promotes Equity and Diversity in Student Selection to Magnet Programs," Magnet Schools of America Conference, February 13, 2006.

21. See Megan Hawkins, "Five School Diversity Plans Detailed," *Des Moines Register,* March 10, 2008; and Davenport Community Schools, minutes from the regular board meeting on February 11, 2008, http://www.davenport.k12.ia.us/schoolboard/minutes/021108R.pdf (describing switch in diversity transfer policy from race to student academic achievement and socioeconomic status).

22. The school includes among its guiding principles: "To build a unified student body, embracing the challenges of gender, economic and racial diversity, fulfilling our commitment to have a student body of at least 40% students from economically

disadvantaged families and 45% women." See the "Vision and Guiding Principles" section of its website: < http://www.scienceandtech.org/about-us/about-vision.php>.

23. See Hawkins, "Five School Diversity Plans Detailed"; and Des Moines Public Schools, minutes of the school board meeting on February 19, 2008, http://www.dmps.k12.ia.us/schoolboard/3-appmin/3-080219appmin.doc (describing shift in diversity transfer policy from race to whether a student qualifies for free or reduced-price lunch).

24. See Application for Federal Assistance, Duval County Public School District, March 11, 2004, 24 (describing magnet school admissions policy in which students who qualify for free and reduced-price lunch and attend a high-poverty Title I school are given preference to attend a magnet school in a non-Title I district, and middle-class children attending non-Title I schools are given a preference to attend a magnet in a Title I district); and Sally Hague, director of Duval County School Choice/Student Assignment Operations, e-mail to Kristen Oshyn, April 10, 2007 (indicating the use of the program at the elementary school level and discussions to extend the policy to middle schools).

25. East Baton Rouge Parish School System uses a weighted-lottery admissions process for its magnet program, which gives consideration to a student's socioeconomic background. See Charles Lussier, "Dufrocq Elementary Adds Magnet Program as Lure," *The Advocate,* June 3, 2009, <http://www.2theadvocate.com/news/46776317.html>, 1B.

26. See Kelly Smith, "Eden Prairie OKs Changing School Lines," *Star Tribune,* December 21, 2010, http://www.startribune.com/local/west/112289839.html (describing a plan in which "boundary lines would be redrawn to balance concentrations of poverty").

27. See "Summary: Board Action on School Choice Access and Options," Eugene Public School District, March 9, 2005 (summarizing decision to provide a preference to low-income students in a lottery for alternative schools that had been utilized primarily by more-affluent students). See also "School Choice Request, 2007–08," Eugene Public School District, 2007, http://www.4j.lane.edu/files/4J_choice_request_2007_0.pdf (outlining priority for students receiving free and reduced-price lunch).

28. See Michael Alison Chandler, "Fairfax School Board Approves Boundary Redesign," *Washington Post,* February 29, 2008; and Fairfax County Schools Policy 8130.5, http://www.boarddocs.com/vsba/fairfax/Board.nsf/0/96e257690b03f37a852 56fcd005278e2/$FILE/P8130.pdf (describing policy in which "Socioeconomic characteristics of school populations" will be taken into consideration when "consolidating schools, redistricting school boundaries, or adopting pupil assignments plans").

29. Farmington Public Schools reestablished school boundaries for the 2010-11 school year with socioeconomic balance as one of its goals. See its "Reconfiguration Plan Info Sheet," <http://www.farmington.k12.mi.us/pdfs/reconfig/reconfiguration_infosheet.pdf> and its "Reconfiguration/School Closings FAQs," updated April 26, 2010, http://www.farmington.k12.mi.us/pdfs/reconfig/reconfiguration_faq.pdf, esp. 4-5 and 7.

30. See Fresno Unified School Board Policy, BP5116.2 "Magnet Schools" (last revised September 6, 2006), http://www.gamutonline.net/4daction/Web_PrintableDisplay/424407 (describing magnet school admissions policy under which FUSD "may use the socio-economic status of students, as determined by eligibility for Free and Reduced Price meals, as one of the factors in the lottery process").

31. Paul Alongi, "Hearings on Students' Schools Set," *Greenville News,* January 27, 2002, 1B, and Paul Alongi, "Meek Offers Proposal on Student Dispersal," *Greenville News,* March 27, 2002, 1B (describing Greenville Board of Trustees vote to adopt a new student assignment scheme that eliminated the use of race but sought to reduce the "concentration of low-income students" and the "concentration of low-achieving students"; the board rejected, however, a more aggressive plan to ensure that no school has more than 50 percent of its students eligible for free or reduced-price lunch). See also Paul Alongi, "School Plan Would Shift More than 1600 Youths," *Greenville News,* February 11, 2003 (describing subsequent redistricting in which committee sought socioeconomic balance in the schools).

32. See Editorial, "Right Decision, But Not a Shared Vision," (Greensboro, North Carolina) *News-Record,* February 25, 2006 (on decision to redistrict schools to increase socioeconomic and racial diversity); and Morgan Josey, "Board Member Pushes Choice on Redistricting," *News-Record,* March 29, 2007 (on proposal by board to water down the earlier decision by allowing greater choice).

33. See U.S. Department of Education, *Creating Successful Magnet Schools* (Washington, D.C.: U.S. Department of Education, September 2004), 44 (describing Hamilton's use of free and reduced lunch data in its magnet school application process to create economically and racially diverse schools).

34. See Linnea Brown, "District Plans 'Gifted' Screening Test," *Hernando Today,* June 10, 2008 (describing plan under which low-income children can qualify for a gifted program under different criteria than most students).

35. The High Tech High goals include: "Serve a student body that mirrors the ethnic and socioeconomic diversity of the local community." See its website: <http://www.hightechhigh.org/about/>.

36. See Adam Emerson, "Hillsborough School Board Approves Boundary Changes," *Tampa Bay Online,* February 10, 2009 (describing redistricting of high school attendance zones in part to create "socioeconomic diversity").

37. See "Choices: A Guide to Jefferson County Public Schools," Jefferson County Public Schools, 2008, http://www.jefferson.k12.ky.us/Pubs/Choices.pdf; and Richard D. Kahlenberg, "The New Look of School Integration," *American Prospect,* June 2, 2008, http://www.prospect.org/cs/articles?article=the_new_look_of_school_integration (describing new plan using census data to create diversity by income, parental education, and race).

38. The Kalamazoo Public Schools Board of Education voted in 2009 to redistrict partly based on "better socioeconomic balance." Ed Finnerty, "Kalamazoo Public Schools Trustees Approve Redistricting for This Fall," *Kalamazoo Gazette,* February 13, 2009.

39. See Kahlenberg, *Rescuing* Brown *v.* Board of Education, 13–28 (describing plan in which elementary school boundaries were drawn to create schools in which between 15 percent and 45 percent of students were eligible for free lunch).

40. See Amanda Bedgood, "Schools Get New Entrance Criteria," *Lafayette Advertiser,* February 21, 2008 (describing switch in weighted lottery admissions program from race to free and reduced-price lunch status).

41. See "Plan for Student Assignment, 2008–09," School District of Lee County, Florida, 36, http://studentassignment.leeschools.net/pdf/2008%20Student%20Assignment%20Plan.pdf ("The District's target for each school is to maintain student enrollment that is within 20 percentage points, plus or minus, of the zone-wide average

of students eligible for Free and Reduced Meals for each level [elementary, middle and high]").

42. See Lee County, North Carolina, Board of Education, "Policy Code: 4150 School Assignment, Reassignment and Transfers," http://policy.microscribepub.com/cgi-bin/om_isapi.dll?clientID=110012429&depth=8&infobase=lee.nfo&record={B40}&softpage=PL_frame (in devising school boundary recommendations, " the superintendent shall consider factors such as school capacity, transportation requirements, geographic features and socio-economic diversity").

43. "Specialty/magnet program assignments" are made via a weighted selection process that uses three factors: "test performance, socioeconomic status (as determined by free/reduced lunch participation) and race." See the "School Choices" section of the district website: <http://lrsd.org/departments1/schoolpages1.cfm?sccode=64&menupagename=School%20Choices&id=1144>.

44. See Andy Hall, "Board Gives Plan F an 'A'; Changes to School Attendance Boundaries on the West Side Are Approved," *Wisconsin State Journal,* March 4, 2008; and "Long Range Planning Considerations When Redrawing Boundary Lines," Madison Metropolitan School District, Appendix C, http://boeweb.madison.k12.wi.us/files/boe/longrange/0506/0506/Considerations.pdf (describing plans to redraw school boundaries that include a provision to avoid creating concentrations of low-income students).

45. See Kahlenberg, *Rescuing* Brown *v.* Board of Education, 36–37 (describing Manatee's policy of integrating schools by socioeconomic status through redistricting and public school choice and magnet schools).

46. See Kahlenberg, *Rescuing* Brown *v.* Board of Education, 37 (describing policy in which middle and high school zones are drawn in order to create socioeconomic diversity).

47. See "Appendix D: Magnet Programs/Schools," in *I Choose: Miami-Dade County Public Schools 2006-2007 Choice Plan,* Miami-Dade County School District, http://choice.dadeschools.net/images/2006_choice_plan.pdf (describing magnet school admissions plan in which 20 percent of slots are to be filled by students from four distinct zones based on school performance and socioeconomic circumstances).

48. See Kahlenberg, *Rescuing* Brown *v.* Board of Education, 37–39 (describing inter-district Choice Is Yours Program, which allows 2,000 low-income Minneapolis students to attend school in more affluent suburban jurisdictions).

49. See "Taking the Jitters Out of Kindergarten Placement," Montclair, New Jersey, Public Schools, http://www.montclair.k12.nj.us/Article.aspx?Id=338 ("a student's eligibility for free and or reduced-cost lunch" may be considered in placements).

50. See "Long –range Educational Facilities Planning: Regulation FAA-RA," Policy Manual, Montgomery County School District, http://www.montgomeryschoolsmd.org/departments/policy/pdf/faara.pdf (outlining that school boundaries and choice plans should be guided in part by "the socioeconomic background of students as measured by participation in the federal FARMS [free and reduced price meals] program"); and "School Assignment Process," Montgomery County Public Schools, adopted June 2003, http://www.montgomeryschoolsmd.org/schools/downcounty/choice/process.shtm (outlining plans for the Downcounty Consortium in which a student's having ever received free and reduced-price meals may be a factor in student assignment).

51. See "Questions and Answers About Changes in Attendance Areas for 2006-2007," Moorpark Unified School District, http://www.mrpk.k12.ca.us/web/PDF/

Boundaries/K-5%20BoundaryChanges06-07QandA.pdf (outlining the school district's decision to redraw school district boundaries to achieve socioeconomic integration); and Marilyn Green, director of special projects for the Moorpark Unified School District, telephone interview with Kelly Dilworth, May 5, 2006 (describing school district's mandate that each school try to closely reflect the district average for free and reduced-price lunch eligibility).

52. See Jillian Jones, "Redrawing the Lines for Local High Schools," *Napa Valley Register,* April 6, 2008 (describing effort to redraw boundaries to create greater socioeconomic integration).

53. See "Application for Federal Education Assistance," New York City Community School District 14, March 2004, 2, 4, Supplement to Table 5 (explaining that weighted lottery to be used in magnet school for consortium of districts 13, 14, and 15 to be used to achieve socioeconomic diversity, using free and reduced-price meals eligibility); "Application for Federal Education Assistance," New York City Community School Districts 20 and 21, March 2004, 4, Supplement to Table 5 (explaining that weighted lottery for consortium magnet school for districts 20 and 21 will use socioeconomic level as a factor in admissions).

54. See Kahlenberg, *Rescuing* Brown *v.* Board of Education, 39–40 (describing Nebraska legislation creating a new metropolitan Omaha "learning district" with a goal of having all schools in the region reflect the socioeconomic diversity of the area, which has a 35 percent free and reduced-price lunch population).

55. See "Student Assignment: Attendance Zone Criteria," Rules of the School Board of Palm Beach County Florida, Palm Beach County School Board, http://www.palmbeach.k12.fl.us/policies/ (describing policy that data on free and reduced-price lunch may be one factor in determining student attendance boundaries).

56. See Policy 10.107, Pitt County Board of Education, "School Attendance Area" (revised September 17, 2007) (providing that socioeconomic status be among the factors used to maintain diversity).

57. See Joe Smydo, "City Magnet School Overhaul Weighed," *Pittsburgh Post-Gazette,* April 29, 2009 ("the district will try to promote diversity with a weighted lottery that gives students extra chances for admission for meeting certain criteria, such as qualifying for free or reduced-price lunches or living in proximity to the magnet").

58. See "4.10.054-AD Student Transfers," Administrative Directive, Portland Public Schools, March 25, 2009, 8, http://www.pps.k12.or.us/directives-c/polreg/4/10/4_10_054_AD.pdf (describing public school choice policy under which "Students whose SES improves the socio-economic balance of the school community shall be weighted in the lottery").

59. See Hawkins, "Five School Diversity Plans Detailed"; and *Postville Community School District Voluntary Plan,* January 2008 (outlining a policy in which "the Postville School District aspires to reduce economic and language isolation by developing plans that may include but are not limited to pairing, clustering of existing classrooms, and adjustment of grade level configuration, and the continuation of existing voluntary programs such as bilingual classrooms, summer school, and Out-reach programs").

60. See "Application for Federal Education Assistance," Proviso Township School District, February 8, 2004, V-52, V-54, Table 5 (describing magnet school lottery system in which socioeconomic status would be a weighted factor).

61. See Michael Perrault, "District Sets New School Borders," *Press Enterprise,* June 25, 2008; and Neal Waner, "Boundary Committee's Goal Was Educational

Opportunities for All," *Redlands Daily Facts,* July 10, 2008 (describing redrawing of high school boundaries in which socioeconomic balance was a consideration).

62. See Kahlenberg, *Rescuing* Brown *v.* Board of Education, 40 (describing controlled choice plan in which schools aim to reflect the socioeconomic diversity of the district, using free and reduced-price lunch as an indicator of economic disadvantage).

63. See "Rock Hill Schools Work to Keep Schools Integrated," Associated Press, May 16, 2004 (school district examined socioeconomic and racial factors in redrawing school district boundaries).

64. See Rockford School District School Board Meeting Minutes, May 17, 2008, http://webs.rps205.com/district/files/36455D3205164FB8A591FC190FF3F885.pdf (discussing the use of "socioeconomic information" to draw middle school zones with aspiration that schools reflect the 70 percent free and reduced-price lunch district average).

65. See Bao Ong, "District Converts 3 Schools to Magnets; Move Intended to Help Desegregation Effort," *St. Paul Pioneer Press,* December 2, 2006; and "District Magnet Enrollment Process," Independent School District 196, Rosemount, Minnesota, http://www.district196.org/magnetschools/2008-09EnrollmentProcess.pdf (describing the use of socioeconomic status as one factor in admissions to three new magnet elementary schools).

66. Bill Hall, e-mail correspondence with Halley Potter, November 8, 2011 (indicating that one of the guiding principles used by the boundary committee was to "seek to balance in SES from building to building, as much as possible").

67. See "Magnet Schools," San Diego Unified School District, http://sandi.net/enrollmentoptions/magnet/enrollment_priority.html (describing priorities in magnet selection program, including for students who are low-income and low-achieving and attending schools in need of improvement).

68. See Kahlenberg, *Rescuing* Brown *v.* Board of Education, 40–41 (describing public school choice program in which oversubscribed schools use socioeconomic diversity as a factor in student admissions, measured by seven criteria).

69. See Larry Sloanker, "S.J. Unified May Look at Income for Diversity," *San Jose Mercury News,* June 20, 2003, A1 (describing board of trustees vote to adopt a plan to allow public school choice using eligibility for free and reduced-price lunch as the main factor in approving or disapproving choice transfers) and "School Board Policies: Voluntary Integration Plan," San Jose Unified School District, http://www.sjusd.org/pdf/districtinformation/Voluntary_Integration_Plan.pdf (describing mechanics of the plan).

70. The student assignment plan for Seattle Public Schools "consider[s] socioeconomic factors when drawing school boundaries." See the "Diversity" section of the New Student Assignment Plan Frequently Asked Questions on the district's website: <http://www.seattleschools.org/area/newassign/faq_diversity.html>.

71. See "Chapter 5.00: Student Assignment," School Board Policy Manual, Seminole County School Board, last revised January 9, 2007, http://www.scps.k12.fl.us/schoolboard/_doc/Policy%20Files%20(PDF)/tableofcontent.pdf (describing Seminole's public school choice program, which weights socioeconomic diversity; transfers are provided when they would bring the school closer to the district's free and reduced-price lunch average). See also Dave Weber, "Seminole, U.S. Agree to Settle Schools Suit," *Orlando Sentinel,* March 1, 2006.

72. See School District of South Orange and Maplewood, *Planning for School Space,* no. 3 (April 30, 1999); Patricia M. Barker (assessment coordinator, School

District of South Orange and Maplewood, New Jersey), letter to author, August 11, 1999 (describing May 1999 school board decision to redraw elementary school district boundaries for better socioeconomic balance).

73. See Megan Boldt, "South Washington County School Board Finalizes Attendance Boundaries," *St. Paul Pioneer Press*, April 24, 2008; and Megan Boldt, "Boundaries May Not Appeal to All," *St. Paul Pioneer Press*, May 21, 2008 (describing change in boundary lines in which student socioeconomic status was factor).

74. See Tracie Dungan, "Language Affect; School Boundaries," *Arkansas Democrat-Gazette*, April 11, 1999, B1 (quoting school board president saying that, for a decade, the district had redrawn school boundaries with an eye toward income integration).

75. Suzanne Robinson, "Schools Adopt Economic Policy," *Vero Beach Press Journal*, January 25, 2001, A12; Paula Holzman, "Growing Schools Seek More Space," *Stuart News/Port St. Lucie News*, August 4, 2002, A1 (describing decision of St. Lucie School Board to modify its controlled choice plan of student assignment to emphasize socioeconomic diversity over diversity by race; under the system, parents are asked whether the family qualifies for food stamps and whether the children qualify for free and reduced-price lunch); and St. Lucie County Public Schools, School Board Policy 5.231 (4), http://www.stlucie.k12.fl.us/districtPortal.aspx?id=iFrame|http://plato.stlucie.k12.fl.us/mis/School+Board+Policies.nsf (describing policy goal that schools should be within ten percentage points of the free and reduced-price lunch average of zone in which school resides).

76. See "Assignment of Students," Stamford Public Schools Board Policy 5117.1, http://stamfordpublicschools.org/filestorage/68/107/801/05Students5000.pdf (providing that "all elementary, middle, and high schools in the Stamford Public School system are expected to meet the district's integration standard to within +/– 10%, as determined annually," with the integration standard "determined by the percent of disadvantaged students [students receiving free/reduced lunch according to federal guidelines, or students identified as English Language Learners according to state guidelines, or students residing in income restricted housing] and the percent of advantaged students, as calculated on October 1 of the given school year).

77. See "Magnet School Admission," Topeka Public Schools, http://documents.topekapublicschools.net/board/policies/8045.pdf (providing a priority in admissions, among other things, for "students from sending schools who will most promote social and economic diversity at the magnet school based upon the difference between the applicant's home attendance area school's residential population SES [determined by the number of students served a free or reduced price lunch] and the magnet school's residential student population SES").

78. See "Student Assignment to Schools," Troup County Public Schools, https://eboard.eboardsolutions.com/ePolicy/policy.aspx?PC=JBCCA&Sch=4162&S=4162&RevNo=1.31&C=J&Z=P (setting a general goal for the "percentage of students eligible for free and reduced price lunch at each elementary school to vary by not more than fifteen percentage points from the zone average percentage of elementary students eligible for free and reduced price lunch").

79. Tucson Unified School District considers "the socioeconomic status of students" in its assignment of students to magnet schools/programs and to non-neighborhood schools via open enrollment "in order to increase the likelihood of diversity." "Tucson Unified School District Post-Unitary Status Plan," adopted by Governing Board on July 30, 2009, <http://tusd1.org/contents/distinfo/pup/Documents/pusp.pdf>, 6.

80. See Brent Champaco, "University Place Will Shift Students to Balance Enroll-ment," *Tacoma News Tribune,* June 24, 2008 (describing plan to rezone students in apartment complexes in order to distribute low-income population more evenly).

81. See Hawkins, "Five School Diversity Plans Detailed"; and Waterloo Com-munity School's Diversity Plan, February 2008, http://www.waterloo.k12.ia.us/files/ CHECKITOUT/Diversity_Plan.pdf (describing transfer plan within school clusters, which are drawn based on economic status, race, attendance numbers, and academic achievement).

82. See Hawkins, "Five School Diversity Plans Detailed" (describing plan, using student native language and income, to limit transfers that would worsen economic segregation).

83. See Gary Mathews, "Beating the Odds with 'Continuous Improvement,'" *New-port News Daily Press,* July 6, 2006, C21 (describing boundary changes to create socioeconomic balance in the schools).

Index

Page numbers followed by letters *f, m,* and *t* refer to figures, maps, and tables, respectively.

achievement gap: at high- vs. low-poverty schools, 2, 12, 31–32, 48, 129, 155; minority student segregation into high-poverty schools and, 181–82, 182f, 183t, 258; No Child Left Behind (NCLB) and pressure to close, 69; socioeconomic school integration and closing of, 30, 40–42, 52, 55, 156, 214; socioeconomic school segregation and, 12, 172–73, 173f, 174, 174t, 258. *See also* readiness gaps

Adequate Yearly Progress (AYP), 223, 250

African-American students. *See* black students

Alabama: accessibility to higher-performing schools in, 255t; prevalence of high-poverty schools in, 166t, 215t; race and high-poverty school enrollment in, 221t; socioeconomic isolation of higher-income students in, 220t; socioeconomic isolation of low-income students in, 217t

Alaska, accessibility to higher-performing schools in, 255t

Allen, Steffani, 67

Alves, Michael, 23, 266, 275, 291

Amherst, Massachusetts, school integration in, 184

ANCOVA approach, 106

Arizona: accessibility to higher-performing schools in, 255t; intradistrict integration strategies in, 187t; prevalence of high-poverty schools in, 215t; race and high-poverty school enrollment in, 221t; socioeconomic isolation of higher-income students in, 170t, 219t; socioeconomic isolation of low-income students in, 217t; socioeconomic school segregation in, 171t; socioeconomic segregation and achievement gaps in, 174t

Arkansas: accessibility to higher-performing schools in, 255t; interdistrict transfer programs in, 136; prevalence of high-poverty schools in, 166t,

215t; race and high-poverty school enrollment in, 221t; socioeconomic isolation of higher-income students in, 170t, 220t; socioeconomic isolation of low-income students in, 217t; socioeconomic school segregation in, 171t; socioeconomic segregation and achievement gaps in, 174t

Asian students, in high-poverty schools, 179–80, 180t, 221t–222t

Aspen Associates, 190

Atlanta, Georgia, hyper-segregated schools in, 167

Barber, Reverend, 267

Basile, Marco, 9

Belfield, Clive, 140, 141, 145

Bell, Courtney, 292

Bergen County, New Jersey, magnet school programs in, 192

Bifulco, Robert, 291

black students: high-poverty school enrollment by, 12, 156, 157, 175–76, 176t, 177f, 182, 221t–222t, 297, 298f; in high-poverty schools, academic performance of, 159; in racially integrated schools, benefits for, 258

Blank, Rolf, 134, 138, 336n43

Borman, Geoffrey, 292

Boston, Massachusetts: charter schools in, 306; interdistrict integration program (METCO) in, 10, 13, 137, 191, 204–5, 211, 319n15

Brooks, David, 303

Brown v. Board of Education, 208, 258, 260

Burkam, David T., 70

Burlington, Iowa, intradistrict school integration in, 184

Burns, Del, 18, 265

business community, and school integration politics, 267–68, 273, 278

"busing": vs. magnet programs, 297–98; political opposition to, 297; vs. socioeconomic school integration, 2, 11. *See also* transportation; travel time

91*f*; measures of, 84–85; omission from preschool policy and research, 116; in publicly funded preschools, 86–87, 87*f*, 88*f*; and quality of program, 91–92; substantive significance of, 107–11
socioeconomic neighborhood integration: and academic outcomes, 5, 7, 31, 295, 317n8; in Montgomery County, Maryland, 4, 5–6, 28–29, 31, 36–37, 295–96; motivations for, 54; vs. school integration, 50
socioeconomic school integration: and academic achievement, 3, 44–46, 45*f*, 51–53, 290, 291; and achievement gap, closing of, 40–42, 52, 55, 156, 214; alternatives to, cost-effectiveness of, 149–50; barriers to, 208, 212–13; benefits of, 139–48, 162, 212, 213–14, 279; case studies in, selection and data gathering and analysis, 261–62; in Champaign Unit 4 Schools, Illinois, 20, 275–77; communication about, importance of, 20, 278; constitutionality of, 161, 358n49; cost-benefit analysis of, 3, 9–11, 128, 147–49, 148*t*; costs of, 10, 133–39, 337n48, 337n49; cumulative effect of, 30, 51–53; demand-side approach to, 73, 117, 118; district size and, 189, 276, 277; effects on higher-income students, 160–61, 293, 294*f*, 299, 359n58; effects on low-income students, 39–42, 39*f*, 41*f*, 293, 294*f*, 299; federal government's role in, 208–10, 279; financial incentives and, 10, 20, 130, 135–39, 190, 209, 298–99; forces driving, 2–3; Harlem Children's Zone (HCZ) philosophy compared to, 304; and high-school graduation rates, 10, 11, 128, 141–44, 142*f*, 146, 147; history of, 129; hybrid approaches to, 18, 185; implementation strategies for, 207–12; instructional demands with, 79–81, 115; vs. investments in high-poverty schools, 48, 53; in Jefferson County, Kentucky, 19, 270–73; in

La Crosse, Wisconsin, 129, 161, 184; limitations of, 213; local resistance to, overcoming, 208–9; magnet schools and, 2, 10, 20, 130, 133–35, 278; and middle-class flight, avoiding, 160–61; need for, 156; vs. neighborhood integration, 50; and parent resources, 22, 33, 76; and peer effects, 51, 74, 76–79; policy debates regarding, 21–24; political challenges to, overcoming, 297–99; political sustainability of, ensuring, 20–21; politics of, 16–20, 257–58, 278–79; in preschool, benefits associated with, 8, 68–69, 74, 104–5, 116, 122, 150; in preschool, feasibility of, 116–19; vs. racial integration, 2, 11, 142, 159, 296–97; research on benefits of, 71–72; return on investment in, 9, 11; school districts adopting plans for, 2, 129, 299, 309*t*–311*t*, 319n14; as school reform strategy, 161–62; selection bias in, 105–6; states' role in, 208, 210–12; supply-side approach to, 73, 117–18; and test scores, international comparison of, 160; "tipping point" in, 6–7, 30, 42, 52, 59*f*–60*f*, 100, 114–15; and turnaround of failing schools, 22, 308; viability of, 12, 14, 156; voluntary approach to, 117–19; in Wake County, North Carolina, 16–17, 129, 161, 263–68. *See also* choice; interdistrict integration strategies; intradistrict integration strategies
socioeconomic school segregation, 259; and achievement gap, 12, 172–73, 173*f*, 174, 174*t*; exceeding level predicted by statewide demographics, 169–70, 171*t*; factors influencing, 170–72, 171*t*; of higher-income students, by state, 169, 170*t*, 219*t*–220*t*; interdistrict choice programs and, 210–11; of low-income students, by state, 166–69, 168*t*, 217*t*–218*t*; patterns of, 212. *See* hyper-segregated schools

About the Contributors

STEPHANIE ABERGER works in Washington, D.C., as a school-based consultant for Expeditionary Learning, where she supports schools in increasing student engagement and achievement for a diverse population of students. She holds a master's degree in education policy and management from the Harvard Graduate School of Education.

MARCO BASILE is a JD/PhD candidate at Harvard University. From 2009 to 2010, he was a program assistant for policy at The Century Foundation's Washington, D.C. office, where he focused on education issues. He holds degrees from the University of Cambridge and Harvard College.

JENNIFER JELLISON HOLME is an assistant professor of educational policy and planning in the Department of Educational Administration at the University of Texas at Austin. Her research agenda is centered on the politics and implementation of educational policy, with a particular focus on accountability, school choice, and school desegregation policies. Her work has been published in

Review of Educational Research (2010), *The Peabody Journal of Education* (2009), *The Equity and Excellence in Education* (2005), and the *Harvard Educational Review* (2002).

RICHARD D. KAHLENBERG is a senior fellow at The Century Foundation and writes about education, equal opportunity, and civil rights. He is the author of books such as *All Together Now: Creating Middle-Class Schools through Public School Choice* (Brookings Press, 2001) and *Tough Liberal: Albert Shanker and the Battles Over Schools, Unions, Race, and Democracy* (Columbia University Press, 2007) and is the editor of *Affirmative Action for the Rich: Legacy Preferences in College Admissions* (The Century Foundation Press, 2010), *Rewarding Strivers: Helping Low-Income Students Succeed in College* (The Century Foundation Press, 2010), and *Improving on No Child Left Behind: Getting Education Reform Back on Track* (The Century Foundation Press, 2008).

ANN MANTIL is a doctoral student in quantitative policy analysis at the Harvard Graduate School of Education. Her research focuses on school composition and its impact on student achievement and other educational outcomes, strategies to promote school diversity, and progressive educational practices. She holds a master's in public affairs from the Woodrow Wilson School at Princeton University and has nine years of teaching experience in urban charter schools.

ANNE G. PERKINS is a research associate at the Massachusetts Department of Higher Education. Her research interests include high poverty schools, reducing achievement gaps in postsecondary education, and PK–20 college readiness initiatives. She received a master's in public administration from the Harvard Kennedy School in 2010.

JEANNE L. REID received her doctorate in early childhood policy from Teachers College at Columbia University in May 2011. Her research has focused on how to foster both equity and excellence in preschool settings. In addition to her work on the relationship between socioeconomic composition and learning in Pre-K classrooms, she conducts research on the content and alignment of state early learning standards. She is currently a postdoctoral fellow at the National Center for Children and Families at Teachers College.

MEREDITH P. RICHARDS is a doctoral student in educational policy and planning at the University of Texas at Austin. Her research explores the social and geographic context of education and the role of schools and educational boundaries in social stratification and segregation. Her educational work has been published in *Review of Educational Research* (2010), *The Peabody Journal of Education* (2009), and the *International Encyclopedia of Education* (2010).

HEATHER SCHWARTZ is an associate policy researcher at the RAND Corporation in New Orleans, Louisiana. She researches education and housing policies intended to reduce the negative effects of poverty on children. She currently leads two projects to study the effects of economic integration on low-income children and their schooling. She obtained her PhD in education policy from Teachers College, Columbia University.

KORI J. STROUB is a doctoral student in educational policy and planning at the University of Texas at Austin. His research investigates the causes and consequences of the persistent patterns of racial/ethnic and socioeconomic inequality in schools. In particular, his research links educational inequality to broader geographic patterns of segregation by race/ethnicity and social class. He is currently conducting research on the effectiveness of integration plans employing geographic proxies for student race/ethnicity.

SHENEKA M. WILLIAMS is an assistant professor in the Department of Lifelong Education, Administration, and Policy within the College of Education at the University of Georgia. Her research examines student assignment policies, school governance, and school and community relations, as they relate to issues of equity and access. Her research on student assignment has been referenced in *EdWeek,* the *Raleigh News Observer,* and *Urban Education.*

DATE DUE

JUL 0 5 2012	
	SEP 1 0 2014
MAR 0 7 2013	
JUN 1 0 2014	